Rājarājeśvarī Devī at Sri Rajarajeswari Peetam, Rush, NY.
(Image credit: Sri Vidya Temple Society)

कल्याणायुतपूर्णचन्द्रवदनां प्राणेश्वरानन्दिनीं
पूर्णां पूर्णतरां परेशमहिषीं पूर्णामृतास्वादिनीम् ।
सम्पूर्णां परमोत्तमामृतकलां विद्यावतीं भारतीं
श्रीचक्रप्रियबिन्दुतर्पणपरां श्रीराजराजेश्वरीम् ॥ १॥

kalyāṇāyutapūrṇacandravadanāṃ prāṇeśvarānandinīṃ
pūrṇāṃ pūrṇatarāṃ pareśamahiṣīṃ pūrṇāmṛtāsvādinīm
sampūrṇāṃ paramottamāmṛtakalāṃ vidyāvatīṃ bhāratīṃ
śrīcakrapriyabindutarpaṇaparāṃ śrīrājarājeśvarīm

"Salutations to her with the face like the full moon that radiates auspiciousness
Who is the delight of prāṇa merging with Īśvara
Who is limitless, complete and infinite as the inseparable tattva of Śiva
Who is the all-encompassing nectar of experience, be it food or thought
Who is the Source of the purest of nectars
Who is the origin of vidyā and non-separate from Sarasvatī
Who exponentially reveals Reality as Herself as we move towards the Bindu of the Śrīcakra
My salutations and oblations to this primordial creative force that is Śrī Rājarājeśvarī"
~ Śrī Rājarājeśvarī Mantra Mātṛka Stavaḥ, Verse 1

Advance Praise

"The first Śrīcakra I ever glimpsed was half a century ago on the back door of a van (the other door sported an ॐ. In the decades since that mystical Devi diagram has spread widely throughout the world, its elegant exoteric symmetries appreciated by almost all and its esoteric meanings understood by almost no one, though its message is displayed in plain sight. This excellent book by Dr. Kavitha Chinnaiyan provides clear keys to that message with explanations well adapted to the modern mind. Both an elucidation of theory and a manual for practice, *Fractals of Reality* provides clear guidance for anyone who wishes to follow the path that leads to Lalitā Devī. Reverence to Mahātripurasundarī for permitting Herself to become so accessible through this text!"

—Robert Svoboda, Ayurvedacharya, author of the *Aghora* trilogy

"Nothing short of a transmission! Kavitha Chinnaiyan's book, Fractals of Reality: Living the Śrīcakra, shines with pristine clarity. It is the most comprehensive, practical, and authentic work on Śrīvidyā. A must for any Devi worshipper. Dive effortlessly and fearlessly into this ocean of wisdom that rises from the heart of a sincere Śrīvidyā upāsakā."

—Indu Arora, author of *YOGA Ancient Heritage Tomorrow's Vision* and *MUDRA The Sacred Secret*

"मातस्ते महिमा वकततुं शिवेनापि न शक्यते
Sage Durvāsa states in the Shakti Mahimna Stotra that the glory of the Goddess cannot be described even by Shiva. In *Fractals of Reality: Living the Śrīcakra*, Kavithaji (Saundaryāmbikā) has taken up a herculean task to give a practical explanation of the Śrīcakra. To say that this book is well researched and written would be an understatement since it is a comprehensive guide to Śrīvidyā, not just for beginners but also for advanced sādhakas. The grace of Goddess Lalitāmbika and the guidance of the Vāgdevatās are evident in this work."

—Jithesh Sathyan (Yugānandanātha), Sriguru at Srividya Tantra Peedom

"This book, *Fractals of Reality: Living the Śrīcakra,* is a magnificent milestone in the modern-day unfoldment of the Śrīcakra, shedding significant light on this ancient practice, and inviting readers into its origins and profound wisdom. There are many wonderful revelations and insights herein. Read it closely, reflect on its content, and let the energy and knowledge that radiate through Kavitha's words penetrate deeply into your consciousness. If you are fortunate enough to read any of Kavitha's books, attend her teaching programs, or simply come into her presence, open your heart and drink in the wisdom that shines forth from her."

—Swami Khecaranatha, founder of the Heart of Consciousness

"*Fractals of Reality* offers the reader a comprehensive overview of yogic and tantric philosophy as the backdrop to unveiling the complexity of the mysterious tantric diagram known as the Śrīcakra. Chinnaiyan has indulged us by sharing her deep knowledge of the ancient teachings hidden within its form."

—Sarah Tomlinson, author of *Nine Designs for Inner Peace* (Inner Traditions publishing)

"In recent times, the Śrīcakra - an ancient and complex tool of esoteric Eastern religious practice - has become increasingly well known, both in India and the West, as an ubiquitous symbol of ... well, something mystical, vaguely "spiritual", perhaps related to Yoga, maybe with a titillating connection to Tantra. If we can never quite un-see such things, we can at least forgive them - for information on the Śrīcakra has historically been exceedingly difficult to come by - and, when found, even harder to comprehend and digest. That ambiguity, I am happy to report, has been firmly and briskly swept away in this extraordinary volume. Dr. Chinnaiyan efficiently collates, sorts, and (very clearly!) explains the vast literature on the topic, aided by the teachings of some of the world's most esteemed living masters. The result is a thrillingly authentic, gratifyingly lucid presentation that manages to fully respect the Śrīcakra's venerable, sacred history, while also offering a much-needed point of easy access for modern readers of every culture, religious background, and level of interest. A stunning achievement, and a highly recommended read."

—Michael M. Bowden, author, *The Goddess and the Guru*; editor, *Gifts from the Goddess*; co-founder, Shakti Sadhana

"Dr. Kavitha Chinnaiyan skillfully weaves scholarly research and her direct experience as a practitioner to lay out the architecture of both the Sri Vidya tradition and the Śrīcakra. *Fractals of Reality* is a much-needed resource for the modern seeker—especially given that the Śrīcakra is a complex esoteric cosmology that traditionally requires guidance. The contemplative aspect of the book is a refreshing invitation for the spiritual aspirant to enter into holographic contemplation and use the Śrīcakra as a tool to embrace the totality of existence and awaken the deity within."

—Janice Craig, Founder, Shakti Shrine

"Kavitha Chinnaiyan's latest book, *Fractals of Reality,* gently carries the reader through increasingly subtle levels of knowledge and practice in the Śrīcakra. Kavitha masterfully weaves together lineage specific understanding with practical "down to earth" engagement in her unpretentious and accessible style. This book will appeal to both established practitioners of the vidyā, as well as those hearing of the all-important cakra for the first time. Much like the Śrīcakra itself, *Fractals of Reality* will satisfy the desires of those who read it and is a much-needed addition to the corpus of available literature on Śākta tantra and Śrīvidyā."

—Brian Campbell, lecturer in the Religious Studies department at California State University, Sacramento and Śrīvidyā upāsaka

"Dr. Kavitha Chinnaiyan unveils the beautiful mysticism inherent in one of the most iconic symbols in the world, the Śrīcakra. This fascinating book dives deep into every aspect of the wisdom to be gained through this study, which can be a spiritual path all on its own. I am enamored."

—Lissa Coffey, author of *Song Divine: A New Lyrical Rendition of the Bhagavad Gita*

"Kavitha Chinnaiyan's book *Fractals of Reality: Living the Śrīcakra* is a powerful, in-depth exploration of the process of devolution and evolution, experienced through the sadhana of the Śrīcakra. It is one of the clearest books I have read on the subject. It takes the reader on a profound spiritual journey, revealing the many stages in which the One undifferentiated primordial consciousness becomes the many -- the vast unseen and seen universes and all that lies within -- and the steps by which each of us can regain the consciousness of our inseparability from the One. She writes with great insight, wisdom and clarity so that even those not familiar with the many Sanskrit terms can follow this journey. The path that she describes is that of the Śrīcakra, a manifestation of the Śakti (Divine Feminine expression), which is, as she says, "the impelling force." She goes on to explain, "She holds creation absorbed within Herself until a desire arises in Her to create—for the One to become the Many. With this initial movement of desire, She separates from Śiva, and time and space come into existence." Of great important is her explanation of why a guru is needed for this spiritual journey of returning to the One source of all. A true guru, a rarity in today's world, is essential for this work of bringing one into deeper experience of the Śrīcakra. *Fractals of Reality* is a book that one must return to again and again in order to absorb the profound wisdom contained within and to apply it to everyday life, as the book enables us to do. Every reader will benefit by taking this book as a lifetime companion, finding new insights and guidance as one progresses on the spiritual path."

—Dena Merriam, author of *The Untold Story of Sita* and *Rukmini and the Turning of Time*

FRACTALS OF REALITY

Living the Śrīcakra

Kavitha Chinnaiyan, MD

Foreword by Sally Kempton

SFAIM PRESS, USA

Illustrations by Rashmi Thirtha Jyoti
www.rashmithirtha.com

Book cover design: Simi Jois and Rashmi Thirtha Jyoti

Printed in the United States of America

ISBN: 978-1-953023-05-6 (hardcover)
ISBN: 978-1-953023-07-0 (paperback)
ISBN: 978-1-953023-04-9 (ebook)

sabda.institute

Sfaim Press

Northville, MI

Contents

Table Guide

Figure Guide

Bhāvanā Guide

Sanskrit Pronunciation Guide

The International Alphabet of Sanskrit Transliteration, IAST is the current standard method of making Devanāgarī, the Sanskrit script accessible to Western scholars, practitioners, enthusiasts, and readers. The following tables provide a layout of the Sanskrit alphabet and a simplistic pronunciation guide.

Sanskrit Alphabet					
Vowels	a ā i ī u ū ṛ ṝ ḷ ḹ e ai o au am ah				
Consonants	Non-aspirated	Aspirated	Non-aspirated	Aspirated	Nasal
Gutturals	k	kh	g	gh	ṅ
Palatals	c	ch	j	jh	ñ
Cerebrals	ṭ	ṭh	ḍ	ḍh	ṇ
Dentals	t	th	d	dh	n
Labials	p	ph	b	bh	m
Semi-vowels	y r l v				
Sibilants	ś ṣ s				
Aspirates	h kṣ				

Letter	English Example	Sanskrit Example	Letter	English Example	Sanskrit Example
a	organ	anuttara	ṭh	light-hearted	kūrmapṛṣṭha
ā	star	ānanda	ḍ	dove	maṇḍita
i	bit	icchā	ḍh	red-hot	Aśvārūḍha
ī	pique	Īśvara	ṇ	fund	Mantriṇi
u	bush	unmeṣa	t	pasta	nirmukta
ū	rule	sthūla	th	path	ratha
ṛ	tree	amṛta	d	thus	Danḍanātha
e	they	prameya	dh	aspirated the	sindhūra
ai	bind, style	Bhairava	n	banana	nayana
o	bore	ojas	p	pine	pūjā
au	bow	mauktikā	ph	uphill	phalapradā
am	stem	saṃsāra	b	baby	bāṇa
ah	aha	Brahman	bh	abhor	abhaya
k	kite	Kuṇḍalinī	m	mother	mantra
kh	Ekhart	Khaḍga	y	yes	yantra
g	gold	Gāyatrī	r	room	Rati
gh	ghoul	ghanāghanā	l	light	līlā
ṅ	sing	śṛṅgāra	v	void	Vāruṇī
c	chair	Śrīcakra	ś	she	Ṣoḍaśi
ch	aspirated c	chandas	ṣ	aspirated sh	Ṣoḍaśi
j	jam	japa	s	savior	sahasrāra
jh	hedgehog	Sarvajhṛṃbiṇi	h	hand	hasta
ñ	onion	ājña	kṣa	makeshift	Kṣobhiṇi
ṭ	tub	aṣṭamī	jña	gnya	ājña

Invocation

चैतन्यश्शाश्वतश्शान्तः व्योमातीतो निरञ्जनः ।
बिन्दुनादकलातीतः तस्मै श्रीगुरवे नमः ॥ ७॥

caitanyaś-śāśvataś-śāntaḥ vyomātīto nirañjanaḥ |
bindu-nādakalā-tītaḥ tasmai śrīguruve namaḥ || 7 ||

"Salutations to the Śrī Guru who is the eternal tranquil consciousness that is pure, transcends space, and bounds of bindu, nāda and kalā."
~Guru Stotra, verse 7

This book is an offering to the lotus feet of my beloved and revered Śrī Guru, who is the personification of auspiciousness, and who carries the grace of the entire Guru maṇḍala in his compassionate gaze. May all who read this book be drenched in the nectar that flows endlessly from him.

Foreword

The Śrīcakra is a yantra, a diagrammatic representation of the cosmic unfolding. It is unquestionably the most well known yantra in the world. It appears not only on the walls of shrine rooms and the covers of books, but also on jewelry--jewelry often admired and worn by people who have no idea that the yantra is the basis for a complex and transformative ritual belonging to a tradition called Śrīvidyā.

For many people, even practitioners in the tradition where the sacred is worshipped as Goddess, the Śrīcakra remains an esoteric mystery. Even the books that purport to explain it don't always help. In fact, the traditional texts on Śrīcakra often provoke even more mystification. One reason for this is that the yantra is supposed to be explained and empowered by a Guru of the tradition, who then initiates you as a Śrīvidyā practitioner. It's through your practice itself that the wisdom in the yantra unfolds for you, often over a period of years. But in addition, to fully understood and appreciate the teachings encoded in the yantra, you actually require an education in the metaphysics of Indian tantra, Vedic wisdom, and yoga.

This, Kavitha offers brilliantly in this book, weaving the philosophical strands of tantric and Vedic philosophy into her descriptions of the journey encoded in the triangles of the yantra. She draws together insights and teachings from the entire spectrum of yogic teachings, especially those that belong to the Śaiva Tantra and Advaita Vedāntic traditions. Her work is precise, clear, and deep, reflecting her years of practice, study and teaching, and also her natural clarity of mind.

When I first came across the tantric narrative—especially the narrative of the 36 tattvas, or levels of manifestation, I was struck by the fact that this story explains what it really means to say "It's all God." Like other students of the Indic traditions, I had heard many teachings about non-duality. But until I learned the 36 tattvas, I knew of no map that truly explained how the infinitely subtle transcendent reality could have become this body/mind that I identified as myself. The teachings of non-dual Śaivism offered the maps I needed to make sense of non-duality. For me, the process of learning was powered by my relationship with an enlightened Guru, who besides downloading meditative awakenings, constantly transmitted experiential insight about how each section of the map could lead me deeper into the truth.

When I came to the study of the Śākta approach to non-duality, I had no such guiding relationship with a Śākta Guru. But the yantra itself, and the mantras that unlocked it, had been empowered for me by a senior Śrīvidyā practitioner. So I learned it from books, but also from practice. And this is its power. Śrīvidyā is a multilayered tradition, but the secret of unlocking it is informed practice. You need the intellectual understanding to unlock its secrets. But most important, you need to practice with it.

Like a mantra, which appears to be a word made of letters and sounds, but which when practiced reveals itself to be a seed-pod containing the fullness of the Absolute, the yantra starts out as a map of the cosmos, and eventually reveals itself within you as the map of your soul.

The Śrīcakra is a symbolic expression of a great non-dual love story, which goes something like this: The one great awareness/love exists eternally, transcendent, ecstatic, glorying in its endless self reflection. Then there comes a moment when these two aspects of the One decide—or maybe it just happens—to create a tiny separation in the oneness. In the tiny separation that ensued, the Awareness side becomes known as Śiva, and the love side as Śakti. In that moment, within Śakti's divine field, the divine powers of will, knowing and action come together in a creative flood, and innumerable rays arise within Śakti's being, each of which becomes an aspect of the multiverse. With all its complexity and all its local features, whatever exists in this multiverse is at its core, made of the host of energies, rays of the great Śakti in her immanant form. Our worlds are permeated by and held within the primordial Śakti herself, united to Śiva as she always is—even when she has allowed her body to become all this. And we hold within ourselves the potential to return with her to rest in the ecstatic truth of what it is that lives this universe.

The Śrīcakra is a diagram of this two-fold process: In the first movement of creation, the manifest world spirals from Śakti/Śiva. In the second movement, the human spirit awakens to the possibility of recognizing his or her inseparability from the divine source. The Śrīcakra shows the way.

Śrīvidyā is both a philosophy and a practice protocol. However, when used in ritual, the yantra is primarily an effective 'device' for making serious contact with the Goddess in the outer and inner worlds. Though there were many different approaches to religion and mysticism in the ancient and medieval worlds, there has often seemed a basic split between two strands. On one side are the traditions—like Vedānta, some forms of Buddhism, and the teachings of western adepts like Plotinus—that approach Spirit through the intellect, through awareness of awareness, or through the process of inquiry into the nature of mind itself.

On the other side are the traditions that use myth, ritual and symbols to create a felt experience of the divine within the human plane. That is what Śrīvidyā accomplishes. Properly performed and properly understood, practice with the yantra, the ritual, and the mantras has the power to draw the experience of the higher worlds to earth. In Śrīvidyā, the ritual space is carefully curated to attract the Śakti of the Goddess and her retinue. The symbols, gestures, and mantras used to invoke Goddess are not meant to compel her, but to attract her. Together they create a kind of landing pad, where she recognizes herself and feels comfortable taking a seat. Once she is present, she reveals her wisdom, her love, and her powers, which are said in the tradition to be the fundamental powers in the universe.

In many of the Śrīvidyā communities in South India, there is an integration of these two 'strands' of spiritual philosophy and praxis. Kavitha holds that balance with enormous insight, bringing together classical Advaita with the ritual, mythic, Śakti-inspired teaching and practice.

Her work in this book is enormously important to the deepening understanding of Śrīvidyā in our time. To have this book is something to be grateful for, whether you are a beginner or an advanced practitioner on this path.

~ Sally Kempton
Author of *Awakening Shakti* and *Meditation for the Love of It*

Preface

Very Big Shoes to Fill

Here it is again... the overwhelming sense of having very, very big shoes to fill with the topic of this book. The *Śrīcakra* is, of course, the most celebrated mystical symbol with countless erudite commentaries by well-known scholars and practitioners. The obvious question that you may have at this point is what makes me qualified to even attempt this book.

The question is a valid one. After all, I'm just an ordinary practitioner of this great *vidyā* (knowledge), not an academician or even a Sanskrit scholar. Mostly, I'm excessively fortunate to have incredible teachers who push me to the limits of my abilities to think, feel, intuit, and function in the world. These extraordinary souls whom I have the great good fortune to learn from are less interested in academic pursuits of vidyā and instead emphasize its application in the very mundane, boring, and ordinary moments of our daily lives. Their incredible grace, wisdom and encouragement have driven this project.

My desire to write this book is fueled by the ubiquitous presence of the Śrīcakra in lay culture; most people have seen it *somewhere*. A while ago, I was chatting with a friend who is a cardiologist and a highly accomplished, ex-military, all-American superstar. I was neck deep into *Glorious Alchemy: Living the Lalitā Sahasranāma* and he was curious about the topic. I casually said it was a book on the goddess who presides over the Śrīcakra. His immediate response was, "Oh, isn't that the symbol with all the triangles?" I was impressed that even someone with no inkling of Eastern traditions knew *something* about the Śrīcakra.

Growing up in India, I encountered the Śrīcakra everywhere, but I wasn't curious or interested in it. It seemed excessively complicated to my convent-educated[1] mind. However, the Śrīcakra circled back into my consciousness decades later, by which time, I was a practicing cardiologist with a busy family life as well as a *Śrīvidyā upāsikā*. This time, my interest in the Śrīcakra increased by leaps and bounds, but the symbology remained formidable, difficult to understand, and even more challenging was the effort to bring its meaning into practice in the moments of my life. Even though I read books, papers, and all the materials I could find, the essence of the Śrīcakra remained elusive and out of reach.

1 Convent schools are run by priests and nuns in India and have a reputation of providing excellent, well-rounded education. They are generally better equipped to provide extra-curricular activities and although of Christian roots, tend to be secular and tolerant.

Some years ago, I was visiting my *Guru* during the fall *Navarātra*[2] and it was my favorite time of the day. The morning festivities and rituals had just ended, and lunch had been served. Aiya[3] sat with a big crowd of disciples, jovially and patiently answering our questions. As always, someone brought up the topic of Śrīcakra *pūjā* (ritual adoration), and Aiya explained its importance and the mental discipline it instills (which we will see later in this book). At the time, pūjā wasn't the medium I was using to engage with the Śrīcakra; it was intellect and reasoning. "Śrīcakra pūjās are long and tedious, Aiya..." I began. He looked at me, his eyes sparkling with humor and affection. "I'm aware," he said with a chuckle.[4] He then proceeded to tell me that I need to do the Śrīcakra pūjā regularly. With a knot in my stomach and fretting about how I was going to find the time, I asked him, "How often?" He replied with a smile, "As often as possible."

Taking his word that I needed this discipline, I returned home equipped with the pūjā *vidhi*[5] and began to worship the Śrīcakra every weekend. As I become more familiar with the ritual, the time it took to perform the pūjā shortened dramatically and an interesting unfolding took place – the concepts I'd imbibed from my research and study fell away and a more dynamic, lived experience of the Śrīcakra began to take shape. The object in front of me began to lose spatiality and I started to become acutely aware of its elements within me. With continued practice, these same elements began to show up in the world, in my interactions with patients, colleagues and family, in world events and natural disasters, as well as in the subtle patterns of thought, speech and action. The Śrīcakra gradually became my reference point for not just pūjā or contemplative practice, but for life. While I had previously dreaded the idea of long, time-consuming rituals, I began to eagerly look forward to the pūjā, which aided the cultivation of a deep reverence by its ability to bestow exquisite mindfulness, concentration, and single pointedness. Every time I engage with the Śrīcakra this way, a new facet of understanding is polished and imbibed.

A year later I was back with Aiya during Navarātra. Once again, we gathered around him after the morning festivities and lunch, bombarding him with questions. This time, I had the lived experience of some of what he was saying in response to the exceedingly vast topic of the Śrīcakra. At one point, he casually turned to me and asked how the Śrīcakra pūjā was going. Trying not to burst into tears, I told him how it had changed my life and perception. Just as casually as he'd asked me to take it up a year earlier, he now told me I could stop doing the pūjā if I wanted. As I looked at him in amazement,

2 *Nava* = nine, *rātra* = nights; the nine nights of worship and adoration of Śakti. There are four Navarātras per year (or more, depending on who you ask).

3 My Guru, Śrī Chaitanyananda Natha Saraswati is affectionately called Aiya, which is a loving and respectful term for a male relative.

4 Aiya is one of the world authorities on the Śrīcakra and author of the celebrated book, *Śrīcakra Pūjā Vidhih.*

5 Vidhi is the detail of the pūjā ritual.

he chuckled and said, "The lesson needed to be learned, Amma."[6] I must have appeared crestfallen for he went on to say, "Of course, you can do it anytime you want. You see, now, the pūjā is no longer a compulsion, but a joyful activity for you."

As my life continued to unfold around the Śrīcakra, the COVID-19 pandemic brought the world to a standstill in the Spring of 2020. My Guru of the *Yoginī* lineage, Dr. Sumit Kesarkar, was visiting me. As luck would have it, travel came to a grinding halt and he was stuck in my home, which was an extraordinary blessing. Over two months of quarantine, he taught me nonstop, escalating my Śrīvidyā *upāsanā* and perception of the Śrīcakra through not just an exploration of texts and theory but its moment-to-moment manifestation and understanding. He stated again and again that he was only helping me internalize Aiya's teachings. Through the relentless application of the exquisite teachings of the Śrīcakra first within and then outside the context of ritual and philosophy, my life and *sādhanā* had permanently shifted. To sit at the feet of one Guru is an immeasurable gift. I've been incredibly fortunate to sit at the feet of two great Gurus, both of whom enthusiastically blessed this book with the emphasis that I *must* write it.

This book is not meant to replace any of the great classics (that we will meet at length), but to provide a window into the broader understanding of the Śrīcakra and most importantly, its assimilation in daily life.

6 Amma is an affectionate term used for mother, and in the South Indian Śrīvidyā traditions, it is the term used to address a woman.

Acknowledgments

This book brings together the teachings and transmissions of my revered Guru *maṇḍala*. My deep bows to my *Śrī* Guru, Śrī Caitanyānanda Nātha Sarasvatī (Haran Aiya), who lovingly introduced me to the Śrīcakra and went on to transmit the understanding and living of its principles. Aiya's love, humor, rigor, grace and generosity have shaped my life and upāsanā in profound and irreversible ways. His emphatic encouragement to write this book gave me the inspiration and strength to delve into the complexities and nuances of the Śrīcakra, which is normally the work of scholars.

My infinite gratitude to my beloved Guru of the Yoginī lineage, Dr. Sumit Kesarkar, whose radical and practical approach to spirituality balances my devotional and intellectual leanings. His teachings have irrevocably shifted my perception of upāsanā and the moment-to-moment arising of life that proliferates from the *Bindu* to the *Bhūpura* of the Śrīcakra. His realistic understanding and transmission of esoterism continue to influence every aspect of my life.

When Aiya said that the entire lineage is supportive of this work, I was immensely grateful even without realizing the depth of his words. Throughout the writing process, all I had to do was leave it to the Guru maṇḍala, and the content manifested by way of dreams, insights during meditation, or "accidentally" coming across a line in a text addressing a particular concept that I was contemplating. Aiya, Guruji (Śrī Amritānanda Nātha Sarasvatī who is Aiya's Guru and therefore my *Parama* Guru) and Sumitji frequented my dreams, where profound conversations and transmissions took place. This book is entirely the product of their vidyā, and the credit for its merits goes entirely to these luminaries. Any faults of this work are mine alone.

My upāsanā has been deeply graced by many incredible teachers over the years. I'm deeply grateful to Swami Chinmayananda whose crystal-clear writings on *Advaita Vedānta* became the lens of my understanding early on in my sādhanā; Greg Goode, whose joyful and profound teachings on the Direct Path resulted in a deep and permanent shift; Śrī Śivapremānandaji who introduced me to Śrīvidyā, which would change my life; and Paul

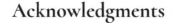

Muller-Ortega and Sally Kempton, whose teachings on non-dual *Śaiva Tantra* illuminated complex and intricate concepts.

This project has been incredibly enjoyable because of the collaboration and support of many. My loving gratitude to my Guru *bhai* (brother), Brian Campbell (aka, Adi Keshava), whose razor-sharp intellect came to my aid when I felt that I was struggling to present a concept clearly. I will always cherish the hours we spent discussing and contemplating *Kāmakalā* and other aspects of Śrīvidyā as two crazed lovers of *Devī*. His love, support and humor are a constant source of joy for me, beyond the context of this book.

My loving gratitude to my beloved friend Rashmi Thirtha, whose illustrations have inspired and moved me throughout the writing process. Her infectious love, enthusiasm and artistic acumen are a gift to my writing and teaching endeavors.

This book would not have been possible without the support of my students who show up willing to apply the teaching in their daily life, which is as challenging as it is freeing. I learn constantly from their graciousness and from the remarkable ways in which they bring about transformation in their lives. Their love for vidyā and Devī inspires me daily. My special thanks to Joanne Tognarelli who transcribed my classes on the Śrīcakra long before the idea for the book arose. She sent them to me with a gentle nudge that they may be helpful for a book *someday*. My gratitude to Holly Robinson for editing the manuscript with love and care, Prashanthi Chitre for creating stunning media to support the book's message, and Shaku Selvakumar and Simi Jois for their dedicated work on the book cover. I'm thankful to my friend Hareesh (Christopher) Wallis, who planted the idea for this book, convincing me it was essential for the broader community of spiritual practitioners.

My heartfelt gratitude to the team at Dartfrog Books for helping me create the book of my vision, including Mark Hobbs for his relentless work on the book cover and some of the illustrations, and Suanne Laqueur and Gordon McClellan for coordinating the details of publication. Deep thanks to Simona Meloni for formatting this book beautifully.

I'm incredibly lucky to have a family that understands my interests and pursuits beyond the extent of my work as a cardiologist. My loving gratitude goes to my husband Arul, our daughters Anya and Annika and our gorgeous pup Bella Māyā. They always find ways to put up with me when I'm juggling a full-time job, a book, and running an institute.

Nothing ever happens without Devī's will, and to her I bow first and last in reverence and awe for making me an instrument of her *icchā* (will).

~ Saundaryāmbikā (Kavitha Chinnaiyan)
Guru Pūrṇimā, 2021, Seattle, WA

Introduction

Before we begin discussing the Śrīcakra, we must first consider the most important question. Why would we even bother studying this esoteric symbol?

Perhaps it would help to start with the quandary of the human condition. We are born and raised in a particular culture, have a certain upbringing and a stream of life experiences. We move through life, sometimes doing what is expected of us, rebelling at other times and we finally arrive at the understanding that life isn't always easy. Experience soon teaches us that life is like a Ferris wheel with incessant ups and downs. There are periods of time when things are relatively easy and others that are challenging or downright difficult. Even on a given day, we seem to go through a potpourri of emotions and end up in the evening with a mindset that's entirely different than the one we started out with in the morning. We can feel wonderful when we receive compliments from friends and co-workers, and anxious or stressed when an angry driver cuts us off on the road an hour later.

Even though we have all the proof and direct experience to know that life is a constant play of ups and downs, we do everything we can to get to a steady state. We obtain an education, get a job, a romantic relationship, have children and spend a lifetime raising them, give back to society, find spirituality, and so on. Every choice we make holds the promise of a steady state devoid of ups and downs, or at least more ups than downs.

Of course, not everyone seeks the ups in this way. Some of us may seek them in substances, risky behavior, or even actively causing harm to others. The *mode* of seeking may differ, but the *goal* of seeking is the same no matter who we are or where we come from. Happiness is the goal we all have in common, which each of us defines differently. In general, happiness has some measures of peace and worth, where our life holds some meaning, and we can leave a legacy or at least be remembered after we die.

One of the greatest sources of our anguish is the uncertainty of life. Even when we are in an upswing, the possibility of things going downhill looms in the background. Moreover, even when we get what we want, it comes with a set of other things that we don't want but must accept. For example, you may long for a stable, intimate relationship, feeling like it is the *one* thing that will solve all your problems. You may find such a relationship, which eventually unveils its own set of problems such as ongoing bickering about minutiae, disagreements, and resentments.

Similarly, you may feel like having a baby is the answer to your sense of emptiness and feel ecstatically happy when the child is born. Soon, however, the child grows out of infanthood, talks back, breaks curfew, disregards your wisdom, and makes bad choices that affect you. In both examples, one set of problems is replaced by another. This phenomenon that leads to the constant cycle of ups and downs is known as *saṃsāra*.

Saṃsāra and Nirvāṇa

The word saṃsāra comes from the root *saṃsṛ*, which refers to going around in circles. In the application of the word saṃsāra here, we must consider two other concepts, including *karma* and transmigration.

> ***Karma is the sum total of all of our past and present actions that determine future outcomes.***

Although popular culture uses karma to mean linear cause and effect, it is hardly that simplistic. In this book we will examine karma at length, but for now and in the context of saṃsāra, karma is the accumulation of *all* our actions – even (and mostly) the unseen ones. The essence of these past actions remains in the subtlest realm of our existence, which is more upstream than the mind. In other words, the essence of karma drives both the mind and the body from an unconscious place (more to come on this throughout this book).

At the end of one lifetime, this accumulated subtle essence doesn't die with the body. Instead, it must find another outlet to live out the effects of those past experiences. This need is not a choice. It's a compulsion where the accumulated essence of karma *must* find continuity through another incarnation to continue to experience the fruit of those past actions. However, this is not the whole story.

Although the body-mind dies at death, there is an eternal, unperishable principle that has begun this whole drama of life and death in the first place. This principle, which is called the soul in some traditions, takes on a particular body-mind in each lifetime to live out the effects of the previous lifetimes. Like an actress discarding her costume and character to don another, the soul transmigrates through countless births, taking on roles and characters to experience the consequences of the drama that has unfolded through the collective actions of the previous roles. It's as if the actress moves on to another play but brings the remnants of her previous roles to the present character. She moves from play to play and character to character, learning along the way and bringing her learning and experience into every role. She may be playing the shrew now, but she can't shake off the *essence* of the time she was Lady Macbeth. The soul is the actress, and the body-mind that the soul inhabits is the character. The consequences of the previous roles that affect the current gig is karma.

Karma (experience and essence of past roles) is thus propagated birth after birth and role after role with no end in sight. Saṃsāra is the process of going through the succession of births and rebirths. Even though it seems like we have distinctly different experiences in each birth, they revolve around the common human themes of survival, validation-seeking, and the search for permanent peace.

What is unique about the human condition is that at some level or other, all seven plus billion of us know there's something greater to life than those common themes. We inherently know there must be something more to life than the constant cycle of ups and downs. What we seek in essence is this something greater, but the problem is we don't know where to look for it. In our innocence, we seek this undefinable something in the usual themes of validation and self-worth. We feel like acquiring our object of desire will be "it" and *this* time, we are on the right track and we will want nothing more. Like the actress in our analogy, we keep hoping we have landed the perfect role which will fulfill us to such an extent that we can permanently remain in character. Since lasting happiness seems to evade us, we continue to be restless in our longing for that *something.* This is the quandary of the human lot whether we can articulate it, live just and moral lives, have criminal records, disabilities, or are abundantly blessed with all riches. We *all* long for that unknown and unclear *something.*

The tradition of the Śrīcakra provides a structure to that indefinable *something* as well as the solution to saṃsāra and the restlessness of seeking. It shows us how to strip off the layers and layers of costumes we have inadvertently put on in our quest for happiness. When we strip off these layers, we realize that what we were seeking was our own true Self![7] This Self, which is the eternal, unchanging and unperishable principle is who we really are. The actress merely needs to realize that she is not the roles she plays.

With this realization, the cycle of saṃsāra driven by karma comes to an end. The end of saṃsāra is called *nirvāṇa*, which is derived from the root *vāna*, which means to blow out.

7 Note the capitalization of S in Self, which is to distinguish from the self that is made up of the roles and attributes that we take to be who we are.

Nirvāṇa refers to the extinguishing of that restless energy of saṃsāra, after which there is no more mistaking the role or the costume for the Self.

Most often, nirvāṇa is explored in the context of religion and spirituality as we tread this path seeking the Divine or God. On the path laid out by the tradition of the Śrīcakra, the search for divinity begins in understanding this mystical symbol and culminates in seeing that our true Self *is* the Divine we were seeking.

While this seems simplistic and straightforward, our way of thinking, feeling and being is complex with layers of intertwined elements. The Śrīcakra is the most elegant and complete representation of this complicated interplay of the gross and subtle factors that keep us bound in saṃsāra. It is a comprehensive layout of saṃsāra that is also the map to nirvāṇa.

In addition to being a flawless map of the microcosm, the Śrīcakra is also an unparalleled representation of the macrocosm.

One of the significant insights of the path of the Śrīcakra is the oneness of the microcosm and macrocosm.

There are many ways to approach the Śrīcakra. Here, we will take a systematic one that brings together its philosophy, practice, and application.

Layout of the Book

This book is organized in three parts. Part I explores the Fundamental Principles of the Śrīcakra with an examination of the elements of sādhanā or practice, which lays down the foundation for Parts II and III. Part II delves into the Śrīcakra as it relates to the *sṛṣṭi krama* or the descent of the unfettered Divine into limited manifestation, the nuances of practice, and the importance of sound and language (*vāc*) in its philosophy. Part III is dedicated to the Practice of the Śrīcakra and makes up the bulk of the book. Here, the Śrīcakra is examined in the *saṃhāra* krama, moving from the limited manifestation of the Divine in and as our lives back to the unlimited, perfect source. Along the way, we will gain deep insights into the nature of our suffering and how to overcome it.

Concepts that are important in the understanding of the Śrīcakra are embedded throughout the book in the relevant sections. This is to avoid the "top-heavy" approach of presenting the often-intimidating body of concepts all at once. Each concept is treated primarily from the standpoint of practice and application as the sādhanā of the Śrīcakra may ordinarily progress. Charts, graphs, and figures are provided in plenty to explain these concepts visually. The first mention of a Sanskrit term in IAST is italicized. Be warned that there is a fair amount of repetition throughout the book, where the same concept is examined in different ways. This is akin to examining a sparkly diamond from every corner and angle of its brilliant cut. Prompts for contemplation and meditation are peppered throughout the book to enhance the understanding and application of these concepts in day-to-day life.

Usually, commentaries on the Śrīcakra focus either on its ritual worship that leads to its understanding and internalization, or on its mystical aspects and the benefits of its sādhanā in terms of wealth, powers, or fulfilment of life goals. In both, there tends to be a paucity of expansion on its profound psycho-physio-socio-cultural correlations with the issues we struggle with, which tend to be removed from ritual and mysticism. In this approach, life and sādhanā remain distinct and separate, where the insights of study or practice remain inaccessible in the moment-to-moment unfolding of life. In this book, I've attempted to make the teaching of the Śrīcakra highly practical and applicable in the trenches of life where it matters most.

The beauty of the Śrīcakra is that each of its various elements keeps us bound in saṃsāra, while also becoming a portal for freedom from it. In this book, we will examine these seemingly opposing shadow and light parts, particularly as they relate to sādhanā. In Part III, you will find tables summarizing the psycho-physiological correlations of the Śrīcakra *āvaraṇas* with suggestions for *bhāvanā* or contemplation on each element. These pointers may seem repetitive, showing up in different āvaraṇas or sometimes, the various elements of the same āvaraṇa. This scheme is intentional and is meant to encourage you to examine the same prompt through ever-deepening insight.

The classical teachings on the Śrīcakra are exceedingly esoteric and highly specific to the Śrīvidyā tradition. While we will stay largely within that framework, I have deliberately chosen to omit the obscure or purely scholarly teachings in favor of the more practical and easily applicable ones. In the Resources section, you will find a collection of books and other publications that may satisfy your curiosity about those omitted parts.

While much of the material for the discussions in this book comes from well-known texts on the Śrīcakra (particularly the *Yoginī Hṛdaya*, *Kāmakalā Vilāsa* and the *Bhāvanopaniṣad*), a large portion is not from texts or books. Rather, it comes from oral transmissions of my Gurus. One of the hallmarks of textual references is that they contain several layers of meanings, ranging from the obvious to the highly secret and esoteric that can only be learned from the Guru, and cannot be elucidated even with a top-notch education in Sanskrit.

The *gūḍārtha* (hidden meaning) often has nothing do with wordsmithing and depends on associations and higher reasoning arising from direct insight. The gūḍārtha is usually hidden in plain sight, cleverly disguised as a play of words, letters or their seemingly casual arrangement, and is revealed as if by magic at a certain level of clarity. Some of the expositions on crucial concepts in this book may be startling or strange to you if they differ from your own oral tradition or lineage. Please bear in mind that there is no *one* way to interpret texts and teachings of any tradition. The lack of a specific way to interpret a teaching lends both challenge and beauty to the Śrīcakra. Being a representation of the fractals of Reality, all possibilities of interpretation exist in its magnificent structure.

Although selected verses from the original texts are included in relevant sections, this book is by no means a commentary on any of them. The purpose of including the verses is to introduce you to the texts – perhaps you will be inspired to study them in their glorious original forms!

How To Use This Book

- Read from cover to cover, stopping to take notes wherever you need. Having read the three parts, commit to practice in the saṃhāra krama of Part III. Spend time with each yoginī with the associated bhāvanā prompt.
- Please note that some chapters (such as those on Sṛṣṭi Krama and Vāc) are necessarily denser than others. I recommend that you return to these chapters frequently, especially once you get into the flow of the saṃhāra krama in Part III.
- Bhāvanā prompts are provided in most of the chapters in Part III for the first yoginī of the āvaraṇa. Apply the same principle to all the other yoginīs as you advance through the āvaraṇa.
- Your contemplation may be greatly aided by directed journaling that examines the areas of your life and psyche where you feel stuck or stagnant and how the bhāvanā needs to be applied.
- Practice the *Śrīṃ* meditation provided in Appendix I as a preparatory step for bhāvanā. This practice opens us to clarity, insight, and joy.
- Identify the yoginī that rules over the particular aspect you are dealing with. Ask for her guidance with humility and reverence. Allow her into your heart and let her perform her magic. Devotion and faith are crucial aspects of Śrīcakra practice.
- In your inquiry, it helps to be radically honest with yourself, especially about your priorities and how you expend your energy, what you really want, and how you are approaching spirituality.
- Listen to the *Khaḍgamālā Stotra*, using it to move your attention and focus from yoginī to yoginī in the Śrīcakra. The lyrics of the Khaḍgamālā Stotra are provided in Appendix II. Approach the Stotra with reverence and humility, opening to its energy and potency and seeking its guidance in your life.
- Perform the *kuṅkumārcana* (worship with *kuṅkuma*[8]), placing a pinch of it at the locations of the yoginīs while chanting (or listening to) the Khaḍgamālā Stotra. The locations of the yoginīs in the Śrīcakra is provided in Appendix II.
- The practice of the Śrīcakra lends itself beautifully to a group of like-minded practitioners. Use this book for practice and study in a group, spending time with each of the yoginīs in the saṃhāra krama.

8 A red powder made by adding slaked lime to turmeric that is used in worship.

- If you have a Guru, discuss the findings of your contemplation with her/him, and seek advice on your practice. If you don't have one, trust that a Guru will find you when you are ready.
- It's extremely helpful and useful to contemplate the Śrīcakra along with the Lalitā Sahasranāma. Chant the Lalitā Sahasranāma daily and study the hymn on a regular basis.[9]
- Become intimately familiar with the nuances of practice and philosophy of the Śrīcakra through repeated study and contemplation.

9 See K. Chinnaiyan, *Glorious Alchemy: Living the Lalitā Sahasranāma* (New Sarum Press, 2020). A recording of the Lalitā Sahasranāma accompanies the book.

PART I

FUNDAMENTAL PRINCIPLES OF THE ŚRĪCAKRA

भवानि त्वं दासे मयि वितर दृष्टिं सकरुणां
इति स्तोतुं वाञ्छन् कथयति भवानि त्वमिति यः ।
तदैव त्वं तस्मै दिशसि निजसायुज्य-पदवीं
मुकुन्द-ब्रम्हेन्द्र स्फुट मकुट नीराजितपदाम् ॥ २२ ॥

bhavāni tvaṃ dāse mayi vitara dṛṣṭiṃ sakaruṇāṃ
iti stōtuṃ vāñchan kathayati bhavāni tvam iti yaḥ ।
tadaiva tvaṃ tasmai diśasi nijasāyujyapadavīṃ
mukunda-brahmēndra-sphuṭa-makuṭa-nīrājita-padām ॥ 22 ॥

"Bhavāni, I approach you as a humble servant desirous of your kind glance and even before I can state my wish, you grant me oneness at your glorious feet that illuminate the crowns of Brahmā, Viṣṇu, and Indra."
~Saundarya Lahirī, verse 22

Chapter 1

Mystical Symbol, Practical Wisdom

By now, you probably know that the Śrīcakra is a conglomeration of geometrical shapes. Even though the Śrīcakra is highly revered and celebrated, its practical and logical wisdom often belies its profound mysticism. The deep metaphysics of the Śrīcakra are inaccessible to the average practitioner since much of the original literature is lost or misplaced, and the oral practice traditions are propagated in secret.

Despite its mysticism, the Śrīcakra lends itself beautifully to understanding the reality of the very mundane aspects of the fundamental human conundrum of suffering and the possibility of freedom from them. In its mystical geometric elements, we will find simple, practical, kind and profoundly wise solutions to our problems.

> ***The combination of its profound mysticism and applicable wisdom renders the Śrīcakra sacred – it is the perfect symbol of the Divine that we approach in sādhanā.***

Sādhanā means spiritual practice that is directed toward nirvāṇa or transcending saṃsāra. However, each of us comes to sādhanā from our unique circumstances that determine how we relate with ourselves and the world. And if the Śrīcakra plays a role in our quest for nirvāṇa, our sādhanā also includes a relationship with the Divine, which determines where we happen to be on the spectrum of practice.

Stages of Sādhanā

When we set out on the path of sādhanā, our initial relationship with the Divine is centered around our wants and needs. We approach the Divine in a give-and-take relationship where we offer prayer or worship for something in return. We tend to believe that our relationship with the Divine will save us from calamities and undesired outcomes. When the Divine doesn't hold up Her end of the bargain, we become confused and angry that bad things can happen to the pious and righteous. Sādhanā at this point remains at the transactional level, where we expect the Divine to accommodate our beliefs and ideas.

In the next stage of sādhanā, we recognize the Divine only in certain forms. In Sanskrit the word for a gross or concrete form is *sthūla*. In this stage, we may feel a stirring in the heart when we look at a picture or idol of the deity. We feel different in a temple or sacred place, especially if we have formed a connection with the deity there. As a result of reliance on the sthūla form of the Divine, we rely on external ritual and worship because we feel different while being engaged in that activity. When the ritual ends, we go back to feeling like our old selves again – restless and uneasy.

At this stage, we are yet to cultivate an understanding of the Divine as the formless Reality that pervades everything, including us. It hasn't dawned on us that existence is a seamless flow and that there is no difference between life and worship. Since the two remain separate, we lack the ability to see the Divine in the mundane aspects of life.

In the next stage, we become acquainted with the Divine in the *sūkṣma* or subtle form. A common example of this relationship is through word and sound as *mantra* (sacred sound). With ongoing practice, the mantra expands beyond the boundaries of the ritual, replacing thoughts, problems, and beliefs with the constant remembrance of the Divine.

As we get into the subtler layers of the mind, the boundaries between the sacred and the ordinary begin to dissolve. Gradually, our perception of ourselves and the world shifts, and we move on to the next stage. While previously we were attached to the sthūla or sūkṣma forms of the Divine, we now delve into the subtlest or the *parā* form. At this stage we don't need external props; there is no *need* for ritual or mantra, sacred place, or a specific form of the deity. Our practice ripens, and we begin to recognize the Divine in everything everywhere, including ourselves. Now when we engage in ritual or other sādhanā, we are immersed in the knowledge that the Divine is both form and formless who is not just out there in the form but is also the one doing the worship or chanting the mantra.

Sādhanā from the sthūla to the parā is the hallmark of all paths and traditions, where we progress from the most concrete and obvious to the subtlest and the hidden. One analogy for the relationship between the sthūla and the parā is that of word and sound, which gives us the basis for understanding the Śrīcakra and how we relate to it in sādhanā.

Sound Becomes Word

We can think of the relationship between sound and word in two different pathways: progressing from sound to word, or from word to sound. If you're in deep sleep and an alarm goes off, the first thing that will land in your awareness is sound, which is diffuse and undifferentiated. For a moment, you know there is *sound* (noise) but can't differentiate it as the *word* (alarm). Even though the noise of the alarm is the same as you come to the waking state, your awareness has shifted from sound to word, from the subtle to the gross.

The most refined example of the sound-to-word pathway is the body of work known as the *Vedas*, (1200-1500 BCE), which are known as *śruti* (heard). The Vedas are the amalgamation of eternal *sound* perceived by highly evolved beings known as *ṛṣis* who made sense of the sound and conveyed their knowledge in the form of language or *word*. Sound is diffuse and generalized. From sound comes word, which is specific and directed. Śruti is the process of the sound becoming the word in this exquisite pathway, which moves from the integral or the whole and unbroken (*samaṣṭi*) to the derivative or the split parts (*vyaṣṭi*). Since the source of the knowledge is sound or the integral, it is applicable to derivatives across time and space. The Vedas as texts may be old collections of words, but the knowledge or *vid* arising from sound contained in them is eternal. The source of the word is sound, which is ever-present and available – even to us – if we can shift from the derivative to the integral or differentiated word to undifferentiated sound. The purpose of sādhanā is to move from word to sound, where we may gain access to vid or eternal knowledge.

Mantra sādhanā is a good example of traversing the word-to-sound pathway, where the specificity of the differentiated word takes us to the diffuseness of sound with committed practice. It is like going from the alarm with its connotations of being annoying, startling or anxiety-provoking to its pure sound devoid of any associations. In mantra sādhanā, a differentiated word, the mantra, eventually dissolves into undifferentiated sound.

The Śrīcakra is the visual representation of both the sound-to-word and the word-to-sound pathways. It expands from the center to the periphery in the sound-to-word pathway, the integral becoming the derivatives and the specifics. In the word-to-sound pathway, the center gathers the derivatives from the periphery back into itself. The Śrīcakra is the dynamic demonstration of sound becoming word, giving meaning and structure to the universe, our body-minds and lives, and the word dissolving back into sound.

The Śrīcakra is the throb of creation arising and collapsing in the sound-to-word-to-sound pathway.

The sādhanā of the Śrīcakra is to first move from the derivative to the integral, or the sthūla to the parā. The sthūla here refers to the word or the specificities of our life that lie at the periphery of the Śrīcakra. Here, we are a tiny part of the fabric of the universe with no access to the whole, which can only be known at the center. The stages of sādhanā correspond to the journey from the periphery to the center as we follow the trail of the word-to-sound pathway.

With this very preliminary understanding of the Śrīcakra and the purpose of sādhanā, we will delve into the specifics of the path known as Śrīvidyā.

Chapter 2

A Primer on Śrīvidyā

Śrīvidyā is comprised of two words, Śrī (auspicious) and vidyā (wisdom) and is a path of philosophy and practice centered on the goddess known as *Lalitā Mahātripurasundarī.*

Although Śrī means auspicious, it refers to the principle of creation that is eternally and universally worshiped. Lalitā Devī (also called Devī in this book) is the personification of the ubiquitous creative force. Whoever we are, wherever we come from and whether we are aware of her or not, we worship Devī in our desire to survive and thrive. The desire to live, create, and prosper drives not only humans but every animate and inanimate form of creation.

> ***Śrīvidyā is the path that brings us to the realization of Śrī, the all-pervading principle at the heart of reality.***

The word vidyā (the feminine noun) also refers to the mantra of a feminine deity. Accordingly, Śrīvidyā also refers to the central mantra of Śrī, which is known as the *Pañcadaśī* (comprised of 15 syllables). Importantly, Śrīvidyā is a path to nirvāṇa or liberation.

The history of Śrīvidyā is difficult to trace, largely due to the many interpretations of its origins, but also because many manuscripts and commentaries that could supplement the data of its origin from the oral practice traditions are lost. Some proponents of Śrīvidyā find its traces in the Vedas, which were compiled into four divisions[10] known as the *Ṛg*, *Yajur*, *Sāma* and *Atharva* Vedas. The Atharva Veda is the newest of the Vedas, dating back to around 900 BCE although some of its content is from the Ṛg Veda. Some scholars trace the Śrīvidyā mantra to the Atharva Veda.

It is possible, however, that what we now know as Śrīvidyā was present as a tribal tradition before the time of the Atharva Veda (or even earlier) and was subsequently incorporated into the Vedas. By some accounts, the cults of worship centered around feminine

10 By the legendary sage Veda Vyāsa, who is also known as the author of the *Purāṇas* (a large body of literature where the complex Vedic knowledge is presented in the form of myths and stories) and the *Mahābhārata* (an epic saga of the Kuru dynasty), among others.

deities are traced to the 5th century CE, where worship may have included possession, occasional sexual rites, and specific codes of conduct and observances. As opposed to mainstream Hinduism, the practices of these cults were not *Vedik* in origin. Instead, the tenets of the path were thought to have been revealed directly by the deities. These texts came to be known as the *Tantras, Āgamas* (tradition, see below) or *Saṃhitās* (collection).[11]

The earliest reference to Śrīvidyā that is closest to its present form appears in the 6th-7th century CE Tamil text known as the *Tirumandiram*, which is attributed to Sage *Tirumūlār*.[12]

Commentaries on the oldest Śrīvidyā text, the *Vāmakeśvara* Tantra, by non-dual *Kashmiri Śaivites* began to emerge. Infludenced by these commentaries, Śrīvidyā acquired the flavors of the *Krama* and *Pratyabhijñā* schools and became established as a sophisticated system of philosophy and practice.[13] Eventually, Śrīvidyā migrated to South India when it was adopted by the *Śaṅkarācāryas*, beginning with *Ādi Śaṅkarācārya* in the 8th century.

If you've heard of Śrīvidyā being a *Tāntrik* path, all this may be confusing since we have been talking about the Vedas up until now. Before we get further into the issue of Vedik vs. Tāntrik with respect to Śrīvidyā, we must understand what Tantra is.

11 See Introduction in André Padoux, *The Heart of the Yoginī: The Yoginihrdaya, a Sanskrit Tantric Treatise* (Oxford: Oxford University Press, 2013).

12 Per some academic experts, linguistic evidence of the currently available version of this text is closer to 13th century C.E.

13 Anna Golovkova, 'Śrīvidyā', in ed. Knut A. Jacobsen et al, *Brill's Encyclopedia of Hinduism.*

Tantra

Tantra has several definitions including to weave. Etymologically, the word Tantra comes from two roots: *tan* (to expand) and *tra* (instrument).

> ***Tantra is an instrument for expansion. It specifically refers to the expansion of the nature of Reality through the particulars of philosophy, code of conduct, and the use of ritual, mantra, and yantra.***

The purpose of Tantra is *svatantra* or absolute freedom from the suffering that is inherent in saṃsāra.

Tantra as a philosophy is diffuse and consists of teachings categorized according to the central deity. Within each category, the central deity is taken to be the ultimate or

Supreme Reality. Although it may seem like the deities are unique and separate, the principle they represent – the Ultimate Reality – is the same. For instance, when the central deity is *Śiva*, the philosophy comes to be known as Śaiva Tantra. Similarly for *Śākta*, *Vaiṣṇava*, *Gāṇapatya* and others where the central deity is Śakti, *Viṣṇu*, and *Gaṇapati*, respectively.

When it comes to the source texts of Tantra, we can think of them in two broad categories: *Āgama* and *Nigama*. Tāntrik texts are presented as dialogues between the central deity who acts as the teacher and a questioner (often another deity) who takes the role of a disciple. The word Āgama refers to a teaching that is handed down in a lineage and generally refers to texts of the Śaiva division. In these texts, the teacher is Śiva and Śakti is often the disciple, whereas in the Tantras (the texts), Śakti is the teacher and Śiva is often the disciple. Texts in which Śakti is the teacher are also known as Nigamas (which means sacred doctrines). However, to further confuse the issue, this classification isn't clear-cut since some of the Śaiva texts are also known as Tantras, and in some Śākta Tantras, Śiva is the teacher.

Tāntrik teachings were developed for initiates that required *dīkṣā* or initiation as the necessary first step. The premise of these teachings was the achievement of both *mukti* (liberation) and *bhukti* (enjoyment), where the adept cultivated supernatural powers that could, at least in theory, dominate the manifest world using mantras, rituals and yantras. Mukti and bhukti were not postponed to the afterlife – they were achievable while still living, and such an adept would be known as a *jīvanmukta*.

As Tāntrik teachings began to expand, they were increasingly adopted by orthodox householder Hindus to such a great extent that there is currently hardly any Hindu tradition that totally excludes Tāntrik elements.

The ritual use of mantra, pūjā or worship that is central to Hindu traditions, the rites and construction of temples, and the use of even the common añjalī mudrā in the greeting "*namaste*" have Tāntrik roots. The later Vedas often refer to practices and philosophy that we now classify as Tāntrik. The important thing to remember is that the philosophy and practice of Tantra comes from a very large body of knowledge, and this is where the issue of Vedik vs. Tāntrik becomes muddled.

While we may be tempted to think that the Tāntrik texts have nothing to do with the Vedas, this would be a considerable misconception on our part. Tantra as a word is mentioned in all the four Vedas in various contexts, as well as in other works that may not be classified as Tāntrik. As much as we would like to neatly separate Tantra from the Vedas, it is nearly impossible to do so.

This understanding is crucial if we want to delve into Śrīvidyā and the Śrīcakra because although some components of this path are Tāntrik, others are based squarely in the Vedas. The important thing to state here is that although this mixing brings up discomfort for scholars and academicians, the majority of contemporary Śrīvidyā practitioners are hardly bothered by it because they are, first and foremost, *upāsakas*.

Śrīvidyā Upāsanā

The practice of Śrīvidyā is most referred to as *upāsanā*, rather than sādhanā. Upāsanā is derived from two roots: *upa* (near) and *āsana* (sit), meaning to sit near or to be in the proximity of the object of our interest. When the "*a*" at the end becomes elongated as in upāsanā, the word assumes a feminine gender, and means worship or devotion that is expressed as a sense of proximity to the object of worship. In Śrīvidyā, the object of worship is Devī (short for Lalitā Devī).

While sādhanā also refers to worship or adoration, the word has the connotation of focus and determination to achieve a particular goal. Both sādhanā and upāsanā require focus and determination, but the *attitude* differs.

> ***For an upāsaka, the very act of being near the object of devotion is the goal, whereas for a sādhaka, the object of devotion is the means to an end.***

There are several aspects of a path that make the path an upāsanā rather than a sādhanā, including constant worship and attendance in the activities of daily life, humility, reverence, service, and renouncing other competing interests.[14] For an upāsaka, every mundane activity such as an interaction with a co-worker or family member, or the need to attend to taxes and bills, is an act of worship. The

14 Ramachandra S.K Rao, *Śrīvidyā Kośa* (Delhi: Sri Satguru Publications, 2013), Chapter 1.

upāsaka doesn't stray too far from Devī; her conduct and behavior are congruent with the focus on constant worship. She gradually renounces competing interests and realigns the rest of her life - work, relationships, finances, and lifestyle - with the mode of constant worship.

While ritual is part of this worship, the significant realignment, focus, determination, and perseverance that the path demands comes from the repetitive turning over of the instruction in the mind, applying the teaching to the nitty-gritties of life, and finding the sweetness and delight of the aspects of ritual in the mundane.

Because it is a constant remembrance, upāsanā gradually realigns our worldview with that of the path. This is a significant occurrence in an upāsaka's life, and one that results in a shift in stance. A stance here is meant by the place from which we approach the world. Ordinarily, this stance or worldview is shaped by influences from our family, culture, media, peers, and other norms. We hold on tightly to our beliefs about ourselves and the world, and how everything "should" be, which is a significant cause of suffering. We tend to rule over the world mentally, silently dictating the behavior of others, our past selves, world events, and natural disasters.

As a result of upāsanā and the constant turning over of the teachings in the mind, our worldview begins to disintegrate and is replaced by the darśana (view) of the path.

Quite insidiously, our old patterns are replaced by the teachings of the path, and our perception begins to change. We stop holding things too tightly and quit dictating the world from our mental thrones. The concepts of the *darśana* will need to eventually disintegrate as well, but for now, the change in our worldview is the exquisite gift of upāsanā.

The practice of the Śrīcakra is an upāsanā, where we constantly engage in its contemplation or bhāvanā and apply its principles in moment-to-moment life. In this book, the words sādhanā and upāsanā are used interchangeably. When the proximity to the practice is the emphasis, the word upāsanā is preferentially used.

Śrīvidyā is not unique in being a path of upāsanā; in fact, this is the central theme of the Āgamas. Although it receives special attention in the Śākta texts, it has components of the Śaiva and Vaiṣṇava streams as well. What is unique about Śrīvidyā is the highly developed philosophy and practice centered on the Śrīcakra.

Several other nuances differentiate Śākta Tantra from other streams, such as the emphasis on lineage-based teachings rather than textual knowledge, as well as on dīkṣā. The stress on lineage-based teachings (known as *sampradāya*) is probably at least in part due to the wide heterogeneity in what constitutes Śrīvidyā. However, because of the considerable influence of Śaivism (of Kashmir) on Śrīvidyā and its subsequent spread to South India, there is a great mix of teachings with regional flavors. Depending on whether the worldview of a stream of practitioners is Vedik, Śaivite or Śākta, the version of Śrīvidyā they practiced became unique to them. Even though the central tenets of Śrīvidyā – the Śrīvidyā mantra, the ritual worship of Devī, and the Śrīcakra – are the same, the *way* in which these aspects are practiced can differ considerably among the sampradāyas. The central principle of a given sampradāya is the exquisite relationship between the Guru and the *śiṣya* (student).

The Guru-Śiṣya Relationship

One of the fundamental tenets of Śrīvidyā is that of the systematic progression of upāsanā under the guidance of a Guru.

There are many meanings of the word Guru (including heavy and prized), but in this context, we consider its two roots: *gu*, which means darkness, and *ru*, meaning confining or obstructing darkness. Taken together, a Guru is one who sheds the light of Self-knowledge that dispels the darkness of ignorance.

Here, ignorance refers to taking ourselves to be this body-mind or the actor in the movie analogy (see Introduction), which is the basis for saṃsāra. A Guru is one who shows us the way out of the ignorance of saṃsāra because s/he has "been there and done that." Various texts describe the ideal Guru as one who has attained Self-knowledge and is only interested in the upliftment of the śiṣya (disciple) to the same level of realization. In other words, a Guru has no other vested interest in the śiṣya, such as building a following, attaining fame, acquiring wealth, and so on.[15]

15 Swami Chinmayananda, *Vivekacūḍāmaṇī* (Chinmaya Mission Trust), 2006. Chapter 1.

A śiṣya must be equally primed to enter this relationship and must have cultivated the essential qualities of wanting Self-knowledge, understanding the difference (at least in theory) between saṃsāra and nirvāṇa, patience, tolerance, some degree of control over the senses, and importantly, devotion.

> ***The ideal Guru-śiṣya relationship is exquisite, where the Guru regards the śiṣya as an equal and the śiṣya honors the Guru as the source of vidyā (knowledge).***

Unlike all other relationships that are based in social and cultural norms, the Guru-śiṣya bond is based in naked vulnerability and mutual love and respect. The śiṣya surrenders to the Guru, becoming progressively empty of her old patterns of thinking and being, and is steadily filled with the darśana of the lineage. Denser patterns are replaced by increasingly subtle and rarefied ones through the study of the philosophy and the practice in which she is instructed.

The concept of the Guru is a delicate one and needs a bit of deliberation here. In the modern era where individualization and personal accomplishment are deeply valued, we may have an issue with the idea of submitting to a Guru. The modern age makes us naturally suspicious of hierarchy, compounded and justified by the abundance of self-proclaimed Gurus who turn out to be charlatans that abuse their followers to fulfill their own unmet needs. If we project the flaws of *some* frauds on *all* Gurus, our cynicism comes in the way of the *upadeśa* (instruction), prohibiting the transmission of vidyā (knowledge).

On the other hand, approaching a Guru with a sycophantic sentiment is not helpful either. Flattery, blind faith, and the lack of an ability to think for oneself are equally problematic obstacles in the Guru-śiṣya relationship. Although a deep devotion and regard for the Guru is needed, the willingness to internalize the upadeśa to practice unceasingly and to work upon our self is far more important for progress. While the Guru imparts knowledge and śakti (power) through the upadeśa, s/he cannot do our work for us.

It's essential to reflect on why we would need a Guru at all. We approach one because we want to be freed of our delusions and ego that keeps us bound in saṃsāra. If we approach the relationship expecting the Guru to soothe and placate the ego, they would not be holding up their end of the bargain, which is to free us from it. Their behavior and instruction must reflect the purpose for which we approached them in the first place, and our expectations must remain congruent with our intention.

Importantly, the Guru is known as a refuge not only because s/he "has our back," but also because it is only in this relationship that we can show up without any posturing. In all other relationships, we are expected to behave in certain ways to maintain the decorum and structure of the relationship. Socially constructed relationships that depend on maintaining harmony demand that we appease each other in word and deed. Showing up naked and vulnerable is challenging when relationships are built on expectations.

With the Guru, however, we can lay down the mantle of pretences and show up as nakedly as we possibly can. S/he acts as a mirror, showing us our limiting patterns and teaching us other ways to think, feel, and behave. In the cultivation of surrender and nakedness our deep grooves of conditioning begin to fill in. It is not enough to intellectualize that everything is Devī in manifestation. In the context of this intimate upadeśa of looking in the mirror that is the Guru, we come to experience this truth first-hand. The Guru becomes the gateway to this experience as we follow the threads of vidyā coming through the upadeśa.

Upadeśa begins with dīkṣā, which is derived from two roots: *dā* (to give) and *kṣi* (to destroy). It can also mean consecration and refers to the process by which the śiṣya becomes initiated into the practice, the philosophy, and the lineage. Although we commonly think of dīkśa as the process in which the Guru imparts a particular mantra, it is much more complex and dependent on the *bhāva* (attitude or disposition) of the śiṣya. The classification of bhāvas is one of the fundamental tenets of Tantra and forms the traditional basis for the differences in the upadeśa between śiṣyas of the same Guru.

Since aptitude determines suitability for specific practices, we will now investigate the sādhanas in Śrīvidyā.

The Sādhanā Spectrum in Śrīvidyā

Practices in Śrīvidyā vary widely according to sampradāya and the inclination of the practitioner. In general, Śrīvidyā involves the worship of other deities along with Lalitā Devī, including Gaṇapati, *Bālā Tripurasundarī* (the form of Devī as a young girl), *Mātaṅgī*, and *Vārāhī*.

Sādhanā involves pūjā or ritual worship of the deities in both their sthūla (such as a *mūrti* or idol) and yantra forms, *nyāsa* or ritual installing of divine forms, mudrā or hand/body gestures to redirect and seal the flow of energy, *tarpaṇa* or libations, *japa* or mantra sādhanā, *homa* or offerings into the fire, visualization, meditation, and bhāvanā.

The ritual worship of the Śrīcakra in Śrīvidyā tends to be highly specific to the sampradāya and must be learned from the Guru. In general, it involves the preparation of the *sāmānyārghya* (the ordinary offering) and the *viśeṣārghya* (the special offering) by invoking various śaktis, deities and *kalās* (digits of the fire, sun, and moon)[16] into them through mantras and nyāsas. The two *arghyas* are reverential offerings used to oblate the Śrīcakra in the process known as tarpaṇa. This process, the contents of the viśeṣārghya, as well as how it is used in the pūjā are sampradāya-specific.

16 See Chapter 11 for the kalās of fire and Chapter 16 for the kalās of the moon.

The Śrīcakra pūjā includes all (or nearly all) the sādhanās in the spectrum and can be a lengthy process.

> ***Through the involvement of the body, mind, and speech in the offerings, chanting, japa, nyāsa, coordination of mantra with procedure, and the intense focus that is required in every step, the Śrīcakra pūjā works as a deep cleansing process. It works on rewiring the brain, the neurohormonal pathways, the flow of thought and emotion, sense perception and perspective.***

Even though the sādhanā spectrum in Śrīvidyā can be daunting, the diversity of practices make sense when we understand the range of bhāvas or inclinations of Śrīvidyā practitioners.

Bhāva

In general, a spiritual aspirant may be of one of the following bhāvas, which will determine which elements of a given path might result in the assimilation of vidyā. The three bhāvas are progressive and denote the change in stance that occurs naturally as a result of dīkṣā and upadeśa in the context of the Guru-śiṣya relationship.

Paśu, which means animal, refers to the bhāva of a herd. Most of us begin here, where our aspirations are inspired by being in the herd of society. These aspirations are familiar and comforting and are informed by the prevailing thought of the family in which we are born, the society in which we are raised and nurtured, and the peers with whom we live, age, share, work, play, and die. As paśus, we follow the common aspirations of our culture such as growing up with a certain set of moral values, accomplishing certain goals such as an education, a job, intimiate relationships, and caring for others in particular ways.

Paśu bhāva also influences our spiritual and religious beliefs, where we follow what we have been taught, and tend to be driven by fear and hope – fearing the consequences of not following a particular belief and hoping for a future outcome that rewards us for our loyalty. Bhāva shapes our perception, establishing clear boundaries between "us" and "them" (of different beliefs and lifestyles). As paśus, we prefer to hang out with our herd even if it causes conflict or discomfort, or if we are shamed or abused, because its familiarity is more comforting than the uncertainty of the alternative.

Vīra, which means valorous, refers to the bhāva of one who is willing to step out of the herd. A vīra (*vīrā* with the elongated a at the end refers to a female practitioner) has cultivated the necessary self-awareness to understand the influence of the herd on their own life, and in thinking and being. S/he becomes willing to go against the grain of the herd and discard the limitations of the social, moral, and cultural conditioning.

With increasing courage, a vīra steps into the discomfort of the uncertainty of leaving the herd. Through the teachings and practices of the lineage, a vīra's perception begins to change, where the world isn't seen as clearly divided into blacks and whites, but as shades of grey. With a loosening of the ideas around right/wrong and good/evil, the vīrā transcends the limitations of her own mind.

With the continuous expansion of the mind beyond the limiting concepts and beliefs of the paśu, the vīra explores the world as a playground. S/he challenges the mind by increasing mental/emotional engagement with what was previously taboo, unthinkable, sinful, or immoral, while still living and working harmoniously in the world. The purpose of such an exploration is never to exploit or harm others, but to continuously ascend the ladder of vidyā by shedding limitations cast by society and learning.

Divya, which means divine, refers to the bhāva of exquisite *viveka* (discernment) and *vairāgya* (non-attachment). A divya has overcome the limitations of the herd, and through the subtle explorations as a vīra, has arrived at the state where s/he is not influenced by the approval or criticism of the world. Through the constant contemplation and application of the darśana in daily life, s/he has risen above the vagaries of saṃsāra.

The paśu's internal landscape is dominated by thoughts and feelings of self-preservation, gaining approval of others, maintaining a self-image, and getting along with the herd. A vīra's internal landscape, on the other hand, is characterized by thoughts and emotions focused on self-expansion through self-inquiry, self-challenge, and self-exploration. In contrast to both, a divya rests in self-assurance, with thoughts and emotions directed toward the Supreme Reality. S/he is able to discern the extremely subtle difference between self-knowledge and self-deception. Viveka, or discernment, goes hand-in-hand with vairāgya, where s/he is unattached to events and occurrences that lead to the latter, being firmly established in wanting and seeking vidyā alone.

Bhāva becomes important in the discussion about dīkṣā since it determines the *ācāra* (code of conduct) of the śiṣya and therefore the type of upadeśa that the Guru may impart upon them.

Ācāra

Traditionally, there are seven ācāras, referring to the various prescribed (and observed) modes of conduct.[17,18]

- *Vedācāra*: the prescription is to conduct our lives with daily rituals, contemplating our inner landscape, and honoring teachers, parents, and other figures of authority. Here, the focus is on understanding our place in society and cultivating a sense of what is right and behaving in ways that are congruent with *dharma* (natural law).[19] At this stage, conduct is dictated by obedience to an external authority and driven by the fear of otherwise incurring their wrath.
- *Vaiṣṇavācāra*: the fear of external authority is increasingly replaced by devotion. The conduct of the previous phase has opened us to awe and faith in the protective power of the Divine. Accordingly, the conduct is shaped by a greater degree of adherence to dharma, particularly as it applies to non-violence and harmony.

17 See also Chapter 11 in K. Chinnaiyan, *Glorious Alchemy: Living the Lalitā Sahasranāma* (New Sarum Press, 2020).

18 Ramachandra S.K Rao, *Śrīvidyā Kośa* (Delhi: Sri Satguru Publications, 2013), Chapter 1.

19 Simply stated, dharma refers to behaviors and a way of living that are in accordance with the natural order of the universe.

- *Śaivācāra:* the devotion of the previous phase is mingled with the courage to explore beyond norms through the acquisition of knowledge. At this stage, we actively seek knowledge and spiritual power because of the cultivation of the body and senses in the previous stages.
- *Dakṣiṇācāra:* ritual worship is undertaken with the application of purity cultivated in the first stage, devotion in the second, and knowledge in the third. Here, we are coming to understand the three primordial energies of creation – icchā, *jñāna* and *kriyā* (more on this to come in the next chapter) in our day-to-day experience.
- *Vāmācāra*: the focus is on the refinement and expansion of viveka and vairāgya.[20] Having passed from fear to valor, those belonging to the Vāmācāra lineages are called to antinomian practices utilizing the *pañcamakāras*, which are the five Ms: *madya* (alcohol), *māṃsa* (meat), *matsya* (fish), *mudrās* (hand gestures)[21] and *maithuna* (ritual sex outside of marriage). The purpose of the makāras is to transcend social, cultural, and moral norms. These transgressive practices are particularly tricky to navigate without the guidance of a Guru because it is easy to fall into the trap of sense gratification instead of using the makāras to transcend them. Vāmācāra also consists of practices such as rituals conducted in cremation grounds, which tend to be dangerous from the psycho-spiritual perspective without a certain degree of attainment and control over the senses.
- *Siddhāntācāra*: we have transcended fear, disgust, pity, hatred, lust, and attachment, and attention rests effortlessly in the essence of Reality. Here, the Guru transmits the innermost secrets of the path because the śiṣya has attained the *pātrata* (competency or worthiness) for this higher teaching.
- *Kaulācāra*: considered the highest among the seven ācāras where we have transcended all norms bound in time and space. A *kaula* roams free in the vast inner space that has become her/his outer reality. S/he sees no differences between the seemingly beautiful and the profane. The microcosm and the macrocosm have become one and s/he has transcended saṃsāra.

The above seven ācāras come to us from the Śākta literature[22] that are kaula in their outlook. The important thing to remember here is that instead of being seven different classes or divisions, the ācāras represent a loose progression from the gross to the subtle, or from paśu to divya. However, this does not mean that they aren't also considered to

20 See Chapter 5.

21 Mudrā may also refer to parched grains because they are said to contain aphrodisiac properties.

22 Such as the *Kulārṇava Tantra*, *Mahānirvāṇa Tantra*, *Niruttara Tantra*, and so on.

be separate streams of practice. Especially after Śaivācāra, we can continue to progress in either the Dakṣiṇācāra or Vāmācāra streams that tend to be lineage specific. Although these ācāras can be considered as stages of spiritual growth, we must remember that this progression need not occur in a single lifetime and is considered to happen over several lifetimes. In each subsequent birth, we pick up where we left off.

In Śrīvidyā, we come across another ācāra known as *Samayācāra*, which is not included in the above classification. The Śrīvidyā lineages arising from Ādi Śaṅkarācārya fall into this category and follow the Vedik text known as the *Śubhāgama Pañcaka*, or the works of the five great seers who were the mind-born sons of *Brahmā*, the creator.[23] In Samayācāra, practices are entirely internal, and all external rituals are disposed of and discouraged. Samayācāra has come to be associated with the Vedik path of Śrīvidyā, often consisting of rigid rules and regulations such as exclusion of women and those of certain castes.[24]

The purpose of reviewing the ācāras is to understand the correlation between bhāva and dīkṣā.

23 *Sanaka, Sanandana, Sanatkumāra, Sānatsujātha* and *Śaṅkara*.

24 Non-Brāhmins are not given dīkṣā in certain Śrīvidyā lineages.

Dīkṣā

Venturing into the spiritual journey often involves appropriate initiations.[25] If we possess paśu bhāva, initiation into Vedācāra and Vaiṣṇavācāra are considered appropriate. Dīkṣā into the Śākta path takes us to Dakṣiṇācāra and is known as *sāktābhiṣeka*, and the next consecration (*pūrṇābhiṣeka*) into the Vāmācāra path occurs when our bhāva shifts to that of a vīra.

Consecrations known as krama dīkṣā and *sāmrājya* dīkṣā occur when our bhāva transitions to that of a divya, entitling us to follow Siddhāntācāra. *Mahāsāmrājya* dīkṣā gives us the eligibility for Kaulācāra, and pūrṇābhiṣeka at this stage marks the final attainment. In Śrīvidyā, there are 32 levels of initiations.

Dīkṣā can occur through various means, such as touch, sight, thought, mantra, and ritual.[26] The choice of the method of dīkṣā rests with the Guru, who also decides on the progressive consecrations based on the *pātrata* or capacity of the śiṣya.

When it comes to Śrīvidyā, mantra is the most common mode of dīkṣā and the Guru decides the most appropriate one for the śiṣya, imparting progressively more advanced

25 Ramachandra S.K Rao, *Śrīvidyā Kośa*, (Delhi: Sri Satguru Publications, 2013), Chapter 1.

26 Arthur Avalon, *Kulārṇava Tantra* (Motilal BanaṚṣidass, 2007), Chapter 10.

mantras over time. The appropriateness of a mantra for a given disciple is based on numerous factors, most of which are subtle and observed only by the discerning Guru. A given mantra must do its work of being comfortable enough to practice regularly *and* challenge the sādhaka to grow beyond the confines of the conditioned mind.

Here, the important thing to remember is that the importance of the Guru cannot be overstated in Tāntrik sādhanā. While it may be tempting to dismiss the Guru in favor of the "inner Guru," which implies a reliance upon one's own (often flawed) intuition, treading the traditional Tāntrik path is to honor the Guru-śiṣya relationship. Taking a mantra out of a book or off the internet does not constitute Tāntrik sādhanā as far as Śrīvidyā adepts are concerned, particularly because the Śrīvidyā mantra lends itself to additional layers of complexity and variation in classifications known as *matas*.

The Śrīvidyā Matas

In general, the Śrīvidyā lineages, rituals and texts were distinguished by three matas[27] – *kādi*, *hādi*, and *sādi*.[28] The mata refers to the beginning syllable of the Pañcadaśī mantra, which can be *ka*, *ha* or *sa*. Each mata has its own ritual manuals and source texts and can contain sampradāyas spanning the various ācāras. Kādi vidyā, referring to the mantra beginning with *ka* is the most widely prevalent form of Śrīvidyā. The Lalitā Sahasranāma, the *Tantrarāja Tantra*, *Bhāskararāya*'s *Varivasya Rahasya*, the Bhāvanopaniṣad and the *Paraśurāma Kalpa Sūtra* are examples of kādi vidyā or *kādimata* texts.

Hādi vidyā or *hādimata* was precepted by *Lopāmudrā*, Sage *Agastya's* illustrious wife.[29] Yoginī Hṛdaya, Kāmakalā Vilāsa and the Khaḍgamālā Stotra are examples of hādi vidyā texts. *Sādi vidyā*, which is no longer in popular use, was precepted by *Sage Dūrvāsa* without any widely known dedicated texts or handbooks on rituals.

Guru Maṇḍala

In Śrīvidyā, Devī is the Supreme Guru from whom the entire *paramparā* (lineage) unfolds in an unbroken chain. The Guru is non-separate from both Devī and the sādhaka.

27 Mata refers to practice or lineage and refers to a variation of the Pañcadaśī mantra.

28 Traditionally, there are 12 variations of the Pañcadaśī attributed to one of the following luminaries: Manu, Candra, Kubera, Lopāmudrā, Kāma, Agastya, Agni, Sūrya, Indra, Skanda, Śiva, and Durvāsa. Of these, kādi and hādi are best known. According to some scholars, there are up to 30 variations of the mantra!

29 See Chapter 1 in K. Chinnaiyan, *Glorious Alchemy: Living the Lalitā Sahasranāma* (New Sarum Press, 2020).

Realizing the oneness of the three is an important milestone in sādhanā. Traditionally, there are 32 levels of initiation in Śrīvidyā, and at a certain stage, the sādhaka is given a new name and is incorporated permanently into the lineage. The Guru maṇḍala, which is a vital aspect of Śrīvidyā, is deeply revered and commands a high level of devotion.[30] In fact, the Guru-disciple relationship is the lifeblood of Śrīvidyā.

30 The Guru maṇḍala is the "network" of the Gurus of the lineage.

For the śiṣya, the Guru maṇḍala begins with the Śrī Guru, the one with whom we cultivate an intimate relationship, who initiates us on the path and graces us with upadeśa. Through the Śrī Guru, we meet her/his Guru, who becomes our Parama Guru, and through her/him, our *Parameṣṭi* Guru. The Parameṣṭi Guru's Guru is our *Parātpara* Guru (see Figure 1). As we will see later, the Guru maṇḍala has a special place and location in the Śrīcakra.

The Guru maṇḍala becomes a constant source of inspiration for the willingness to go the distance. The Guru maṇḍala that is central to the practice of Śrīvidyā is dependent on sampradāya and *āmnāya*.

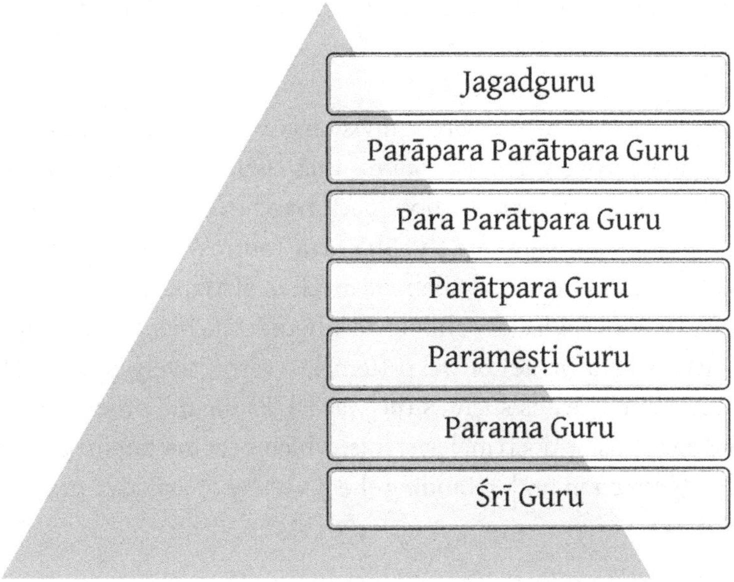

Figure 1. Guru Maṇḍala

Sampradāya and Āmnāya

The history of Śrīvidyā lends itself to equal parts of confusion and inspiration. While a deep academic exploration of the topic is not necessary for most upāsakas, understanding some of its nuances does enhance practice and engagement with the Śrīcakra.

The Tāntrik Śākta-Śaiva canon splits at the outset into two distinct paths – *Atimārga* (extreme or superior path, referring to upāsakas who live and practice outside the norm of the householder path) and *Mantramārga* (path of mantra) (see Figure 2). In Atimārga, which consists of several streams such as *kapālika* and *lākulīsa*, the emphasis is entirely on transcending saṃsāra. Here, mantras are used to accomplish this goal and not for gaining any other power or worldly goal.

In Mantramārga, mantras are the vehicles for not only transcending saṃsāra but also for various accomplishments and perfections known as *siddhis*. In fact, a mantra is the deity in sonic form, worthy of propitiation and worship. Additionally, Mantramārga was open to non-*Brāhmins* and women, whereas only Brāhmins qualified for Atimārga.[31] Moreover, Mantramārga held the promise of bhukti and mukti, as opposed to Atimārga, which shunned bhukti in favor of mukti.[32]

Mantramārga is divided into two broad divisions – *Siddhānta* and non-Siddhānta, which are based on texts known as *Bhairava Tantras* that contain transgressive practices such as the pañcamakāras (see above) or those performed in cemeteries (see Figure 2). The Siddhānta stream does not venerate the Bhairava Tantras, whereas the non-Siddhānta stream does. The non-Siddhānta or Bhairava division of Mantramārga is further divided into *mantrapīṭha* and *vidyāpīṭha*, depending on whether the mantra (and the corresponding central deity) is Śiva (male) or Śakti (female), respectively. Within Mantramārga, we find nine different streams such as the *yāmala*, kaula and others. Within the kaula system are the āmnāyas or doctrinal systems, which become important for those of us who might be interested in understanding the diversity of Śrīvidyā practices and ritual *paddhatis* (methods).

31 Brāhmin, Kṣatriya, Vaiśya and Śūdra are the four divisions of society that over time have come be known as castes. Although caste was originally understood as the classification of societal roles based on guṇa (aptitude) and karma (vocation), it eventually became a social division of hierarchy, where Brāhmins proclaimed themselves to be superior and worthy of knowledge, segregating other castes as inferior. See *Bhagavad Gītā* Chapter 4 and *Chinnamasta* in K. Chinnaiyan, *Shakti Rising* (Nonduality Press, 2017).

32 See The Path of Bhukti and Mukti in Chapter 6.

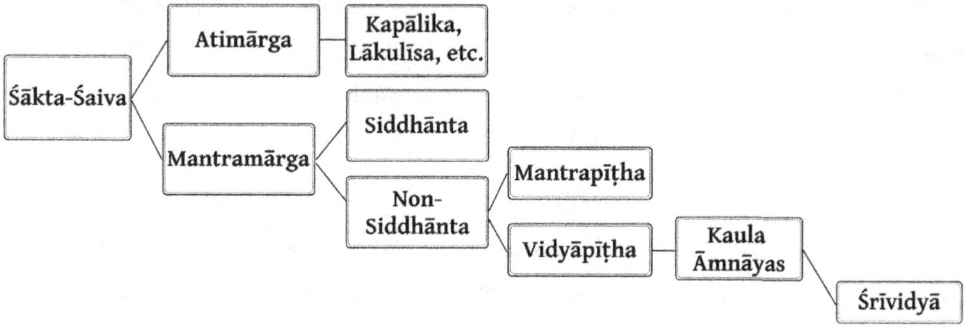

Figure 2. Classification of the Tāntrik streams

The four principal āmnāyas are named after the four directions and are centered on particular deities. Each āmnāya is associated with a Guru maṇḍala, darśana, rituals and practices, and the corresponding fruit of sādhanā (see Table 1). The northern doctrine or *Uttarāmnaya* is known as *Kālī Kula* or Krama and is centered around *Kālī*. The eastern doctrine or *Pūrvāmnāya* is *Trika*, centered around three deities – *Parā*, *Parāparā* and *Aparā*. The western doctrine or *Paścimāmnāya* is *Kaubjikā* Tantra, centered around goddess *Kubjikā*. The southern doctrine or *Dakṣiṇāmnāya* is Śrīvidyā, centered around Mahātripurasundarī.[33] Each āmnāya has its own philosophy, text(s) and ritual paddhati that is unique and specific to the stream, with significant overlap amongst the doctrines. In addition, some authors correlate each āmnāya to one of the four primary Śakti *pīṭhas* (seats) – *Oḍḍiyāṇa*, *Pūrṇagiri*, *Jālandhara*, and *Kāmarūpa*.[34]

33 The Dakṣiṇāmnāya was historically centered around Kāmeśvarī. Śrīvidyā took over this stream and Mahātripurasundarī became its central deity. Śrīvidyā is the latest stream with elements adopted from Trika, Krama and Kaubjikā streams, all of which are still present and practiced in it.

34 Pīṭha refers to the sacred site of Śakti and can vary greatly in number depending on the text/tradition. The four referred to here are geographical locations in the Indian subcontinent that are of great importance for Śakti sādhanā and are said to be infused with the presence of the goddess. They also correspond to centers in the subtle body.

Table 1. A Summary of the Four Āmnāyas

Āmnāya	Uttarāmnāya	Pūrvāmnāya	Paścimāmnāya	Dakṣiṇāmnāya
Direction	Northern	Eastern	Western	Southern
Tradition	Krama	Trika	Kaubjikā	Śrīvidyā
Deity	Kālasaṅkarṣinī Kālī	Parā Aparā Parāparā	Kubjikā	Tripurasundarī
Pīṭha	Oḍḍiyāṇa	Kāmarūpa	Jālandhara	Pūrṇagiri
Text(s)	Jayadhratayāmala	Mālinīvijayottara	Kubjikāmata	Vāmakeśvarīmata

Two other āmnāyas are invoked primarily in the Śrīcakra pūjā: *ūrdhva* (upwards) and *Anuttara* (supreme). Upāsakas of Śrīvidyā consider this path the supreme or most evolved revelation that includes elements of all the āmnāyas. From an upāsaka's point of view, Śrīvidyā is holistic and inclusive because the deities of all āmnāyas find a place in the Śrīcakra, and many of the mantras from other āmnāyas are included in various Śrīvidyā teachings.

An alternative explanation of the āmnāyas comes from the legend of Lord Śiva who is said to have five faces, four facing the four directions and one facing upward. Each of his faces gives rise to one of the āmnāyas, Anuttara being his secret or hidden face.

While the above description of the āmnāyas from the standpoint of classical Tantra helps us place Śrīvidyā in the broader context of *Śāktism*, we must realize that this takes a different turn in what is known as the *Āmnāya Samaṣṭi pūjā*, which is part of the Śrīcakra pūjā. Here, the four principle āmnāyas correspond to the four Vedas, while the Ūrdhvāmnāya is the sum total of the knowledge of the *Upaniṣads*, and the Anuttarāmnāya is the implied, felt-sense of vidyā. Together, the six āmnāyas are said to contain 70 million mantras, and the purpose of invoking them in the Śrīcakra is to realize that all mantras of all āmnāyas are but different emanations of Lalitā Devī, who is the Supreme Reality or *Brahman*.

It must be noted here, however, that although all āmnāyas are worshiped in Śrīcakra pūjā, it does not mean that the specific paddhati of each doctrine (Trika, Kaubjikā or Krama) is followed. Instead, lineage-specific Śrīvidyā paddhatis are used to invoke the āmnāya deities in the Śrīcakra.

Sampradāya refers to the combination of darśana and upāsanā that is transmitted from one generation of adepts to the next. This transmission ensures continuity while allowing for revisions and updates within the community of practitioners. The three primary Śrīvidyā sampradāyas are *Dakṣiṇāmūrti*, *Hayagrīva*, and *Ānandabhairava*. Within each sampradāya are various Guru paramparās, with further variations in paddhatis. The construction and adoration of the Śrīcakra can differ between sampradāyas and within the same sampradāya among the Guru paramparās. Dīkṣā into the Guru paramparā enables us to become part of the sampradāya.

The given approach, rituals, and practice of the Śrīcakra are thus dependent on the āmnāya, sampradāya, Guru paramparā and the ācāra of that lineage (see Figure 3).

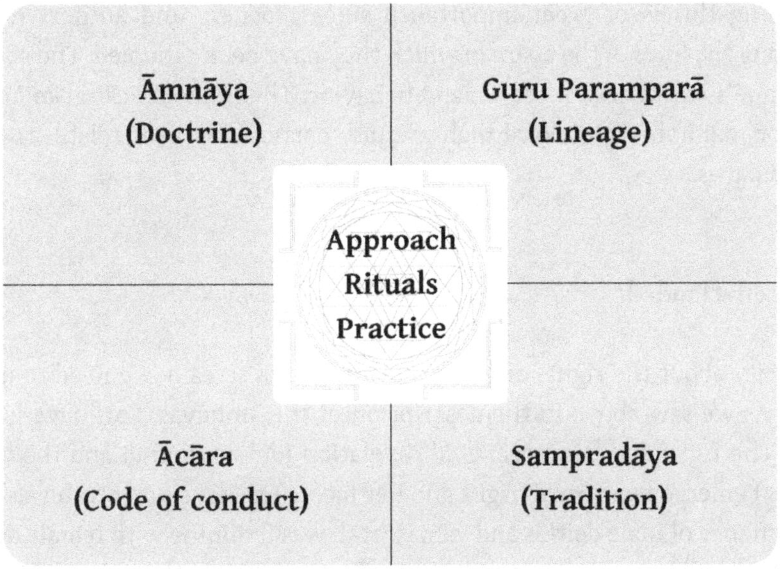

Figure 3. The Intricacies of Śrīcakra Practice

As we see through this brief exploration, the history of Śrīvidyā is exceedingly complex. Although we see its early origins in the Kaula stream, Śrīvidyā became incorporated into the monastic order of Ādi Śaṅkarācārya of Southern India over the next several centuries while also continuing to develop along its original roots among householders.

With Śaṅkarācārya, Śrīvidyā of the monastic order or Samayācāra (see above) was stripped of the antinomian Tāntrik hues, such as the use of mantras for magic and dominion, sexual rites, and other transgressive practices. It was made more acceptable for the masses by imbibing it with socially and morally acceptable norms, with an emphasis on cultivating *sattva* (more on this later).

A given Guru paramparā may lean toward a particular ācāra, leading to a corresponding adaptation of the darśana and upāsanā. In the monastic order, the Kaula darśana of Śrīvidyā was gradually replaced by that of Advaita Vedānta and adopted along the lines of Dakṣiṇācāra, which continues to present day. In general, except for a few such paramparās that tend to be purist when it comes to ācāras, most adopt a mix (*miśrācāra*). Understanding this is of great importance since teachers and authors expound on Śrīvidyā along the lines of the ācāra in which they have been schooled. The ācāra greatly influences one's worldview, lifestyle, and behavior. The issue of ācāra can also become the basis for maintaining a moral high ground, particularly as it relates to right- and left-handed paths.

Right- or Left-Handed?

To gain clarity about the right- or left-handedness of a stream, we need to understand its origins. As we saw above in the description of the āmnāyas, Lord Śiva is said to be five-faced. The right and left streams of revelation (*dakṣiṇasrotraḥ* and the *vāmasrotaḥ*, respectively) emerge from Śiva's right and left faces. The dakṣiṇasrotraḥ was masculine with a dominance of male deities and vāmasrotaḥ was feminine with female deities. This classification was given shape by Mantramārga (see above) with its distinctions of mantrapīṭha and vidyāpīṭha centered around male and female deities, respectively.

The original divisions between right and left had little to do with modes of conduct or practice, but with the classification of Tāntrik revelations. Although some debates on ācāras may have sprouted and grown over time, it wasn't until the 19th century that the idea of right- and left-handedness took hold and grew, propagated by the writings of Madame Blavatsky of the Theosophical Society. This new division created the idea of the right-handed path being benign, safe, and pure, and the left-handed as being dangerous and impure. Accordingly, left-handed became associated with black magic as well as transgressive practices such as ritual sex and consumption of meat or alcohol.

However, the definition of transgression is highly dependent on the ācāra one follows, which in turn falls upon the Guru paramparā and the practitioner's inclinations. To add to the confusion, practitioners within the same paramparā may differ in their approach to practice and "handedness," settling for one stream or another, particularly after *pūrṇadīkṣa* (see Dīkṣā above). Table 2 *loosely* summarizes some ways in which the two streams are differentiated, based on whether one is a monk or a householder, and the *mārga* (in the broad classification of Śaiva texts, see above) or ācāra one follows.

Table 2: Broad Classification of Right- and Left-Handed Paths

Classification	Right-handed	Left-handed
Monastic	Monastic	Householder
Mārga	Saiddhānta	Non-Saiddhānta, Atimārga
Ācāra	Dakṣiṇācāra Samayācāra Vedācāra Vaiṣṇavācāra Śaivācāra	Vāmācāra Kaulācāra
Esoteric practice	The ascent of Kuṇḍalinī in a rightward loop	The descent of Kuṇḍalinī in a leftward loop

Ultimately, what is left-handed can be interpreted as anything that is transgressive to one's moral and social inclinations. If our moral conditioning around spirituality is that of celibacy, being sexually active can *appear* to be transgressive. If it is vegetarianism, eating meat becomes a transgression, and so on.

The beauty of the Śrīcakra is that it accommodates all the ācāras, beliefs, social and moral norms, and cultural labels. The goal of the practice is to start wherever we find ourselves on the spectrum of these specifications and work our way through them.

An esoteric way of understanding the right- and left-handed paths is through the concept of *cakras* and *Kuṇḍalinī*.[35] The six cakras of the subtle body are visualized as

35 See Prāṇa Nāḍīs, Cakras and Kuṇḍalinī, Chapter 11.

lotuses with specific numbers of petals (*mūlādhāra* – 4, *svādhiṣṭāna* – 6, *maṇipura* - 10, *anāhatā* - 12, *viśuddha* - 16 and *ājñā* - 2), totalling 50 and corresponding to the 50 Sanskrit letters.[36] They are placed in a clockwise direction in each cakra. In meditative practices, particularly those involving a mantra, the practitioner is taught to visualize each petal in succession beginning in the mūlādhāra and ascending to the ājñā in an anti-clockwise direction or rightward loop. At the ājñā, this loop is reversed and the sādhanā continues in a clockwise direction back to the mūlādhāra in a leftward loop.

The idea here is that we begin to ascend as vīras beyond our limitations of the socially and morally acceptable conduct of paśus. However, as we reach the expanses of Being beyond the dualistic mind at the ājñā, we come to realize that moral and social norms are in place to maintain societal harmony. Instead of being imposed externally through rigid rules, our behavior is cleansed and aligned with Divine Will, free-flowing and spontaneous in love, compassion, inclusivity, and delight.[37] The right-handedness of externally imposed limitations is transmuted to the left-handedness of spontaneous alignment with dharma through the transcendence of moral and social norms.

With this primer on the Śrīvidyā, we are now equipped to begin the exploration of the Śrīcakra.

36 In practice, the thousand-petaled sahasrāra cakra is assigned one petal, which makes it 51 Sanskrit letters.

37 See Chapter 18.

Chapter 3

The Auspicious Śrīcakra

The Śrīcakra is a cakra, a yantra and a maṇḍala, each word carrying a slightly different connotation. Even though we use the words Śrīcakra and *Śrīyantra* interchangeably, understanding the subtle differences between the terms may be helpful in practice. It is a cakra in that it includes elements that embody the cyclical movement of kinetic and potential energy, a yantra in that it is an instrument for Self-knowledge, and a maṇḍala in that it holds the space for a group of energies.

Cakra

The word cakra refers to various things, including cyclical phenomena and whirlpools. Relevant to our current topic is its meaning as a wheel, which, being circular, allows for the arrangement of various elements that cohesively and effectively work together. Just like a wheel, the various elements that make up a cakra are compactly held together by the centripetal force of the center.

> ***The cakra transcends and surpasses the sum total of the parts, and functions as one unit even though each element exerts its own power and influence upon the structure.***

Even though cakra refers to circular structures, the word also applies to purely metaphorical concepts such as the cakra or wheel of seasons, time, astrological bodies, or mantras. The synergy within the Śrīcakra works similarly. Each element in the Śrīcakra stands alone and yet exerts its influence over the entirety. The Śrīcakra is held together by the unifying force of the Bindu from which all the elements emerge and disperse into its farthest reaches. If the Śrīcakra is the whole of creation, each of its elements is a fractal, holding within itself the potential for totality. Each element is a fractal of reality and a portal to wholeness.

A familiar use of the word cakra is its association with the subtle centers that play an important role in Tāntrik sādhanā.[38] Cakras refer to subtle psycho-physiological centers that ground and trap the issues that keep us bound in saṃsāra. Ordinarily, our *saṃsārik* troubles keep our energies so engaged and entangled that the cakras are dull and stationery. Instead of whirling freely, it is as if they are stuck in mud. Sādhanā involves resolving the associated issues so that the cakras can behave as wheels, resulting in a release of stuck and pent-up energy that becomes available for increasingly advanced practices.[39]

38 See Chapter 7, 'Cakras and Kuṇḍalinī' in K. Chinnaiyan, *Glorious Alchemy: Living the Lalitā Sahasranāma* (New Sarum Press 2020).

39 See The Vāyus in Practice in Chapter 12.

There are many ways to classify the cakras, which depend on tradition and lineage. In Śrīvidyā, we focus on seven primary cakras that lie along the spine. The āvaraṇas of the Śrīcakra correlate to the psycho-physiological cakras; however, this correspondence tends to differ according to the sampradāya.[40] In Chapter 5, we will briefly examine one such correspondence from my lineage. The specifics of āvaraṇa-cakra correspondence are less important - what is more fruitful in personal practice is the appropriate internalization of knowledge to transcend the preoccupation with the issues of the related cakra/āvaraṇa. We will explore these relationships at length in this book.

40 See The Ṣaṭcakra and the Śrīcakra in Chapter 5.

Maṇḍala

In general, the word maṇḍala tends to be synonymous with cakra - an aggregation of individual elements. However, there are subtle differences between the two. A cakra can be thought of as a structure replete with kinetic and potential energy which is to be internalized (or rather, realized to be an internal phenomenon).

A maṇḍala, on the other hand, is a field or domain delineated in space. We can think of this domain to contain a particular type of energy, which can fall anywhere in the very broad spectrum of entities, deities, persons, or principles. Some examples of maṇḍalas are *sūrya* (solar), *candra* (lunar), *bhū* (earth), and Guru. Each of these maṇḍalas is an aggregate in space of the energies of the particular entity after which it is named.

Importantly, a maṇḍala is the *space* in which a cakra can be invoked. Certain rituals are performed by a group of practitioners. For example, a group of sādhakas invoking and worshiping a cakra (such as the Śrīcakra) is a maṇḍala.

Yantra

A yantra is a visual representation of the internal forces that make up a cakra. The literal meaning of the word yantra is contraption or device. In this context, a yantra is a contraption that works in a particular way when fueled by a mantra. Through the medium of sound (mantra) and vision (yantra), the external representation of the forces become internalized. In other words, a yantra is the external tool that facilitates the recognition of the internal cakra.

Japa is the process of working with a mantra, which is practiced in increasing levels of subtlety beginning with chanting it aloud, which involves the vocal apparatus. The practice eventually evolves to thinking the mantra without employing the lips, tongue, palate, or vocal cords. After a variable amount of time (usually several years), the mantra becomes so deeply entrenched in our system that no effort is needed in japa at all. The mantra arises on its own and runs on automatic, at which time it is said to have become *ajapa* japa – japa occurring without the conscious effort of japa.

Of particular significance in Tāntrik sādhanā is the understanding of the body as a yantra. By body, we mean not just the physical body but also that which includes the subtle planes, the fuel for which is the breath. The sound of the breath (*soham*) is known as the *Ajapa Gāyatrī* - *so* on the inhale and *ham* on the exhale. Since the breath is automatic and requires no conscious effort on our part, its sound is ajapa, and a great tool for sādhanā.

> ***The body that is a yantra is fueled by the breath that is the mantra, and the relationship between them is Tantra.***

The Śrīcakra

The Śrīcakra is known also as the Śrīyantra because it is both a cakra of seemingly different elements and a yantra or an instrument.

> ***As a yantra, the Śrīcakra is the contraption that is enlivened through the practice of the Śrīvidyā mantra, which leads us to its realization in the cosmos, the unity of the microcosm with the macrocosm, and of both with Lalitā Mahātripurasundarī.***

It is also a maṇḍala, being the aggregate of Lalitā Devī's energies.

The employment of yantras in worship or spiritual practice is not new; many cultures use implements for this purpose. In temples and places of worship, the consecration of a deity involves placing the likeness of the mūrti on the corresponding yantra, where its energy becomes contiguous with that of the deity. This is because the yantra *is* the deity. Accordingly, the Śrīcakra is the most mathematically correct form of Lalitā Devī.

> ***The cosmos is her body, which means that the Śrīcakra = Lalitā Devī = cosmos.***

The elements of the Śrīcakra are ruled by a retinue of goddesses, all of whom are rays of Devī.

The widespread presence of the Śrīcakra in temples and Śakti pīṭhas (sacred sites) gives us an indication about its importance in the Śākta tradition. Even though the Śrīvidyā mantra and philosophy are relatively less known, the Śrīcakra has become ubiquitous in all parts of the world. It's not uncommon to own a Śrīcakra as a charm or talisman for good luck or to associate superstitions with it. Accordingly, the vidyā of the Śrīcakra has become dilute and is replete with misinformation. There's an explosion of methods and ways to understand the Śrīcakra, and some stray considerably from its original teachings.

A significant problem here is that not much is known about the earliest descriptions of the Śrīcakra, and its treatment depends on the sampradāya. One of the earliest depictions of the Śrīcakra is in Sringeri Maṭha, which was established by Śrī Ādi Śaṅkarācārya in 8th century CE.[41] A Buddhist inscription in South Sumatra mentions the Śrīcakra as early as 7th century CE. Following its description in the Atharva Veda in 12th century CE as the structure composed of the nine triangles, the Śrīcakra was adopted in texts and ritual manuals in various sampradāyas.

A vast body of literature deals with the Śrīcakra and Śrīvidyā in numerous ways. Important among these texts are the *Tripurarahasya, Vidyārṇava Tantra, Gandharva Tantra Śaktisaṅgama Tantra, Saundaryalaharī,* as well as the Śākta Upaniṣads such as the *Tripurā* and the *Bhāvanā* (also known as Bhāvanopaniṣad). The Vāmakeśvara Tantra is of great significance in the Śrīvidyā tradition as one of its original texts, consisting of two parts – *Nityāṣodaśikārṇava* and the Yoginī Hṛdaya. The Yoginī Hṛdaya (translated as the heart of the Yoginī, which refers to Lalitā Mahātripurasundarī) is a classic in the understanding of the darśana and practice of the Śrīcakra.

The Bhāvanopaniṣad is a short text that is included in the Śākta Upaniṣads and is ascribed to the Atharva Veda. Bhāskararāya Makhin, the extraordinary 18th century Śrīvidyā adept and polymath composed a commentary on the Bhāvanopaniṣad, providing the framework for understanding the Śrīcakra as a psychophysiological model that parallels the macrocosm. The Kāmakalā Vilāsa is another central text of Śrīvidyā that was composed by Śrī Punyānanda Nātha of the hādimata[42] describing the Śrīcakra with the sun as the mingling of Śiva-Śakti as Devī's face, the fire and moon as her and breasts, and the emission of creation as the resonance of *Īm* as *Aham (I)*.[43] Broadly speaking, while the Yoginī Hṛdaya and the Kāmakalā Vilāsa refer largely to the cosmology (*brahmāṇḍa*) aspect of the Śrīcakra, the Bhāvanopaniṣad treats its microcosmic (*piṇḍāṇḍa*) aspect.

The ritual worship of the Śrīcakra is described and dealt with in many texts including the Paraśurāma Kalpa Sūtra, which is a kādimata classic. Modern and contemporary ritual manuals treat the Śrīcakra in various ways as well.[44]

Drawing the Śrīcakra

In general, there are two broad ways of drawing or creating the Śrīcakra – the kaula and the samayā methods. The Śrīcakra is especially challenging to construct and the intersecting lines must be exact to maintain the integrity of the *sandhis* and *marmas*.[45]

41 This pīṭha of Goddess Śārada is situated in the southern Indian state of Karnataka and is at a distance of about 320 kilometers from the capital city of Bengaluru.

42 See The Śrīvidyā Matas in Chapter 2.

43 See Kāmakalā in Chapter 4.

44 Among contemporary ritual manuals, the most comprehensive one is *Śrī Cakra Pūjā Vidhiḥ* by my Guru, Śrī Caitanyānanda Nātha Sarasvatī.

45 See Sandhis and Marmas in Chapter 4.

Accordingly, the methods of drawing a Śrīcakra are perfected and passed on from generation to generation to maintain its integrity.

The kaula method is to construct the Śrīcakra with the *Trikoṇa* (the innermost triangle) being downward facing. In the samayā method, the Trikoṇa faces upward. This changes the position of the Bindu as well. In the kaula method, the Bindu is at the center of the innermost triangle, whereas in the samayā method, it is in the center of the *Vasukoṇa*, the eight-triangled āvaraṇa.

The construction of the Śrīcakra in the different methods tends to be highly lineage specific, including the size and points of contact between the triangles and the circles. The worship and meditation on the Śrīcakra also determine its construction and must be learned from the Guru to remain consistent within the sampradāya. The important thing to remember is that any deviation from the symmetry creates flaws in the sandhis and the marmas and renders the Śrīcakra unsuitable for worship. At best, it won't lead to the desired results and at worst, it will create corresponding fatal flaws in the psycho-physiological system.

The Śrīcakra can be constructed in gold, silver, copper, or a combination of the three. A Śrīcakra constructed without flaws in gold can retain its energy for a lifetime. Silver Śrīcakras can last a few decades and copper ones for a few years. Śrīcakras constructed with these metals are said to provide specific benefits such as prosperity, abundance, and health. It can also be drawn on paper or parchment. The colors used for the Śrīcakra are significant from the standpoint of the congruence between mantra frequency and the color spectrum. Rare scientific experiments have been published where the resonance of the mantra *AUM* creates a particular color frequency that creates and permeates a Śrīcakra.

When drawn and prepared on a flat surface as a 2-dimensional model, the Śrīcakra is known as a *bhūprastha*. When constructed as a 3-dimensional model, it is known as a *meru*, where each āvaraṇa is at a different level. The sṛṣṭi, *stithi* and saṃhāra krama āvaraṇas[46] can be grouped in distinct levels as well.

46 See The Krama of the Āvaraṇas in Chapter 4.

A Śrīcakra that is prepared or acquired for worship should never be hung on a wall but always placed horizontally with the apex of the Trikoṇa facing the practitioner in the kaula system or facing away from them in the samayā system. Since the Śrīcakra represents the emanation of the universe from the Bindu in a vertical configuration, hanging it changes the orientation and renders it challenging for practice. If not used for ritual worship, it's fine to hang it vertically.

Components of the Śrīcakra

The main structure of the Śrīcakra consists of nine intersecting large triangles – four of Śiva facing upward and five of Śakti facing downward.[47] The intersection of the nine triangles gives rise to 44 smaller triangles. This matrix of triangles is surrounded by the *Aṣṭadalapadma* or the eight-petaled lotus, the *Śodaṣadalapadma* or the 16-petaled lotus, the *Trivṛtta* or the three concentric circles, and finally the Bhūpura or the square consisting of three parallel lines. In a three-dimensional Śrīcakra meru, the components are situated at different levels, the Bindu projecting skyward.

47 See The Structure of the Śrīcakra in Chapter 4.

Lalitā Mahātripurasundarī resides in the Bindu in her unabashed splendor, while her infinite emanations become the components of every āvaraṇa. Nine forms of Lalitā Devī, all closely resembling her, reign over each āvaraṇa as its *Cakreśvarī*. The āvaraṇas are cakras and are named to denote their function in creation (See Table 3). The smaller components (such as the petals or the triangles) of each āvaraṇa are ruled by forms of Devī known as yoginīs. Each āvaraṇa is accompanied by a *Mudrā Devī* who seals its energy as well as a *Siddhi* who grants a particular attainment when the āvaraṇa yoginīs are pleased with our sādhanā. The upāsanā of an āvaraṇa bestows a specific *rasa*.

All aspects of the āvaraṇas are significant in our upāsanā, especially the yoginīs who rule over specific aspects of the macrocosm and microcosm. They unify the seeming opposites of Śiva-Śakti or *Prakāśa-Vimarśa* within their sphere of influence.[48] Being of the nature of saṃsāra and nirvāṇa, the yoginīs embody both a shadow and a light aspect; their shadows entrench us in saṃsāra, and their light liberates us from it.

48 See Prakāśa and Vimarśa in Chapter 4.

When we attain their grace, the yoginīs move us from shadow to light within the individual components and when we have resolved the shadows of the entire āvaraṇa, we arrive at the feet of the Cakreśvarī. The Cakreśvarī bestows a holistic insight that reconciles the shadow and light aspects of all the yoginīs of the āvaraṇa and propels us along the path of upāsanā.

The Mudrā Devī of each āvaraṇa determines the flow of energy in the āvaraṇa in its shadow and light aspects. When entrenched in saṃsāra, the energy is sealed in limited ways and when the yoginīs transform the contraction to expansiveness, the Mudrā Devīs bestow their grace and seal the flow of energy in the newly forged neurohormonal pathways.

Although the Siddhis are stationed in the Bhūpura, they are also present in each āvaraṇa as the subtle essence of attainment that arises from the release of particular limitations. Each Siddhi grants the boon of a particular rasa at each āvaraṇa, which is the result of deepening insight in daily life.

Table 3. The Āvaraṇa Devīs of the Śrīcakra

Āvaraṇa	Cakra	Yoginī	Cakreśvarī	Mudrā	Siddhi	Rasa
Bhūpura	Trailokyamohana	Prakaṭa	Tripurā	Sarvasankṣobhiṇī	Aṇimā	Śṛṅgāra
Śodaṣadalapadma	Sarvāśāparipūraka	Gupta	Tripureśī	Sarvavidrāviṇī	Laghimā	Vīra
Aṣṭadalapadma	Sarvasankṣobhaṇa	Guptatara	Tripurasundarī	Sarvākarṣiṇī	Mahimā	Kāruṇya
Manvaśra	Sarvasaubhāgyadāyaka	Sampradāya	Tripuravāsinī	Sarvavaśaṅkarī	Īśitva	Bhayānaka
Bahirdaśara	Sarvārthasādhaka	Kulottīrṇa	Tripurāśrī	Sarvonmādinī	Vaśitva	Bībhatsa
Antardaśara	Sarvarakṣākara	Nigarbha	Tripuramālinī	Sarvamahāṅkuśa	Prakāmya	Raudra
Vasukoṇa	Sarvarogahara	Rahasya	Tripurāsiddhā	Sarvakhecarī	Bhukti	Hāsya
Trikoṇa	Sarvasiddhipradā	Atirahasya	Tripurāmbā	Sarvabījā	Icchā	Adbhuta
Bindu	Sarvānandamaya	Parāpararahasya	Mahātripurasundarī	Sarvayonī	Prāpti	Śānta

One of the ways to worship and internalize the deities of the Śrīcakra is through the Khaḍgamālā Stotra, which we will explore next.

Khaḍgamālā Stotra

The Khaḍgamālā Stotra is a hymn that is known as a *mālā* mantra, where mālā refers to a garland of mantras. *Khaḍga* means sword, and this hymn is a garland of sword-like mantras that cut through our limitations and propel us toward the Bindu.

The Khaḍgamālā Stotra invokes the deities of the āvaraṇas in the saṃhāra krama, and in its meditative aspect, allows us to move from element to element in a systematic way that takes us from the darkness of ignorance to the light of vidyā.

> ***The Khaḍgamālā Stotra is a sequence of the names of the principal deities of the Śrīcakra in the saṃhāra krama.***

Although various texts refer to the Khaḍgamālā Stotra, its original source is largely unknown. While the Khaḍgamālā we will explore here is a hymn that invokes Lalitā Mahātripurasundarī in her emanations as the deities of the Śrīcakra, there are several other Khaḍgamālā Stotras dedicated to deities such as Kālī, Tvaritā, Mātaṅgī, and others.

Classification of Khaḍgamālā Stotra

Since Lalitā Mahātripurasundarī is the form of Prakāśa-Vimarśa or Śiva-Śakti, she is invoked through the Khaḍgamālā in three forms – Śakti, Śiva, and Śiva-Śakti together. Each of her three aspects can be invoked in five different iterations of the Khaḍgamālā, which are used in different modes of worship (see Table 4). The 15 total iterations of Khaḍgamālā (five each for Śakti, Śiva and Śiva-Śakti) correspond with the 15-syllabled Pañcadaśī mantra as well as the 15 *Nityā Devīs* that represent the moon phases or *tithis*.

Table 4. Khaḍgamālā Stotra Classification

Type*	Suffix	Worship Mode
Sambudhyanta	None	Japa
Nāmonta	Namaḥ	Arcana (flowers)
Svāhānta	Svāhā	Homa (fire offerings)
Jayanta	Jaya jaya	Praise
Tarpaṇānta	Pūjayāmi Tarpayāmi Namaḥ	Tarpaṇa (water)
*Each set of five for Śakti, Śiva and Śiva-Śakti together makes up 15, one for each moon phase		

The use of the Khaḍgamālā according to the moon phases depends on the lineage and must be learned from the Guru. The Śakti iterations of the stotra invoke the Śrīcakra deities with feminine endings, the Śiva versions with masculine endings, and the Śiva-Śakti versions contain sequential masculine-feminine endings.

Each iteration of the stotra has a different suffix, except the *sambudhyanta* version that is used for japa or internal worship. The suffix determines the mode of worship that is used on the corresponding tithi or moon phase. For example, in the *Svāhānta mālā*, every deity name is followed by "*Svāhā*!" and this version is used in fire rituals known as homa, where the deities are invoked in the fire.

Three additional Khaḍgamālā Stotras are imparted to advanced practitioners that invoke Lalitā Mahātripurasundarī directly and must also be learned directly from the Guru.

The classification of the stotra and the correspondence of the 15 iterations with the moon phases are significant for the exercise known as *puraścaraṇa*.

Puraścaraṇa

Puraścaraṇa is a preparatory exercise for advanced practices and involves a somewhat complex procedure where a mantra is practiced in specific ways. The procedure is to repeat the mantra 100,000 times for each syllable in the mantra. Depending on the number of syllables in the mantra, the total number of required repetitions can run in the millions. As an example, puraścaraṇa of the 15-syllabled Pañcadaśī requires a minimum of 1.5 million repetitions.[49] However, this is a general rule, and some texts prescribe other numbers of repetitions that don't necessarily adhere to 100,000 per syllable.

49 This is an approximate number, essentially emphasizing the very large number of repetitions required to attain mantra siddhi.

The purpose of puraścaraṇa is to enable mantra siddhi, where the mantra opens itself to the practitioner with all its hidden secrets and blessings.

Puraścaraṇa follows the ten percent rule where ten percent of the total number of repetitions is to be performed as homa with fire offerings, ten percent of the homa repetitions as tarpaṇa with water offerings, ten percent of the tarpaṇa as *mārjana* or self-oblation, and ten percent of this as *bhojana* where a corresponding number of those with siddhi in the same mantra are fed and respectfully honored. The five types of the Khaḍgamālā Stotra conveniently adhere to the scheme of puraścaraṇa, where they can be used specifically in the said rituals.

Each of the fifteen Khaḍgamālās represents one syllable of the Pañcadaśī mantra, beginning with the syllable K in the kādi tradition. The meditative verses of each Khaḍgamālā define the syllable, the deity (Śakti, Śiva, or Śiva-Śakti), the composer of the Stotra (ṛṣi) and the meter (*Chandas*). The practice of the 15 Khaḍgamālā according to the moon phases is one of the various ways of performing Nityā Devī sādhanā, which differs according to the lineage. In general, because each of the Khaḍgamālā Stotras involves a syllable of the Pañcadaśī, the practitioner must be initiated into the mantra.

The sambudhyanta version of the Khaḍgamālā Stotra is provided in Appendix II of this book, including the meditative verse and the nyāsa.

Nyāsa

Nyāsa means to place, and it is the procedure of inviting the deity into various body parts through ritual touch. The purpose of nyāsa is to realize the unity of the deity and self. There are many types of nyāsas that are specific to the ritual, hymn, or procedure. Traditionally, no chant or ritual is complete without nyāsa, which bookends the procedure. It is a way to invite the ṛṣi or composer, the deity, the meter, the seed (*bīja*), the power (Śakti), and the key (*kīlakam*)[50] in a procedure known as *Ṛṣyādi* nyāsa followed by *viniyoga*, which is the prayer to the deity to actualize the effects of the procedure. In the case of the Khaḍgamālā, the viniyoga is Khaḍga siddhi, or the attainment of the sword that cuts through the darkness of ignorance.[51]

Nyāsa is followed by meditative verses known as dhyāna. In the Khaḍgamālā, the dhyāna mantra sets the following intention, "May I be granted your sword that I keep handy and through which I become the empress of the islands in all eight directions."[52]

The dhyāna mantra is followed by mental worship, where the deity that is invoked is worshiped through the five elements. The Khaḍgamālā then begins with the invocation of the 16 Nityā Devīs around the Trikoṇa, followed by the Guru Maṇḍala between the Trikoṇa and Vasukoṇa. Each of these Gurus also represents a power or Śakti, which is an emanation

50 Even though commonly thought of as a key, kīlakam is like the pin that holds the door onto its frame and allows it to swing open.

51 My Guru says that the Khaḍgamālā cuts through linear time, which is the source of ignorance.

52 See the Khaḍgamālā Stotra in Appendix II.

of Devī. The Stotra then begins with the first deity of the Bhūpura, *Aṇimā Siddhi.*

The Khaḍgamālā Stotra enlists the names of 98 principal deities in the Śrīcakra distributed among the āvaraṇas. However, the Śrīcakra is said to be comprised of 64 crores[53] yoginīs, denoting its comprehensiveness.

53 1 crore = 10 million.

Memorizing this hymn makes it easier to contemplate the Śrīcakra deities in meditation. With ongoing practice, we become adept at recognizing our limiting patterns, where in the Śrīcakra they appear, how they are connected to our deepest fears and pain, and how they affect our behavior in the world. With constant contemplation, the yoginīs of each element appear in the mind's eye with the arising of the pattern, showing us the way out of the darkness of limitation into the light of freedom. The grace of the Śrīcakra deities thus allows us to realign with upāsanā and its constant application.

Now that we have explored Śrīvidyā and the overall structure and importance of the Śrīcakra, we are prepared to journey into its deep secrets. In the next section, we will investigate the Śrīcakra in the sṛṣṭi krama, or the descent of the Divine into creation as this magnificent, mystical symbol.

PART II

THE SECRETS OF THE ŚRĪCAKRA

चतुर्भिः श्रीकण्ठैः शिवयुवतिभिः पञ्चभिपि
प्रभिन्नाभिः शम्भोर्नवभिरपि मूलप्रकृतिभिः ।
चतुश्चत्वारिंशद्-वसुदल-कलाश्र त्रिवलय-
त्रिरेखभिः सार्धं तव शरणकोण: परिणताः ॥ ११ ॥

caturbhiḥ śrīkaṇṭhaiḥ sivayuvatibhiḥ pancabhir api
prabhinnābhiḥ saṃbhor navabhirapi mulaprakṛti-bhiḥ |
catus catvārimśad vasudalakalāśratrivalaya
trirekhabhiḥ sārdham tava śaraṇakoṇaḥ pariṇatāḥ || 11 ||

"Your abode is the triangle made by the four of Śiva and five of Śakti comprising the nine primary triangles of Nature and resulting in forty-four, the eight and sixteen petals, the three circles and the three lines."
~ Saundaya Laharī, Verse 11

Chapter 4

Sṛṣṭi Krama: The Descent

To understand the Śrīcakra in sṛṣṭi krama, we must become aligned with its darśana. Since the darśana is nonlinear, there is no beginning or end, which means that we must start somewhere and eventually make our way back to that point.

In many Eastern traditions, time is circular and recurring, and is both linear and non-linear. Let's assume that time begins with a concrete activity such as the Big Bang (or any other theory, for that matter) and that prior to this seminal event, there is "nothing." In this tradition, the nothingness is the result of the *previous* cycle of creation being absorbed into quiescence.

> ***At the end of a cycle of creation that occurs at the end of a Mahāyuga,[54] the cosmos is absorbed back into its seed form in a process known as pralaya. This is the "nothingness" from which the next creative cycle begins.***

54 Yuga is a unit of time, occurring cyclically. A Mahāyuga is an aggregate of 4,320,000 years made up of four yugas: Satya, Tretā, Dvāpara, and Kālī.

In this state of quiescence, nothing is happening since time and space haven't yet been birthed. Here, the Absolute Reality or the Divine Śiva-Śakti is undifferentiated where Śiva and Śakti are said to be in perfect union, blended inseparably, and absorbed in each other.

> ***Śiva is the ground of being and is without any attributes. Śakti is energy and all attributes.***

In other words, anything we assign to Śiva – such as him being awake, pale, transcendent, aloof, compassionate, and so on – is Śakti, for he is without form of *any* kind. Anything that Śiva says, feels, thinks, or does is Śakti. She is his energy. Being all attributes of Śiva, and therefore of creation, Śakti is the creator, sustainer, and destroyer of all in existence. When we worship Śiva, we are worshiping Śakti because he is beyond worship as the formless.

Śakti is the impelling force that begins the next cycle of creation. She holds creation absorbed within herself until a desire arises in her to create – for the One to become Many. With this initial movement of desire, she separates from Śiva, and time and space come into existence.

Prakāśa and Vimarśa

One way to understand the relatively complex relationship between Śiva and Śakti, other than as masculine and feminine principles, is through the concepts of Prakāśa and Vimarśa, which are more aligned with this darśana.[55]

55 See also Chapter 3 in K. Chinnaiyan, *Glorious Alchemy: Living the Lalitā Sahasranāma* (New Sarum Press, 2020).

> ***Prakāśa is illumination, which refers to the light of consciousness or pure subjectivity – the Self or I, also known as Aham. Vimarśa is self-reflection, which refers to the Self knowing Itself as Idam.***

Vimarśa is described as the pure mirror in which Prakāśa knows itself. Think of it this way – for you to know or cognize an object, you must first cognize yourself. You know you exist, which is the most fundamental knowledge. You always have a sense that you are. This is the inherent Self-consciousness of our experience, which is not the same as being self-conscious, say, in front of people. Self-consciousness here is the I or Aham cognizing itself, where what it cognizes (itself) becomes an object or Idam. When you know yourself, one has become two – the one who knows (Aham, the subject) and the one that is known (Idam, the object). Śakti is the self-recognition of Śiva; she is Śiva knowing himself.

The nothingness prior to time is the state of oneness. There is nothingness here because experience requires both the observer or knower and the observed or known. When Śiva and Śakti are fully merged, there is no dichotomy between the observer and the observed. For creation to occur, Śiva and Śakti must necessarily separate, where he becomes the observer, and she, the observed.

Śakti, out of her own power of Absolute Freedom known as *svātantrya śakti*, becomes the cosmos with the 36 *tattvas*. To become many, she must impose several limitations upon herself, which begins at the instant of separation from Śiva, and progressively crystallizes through the devolution of the tattvas. At the *Māyā* tattva, she takes on five specific contractions or limitations known as *kañcukas*, beyond which her separation from Śiva is clear and obvious. Until she limits herself at the Māyā tattva, Śiva looks in the mirror and sees himself as Śakti in her limitlessness. Once Māyā's limitations are placed, objects of the universe become distinct and separate; he looks in the mirror and sees himself as Śakti in her limitations as the world.

The world is Śiva's reflection, and that reflection is Śakti.

Śakti, the power of self-recognition, brings forth creation from Śiva, the power of illumination. In other words, everything in manifestation arises from Śiva, the father and Śakti, the mother. Śiva-Śakti are one, like water and wetness or fire and heat. They cannot be separated at any level, and any sense of separation is the play of Māyā, which is the projection of Śakti. One question that comes up often when we study cosmology is, "Why does the Divine project this separation that causes so much strife and conflict?" The answer is in svātantrya śakti – the power of Absolute Freedom – the Divine does whatever just because the Divine *can*! As we progress in sādhanā, questions like these disappear and stop making sense.

The separation and coming together of Śiva and Śakti in the creation of the world with the 36 tattvas is depicted in the highly esoteric Kāmakalā.

Kāmakalā

सितशोणबिन्दुयुगलम् विविक्तशिवशक्तिसन्कुचत् प्रसरम्
वागार्थस्ष्टिहेतुः परस्परानुप्रविष्ट विस्पष्टम् ॥ ६ ॥
बिन्दुरहङ्कारात्मा रविरेतन्मिथुनसमरसाकारः ।
कामः कमनीयतया कला च दहनेन्दुविग्रहौ बिन्दू ॥ ७ ॥

sitaṣoṇa-bindu-yugalaṁ vivikta-śivaśakti-saṁkucat-prasaraṁ |
vāgartha-sṛṣṭi-hetuḥ parasparānupraviṣṭa vispaṣṭam || 6 ||
bindur-ahaṅkārātma raviretanmithunasamarasākāraḥ |
kāmaḥ kamanīyatayā kalā ca dahanendu-vigrahau bindu || 7 ||

"The white and red bindus are Śiva and Śakti who unite in secret, expanding and contracting in mutual enjoyment. They are the source of vāc and artha, entering and separating from each other. The union of the white and red bindus is the sun, which is the ahaṅkāra (Ahambhāva). The sun is kāma because of its desirability and the moon and fire are the kalās."
~Kāmakalā Vilāsa, verses 6-7

Sṛṣṭi krama is the descent of the Divine into creation, and in the Śrīcakra, the devolution from the Bindu to the Bhūpura. The Bindu is the dynamic source of the Śrīcakra, which is all of creation. It is where Śiva and Śakti sport to bring forth all of creation, not just as the progressive linear devolution of matter but primarily the moment-to-moment emission and resorption of existence. Since creation is the play of illumination and self-recognition (Prakāśa and Vimarśa), everthing in existence is merely the sporting of Śiva and Śakti.

The entire Śrīcakra is the Bindu, since every aspect of creation reflects the interaction between Śiva and Śakti.

In other words, Śiva-Śakti is all that exists, despite the infinite variety of form in creation. The Bindu is the source of creation, which *is* the Śrīcakra.

Even though the Bindu of the Śrīcakra is represented as a dot, it is dynamic and multi-faceted, the container for the unfolding of the Absolute Reality and the womb that births creation. The process by which Absolute Reality becomes the source or Bindu of the Śrīcakra is described by the Kāmakalā. *Kāma* is desire and kalā is digit or part of the whole, and Kāmakalā refers to the orgasmic process in which creation emerges as a part or digit of the limitless Absolute Reality.

Remember that at the level of Absolute Reality, Śiva-Śakti are indistinguishable from each other and this level is known as Anuttara or Supreme. At this Absolute level, Śiva-Śakti as the Divine is called *Kāma-Kāmeśvarī*, existing as the *Mahābindu* or Supreme Bindu (see Figure 4). With the stir of desire in Anuttara, the Mahābindu expands or swells as Prakāśa and Vimarśa.

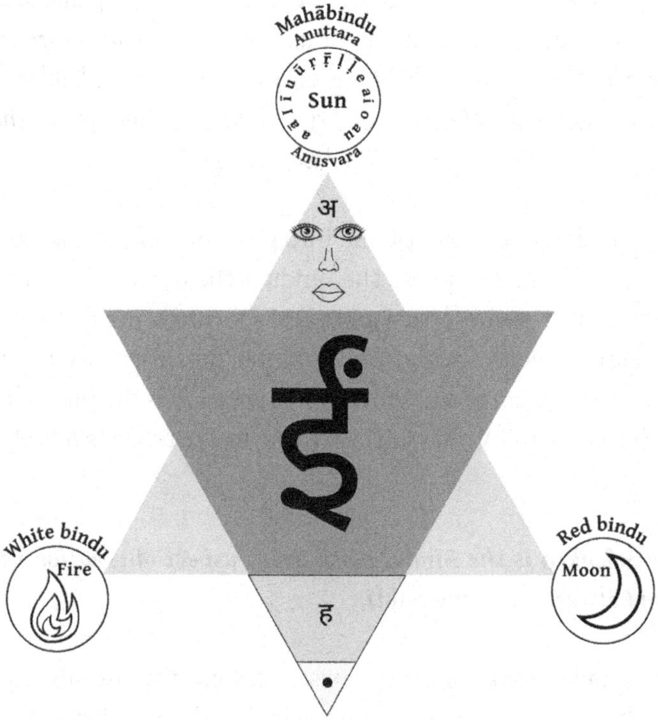

Figure 4. Kāmakalā

Prakāśa is known as the fire principle and is denoted by a white bindu, while Vimarśa is the moon principle denoted by a red bindu. As we saw earlier, Prakāśa (the white bindu or fire) is attributeless and formless illumination, while Vimarśa (the red bindu or moon) is replete with all attributes and forms. Vimarśa then is the body of Prakāśa, containing within itself all of creation. The white bindu (Prakāśa) penetrates the red bindu (Vimarśa), which is to say that Śiva as illumination diffuses into his body, which is Śakti. Just as enthusiastically, the red bindu of Vimarśa, the Supreme Śakti, penetrates the white bindu of Prakāśa, which is contained within herself. The resulting mixed bindu is poised for creation. This sporting of Śiva and Śakti occurs after they separate as the white and red bindus, where they re-unite in equal delight and desire. Creation is the result of this sexual union, which occurs as the interpenetration of the two bindus.

The white and red bindus are said to frolic secretly in mutual enjoyment, contracting towards each other and expanding away towards creation. The sun is of the mixed character of the fire and the moon because fire enters it during the daytime and the new moon disappears into it. The upper Mahābindu (sun) is kāma, the absolute desirability of existence, which splits into the two digits (kalās) of the fire and the moon.[56] The mixed bindu gives rise to *Nādātmika Śakti* or the primordial sound/resonance, which takes a pyramidal form with a triangular base (*Śṛngāṭaka*), containing within herself all the tattvas and creative energies in the seed (bīja) form.[57] This process of one (sun) becoming two (fire and moon) is represented in the Kāmakalā with its three bindus and two overlapping triangles with their apices turned away from each other. The Kāmakalā is a representation of the visual and sonic forms of Śiva-Śakti engaged in the creative process. This creative process is the central tenet of the Śrīcakra, which is a visual representation (yantra) of the primordial resonance (mantra).

The sun or Mahābindu encases the aggregate or mass of the Sanskrit phonemes (word or *Mātṛkā*), beginning with "*A*" and ending with "*Ha*" and is known as Anuttara or the Supreme, referring to the Absolute Reality. At this point, we need to realize that the same principle occurs at all levels. At the level of Absolute Reality, the occurrence of a principle or phenomenon refers to its samaṣṭi *rūpa*, where the aggregate is greater than the sum of its parts. Below the Absolute Reality level, the principle refers to its vyaṣṭi rūpa or individual form. Accordingly, the Mahābindu is Anuttara, containing creation in its seed form as the samaṣṭi of the Sanskrit phonemes from *A* to *Ha*, which become Aham or I, the Self.

56 The source texts disagree on the assignment of the red and white bindus to the fire and the moon. In some, the white bindu corresponds to the fire and the red to the moon. In others, it's the opposite.

57 See Arthur Avalon, *Kāmakalā Vilāsa by Puṇyānanda Nātha with the commentary of Naṭanānanda Nātha.* (Madras: Ganesh and Co (Pvt) Ltd, 1961) for a comprehensive examination of Kāmakalā in English.

As we have seen earlier (see Chapter 1), creation occurs in the sound-to-word pathway. The blueprint of creation rests in the Mahābindu as sound-that-is-yet-to-become-word as the mass of phonemes in their samaṣṭi rūpa known as Mātṛkā Cakra. As we will see in Chapter 6,[58] the Mātṛkā Cakra is at the level of *parāvāk*. The progressive gathering of the vowel potencies from *a* to *au* within the Mahābindu results in its "swelling" (see Figure 4). The vowel *am* is the intense focusing of charged energy at a single point and is known as the *anusvāra*, which will emit as the *visarga*, the separation of the white and red bindus. Anusvāra is depicted by a single dot (.) whereas visarga by two (:), demonstrating the split of the One into two, the primordial duality.

58 See Vāc in the Śrīcakra, Chapter 6.

In the Kāmakalā, the *A* or Anuttara resides in the sun at the apex of the upward-facing triangle, pervading the Mātṛkā Cakra and poised for creation as the anusvāra, while the visarga is represented by the fire and moon bindus. The resonance of visarga is known as the *hārdakalā*, which resides as *Ha* at the bottom of the downward-facing triangle. The tip of the downward facing triangle is pregnant with the bindu or drop (.), the *m* that brings together *A* and *Ha* as Aham, which means I and refers to the Supreme I-consciousness. Stretched between *A* (the first letter) and *Ha* (the last letter) is the entire spectrum of *nāda* or resonance as the Sanskrit letter *Īm*, encompassing containing all the Sanskrit phonemes the represent the 36 tattvas from Śiva-Śakti to *pṛthvī* (earth). In other words, the nāda of every form of creation is contained and encased within *Īm*. Another word for this primordial nāda is Kuṇḍalinī, which shines forth as the source and fuel of creation. The entire structure of the Kāmakalā is the Bindu of the Śrīcakra, which is Aham or I. In other words, Devī is identical with the creation she emits. She is the Aham or I that subsumes the subject-object duality; she is all that exists.

> ***Devī resides in the Kāmakalā as the source of creation arising from the white, red, and mixed bindus. Her face is the sun, the fire and moon at the two corners of the triangle are her breasts, and the apex of the downward-facing triangle is her yoni or womb.***

Creation is emitted when the red and white bindus expand away from each other and the anusvāra splits into the visarga; creation emerges out of her yoni as the visarga and is nourished by her breasts. When the red and white bindus contract toward each other, the anusvāra unites the two dots of the visarga and becomes Anuttara, diffusing into the Mahābindu.

As we will see throughout this book, the pulsing of Śakti between Śiva and creation is the characteristic of the Bindu. The intermingling of the red and white bindus is Śakti turning toward Śiva; it's as if she closes her eyes, turning away from creation as the anusvāra. The expansion of the red and white bindus away from each other is Śakti turning away from Śiva; she opens her eyes turns toward the world and creation comes into being in the visarga. This movement between the anusvāra and visarga is known as *spanda*, the throb of consciousness. The rhythmic movement from *A* to *Ha* becomes Aham by the addition of *m* at the end, which is the point of contact between them.

> ***All aspects of the Kāmakalā are Mahātripurasundarī as Aham, the subject; she is the Mahābindu becoming the Bindu of the Śrīcakra through the three bindus, the Nādātmika Śakti, the emission of creation as the visarga and its resorption as the anusvāra.***

At this point, the Aham or the Supreme I-consciousness in the Kāmakalā needs a bit of deliberation. At the Mahābindu, the Aham is the entity in which the world and I are synonymous. Here, the subject-object differentiation of I and myself doesn't exist and Śiva-Śakti are entirely dissolved in each other. With the swelling of the sun or Mahābindu into the fire and moon, one becomes three where the Aham at the sun is I (the subject) and at the moon is myself (the object), while fire is I knowing myself – the process of self-recognition.[59] This process goes on in your internal landscape as well – you are aware of your body-mind, where your awareness is the *I* (the watcher) and the body-mind is the *myself* (watched).

> ***Creation is the body-mind of Devī as the moon that is perceived or known by her Aham, the fire. The unity of her body-mind and her Aham is the Supreme I, the sun.***

The Aham in the Kāmakalā is "I know myself," which is projected as the universe in the āvaraṇas of the Śrīcakra. This principle is known as *Ahambhāva*, where the world (moon)

59 Note that the assignment of knower, known and knowing to the sun, moon, and fire is not consistent across traditions. In some, fire is the knower, moon the known and sun the knowing. It's best to follow your own lineage and tradition for this classification.

and self (fire) are united in the I or Aham (sun). With the projection of the Kāmakalā as the universe, "I know myself" shines in all forms of creation. From the grossest to the subtlest, Śiva-Śakti are in continuous union as Aham, which is the interaction of the *A* and *Ha* coming together through *m* (see the later chapters on the Trikoṇa and Bindu for an in-depth understanding of this principle).

In the sound-to-word pathway, nāda or sound (*śabda*) gives birth to the world of objects,[60] which contain the meaning (*artha*). Śabda arises in the form of *varṇa* (letters of the Sanskrit alphabet), *pada* (words) and mantra (deliberation), whereas artha manifests as kalā (digits of time and space), tattva (the 36 tattvas) and *bhuvana* (the innumerable worlds). Arising from the mixed bindu, śabda and artha are irrevocably bound together and arise, stay awhile, and dissolve as one.

60 See Chapter 6 and Śabda and Artha in Chapter 14.

We can also understand the relationship between the Mahābindu and the Bindu as the transformation of potential energy to kinetic energy. Potential energy with no directionality is the state of the Mahābindu, which is symbolized by the syllable AUM, which has a measure (*mātrā)* of 3.5.[61] AUM is known as the *praṇava* or primordial sound, with *A*, *U* and *M* comprising the first three mātrās that are devoid of nāda, which is kinetic energy. The anusvāra makes up the final half mātrā of AUM that is its nāda or kinetic energy. In the Kāmakalā, kinetic energy is represented by the syllable *Īm*, which stretches between *A* and *Ha*. The Kāmakalā, which is the Bindu of the Śrīcakra, is the resonance of the Mahābindu. Advanced mantra sādhanā involves the ascent from the Bindu to the Mahābindu through eight intervening stations, where nāda becomes absorbed into *nādānta* (end of nāda).[62] As we will see later, the kinetic energy of Kāmakalā or the *Īm* is Kuṇḍalinī, which pulses as the contraction and expansion between *A* (bindu) and *Ha* (visarga) to become Aham that unifies śabda and artha, I and myself, and subject and object.

61 See Kuṇḍalinī and Nāda in Chapter 11.

62 See Mantra Sādhana in Chapter 6.

Īm as the kinetic energy descends into creation, exploding as the Śrīcakra, which is why it is known as the Śakti Praṇava.

The Descent of Creation

The three bindus of Kāmakalā make up the primordial triad of creation, and Devī is the supreme beauty that permeates them as Mahātripurasundarī (*mahā* = great, *tripura* = three cities, referring to triads, *sundarī* = beautiful one).

The Trikoṇa comes into being when the mixed bindu divides three ways into the three bījas or seeds of creation – *Vāgbhava, Kāmarāja* and Śakti. These divisions also refer to the three *kūṭas* or peaks of the 15-syllabled Pañcadaśī mantra, which is the subtle form of Lalitā Mahātripurasundarī. As the Vāgbhava kūṭa, she is jñāna śakti; as Kāmarāja, she is kriyā śakti; and as Śakti, she is icchā śakti.[63] These three bindus also make up the primordial triad of the knower (*mātṛ*), known (*meya*) and knowing (*māna*) that make up the Trikoṇa, which is Prakāśa interacting with Vimarśa as the knower and the known, both being Aham. This is the triad of *sat-cit-ānanda* or being-consciousness-bliss, which is the very nature of the Divine. The Trikoṇa comprises the three pīṭhas or seats of Devī, which are both esoteric nonlocalized stations of her icchā, jñāna and kriyā as well as geographical locations of spiritual significance in Śāktism.

63 See *Kāmakalā Vilāsa*, verse 12. In some lineages, this order may be different, where Vāgbhava is icchā śakti, Kāmarāja is jñāna śakti and Śakti is kriyā śakti.

In every triad of forms in the Trikoṇa, Devī herself remains unchanging, immutable, and constant as the transcendent fourth.[64]

64 See The Fourth and the Fifth in Bindu, Chapter 17.

Because of her constancy and immutability, she can create the myriad forms, nourish them, and reabsorb them into herself.

The 15 syllables of the Pañcadaśī mantra make up the 15 attributes or *guṇas* of the five great elements or the *pañca mahābhūtas*,[65] which are the *tanmātras*. Sound, touch, form, taste, and smell are the tanmātras or attributes of space, air, fire, water, and earth. *Ākāśa* or space has the single attribute of sound. *Vāyu* or air, the next element, has the two attributes of sound and touch; *agni* or fire has sound, touch, and form; *apaḥ* or water has sound, touch, form, and taste; pṛthvī or earth has sound, touch, form, taste, and smell. Each guṇa or attribute subsumes the subsequent ones.

65 See Trikoṇa, Chapter 16.

Taken together, there are 15 attributes spanning the five elements, and they correspond to the Nityā Devīs that are emanations of Lalitā Mahātripurasundarī surrounding the Trikoṇa.

The Nityā Devīs correspond to the tithis or moon phases, each being a particular characteristic of time. They are symbolic of the circular, ever-changing nature of time and space against the backdrop of the constancy represented by Mahātripurasundarī herself. The 15 tithis symbolize the union of Śiva-Śakti in time and space, gaining attributes with each passing phase to become replete with them as the Pañcadaśī mantra.

As we have seen earlier, the three bindus make up the entire Sanskrit alphabet, which is the body of Mahātripurasundarī. The Pañcadaśī mantra consists of 36 letters that make up the 15 syllables, which correspond with the 36 tattvas. Devī herself is both immanent in creation and transcends the tattvas as *tattvātīta*.[66] The Śrīcakra is the body of Devī, containing all the tattvas in their gross and subtle (as śabda and artha) forms.

66 See Bhāskararāya's *Varivasya Rahasya* for the different implications and treatments of the Pañcadaśī mantra in the kādi tradition, and the Kāmakalā Vilāsa for the same in the hādi tradition.

Kāmakalā is the process of creation that is facilitated in the Bindu, which explodes as the Śrīcakra.

Kāmakalā unites the visual and phonic aspects of the womb of creation, which are the essence of the sādhanā of the Śrīcakra.

Understanding creation through its visual and phonic aspects and the unity of the two forms another triad at the Trikoṇa. The Bindu and the Trikoṇa make up the first five of the 36 tattvas, which propagate and differentiate into the others.

The Tattvas

Tattva means essence or principle, referring to the fundamental aspects of creation. Essentially, tattva refers to a principle that is pure and distinct on its own. The tattvas combine in infinite ways to manifest the countless forms of creation. Śrīvidyā gives us a map of 36 tattvas that differs from the 25 of the *Sāṅkhya* tradition by the addition of 11 above the level of the *Puruṣa* tattva (see Figure 5).

The first two tattvas are Śiva and Śakti coming together as Prakāśa and Vimarśa in the Kāmakalā, while icchā, jñāna and kriyā are tattvas 3-5. At this point, Śiva-Śakti are non-separate, where objects of creation (Idam) are not separate from the subject (Aham).

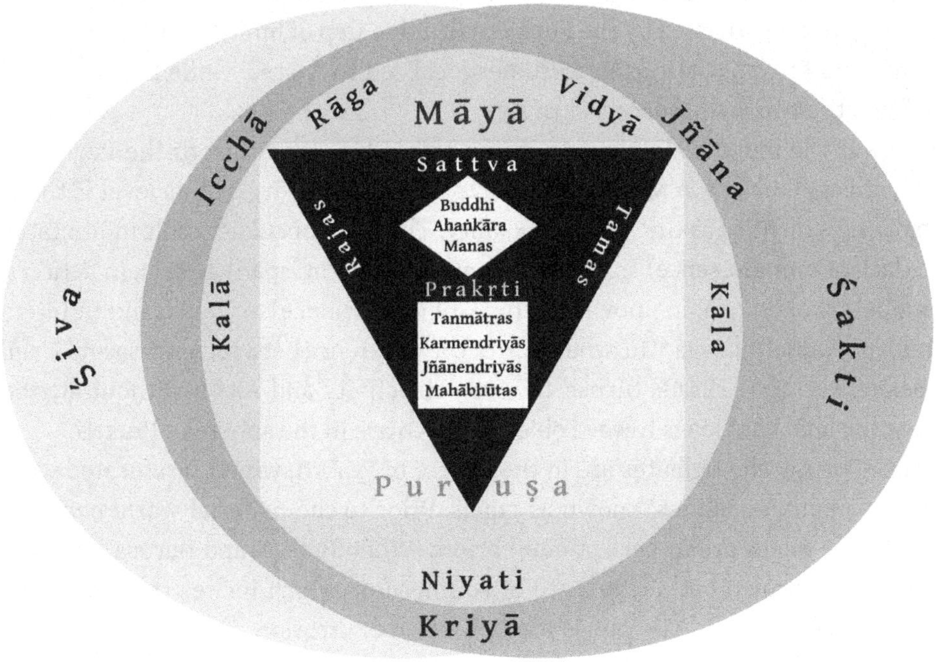

Figure 5. Tattva Map

The next step in devolution is critical, where the separation between Aham and Idam occurs with the veiling known as Māyā, which is tattva six. As we will see in Chapter 9, as Māyā, Śakti puts on five layers of armor known as kañcukas (tattvas 7-11). She limits her icchā, jñāna and kriyā as *rāga*, vidyā and kalā, respectively, along with two other kañcukas – time as *kāla* and causation as *niyati*.

With Māyā and the kañcukas, the Aham of Prakāśa becomes limited as Puruṣa (tattva 12) and the Idam of Śakti as Prakṛti (tattva 13).[67]

As we will see later, Puruṣa is the individual subject or the I that witnesses the body, mind, and the world – all of which make up Prakṛti. Prakṛti is Nature and comprises everything that is witnessed by the Puruṣa. With this step of limiting the Aham and Idam to Puruṣa and Prakṛti, the subject becomes localized to "here," while the world is "out there," and the two are rendered separate.

Puruṣa is the individual witness with no attributes. Even though the Puruṣa is the witness, it is still bound in Māyā and the five kañcukas.[68] Māyā at this level is the ignorance of one's identity as the Absolute Reality. The five kañcukas result in limitation in space (lack of omnipresence) as niyati, in time (age and lifespan) as kāla, in action (lack of omnipotence) as kalā, in knowledge (lack of omniscience) as vidyā, and in intention (beyond individual) as rāga.[69] In other words, the difference between Puruṣa and *ahaṅkāra* (see below) is that Puruṣa is turned toward subjectivity and Aham without attributes, whereas the ahaṅkāra leans toward objects, which are in the sphere of Prakṛti.

Unlike Puruṣa, all attributes are in the sphere of Prakṛti, which is saturated with the three fundamental qualities, known as guṇas. Prior to the material world coming into existence, the guṇas are in perfect equilibrium. When Prakṛti and Puruṣa intermingle, the guṇas are thrown out of the state of equilibrium, which incites the manifestation of the material universe. The guṇas are the fabric of creation, permeating all the subsequent tattvas. Note that the guṇas are not separate tattvas but are the properties or attributes of Prakṛti.

Sattva is the inherent intelligence of the cosmos, an organization, an organism or the smallest subatomic particle or wave. It is the essence or clarity inbuilt in the design of creation. *Rajas* is movement and dynamism which drives the expansion of the universe, the growth, change and evolution of systems, the firing of electrical signals, the release of chemicals in cells and the revolution of the electron in an atom's orbit. *Tamas* is the structure of matter, from the roundness of the planets to the shape, size and heaviness of forms, and the highly efficient make-up of cells and subcellular organelles.

67 Note that this is where the tattva "map" of the Sāṅkhya system begins.

68 Note that this scheme applies to the nondual Śaiva-Śākta traditions with the darśana of 36 *tattvas*. In other traditions such as Sāṅkhya, Puruṣa is the pure I or Aham without limitations.

69 See 'Tattvas' in Swami Lakshmanjoo, *Kashmir Shaivism: The Secret Supreme* (Universal Shaiva Fellowship, 2007).

Sattva, rajas and tamas are embedded in our psychophysiology from the functioning of the organs and organ systems to the way we think, feel, speak, and behave.

In the microcosm, particularly our inner landscape, tamas is inertia and stagnation that prevents us from making meaningful progress in life or sādhanā. This is because tamas is heavy with ignorance, where the identification with the body-mind is tight and we are contracted in this identification. Rajas, on the other hand, is the frenzied energy of hyperactivity and distraction, and the inability to sit still physically or metaphorically. When afflicted by high rajas, we hop from teacher to teacher, tradition to tradition, and technique to technique in endless loops because we lack the maturity to take up serious sādhanā for any amount of time.

A high level of sattva in the inner landscape is required for progressive cultivation of viveka and vairāgya, clarity of the *buddhi* (see below) and most importantly, to make progress in Śrīcakra upāsanā. Tamas and rajas keep us on the periphery while sattva turns us to the radius toward the center.[70] This principle becomes exceedingly important in upāsanā, where the goal is to cultivate increasing levels of sattva through discipline, focus, commitment, and surrender.

70 See Becoming Versus Being in Chapter 5.

In the scheme of the tattvas, Prakṛti's guṇas are reflected on the buddhi, tattva 14. Think of the buddhi as a clear, glassy windshield that reflects the unconditioned I or witness that is the Puruṣa. It is the discerning faculty, the one that chooses, reasons, and decides between this and that. Our *samskārās* or conditioned patterns live at this level, obscuring the clear glass and preventing the reflection of the witness. Samskārās that are tāmasik are like a thick and heavy layer of muck on the windshield, while those that are rajāsik are like the constant rain in a thunderstorm. Sattva is a clear windshield that allows the Puruṣa to be reflected. Effective sādhanā that puts us on the path to upāsanā is like a wiper that clears the windshield of the tamas and rajas to allow the clarity of sattva.

Buddhi at the macrocosmic level is known as *mahat*, which reflects to the ahaṅkāra, tattva 15. This is the level where every form in creation is individuated, becoming separate and distinct from all others. It is because of the ahaṅkāra that a leopard, a mosquito, and a cobra are unique and distinct from each other.

Ahaṅkāra means I-maker, which is an important concept for us at the microcosmic level. This is the tattva in us that "makes" the Aham or I out of experience. Think of it as a filing clerk who puts all the memos, notices, notes, and bills into one bin that is labeled "me." Remember that the I is the Puruṣa that is unconditioned and without attributes such as name, sex, culture, role, memory, achievements, loss, pain, and preferences. *All* attributes are Prakṛti, as we will see in Chapter 9. The ahaṅkāra misfiles attributes of Prakṛti as the I because it reflects the buddhi that is obscured with its samskārās. The ahaṅkāra reflects on tattva 16, the *manas*.

Manas is mind, the faculty through which we take in sensory input from the world and process it. As you might suspect, the way we process sensory input is determined by the samskārās at the buddhi level. In the windshield analogy, your glass (buddhi) is uniquely distorted by where you've been driving, collecting remnants of your experience (samskārās). The distorted windshield affects your visibility as you drive along, becoming more distorted as you bump into others, miss turns, and run over potholes (manas).

The ahaṅkāra sits between the manas that takes in the world and the clouded buddhi, interpreting the world according to past experience and creating the me-story through memory, thought, and feeling. The buddhi, ahaṅkāra and manas together make up what is known as *citta*, the field of thinking and feeling that gives rise to the me-story.

The manas takes in the world through the *jñānendriyas* or the sense organs (nose, tongue, eyes, skin, ears), which are tattvas 17-21. The citta operates in the world through the *karmendriyas* or organs of action (speech, manipulation, locomotion, reproduction, excretion), which are tattvas 22-26. For the external world to be detected by the senses, the citta must contain subtle properties that correspond with each sense. For example, we can have skin, but without the property of texture, we would not be able to experience touch. These subtle elements (sound vibration, texture, form, flavor, and smell) are called tanmātras and are tattvas 27-31. They are the bridge between our senses and the external world that is comprised of the pañca mahābhūtas or the great elements (space, air, fire, water, and earth), which are tattvas 32-36.

Understanding the scheme of the tattvas is crucial in the tradition and lays out its darśana. From this map, we can see that samskārās are created in an endless loop of the ahaṅkāra misfiling experience as the me-story that clouds the buddhi to result in ongoing misfiling. How and why this misfiling occurs is systematically laid out in the Śrīcakra along with the tools to reverse engineer the process. As we will see,

> ***Śrīcakra upāsanā is to go from the ahaṅkāra at the periphery to the Ahambhāva of the center.***

The Structure of the Śrīcakra

बैन्दवं चक्रमेतस्य त्रिरूपत्वं पुनर्भवेत् ।
धर्माधर्मौ तथात्मानो मातृमेयौ तथा प्रमा ॥ १२ ॥
नवयोन्यात्मकं चक्रं चिदानन्दघनं महत् ।
चक्रं नवात्मकमिदं नवधा भिन्नमन्त्रकम् ॥ १३ ॥

Baindavaṃ cakram-etasya trirūpatvam punar bhavet /
dharmādharmau tathātmanau mātṛ meyau tathā pramā //12//
navayonyātmakam cakraṃ cidānandaghanaṃ mahat /
cakraṃ navātmakam iḍaṃ navadhā bhinnamantrakam //13//

"The throne of the Bindu is the birthplace of the threefold aspect. Made of dharma and adharma, the four ātmas, and the perceiver, perceived and perception, the (Śrīcakra) that is the ninefold womb is a mass of consciousness and bliss that corresponds with the ninefold mantra."
~Yoginī Hṛdaya 1:12-13

The entire Śrīcakra is constructed around the Bindu with the Kāmakalā. In fact, it would be totally appropriate to state that the Bindu *is* the Śrīcakra. By now, we see that although depicted as such, the Bindu isn't the little central point we see in the middle of Śrīcakra images – the point is merely its graphical representation. The Bindu is non-localized and is found in every component of every āvaraṇa.

Being nonlinear, the Bindu pulses everywhere and nowhere simultaneously, pulling and gathering all of creation within itself, and organizing it into what we see as the Śrīcakra pattern.

Contained within the Bindu is the map of creation at both the macrocosmic and the microcosmic levels. Creation pulses in the Bindu and is orgasmically emitted in the process known as *sphurattā*. Conversely, the Bindu pulsates in the macrocosm and the microcosm, which mirror each other.

For all practical purposes, the Trikoṇa is automatically included in our consideration of all the other āvaraṇas. Without the split of the One into the triad of the Trikoṇa, none of the other structures would arise, and they would be absorbed in Śakti's womb in the seed form. Sphurattā is the process where Śiva and Śakti begin the play of I and myself in the forms of creation. Therefore, when we consider any other āvaraṇa, the Bindu and Trikoṇa are implied.

The Bindu is graphically represented as the central point of nine intersecting triangles. In the tradition we are exploring here, there are four upward-facing dissolution triangles of Śiva and five downward-facing creation triangles of Śakti.[71] The Śiva triangles are named after four masculine deities – *Brahmā, Rudra, Īśāna* and *Sadāśiva*. The Śakti triangles are named after the feminine deities Tvaritā, *Pārijāteśvarī, Tripurā, Śūlinī*, and *Pancabāṇeśī*.

71 In other traditions, particularly of the Samayācāra, there are five upward-facing triangles of Śiva, and four downward-facing triangles of Śakti. Here, the emphasis is on dissolution, as opposed to creation in the other traditions.

The Śrīcakra is known as the Navayonyātmaka Cakra, which means the pattern that consists of nine triangles or yonis (here, yoni refers to the triangular shape that is reminiscent of the womb).

The nine intersecting triangles give rise to 43 small triangles (See Figure 6). If we include the central Bindu, it becomes 44 small triangles. However, as we have seen above, the Bindu is everywhere and confining it to a small triangle can be misleading.

The structure made up of the nine triangles giving rise to 43 smaller ones is surrounded by two circles of lotus petals and a large square. The smaller triangles coalesce into four rhombi and one central downward-facing triangle immediately around the Bindu (see Śrīcakra.png). Each of these components – the inner most triangle (Trikoṇa), the four rhombi (Vasukoṇa with eight small triangles, *Antardaśara* and *Bahirdaśara* with ten small triangles, and *Manvaśra* with 14 small triangles), the two circles of lotus petals (Aṣṭadalapadma with eight petals and Śodaṣadalapadma with 16 petals) and the square (Bhūpura) becomes an āvaraṇa or covering around the Bindu.

Figure 6. Śrīcakra

Navayoni

The *navayoni* or the group of nine *yonis* carry different meanings. Yoni refers to not only the womb or source, but also a portal to the source. Accordingly, the nine triangles result in groupings of portals into the Śrīcakra. For example, the human body with the nine openings [72] is a navayoni, where each has the potential to become a portal to vidyā through the right view and practice.

The navayoni also corresponds with the mantras of the nine Cakreśvarīs and from a holistic perspective it is the grouping of nine overarching principles: the triad of the perceiver, perceived, perception, dharma, adharma, and the four levels of Self or Aham (the Absolute Reality, the inner self that experiences the external world, the inner self that experiences the inner world, and the self that is the same as the person).[73] This grouping is significant for several different reasons, including their pervasiveness in every level of creation. As we have seen earlier, the Trikoṇa of the perceiver-perceived-perception pervades creation as its fundamental principle.

The inclusion of dharma and adharma in the fabric of creation gives us deep insight into its nature. Dharma has many definitions and in the context of the Śrīcakra, we can think of it as the way of harmony. For a system to be in harmony, its elements must fit and work together as a cohesive whole. Social order, moral norms and the basic tenets of any path that include ideals and injunctions strive for dharma. The harmony of any social structure - be it a family, a community, or a country - depends on maintaining equilibrium by honoring fairness and consideration for others in the system.

Adharma is disharmony, which arises from the lack of regard for the overall system by one or more of its elements, which disrupts the equilibrium of the system by introducing chaos and uncertainty.

The navayoni is formed by the mingling of dharma and adharma that propagates throughout the Śrīcakra, showing us that harmony and chaos arise together.

In the Śrīcakra's exquisite pattern, we see that creation must necessarily include both shadow and light. One cannot be had without the other, and it is in the inseparability of the two that we must find beauty, peace, and freedom.

72 Two eyes, two nostrils, one mouth, two ears, one urinary/reproductive and one anus - note that this does not account for the separate openings for the urinary tract and the genital in the female anatomy.

73 See verses 12-13 in Chapter 1 'Cakrasaṃketa' of *Yoginī Hṛdaya.*

Since the Śrīcakra is the most auspicious symbol, we may tend to assign only those qualities to it that we consider wholesome. However, the Śrīcakra transcends human concepts of dharma and adharma while accounting for both. In fact, it is because it accounts for the dualities of shadow and light that the Śrīcakra is supremely auspicious and sacred.

Sandhis and Marmas

The point where two lines intersect is known as sandhi, and there are 24 of them in the Śrīcakra (see Figure 7). The sandhis represent union of the perceiver and the perceived, which occurs throughout the Śrīcakra.

Figure 7. Sandhis in the Śrīcakra

The point where three lines meet is known as marma and there are 18 of them in the Śrīcakra (see Figure 8).[74] A marma is a vital point, depicting the harmony between Śiva and Śakti throughout the Śrīcakra. Marmas in the microcosm occur at the coalescence of *nāḍīs*[75] and are delicate and sensitive points that when damaged through trauma can result in significant derangement of *prāṇa* leading to disability, chronic pain, or death.

74 Depending on the tradition and the construction of the Śrīcakra, there are up to 54 marma points. In this case, when taken to represent Śiva and Śakti (54 x 2), there are 108 that correspond with the 108 common marma points in the body.

75 See Prāṇa Nāḍīs, Cakras and Kuṇḍalinī, Chapter 11.

Figure 8. Marmas in the Śrīcakra

In mantra sādhanā, these marma points become conductors of energy, leading us through the āvaraṇas into the Bindu. The marma *sthānas* (positions) are the seat of life, and the very essence of the Śrīcakra since they represent the coming together of Śiva-Śakti in our lived experience.[76]

> ***The Śrīcakra comes to life through our sādhanā through the formation of novel neurohormonal pathways, bringing together our understanding of the āvaraṇas into a coherent whole.***

Notice that the sandhis and marmas refer only to the part of the Śrīcakra with the triangles. This is because the earliest descriptions of the Śrīcakra included only the triangles and the other elements such as the lotus petals, the Trivṛtta (see below) and the Bhūpura were added later. Even now, some sampradāyas (such as the Hayagrīva sampradāya) only include the triangles. In the Ānandabhairava sampradāya, the other elements are included but not utilized in worship, whereas in the Dakṣiṇāmūrti sampradāya, all the elements are worshiped and used in sādhanā.

76 In some lineages, it is common to consider a specific number of marma points corresponding with the syllables of a mantra. In mine, 28 are considered important, corresponding to the Mahāṣoḍaśī mantra of 28 syllables.

Śakti's Infinite Powers in the Śrīcakra

The Śrīcakra is the geometric form of Lalitā Devī, and every one of its aspects is an emanation or ray of her light. She holds court over her emanations from her seat in the Bindu where she resides as Kāma-Kāmeśvarī representing the union of Śiva and Śakti.

> ***Lalitā Devī is the red-hued, resplendent goddess seated on a throne that is held up by Brahmā the creator, Viṣṇu the sustainer, Rudra the destroyer, and Īśāna the concealer. The throne's seat is Sadāśiva the revealer, and Devī sits atop this emanation of Śiva, in sexual union with him.***

Out of her own svātantrya śakti, Devī performs the five functions of creation, sustenance, dissolution, concealment, and revelation through the five primary deities. She creates as Brahmā, sustains as Viṣṇu, and destroys as Rudra. As Īśāna, she conceals Reality in Māyā, keeping us bound in saṃsāra and suffering. As Sadāśiva, she bestows her *anugraha* or Grace that imparts the knowledge of Reality.

All the deities of the Śrīcakra are emanations of Lalitā Devī, reigning over every aspect of the various āvaraṇas. The subtle form of the Śrīcakra is identical with the gross form of the deity, and they arise together. From *Tripurāmbā* ruling over the Trikoṇa to Tripurā reigning over the Bhūpura, Devī becomes the Cakreśvarīs of each āvaraṇa. The yoginīs of each āvaraṇa are the subsidiary emanations of Lalitā Devī and they govern over unique aspects of creation. The Mudrā Devīs reign over the flow of creation in specific ways.

Some traditions describe 64 crores of yoginīs in the Śrīcakra, eight crores arising from each of the eight Mātṛkās. The Mātṛkās, in turn, are emanations of Lalitā Devī, and they rule over the groups of Sanskrit phonemes. The inclusion of 64 crore yoginīs in the Śrīcakra depicts the incomprehensible number of unique vibrations of vāc in creation.

The Tattvas in the Śrīcakra

To enable our understanding of the Śrīcakra as it relates to the tattvas, we must make assumptions and loose associations since there is no consistent description of this scheme. The description here is a general understanding and may differ from yours and from other sources. The important thing to realize is that all tattvas are accounted for in the Śrīcakra elements (see Figure 9).

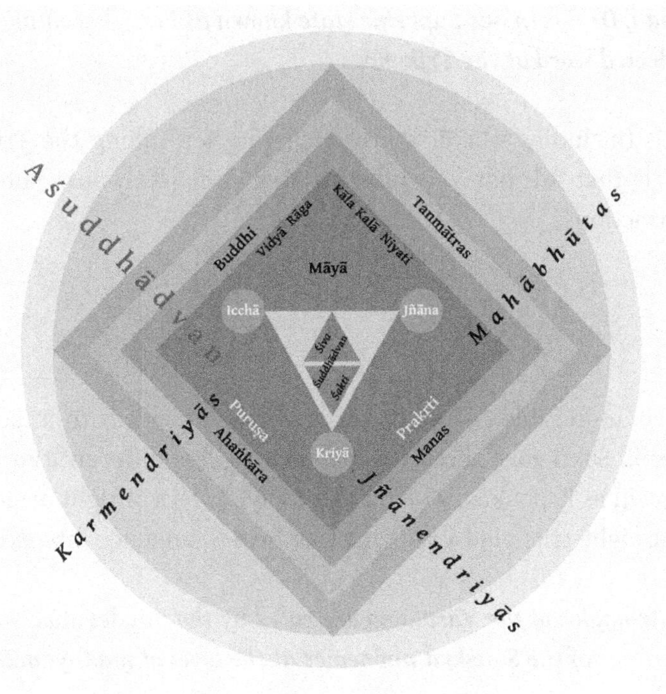

Figure 9. Tattvas in the Śrīcakra

Bindu and Trikoṇa

As we have seen earlier, in the beginning, there is the Absolute Reality in which arises the will to become many. This results in the split of the Divine into Śiva or Prakāśa, and Śakti or Vimarśa in the Bindu as Kāmakalā. The initial will of the Divine to become many condenses into icchā, deliberation as jñāna, and action as kriyā. Devī's icchā for creation actualizes as kriyā into the remaining tattvas through the intermediate tattva of jñāna. The Kāmakalā of the Bindu where Śiva-Śakti are in union as Lalitā Devī split into the Trikoṇa, or the primordial triangle made up of the perceiver, the object of perception, and the interaction between the two.[77]

77 See Trikoṇa, Chapter 16.

At the Bindu, Devī is in her Supreme state known as Parā, becoming paśyantī or the reflected word at the Trikoṇa.[78]

78 See Vāc in the Śrīcakra in Chapter 6.

The 16 Nityās (including Mahātripurasundarī herself) along the Trikoṇa also represent the vowels that are not yet differentiated completely into subject-object and word-object distinctions.

Vasukoṇa

For the unlimited, indivisible Divine to become many, it needs to impose certain limitations upon itself. Śakti goes about this by creating five different types of limitations upon herself known as kañcukas, which are like five layers of tight armor. The Trikoṇa devolves into the eight-triangled Vasukoṇa that brings language into existence.

The eight triangles of the Vasukoṇa are ruled by the Vāgdevatās, who represent the groups of the Sanskrit phonemes at the level of madhyamā.

The Bindu becoming the Trikoṇa devolves into the power of expression at this āvaraṇa. In this scheme, the Trikoṇa and Vasukoṇa manifest almost simultaneously since language is the basis of creation.

Language or the power of expression in the Vasukoṇa gives rise to the five kañcukas and the Māyā tattva. Language is the supreme power that veils Reality as Māyā. It is also the basis for individuation, where every form of creation vibrates at its own specific frequency that makes it unique and separate. In this devolution, the previously unlimited and expansive Divine becomes contracted in intention as rāga, wisdom as vidyā, space as kalā, time as kāla, and causation as niyati.

The kañcukas give rise to a predicament. Prior to this, in the Trikoṇa, the subject-object division is non-localized, where Śiva looks at Śakti in the mirror, but this reflection is simultaneously everywhere and nowhere. The kañcukas contract this *global* awareness into *individual* awareness known as the Puruṣa and the objects witnessed *by* Puruṣa into

Prakṛti. Here, in the Vasukoṇa, creation splits into these two primordial principles – Puruṣa and Prakṛti.

> ***The kañcukas contract Śiva, the Supreme Prakāśa into individual awareness known as the Puruṣa, and the objects witnessed by the Puruṣa into matter known as Prakṛti.***

Puruṣa is the knowing subject and the witness of Prakṛti, which makes up the body, mind, and the world – the rest of the āvaraṇas. Here in the Vasukoṇa, Puruṣa comes into being as the individual "I" or subject, which is the localization of the "me here" while the world is "out there," and the two are separate.

The Guru Maṇḍala

Devī manifests as the Guru maṇḍalas of the divya, *siddha* and *manava* groups in the space above the upper horizontal line of the Trikoṇa. The *divyaugha* Guru is the Divine being or deity of the paramparā, the *siddhyaugha* Gurus are the ones that have attained the highest siddhis, and the *manvaugha* Guru is the one that is constantly worshiped in upāsanā, and the one that with whom we have the most contact. From their position, these Gurus, who are the forms of Devī herself, direct the sādhanā and opening of aspirants, taking them progressively through the āvaraṇas to the navayoni cakra, and granting the Grace to traverse the Vasukoṇa and Trikoṇa into the Bindu. In the saṃhāra krama, the Guru maṇḍala bestows the realization of the oneness in the Devī-Guru-Self triad.

Antardaśara

The Vasukoṇa, Trikoṇa and the Bindu make up another navayoni that becomes the source of the rest of creation, beginning with the Antardaśara, the inner group of ten triangles where the next three tattvas – buddhi, ahaṅkāra and manas manifest. The Antardaśara is the āvaraṇa where agni, the primordial power of transformation comes into perceivable being. The clearly discernible forms of creation are at the level of *vaikharī*, extending to the Bhūpura.

Puruṣa in the Vasukoṇa is the individual pure witnessing awareness that is without attributes. In other words, it is Śiva at the individual level, the subjectivity of *individual* experience. On the other hand, *all* attributes belong to Prakṛti and are merely the interaction of the three guṇas that saturate her. At the microcosmic level, the first tattva downstream of Puruṣa-Prakṛti is buddhi, that is endowed with reasoning and discernment to know the difference between witnessing awareness that is Puruṣa and the objects it perceives – Prakṛti. The next tattva is ahaṅkāra.

Ahaṅkāra is the "I-maker," where the vast array of experiences and attributes that belong to the sphere of Prakṛti are mistakenly assigned to the I or Puruṣa. These attributes of Prakṛti include our history, culture, past stories, future dreams and hopes, genetics and upbringing characteristics. What we really are is witnessing awareness (Puruṣa) but instead, we take ourselves to be everything in the realm of Prakṛti with her guṇas or attributes.

Moving from the ahaṅkāra to the Ahambhāva is the goal of the path.

The ahaṅkāra is reflected onto the next tattva, the manas or mind. The manas is the filter that allows us to process and interpret the world that we take in through the senses, as well as the way we interact with the world. The functioning of the manas is determined by both the ahaṅkāra and the buddhi.

The Antardaśara with the tattvas of the buddhi, manas and ahaṅkāra comprises the power of transformation or agni, which projects onto the next āvaraṇa, the Bahirdaśara.[79]

79 See Agni in Chapter 13.

Bahirdaśara

From the agni of the Antardaśara arises the Bahirdaśara with the primordial power of movement, vāyu. The inner apparatus comprising the buddhi, ahaṅkāra and manas must interact with the outer world, and this occurs through the tanmātras or subtle elements including sound vibration, texture, form, flavor, and smell. The tanmātras are nourished by vāyu and are the bridge between our five senses and the pañca mahābhūtas or the great elements – space, air, fire, water, and earth.

Between the five tanmātras of our inner landscape and the pañca mahābhūtas of the external world are two other sets of tattvas – the karmendriyas and the jñānendriyās, which are the organs of action and the five sense organs. These ten *indriyas* or senses are the intermediaries between us and the world. The world is taken in through our jñānendriyas and our energy is sent out into the world through the karmendriyas. The four groups of tattvas are found throughout the remaining āvaraṇas at different levels of subtlety.

For example, agni and vāyu are the primordial forces of creation as the powers of transformation and movement that drive the initial split of Śiva and Śakti. At the Bindu, they are at their subtlest levels as icchā, jñāna and kriyā. Starting at the Antardaśara and the Bahirdaśara, agni and vāyu become increasingly perceptible with the progressive differentiation of forms. Similarly, we see that the attributes of the pañca mahābhūtas were present in the Trikoṇa as the Nityās at their subtlest levels. At the Bhūpura, on the other hand, they are experienced in their most obvious forms.

Manvaśra and Trivṛtta

At the Manvaśra, the elements of the previous āvaraṇas are channelized into differentiation through the power of prāṇa, which is a function of agni and vāyu. With increasing demarcation between unique forms, there arises a distinction between the subtle and the gross, represented by the Trivṛtta.

Various classes of elements and deities are assigned to the Trivṛtta, including the groupings of letters and the triad of knower, known, and knowing. Once again, this scheme of duplicating or triplicating the presence of the same elements in the various āvaraṇas represents varied levels of subtlety. As an example, the triad of knower, known and knowing here at the Trivṛtta is at a grosser form than at the Trikoṇa. As our sādhanā progresses, the division between these levels of subtlety dissipate and the Trikoṇa and Bindu begin to arise in every element of every āvaraṇa.

Aṣṭadalapadma

At the Aṣṭadalapadma, the sense of separation from the world is complete through the action of the five kañcukas and the three *malas* that result in agitation and restlessness. Agitation is projected onto our own internal landscape at the Śodaṣadalapadma and upon the external world at the Bhūpura.

Śodaṣadalapadma and Bhūpura

The agitations of the Aṣṭadalapadma give rise to the deep longing to fulfill our wishes, which manifests as the *ākarṣiṇīs* of the Śodaṣadalapadma. Fulfilling our wishes requires us to interact with the world since the senses are by nature turned outward. The gross world comes into existence here as the Bhūpura.

Sṛṣṭi Krama in the Microcosm

At the level of piṇḍāṇḍa or the microcosm, the three bindus of the Kāmakalā represent the creation of the individual at birth.

> ***The red bindu is ārtava, representing the ovum that is matured through menstrual cycles. The white bindu is semen, and the mixed bindu is the union of the ovum and sperm poised to give birth.***

In Śrīvidyā, Lalitā Mahātripurasundarī is Śiva-Śakti at the level of Absolute Reality and even the masculine aspects of creation are her emanations. The father or the contributor of the white bindu here, in the place of Śiva, is Vārāhī, whereas the mother who provides the ovum is *Kurukullā* in the place of Śakti. Vārāhī and Kurukullā contribute the different *dhātus* or tissues of the fetus.

While Vārāhī contributes marrow, reproductive fluid, prāṇa and *jīva* (individual soul) to the fetus, Kurukullā provides flesh, fat, skin, blood, and bone. The fetus is provided consciousness through orgasm, with the union of the red and white bindus. The coming together of the sun, moon, and fire in the orgasm of Kāmakalā explodes into the psychophysiological being – the piṇḍāṇḍa that is the perfect mirror of the macrocosm or brahmāṇḍa.

Vārāhī's four upward-facing triangles represent the 12 kalās of the sun, which at the piṇḍāṇḍa translate to the sidereal constellations, whereas Kurukullā's five downward-facing triangles make up the 15 lunar tithis. Embedded in these time-space signatures, the microcosm develops and grows, bringing in the conditioning of the past that was in the seed form at the end of its individual *pralaya*.[80]

At the end of the previous lifetime, all our karmas are absorbed into the Bindu in seed form. With the orgasmic creation of the next life through the confluence of the two bindus, the seeds are primed to sprout and grow in the subtleties of the āvaraṇas between the Bindu and the Bhūpura. Propelled by the condensation of vāc from parāvāk to vaikharī, the seeds fully sprout and manifest at the Bhūpura, becoming the stimuli for our karma and destiny.

80 Process of dissolution when all of creation is reabsorbed into the seed form and becomes unmanifest; deluge.

The Krama of the Āvaraṇas

Krama means sequence, and traditionally, the nine āvaraṇas of the Śrīcakra are divided into three groups of three. The Bhūpura, Śodaṣadalapadma and Aṣṭadalapadma make up the sṛṣṭi (creation) cakra, symbolizing the manifestation of the world in its gross, largely perceivable form.

The next three āvaraṇas, including the Manvaśra, Bahirdaśara and Antardaśara make up the stithi (sustenance) cakra, because they are the inner workings of the sṛṣṭi cakra that provide the appearance of constancy. They are largely hidden unless we cultivate awareness through the right sādhanā.

The saṃhāra (dissolution) cakra is made up of the three innermost āvaraṇas including the Vasukoṇa, the Trikoṇa and the Bindu. The universe as we know it dissolves in this cakra, returning to the Source, the Bindu. The saṃhāra cakra is entirely hidden from our ordinary perception and can only be accessed in advanced sādhanā.

It is critical to understand that this classification is relevant only from the standpoint of the saṃhāra krama. In the sṛṣṭi krama, all the āvaraṇas originate from the Bindu. In both movements, the understanding of the saṃhāra cakra is that it is the primary yoni - the womb that creates and dissolves creation. Since creation is only possible through dissolution, the innermost āvaraṇas are the supreme destroyers at the Source. So too in the saṃhāra cakra, where constant dissolution occurs to give birth to the new in the sṛṣṭi cakra and the appearance of constancy is provided by the stithi cakra.

The three primary modes of cosmogony – sṛṣṭi, stithi and saṃhāra – expand into the nine āvaraṇas making up the three krama cakras. The sṛṣṭi cakra is of the nature of fire, and within the scope of sṛṣṭi are the three modes of sṛṣṭi, stithi and saṃhāra (see Figure 10). The stithi (sun) and saṃhāra (moon) cakras similarly encompass the other modes, demonstrating their intermingling in creation. Destruction is a necessity for creation where everything arises as the Śrīcakra, stays a while and dissolves into the Bindu.

> ***Linear creation arises from the nonlinear, nonlocalized Bindu, and linearity is dependent on dissolution.***

This moment must dissolve to give rise to the next. Evolution, aging, seasons, the cycles of day and night, the microscopic processes of digestion, respiration and cellular metabolism are all based on destruction, where one must die to make way for the new.

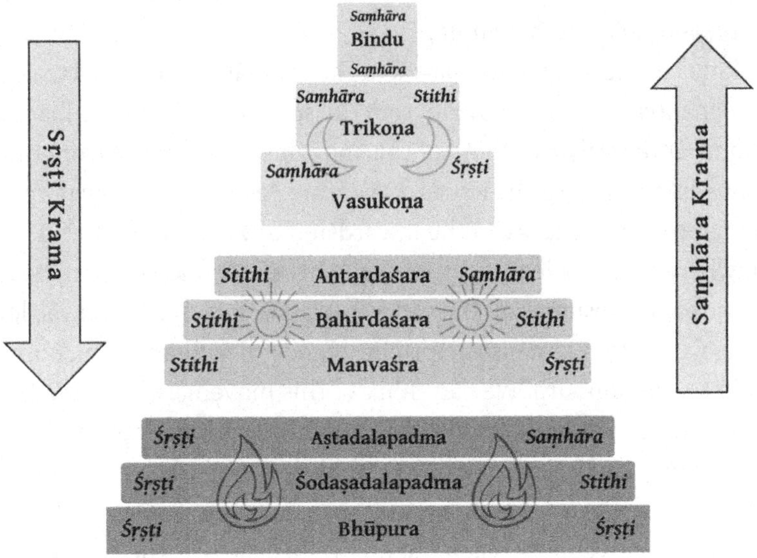

Figure 10. The Krama of the Āvaraṇas

As we move from Bhūpura to the Bindu in the saṃhāra krama, the first significant stage of practice is the resolution of the fire (knower), which is to resolve the subject by separating it from subtle objects that we take to be the self (I). Our developing discernment and dispassion help us see that the I is not the objects we previously thought it was, such as roles and attributes. It's known as the sṛṣṭi cakra because this is where we manifest the world through our own projections.

Saṃhāra krama in the stithi cakra gives us the insight that the world is indeed WITHIN us. In the sṛṣṭi krama of this cakra, our world is seen as a continuous cycle of destruction and creation that occurs ecstatically and non-linearly within us, giving the *appearance* of linearity and continuity. This is the sphere of the sun, in which the known occurs in the knower.

In the saṃhāra krama of the saṃhāra cakra, objects (the known) dissolve fully into the subject, where the world IS us. There is no separation between the world and the self, the distinction having been resolved. This is the sphere of the moon or the known dissolving into the knower or fire. In the sṛṣṭi krama of this cakra, the nonlinear nonseparation persists even while progressing into the stithi and saṃhāra cakras. Linearity is subsumed by nonlinearity, and separation by unity.

The three kūṭas of the Pañcadaśī mantra in the saṃhāra krama lead to three progressive insights in mantra sādhanā, moving from the sṛṣṭi cakra to the saṃhāra cakra in the *nivṛtti* direction.[81] Ordinarily, we think of this movement occurring from the mūlādhāra to the sahasrāra cakras, where the issues of each are resolved from *upasarga* to *apasarga*, gathering momentum and energy in the inward and upward direction.[82] This is the path of Kuṇḍalinī, where upāsanā leads us from vaikharī to parā at the nonlinear sahasrāra, which transcends and subsumes all the other āvaraṇas, *ṣaṭcakras*[83] and vāc levels.

81 See Pravṛtti and Nivṛtti in Chapter 5.

82 See Upasarga and Apasarga in Chapter 5

83 See The Ṣaṭcakra and the Śrīcakra in Chapter 5.

In some lineages, sṛṣṭi krama is the primary mode of sādhanā, which involves going from the Bindu to the Bhūpura. We can think of this movement as going from the integral to the derivative, where all possibilities exist at every level of devolution. This sādhanā is necessarily challenging without a stable stance in the nondual understanding of Absolute Reality and Śiva-Śakti. In sṛṣṭi krama sādhanā, we are at the center at the Bindu, and our perspective must reach the furthest corners of the Bhūpura. For this, we must have the ability to set aside our conditioning of how things *should* be and cultivate the broadest possible perspective. As you might imagine, sṛṣṭi krama requires us to be advanced practitioners *and* to work under the direct guidance of a Guru.[84]

84 Guru's guidance is imperative for any Śrīcakra upāsanā.

Stithi krama as sādhanā also requires a high degree of discernment to be able to understand the integral and the derivative together. Here too, we must have the capacity to set aside our conditioning to be able to find the integral in the derivative – the Trikoṇa in every element of the Śrīcakra.

The saṃhāra krama is the easiest of the sādhanās since it allows us to enter the Śrīcakra from the seat of our contraction and find our way to the Bindu *through* it. Here, the very contraction that keeps us in saṃsāra becomes the path to freedom. Since the saṃhāra krama is the most prevalent way of understanding the Śrīcakra, it will be the approach for the remainder of the book. However, to even enter the Śrīcakra, we will need to deeply understand the purpose of sādhanā and its fundamental tenets, which we will explore next.

Chapter 5

Nuances of Practice

In this chapter, we will explore the nuances and pitfalls of sādhanā but before we get to it, we must examine the purpose of sādhanā, especially as it relates to the Śrīcakra. This will make all the difference as we move along, particularly in the saṃhāra krama.

Becoming Versus Being

Our ordinary way of being is a becoming, arising from the fundamental split of the One into two or duality. It is the very nature of creation to impose a self-limitation so that it can experience Itself in every possible permutation and combination. In other words, our ordinary way of being at the highest level is the Divine experiencing Itself.[85] However, we don't know this because of the self-imposed kañcukas and malas of the Divine. These limitations projected upon us create the illusory creation of a separate "I" through the action of the ahaṅkāra. Innocently, we come to believe that we are the limited self instead of the Divine.

85 See Prakāśa and Vimarśa, Chapter 4.

The inherent limitation results in a sense of something missing as we go about life. We know, on some level, that there must be more to our existence than the obvious. This fundamental sense of lack known as the *āṇava mala* drives our way of being, which is to become something other than what we already are.[86] The sense of "I" created by the ahaṅkāra is superimposed on the supreme I that is Ahambhāva (see Figure 51, Chapter 16), resulting in a split between *what is* and what *should be.*

86 See Kañcukas and Malas, Chapter 9.

Our sense of what *should be* is the result of our contractions arising from our past conditioning that clouds the buddhi tattva, making it difficult, if not impossible, to see things as they *are*. Our contractions keep us entrapped in our ordinary experience that occurs at the surface level, and the Source remains hidden. One way to understand this dichotomy between being and becoming is through the example of a circle.

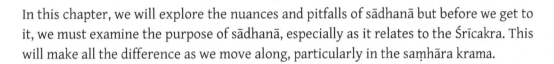

A circle has three primary elements – the outer circumference or the periphery, the central point, and the infinite radii that connect the two.[87] The circumference is the sthūla or gross, the radius is the sūkṣma or subtle, and the center is the *kāraṇa* or the cause of both.[88] Our ordinary experience lies at the circumference or sthūla, where the radius remains hidden, and the center is entirely inaccessible. We go about life trying to understand the surface without ever delving into the center. The paradox here is that if we knew the center, we'd know the whole circle. However, because we never venture too much onto the radii, our whole experience remains limited to a tiny slice of the circumference that is available to us at any given moment.

87 See 'Introduction' in Swami Pratyagatmananda Saraswati, *Sādhana for Self-Realization* (Ganesh Publishers, 1963).

88 See Chapter 7.

The quest for the center drives creation. Evolution and advances in medicine, technology, science, economics, or world politics occur because humankind is constantly trying to find the Source. Research and development in any arena are the methods of finding the radii that connect the surface to the center.

The circumstances, behavior, and outcomes at the sthūla level become the focus of study and exploration along the radius, which drive all human endeavors, including spirituality.

Our normal way of being is such that all our actions and interactions remain at the sthūla level. In all our endeavors, we seek the center, the Source, which will be "it," the one thing that will resolve all the angst at the periphery. However, we often mistake the circumference for the radius. As we set out to find the center, the impelling force of becoming creates more interactions and turbulence at the periphery, which keeps us engaged there. We mistakenly think we are traversing the radius when actually we are caught up in the turbulent waves at the surface. The spiritual path is like scuba diving, where the goal is to dive down from the surface with its choppy waves to the calmer waters underneath to land at the ocean floor.

In the analogy of the circle, the sthūla at the rim reflects the sūkṣma that is the radius.

Our external circumstances reflect our internal state.

For the sthūla to change, the sūkṣma must change. Importantly, we must know the difference between the two. The reason we don't seem to make progress on the spiritual path is that our energy is dissipated in trying to find solutions to problems at the sthūla, creating more surface turbulence without delving into the sūkṣma that caused them in the first place.

The path of sādhanā requires us to get off the circumference and dive into the radius toward the center. The center is the source of knowledge and illumination that shows us how things *are*, which is known as *satyam* (truth). The process by which satyam unfolds to the becoming at the surface is known as *ṛtam* (law).

> ***Ṛtam is the law of satyam, and the path of sādhanā is most useful and successful when we understand the ṛtam so that we can reverse engineer our way through it.***

If the ṛtam of creation is to move from being at the center to becoming at the surface, sādhanā moves us in the opposite direction. By deeply understanding the ṛtam of becoming, we move to the satyam of being, where the gap closes between what is and what should be.

The Śrīcakra is the perfect representation of this analogy where the center, kāraṇa or satyam is the Bindu. The radii as the ṛtam emanate from the Bindu as the systematic layers of sūkṣma, unfolding as the becoming from the being. The Bhūpura is the circumference, the sthūla field where becoming is fully manifest. In the saṃhāra krama of reverse engineering, we move from the sthūla at the Bhūpura along the radii of the intervening āvaraṇas to the Bindu at the center (see Figure 11).

> ***The Bhūpura is where our dramas play out, keeping us engaged and interested in our circumstances, strife, outcomes, disappointments, and satisfaction. It is where we seek completion – the becoming.***

The other word for becoming, is of course, saṃsāra. The Bhūpura is where we experience the conflict between what is and should be.

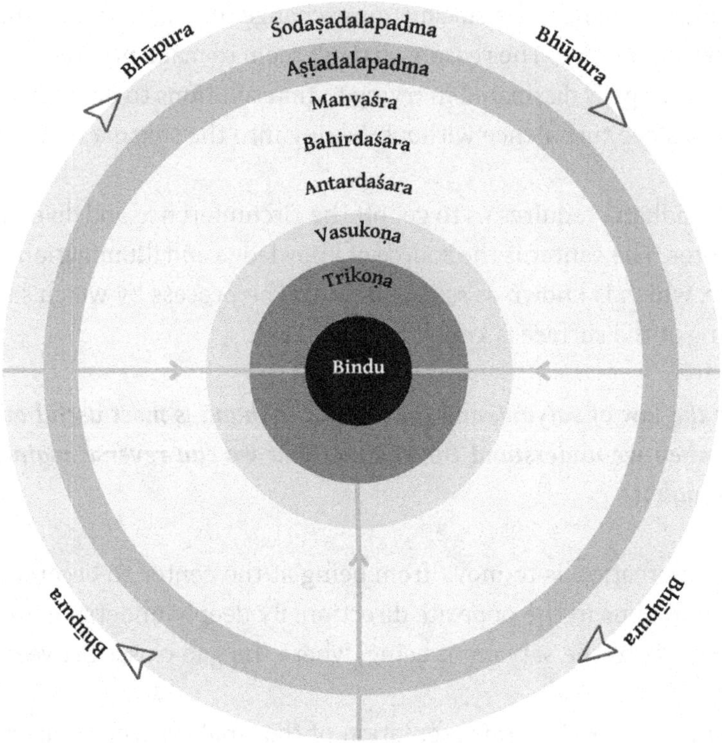

Figure 11. The Circle Analogy For Śrīcakra Upāsanā

The inward path from the Bhūpura through the intervening āvaraṇas take us toward being – as long as we follow the procedure through the right discernment. Often, it is easy to be fooled into thinking we are going inward when we are still very much at the surface. The tenets of Śrīcakra sādhanā prepare us to understand bhāvanā (see later in this chapter) and the critical difference between two types of practice – the first that keeps us entrapped in the circumference, and the second that catapults us onto the radius. One way to understand the difference between the two is through the concepts of *parā* and *aparā vidyā.*

Parā and Aparā Vidyā

To understand the difference between parā and aparā vidyā, we must explore the distinction between transactional and Self knowledge. Our day-to-day interactions constitute transactional knowledge, which refers to the interaction between the I or subject and the That, the world of objects. Our routine way of being is transactional, where we gather information through the senses, make some sense of it, and respond back through the organs of action. However clever and astute we are in the way we interpret the world and interact with it, the knowledge is still transactional, where the I is transacting with the world. In transactional knowledge, the I refers to the ahaṅkāra, and the way we interpret the world and interact with it has largely to do with feeling a certain way about our self, and maintaining the self-image. Here, the attention is on objects or That as the support or basis for the subject, the I. This is known as aparā vidyā, where aparā means inferior. Aparā vidyā keeps us on the circumference of becoming.

Parā vidyā is Self-knowledge, where our interest is in the subject, the I. Here, even when we understand the difference between Puruṣa and Prakṛti only intellectually, we are willing to relinquish the self-image made of objects in favor of the I, the subject. In parā vidyā, we are on the radius toward being, rather than the circumference of becoming. Even when interacting with the world, we favor freedom from the self-image and its maintenance, willing to let go of aparā vidyā.

Having extensive academic or scholarly knowledge about the Śrīcakra doesn't automatically make it parā vidyā. In the ultimate analysis, academic knowledge is no different than owning a Śrīcakra for good fortune. Both are aparā vidyā when the knowledge is acquired or the action is performed to placate a self-image (being knowledgeable in the first example and needing luck in the second, both of which refer to the ahaṅkāra).

The issue here is that it takes increasingly refined discernment to know the difference between aparā and parā vidyā. Two people in the same sampradāya can be engaged in an identical practice or ritual, where one is favoring aparā and the other parā. When a practice, ritual or approach is used to create and maintain a particular self-image, it becomes aparā even when appearing to be advanced or elevated to others. On the other hand, a simple practice or mantra can become parā when we are on the radius. This difference is one of the many reasons for needing a Guru who can continuously place us on the radius by imparting the right view, the right thinking, and the most appropriate practice.

To head out in the right direction in upāsanā, it is helpful to understand its basic tenets and the preliminary attitude that we must cultivate in order to make progress.

Tenets of Śrīcakra Upāsanā

As we have seen earlier, the upāsanā of the Śrīcakra is highly dependent on the sampradāya, which in turn depends on the āmnāya and ācāra to which it subscribes. Accordingly, the process or ṛtam of turning inward onto the radius can differ and is highly individual, depending on the practitioner's degree of discernment and clarity of buddhi.

The following tenets are generic and applicable to all sampradāyas, and in fact, to every spiritual path that seeks the Source. They are adapted from the dharma or principles of the Paraśurāma Kalpa Sūtras which convey the preliminary stance of an aspirant through pithy aphorisms. Table 5 includes 15 tenets that are included in these aphorisms with my brief commentary on each.[89]

89 See *Paraśurāma Kalpa Sūtras*, 1 and 6-29. The most widely available English translation and commentary is by M.P.Pandit (Dipti Publications, 1972).

Table 5. Tenets of Upāsanā

TENET	COMMENTARY	TENET	COMMENTARY
Dīkṣā (Initiation)	Initiation is the first step in upāsanā, where the aspirant is energized by the Guru's knowledge and light. Since the Śrīcakra is the parā or subtlest form of Lalitā Devī, dīkṣā into the Pañcadaśī is a requirement for its ritual sādhanā in most lineages. *	**Ekāgratā (Single pointedness)**	Single pointedness in sādhanā must be cultivated to such an extent that our interest in becoming naturally dissolves. Progress in sādhanā must be favored over greed, petty desire, envy, anger, hatred, and destructiveness.
Guru (Preceptor)	Cultivation of intimacy with the Guru is crucial in Tāntrik sādhanā. The non-separation between Devī, Guru and self is accepted intellectually, which becomes a lived experience through ṛtam.	**Eṣaṇā lakṣya (Awareness of Eṣaṇas)**	Our three eṣaṇas keep us entrenched on the surface or sthūla level. They must be fulfilled to a certain degree before we can turn to the radius. Cultivating stark honesty about our eṣaṇas hastens this process.
Darśana (View)	Aligning with the darśana is crucial for progress, including the understanding that our true nature is Śiva-Śakti, which is currently obscured by the āvaraṇas. Other aspects of the darśana, such as the 36 tattvas, kañcukas, malas, karma, saṃsāra as the cause of suffering, and the meaning of liberation must be clearly understood through constant reflection.	**Bhāvanā (Contemplation)**	We must become adept at bhāvanā or self-inquiry that takes us to the sūkṣma, where we understand the workings of the sthūla. Bhāvanā must catapult us out of our mind stories and analysis that revolves around eṣaṇā fulfilment to the calm and detached observance of the psychophysiological mechanisms represented in the āvaraṇas between the Bhūpura and the Bindu.
Śraddhā (Faith)	Faith in the Guru and the path must be to the extreme. Other paths must not be criticized but the focus must be on one's own path and Guru.	**Vairāgya (Dispassion)**	Dispassion is required to ignore the juicy drama of the Bhūpura in favor of the logical, mechanistic process of the ṛtam.
Puruṣārtha (Objective)	The objective of sādhanā must be clear and not confused with the temporary fulfilment of life goals at the surface. The goal of sādhanā is mokṣa, which is to realize our true nature, which is unfettered and unlimited as Śiva-Śakti.	**Viveka (Discernment)**	Discernment is the ability to know the difference between the sthūla and the sūkṣma. It is the difference between aparā and parā vidyā. As we move closer to the Source, it is the difference between ahaṅkāra and Ahambhāva.
Tapas (Perseverance)	The practice and lifestyle prescribed by the Guru must be upheld at all costs. Sacrifices will have to be made, and expectations adjusted for tapas.	**Vīrya (Courage)**	Fearlessness must be cultivated by a serious upāsaka of the Śrīcakra, which is enabled by unshakable faith in the Guru and the path.
Avadhāna (Mindfulness)	Mindfulness is the continual redirection of attention from the drama of life to a curious witnessing of one's inner landscape.	**Śaraṇāgati (Surrender)**	Surrender is the stance of humility and softness, where we empty our cup and allow the Guru to fill it.
Titikṣa (Forbearance)	Forbearance and cultivation of patience aids the path greatly. It is helpful to remember that conditioning occurs over lifetimes and takes nearly as long to dissolve. It also helps to remember that anugraha occurs according to Devī's timeline, not ours.	**Sthūla is the anthropomorphic form, sūkṣma is the mantra, parā is the yantra and subtler still is Devī as Kuṇḍalinī. The Pañcadaśī mantra and the Śrīcakra are Devī's subtle and parā forms, respectively, which is why dīkṣa is required for the ritual worship that brings the mantra and yantra together.*	

Even though the tenets of practice are preliminary to the rituals and meditations, their importance can hardly be over-emphasized. They are exceedingly crucial for advancement on the path of ṛtam. Without the cultivation of these tenets, it's impossible to advance in mantra or yantra (and therefore, Tantra) sādhanā. This principle becomes evident in the understanding of prāṇa,[90] which is constantly wasted in the process of becoming at the surface, which is driven by our *eṣaṇas.*

90 See Prāṇa Vāyus in Chapter 12.

The Eṣaṇas

Ordinarily, we strive to find fulfilment in the world of objects, driven by the cycles of desire, which, in turn, arise from our past experiences. Our desires fall into three general categories known as eṣaṇas (longings): *prāṇeṣaṇā*, *dhaneṣaṇā*, and *(para)lokeṣaṇā.*[91] Prāṇeṣaṇa is the inherent desire for survival, longevity, and health, while dhaneṣaṇā is the longing for resources and wealth. Paralokeṣaṇā is the desire for a favorable future outcome of the actions we engage in today. It is the very stimulus for our action, where the vision of a future outcome impels us to do what we do.

91 See *Caraka Samhita, Sūtra Sthāna* Chapter 11.

However, paralokeṣaṇā is closely related to *lokeṣaṇā*, which is the longing for validation and to be seen and recognized in our current action and behavior. We not only want a good outcome in the future, but we also want to feel like our efforts are worth something, that we are recognized by others, and most of all, that we feel self-fulfilled. Lokeṣaṇā is the fundamental cause of many mental health imbalances, including anxiety, depression, self-doubt, guilt, blame, shame, the imposter syndrome, and the general sense of dissatisfaction even when things are going well. The need for approval from others and ourselves drives us in all the three *puruṣārthas* or universal aspirations.[92] Lokeṣaṇa determines our self-worth, how we view ourselves and others, and whether we are psychologically well-adjusted.

92 See Puruṣārthas in Chapter 8.

Lokeṣaṇa is the driving force of spiritual materialism, where we use spirituality, practices, and knowledge to feel better about ourselves.[93] It impels us toward creating a self-image, maintaining it, and propagating it in whatever we do. If our lokeṣaṇā is fulfilled by the self-image of being virtuous, we organize our life and circumstances to fulfill it. If it is the self-image of being carefree or adventurous, we take risks to

93 Coined by Chogyam Trungpa, the term spiritual materialism refers to the concept of pursuing the spiritual path to fulfill ego-based desires.

propagate that. Whether the self-image is one of being rich and successful or humble and surrendered, lokeṣaṇā is the primary force of the image-making, which is greatly amplified in the age of social media and the seeking of fifteen minutes of fame.

> ***In the sādhanā of the Śrīcakra, understanding the eṣaṇas is critical, since spirituality becomes the hook, trapping us in the sphere of becoming at the periphery.***

The tricky thing about eṣaṇas is that they cannot be denied or bypassed. Instead, they must be acknowledged and fulfilled to a degree where they naturally die away and place us on the radius. For this, a clear understanding of what we can do to achieve them is critical. For example, if you were born with a genetic disorder that requires a lifetime of treatment, it is unreasonable to want perfect health. Here, an attitude adjustment is required where a broad perspective of the darśana or view of the path can help you understand how to make the most of your health problem and to use it as a sādhanā. On the other hand, working on fulfilling eṣaṇas that are at least partly under your control is critical, such as those of being an artist, a parent, a designer, or whatever gives you the sense of being sated. The spiritual path does not work as a good substitute for fulfilling eṣaṇas, particularly if we wish to bypass our predicament.[94]

94 See The Path of Bhukti and Mukti in Chapter 6.

There is a point at which the fulfilment of the eṣaṇas makes us feel content enough to withdraw from the enchanting drama of the periphery and turn towards the center. If the eṣaṇas haven't been fulfilled to this critical point, we continue to be ensnared in saṃsāra. With their fulfilment to the critical point, our attention turns upon itself through the right kind of questioning, placing us on the radius. The eṣaṇas make all the difference when it comes to the two ways in which the Śrīcakra is viewed and practiced – *pravṛtti* and nivṛtti.

Pravṛtti and Nivṛtti

Thus far, we have examined the various ācāras, āmnāyas and sampradāyas as they relate to practice. One way to simplify the details is to think of sādhanā in two ways – pravṛtti and nivṛtti, both of which refer to *vṛttis* or tendencies.[95] Pravṛtti is the multiplication of vṛttis, and nivṛtti is their cessation. We will examine vṛttis in great depth in the Aṣṭadalapadma, but for now, we will touch upon pravṛtti and nivṛtti as somewhat distinct paths.

95 See Citta Vṛttis in Chapter 10.

Pravṛtti is the path of sṛṣṭi krama, where vṛttis are produced in an explosive and exponential pattern, each layer of creation giving rise to infinite other layers. It is the path that progresses from the center to the periphery, from being to becoming. Nivṛtti is the path of saṃhāra krama, which proceeds from the periphery to the center, with the progressive loss of vṛttis. It is the path from becoming to being.

Pravṛtti is to engage with the vṛttis to produce an increasing number of forms, whereas nivṛtti is the path back to the center from form to the formless.

Ordinarily, the pravṛtti and nivṛtti mārgas (paths) are understood as the householder and the renunciate paths, respectively. The idea here is that the householder is engaged in the world of objects and the renunciate is detached from them, and each must find the way back to the Source within their chosen spheres. However, it's not as simple as being a householder or a renunciate.

A renunciate may eschew the world externally and yet remain on the circumference, seeking validation and self-worth in the act of renunciation and spiritual ideals. In this case, s/he is still on the pravṛtti mārga. On the other hand, a householder that is continuously engaged in the world of objects may have no interest whatsoever in fulfilling eṣaṇas and is naturally turned toward the radius. In this instance, the householder is on the nivṛtti mārga.

Pravṛtti and nivṛtti have little to do with lifestyle choices or external circumstances. Instead, they have to do with whether we are trapped on the surface of the ocean where waves beget waves, or we traverse the radius. We can turn toward the radius only when we have made peace with the surface, at least to a certain degree. If our hunger for the eṣaṇas isn't fulfilled, spirituality becomes yet another avenue to fulfill them. In this case, we remain on the surface but fool ourselves into thinking that we are on the radius.

At this point, we must clarify the issue of Tantra being a householder path. Tantra is a discipline that excludes nothing. All aspects of our life, thought, emotion, speech, relationships, health, finance, values, and goals become portals to Tantra sādhanā. In Tantra, the very thing that binds us becomes the thing that liberates us. What is tricky here, however, is that although everything has the *potential* to liberate us, it also has the power to bind us.

> ***Since nothing is excluded in Tantra, it is exceedingly easy to think of it as licentiousness, particularly when we are on the surface.***

And here, on the surface, the thing that binds us does keep us bound!

Pravṛtti becomes a mārga for liberation when we are fully engaged in the circumference, using every experience as a portal to the radius. Until then, pravṛtti is not a mārga for liberation; instead, it traps us in saṃsāra by creating a cascade of never-ending vṛttis. When we approach this with honesty about fulfilling our eṣaṇas without attaching spiritual labels to our problems, we gain a huge advantage. Being honest and humble about our predicament allow us to fulfill our eṣaṇas on the circumference and places us on the radius, shifting us from pravṛtti to nivṛtti. The true pravṛtti mārga of Tantra is about finding the center in the periphery, or the Bindu in moment-to-moment awareness. This only happens when nivṛtti is attained by way of dispassion and discernment.

> ***The pravṛtti of Tantra is the path from here to HERE, from now to NOW, from linearity to the nonlinear, from the derivative to the integral.***

The crucial thing to understand is that whether we are a householder or a monk, renunciation is a requirement for progress in sādhanā (see Tenet #12 in the table above). Through the tenets, we learn to conserve energy that can be used in the process of ṛtam that leads us from pravṛtti to nivṛtti.

Upasarga and Apasarga

Another way to understand the critical difference between pravṛtti and nivṛtti is through that of *sarga*, which means nature or tendency. Upasarga (upa = superimposed, sarga =

tendency) is the process where tendencies sprout from underlying tendencies, mushrooming at the surface level (see Figure 12). The triad of icchā, jñāna and kriyā proceed in erratic directions toward the surface, driven by the predominant tendencies or samskārās.

Apasarga (*apa* = destruction, sarga = tendency) is the process by which the surface tendency is traced back to its root and destroyed in the process.

> ***Upasarga is like a ripple on the surface of water that creates innumerable other ripples and apasarga is the examination of how the original ripple occurred in the first place.***

While this difference may seem clear in theory, it is exceedingly difficult in practice. We can feel like we are engaging in sādhanā on the radius but may be caught up in the loops of mind stories, justifications, and validations creating the ripple effect on the surface.

The foundational tenets of sādhanā are meant to turn us from upasarga to apasarga, and because our sargas or tendencies are so tenacious, working with a teacher eases the process. The Guru points out the difference between the two in our day-to-day life, continuously redirecting us from upasarga to apasarga.

The concepts of pravṛtti and nivṛtti, and upasarga and apasarga are significant in understanding the meaning of saṃhāra krama of the Śrīcakra, which is often correlated with the cakras of the subtle body in a linear way. Once we appreciate the difference between pravṛtti/nivṛtti and upasarga/apasarga, we are in a better position to understand the purpose of the saṃhāra krama.

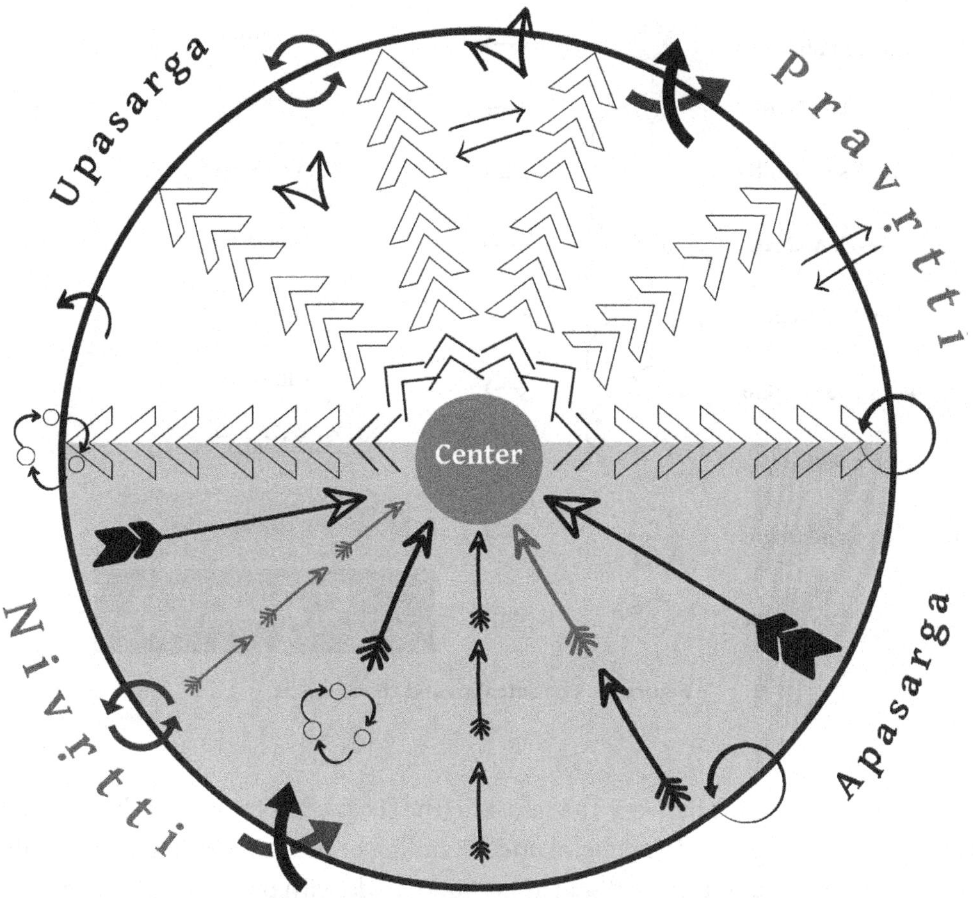

Figure 12. Pravṛtti and Nivṛtti

The Ṣaṭcakra and the Śrīcakra

In Chapter 3, we briefly explored the correspondence of the Śrīcakra āvaraṇas with the subtle centers known as cakras (see Figure 13). The correspondence of the āvaraṇas with the cakras differs according to the text and tradition.[96] The specific way of practicing with this correlation must be learned directly from the Guru.

96 See M. Bowden (ed.) *Gifts from the Goddess: Selected Works of Śrī Amritananda Natha Saraswati* (45th Parallel Press, 2019) for a description of this correlation in my lineage.

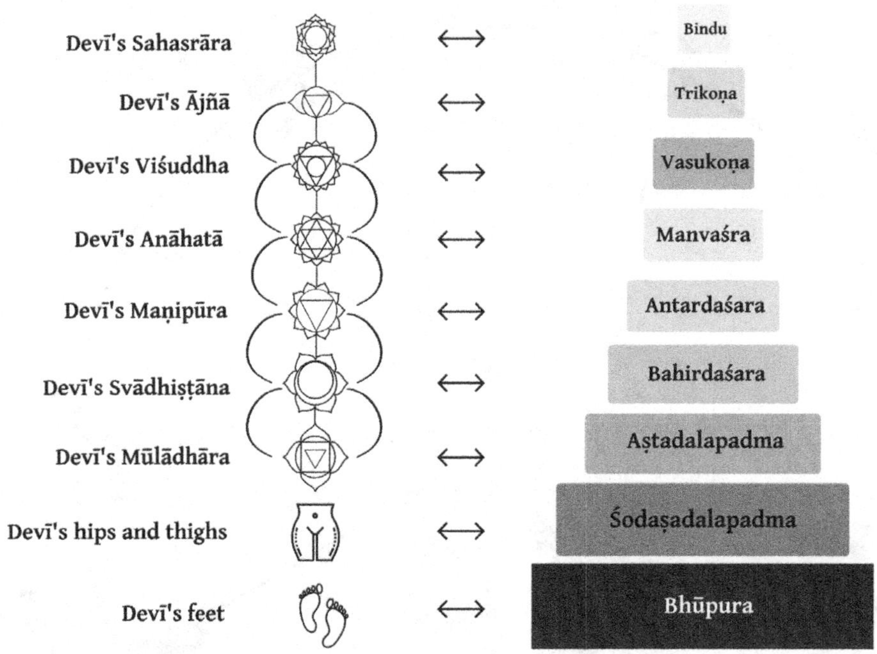

Figure 13. The Ṣaṭcakra and the Śrīcakra

While the association between the ṣaṭcakra (the six cakras of the subtle body) and the āvaraṇas can be helpful in the general understanding of the progression of the saṃhāra krama from the Bhūpura to the Bindu, it has more to do with pravṛtti and nivṛtti, which is a subtle distinction.

Since creation is necessarily dualistic, all its aspects have the power to bind us in saṃsāra or lead us to nirvāṇa. Every deity of the Śrīcakra displays the dual sides of shadow and light that either keep us on the surface or lead us through ṛtam to satyam.

The ṣaṭcakras are described variously depending on the lineage and the influence of modern psychology, correlations with neurohormonal biology and their presumed functions. These descriptions can be useful to make some sense of our behavior and patterns, and to gain some understanding of the ṛtam of creation. However, much of this knowledge remains at the pravṛtti level where it becomes a subtle trap that keeps us engaged at the periphery.

Take, for instance, the mūlādhāra cakra, which is the manifestation of the earth element in the subtle body. In popular culture, the mūlādhāra is assigned the task of survival, where the heaviness of the earth element is correlated with the concept of being grounded and secure. The point of this scheme of progression from earth, the grossest element, to space, the most subtle is to turn from pravṛtti to nivṛtti. However, each cakra contains the dual aspects of pravṛtti and nivṛtti in it, where pravṛtti is the shadow and nivṛtti is the light. In other words, the ṣaṭcakras are nonlinear and any linearity we assign to them becomes a trap.

If we were to assign groundedness to the mūlādhāra, we may overlook the fact that survival is more than physical. Our attachments to food, lifestyle choices, comfort, body image, aging, family history, cultural practices, fear of death and illness, our countless insecurities and many "wholesome" qualities define our survival beyond the physical. Evolution hasn't changed the *response* of our neurohormonal pathways. The chemical and electrical signals that kept us safe from being hunted continue to drive the body-mind – only the *context* has changed. Survival is less about being eaten by wild animals and more about keeping up appearances and being validated for how we see ourselves. Our insecurities that drive the upkeep of the self-image bring up the same biological response as being chased by a predator. We are still fighting for survival; only the context has changed.

When we come to the spiritual path, our survival instinct doesn't magically dissolve. The neurohormonal pathways are rearranged to the new context, and the innate sense of wanting to exist and be seen in a certain way presents itself in the spiritual garb. Now we want to be seen as spiritual, wise, disciplined, or as someone who has overcome limitations. The me-story continues to be written on a different storyline, creating all-new samskārās and finding new ways to remain entrapped in saṃsāra. Replacing one persona with another, we think we have resolved the issues of the mūlādhāra when in fact, most of our energy is still trapped in the survival mode of the self-image.

In this sense, we can see why the association between the Śrīcakra āvaraṇas and the cakras differs between teachings and can be problematic. In this book, which is based in the oral practice tradition of practical application, we will hold these associations loosely and instead, focus on whether we are at the periphery or the radius. Here, whether we are entrapped in survival issues (mūlādhāra), lack creative energy (svādhiṣṭāna) or manipulate experience to feel good about ourselves (maṇipura), we are at the Bhūpura and operating at the periphery. The journey toward the center doesn't even begin until our energy is freed up from seeking approval or validation from others or ourselves.

Bhāvanā

Whether we are engaged with the Śrīcakra in ritual, mantra, contemplation, or any of the practices in the sādhanā spectrum, bhāvanā is the key that leads to progress in the saṃhāra krama. Bhāvanā can mean thought, supposition, or direct knowing, and in the upāsanā of the Śrīcakra, it is *right* contemplation.

Right contemplation takes us from becoming to being, upasarga to apasarga, from pravṛtti to nivṛtti, and from the periphery to the center. It necessarily requires the application of all the tenets of sādhanā, particularly viveka and vairāgya.

Firstly, we must know if our inquiry is leading us to upasarga or apasarga. Moreover, we must have non-attachment for the upasarga so that we can proceed along apasarga. As long as our eṣaṇas are unfulfilled, our natural inclination will be toward upasarga and the drama at the surface. However, viveka and vairāgya play a role in eṣaṇā fulfilment as well and arise from being honest about them without bypassing them or using spirituality to explain them away.

Let's explore this with an example. Your mother was not encouraging of your talents in childhood and was probably even negligent at times. You have carried the hurt and anger with you and it colors not only your relationship with her but also how you perceive yourself. You embark on the journey of self-inquiry and begin to explore the relationship by reflecting on your childhood. As the memories come up, they dredge up the pain and thoughts mushroom. At that party when you were ten and offered to sing, she laughed when she should have been supportive and loving. In your self-inquiry exercise, you land at a point where this knowing of what she *should* have done makes you feel bad that it happened at all, and good that you have an explanation for your pain. The good and the bad feelings lead you on tangents, sometimes with compassion for your mother ("she had a hard childhood too") and at other times, rage ("so what, she shouldn't have had kids if she didn't know how to raise them"). This is the path of apasarga, where mental modifications keep us on the surface.

At every point in this exercise, viveka is the ability to see that we are indeed thrashing on the surface. Vairāgya here is tricky, because it is so *juicy* and enticing for the mind to stay on the surface. We feel vindicated and satisfied in landing *somewhere* and this adds to our self-image, even when it is painful. In fact, self-image isn't always about uplifting ourselves. The self-image of being a loser isn't necessarily better than more grandiose ones when it comes to the inner journey. The continuous creation and maintenance of *any* self-image is the issue of pravṛtti or becoming.

In addition to viveka and vairāgya, meaningful bhāvanā requires the cultivation of sound or higher reasoning known as *sattarka*. As we explored in the previous chapter, our choices normally arise from the buddhi, which is tainted by our samskārās. Our choices are dependent on our preferences, the grudges we hold and the hope of achieving specific outcomes, which is why the idea of free will must be examined. If we are held hostage by our samskārās that drive all our choices, how free are we, really?

This is where sattarka (*sat* = pure, unconditioned, *tarka* = reasoning) comes in, where the buddhi is not influenced by the remnants of the past or the hope for the future, but by the ability to see things as they are. Say you run into an old friend on the street and she exclaims, "Oh, you look tired! Are you ok?" You had been feeling well until that point and had no idea you were looking tired or ill. If you are attached to the idea of looking a particular way, you'll be surprised, hurt, angry, or self-conscious, and your mind will tend to fixate on the *content* of her words. The memory of the content will create loops of thought and emotion in your citta, and the next time you see her you'll be armed with a reaction. Notice how you've created samskārās that will drive your action.

On the other hand, if you operate from a stance of sattarka, you might thank her, self-reflect a bit, and say, "Ha! I had no idea I looked tired. Thank you." Your joy of seeing her is untainted, and *what* she says is irrelevant. Your citta remains undisturbed, you have created no new samskārās or karma, and your future encounters with her remain fresh.

Sattarka requires the ability to discern between increasingly subtle objects such as a word and its meaning. In the above example, it's the difference between a *statement* and its *content*. Normally, we are tripped up by the *content* of words and experiences that stir up our samskārās and drive our choices. With increasing inner stillness, we learn to recognize the difference, seeing that most of our reactions are in response to the implied meaning of speech and experience. At the Vasukoṇa, we will see how sattarka becomes the sharp edge of a sword that cuts through misperception with clear and perfected reasoning.

Sattarka requires both inference and direct experience. Inference is the ability to apply the darśana in moment-to-moment experience when it has not yet become our reality. We must accept the darśana and rearrange our thinking. Direct experience occurs through constant application, with a continuous stream of *Aha!s* when we learn to recognize the various elements of the darśana.

Bhāvanā with its elements of viveka, vairāgya and sattarka applies to the self-image of sādhanā as well. Upasarga presents as the whetting of the spiritual self-image, where our practices and knowledge keep us on the surface. Replacing the old non-spiritual self-image with a spiritual one that is still in the sphere of eṣaṇas doesn't help us in bhāvanā. To know that our contemplation adds to our self-image in *any* form is viveka, and the ability to relinquish the self-image ingredients is vairāgya.

Bhāvanā is a delicate process which must proceed along a series of conjunctions between the arising thought and the next one. As we will see later, these are the sandhis and marmas of the Śrīcakra, where the energy can flow in either direction. The cultivation of the fundamental tenets opens us to anugraha, where the energy at these confluences keeps us moving in the direction of apasarga, changing the vector of our inquiry from the periphery to the radius. Every element of the Śrīcakra lends itself to the exquisite practice of bhāvanā, progressing systematically from the rim to the center. In Part III, you'll find examples of bhāvanā that may inspire you to work with each of the yoginīs in your own upāsanā.

With this understanding of the foundational tenets of sādhanā, we are now equipped to explore one of the most important concepts of the Śrīcakra – its associations with vāc or language.

Chapter 6

Vāc

Vāc means speech, usually referring to the deification of expression *as* manifestation. Thus, creation is Śakti expressing herself as the infinite forms of the universe.

Think of expression in terms of frequencies and wavelengths. From the subtlest to the grossest, every manifested form comprises a specific frequency and wavelength that morphs, devolves, or evolves in every experience. The birth of forms from the formless occurs at four somewhat distinct levels of vāc.

The Four Levels of Vāc

Śakti as vāc is the entire spectrum of expression in its various states of density and rarefication. The highest level of vāc is in the Bindu as parāvāk,[97] where she resides in two forms. The first is the bindu or anusvāra,[98] where Śakti faces Śiva and creation doesn't exist. The second is visarga, where Śakti turns away from Śiva toward manifestation.[99] In both bindu and visarga, parāvāk has to yet to split into the Trikoṇa. At this highest level of vāc before manifestation, Devī is known as *Ambikā*.

Devī divides herself into the subject and the object at the Trikoṇa where she becomes *paśyantī* or the perceiving word and is known as *Vāmā*, the one who emits the Śrīcakra out of her being. Thus, one becomes three distinct points – the unchanging subject (*pramatṛ*), the everchanging object (*prameya*), and the relationship between the two (*pramāṇa*). While pramatṛ and pramāṇa remain constant, prameya divides into the precursors of the infinite forms at the Vasukoṇa where Devī is known as *Jyeṣṭhā*, the elder.

At the Vasukoṇa, paśyantī devolves to *madhyamā*, the middle. Here, prameya organizes into the eight groups of the Sanskrit letters that will crystallize into the frequencies and wavelengths of countless forms (see Vāc in the Śrīcakra, below). Jyeṣṭhā is the eldest and the first of the conditions at the Vasukoṇa.

97 Vāc is the plural of vāk.

98 Anusvara or am is the 15th vowel that is represented by a dot (.) that is also known as a Bindu.

99 See Kāmakalā in Chapter 4.

The younger and the youngest forms of vāc arise from the Vasukoṇa in the next six āvaraṇas as vaikharī. Here, Devī is known as *Raudrī*, the fierce one who manifests increasing numbers of forms at every level of interaction and experience. From the Antardaśara to the Bhūpura, the subject-object distinction becomes increasingly apparent.[100]

100 See also Chapter 8: 'Vāk' in K. Chinnaiyan, *Glorious Alchemy* (New Sarum Press, 2020).

With this brief exploration of vāc in the Śrīcakra, we must now necessarily delve into its intricacies and nuances, beginning with its relationship with the different states of consciousness known as *avasthās*.

Avasthā: States of Consciousness

The three states of consciousness that are commonly available to us are *jāgrata* (waking), *svapna* (dreaming), and *suṣupti* (deep sleep). In the Śrīcakra, these three states make up the fundamental fabric of creation that supports the birth, play, and dissolution of its countless forms.

Jāgrata

We usually think of jāgrata as the ordinary waking state where we interact with the world at the vaikharī level. This is an accurate description of biological wakefulness, where we are oriented to time, space and person, and the separation between "I" and "not I" is most clearly apparent. However, jāgrata, like the other avasthās, is usually mixed in with svapna avasthā or the dream state.

Svapna

Svapna or dreaming is a stage of sleep where we are oriented toward the subtle objects of the subconscious mind. While sleeping, svapna presents as dreams, and while awake as the reveries and constant flitting between the objects of the world and the mind. Here, vāk is at the madhyamā level.

Suṣupti

Suṣupti is deep sleep where biologically, we have no cognition of objects. The subject-object distinction present in jāgrata and svapna doesn't exist in suṣupti. Instead, both the subject and the object disappear into the dark recesses of the unconscious mind. Suṣupti occurs at the paśyantī level.

Turya

Turya is the fourth state[101] in which the other three conditions occur and is at the level of parāvāk[102] turned toward manifestation as the visarga. This is the state of the Bindu poised to explode into the Śrīcakra. Thus, Śakti has turned away from Śiva toward expression, but the split into the Trikoṇa hasn't occurred yet.

101 See the Fourth and the Fifth in Bindu, Chapter 17.

102 Vāk is singular and vāc is plural.

Turyatītā

Turyatītā is the fifth state where the Bindu reabsorbs the Śrīcakra into itself. Here, Śakti turns toward Śiva, and creation ceases to exist. All the āvaraṇas are subsumed and dissolved into the Bindu, where Parā shines as the sole Self. The path from turya to turyatītā is known as *śuddhādvan*, with increasing non-separation of Aham (I) and Idam (That). [103]

103 See The Pure Path in Bindu, Chapter 17.

Avasthās in the Śrīcakra

When we delve into the study and understanding of the avasthās, particularly as they relate to the subject-object relationship in the Trikoṇa, the entire Śrīcakra and its darśana begin to reveal itself.

All forms in existence belong to one of the three common avasthās – jāgrata, svapna, and suṣupti. The brahmāṇḍa (macrocosm) and the piṇḍāṇḍa (microcosm) are reflections of the avasthās and understanding this concept can be extremely helpful in upāsanā.

The three avasthās arise from the Trikoṇa and align with the triads of icchā-jñāna-kriyā and pramāṇa-prameya-pramatṛ at every level of the Śrīcakra.

However, our understanding of the sṛṣṭi and saṃhāra kramas can be greatly aided if we consider the avasthās at two levels: the Absolute level of Śiva-Śakti, and the individual level. For this, we'll examine the avasthās in the sṛṣṭi krama from the standpoint of Devī's avasthās, and the saṃhāra krama from the perspective of the upāsaka's.

Avasthās in Sṛṣṭi Krama

जाग्रत्-सुषुप्तिकृत्-दक्षिण-वाम-भागाम् ।
स्वप्न स्वभाव-परिक्लृप्त-जघन्य-भागाम् ।
तुर्यातितुर्य-घटितानन-हृत्प्रदेशाम् ।
प्राणेश्वरीं परशिवस्य परामृशामः ॥ १ ॥

jāgrata -suṣuptikṛt-dakṣiṇa-vāma-bhāgām |
Svapna svabhāva-pariklṛpta-jaghanya-bhāgām |
Turyātiturya-ghaṭitānana-hṛtpradeśām |
Prāṇeśvarīṃ paraśivasya parāmṛśām || 1 ||

"She, whose right side is jāgrata and left is suṣupti, womb is svapna, face is turya and heart is turyatītā is the prāṇa deliberation (Vimarśa) of Śiva."
~ Śrī Mātṛkācakra Vivekaḥ, verse 1

In the Bindu, the avasthās make up Devī's body – jāgrata is her right side, and suṣupti is her left, turya is her face, turyatītā her heart, and svapna is her womb. Her heart is united with Śiva, and her face is turned to creation.[104]

104 See Giri Ratna Mishra, *Śrī Mātṛkācakra Vivekaḥ* (Chaukhamba Surbharati Prakashan, 2016).

The icchā to create arises in her left side of suṣupti. Knowledge of the cosmos or jñāna is birthed in her womb as svapna and explodes as infinite forms from her right side of jāgrata as kriyā. This five-formed description is the nature of Śakti, who is Vimarśa.

Suppose we think of creation occurring between the polarities of her left (suṣupti) and right (jāgrata) side, and the other two states of *svapna* and *turya* are the result of the two polarities co-mingling. Suṣupti is the avasthā of rest and jāgrata of action. When action arises in suṣupti, the resultant avasthā is svapna. When rest arises in jāgrata, the resultant avasthā is turya. The intermingling of the avasthās creates the dual conditions of vidyā or nirvāṇa, and *avidyā* or saṃsāra.

Recall the concepts of bindu and visarga from Chapter 3.[105] Bindu or anusvāra is the contraction of the white and red bindus towards each other, or Śakti turning toward Śiva. Here, Śakti as Vimarśa is united with Śiva as Prakāśa and absorbed in turyatītā. Visarga is the expansion of the two bindus away from each other, where Śakti turns toward creation. Her icchā to create stirs her suṣupti and jāgrata, resulting in svapna and turya. The blend of avasthās arising from her icchā-jñāna-kriyā explodes as creation.

105 See Kāmakalā in Chapter 3.

The combination of the avasthās as visarga results in pravṛtti, devolving from the nondual center to the dualistic surface where the separation between the Aham and Idam is fully manifested as vaikharī at the Bhūpura.

When Śakti is turned toward Śiva, the avasthās evolve from the dualistic periphery to the nondual center in the direction of nivṛtti.

The fully manifest Aham-Idam separation at the periphery dissolves as Parā in the Bindu. In nivṛtti, the four avasthās return to Devī's original state. The anusvāra is the path of nivṛtti and the visarga is the path of pravṛtti.

Turyatītā, the fifth avasthā, is her heart united with Śiva at the Absolute Level, which transcends and subsumes both the dual and the nondual (see Figure 14). In all avasthās and forms, she is eternally united with him.

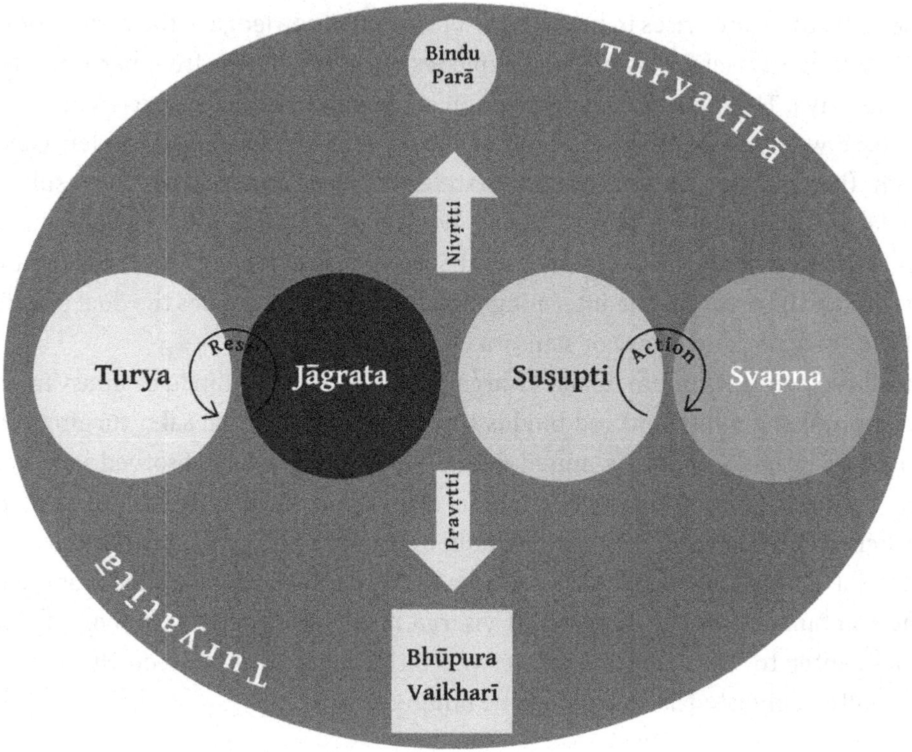

Figure 14. Avasthās and Vāc

Avasthās in Saṃhāra Krama

We can think of the sṛṣṭi krama as the transition from Devī's suṣupti to jāgrata avasthā, which is the path of visarga from the Bindu to the Bhūpura. The saṃhāra krama is the transition from our jāgrata to suṣupti, which is the path of the anusvāra from the Bhūpura to the Bindu. The key here is that there is a difference between Devī's avasthās and ours.

The Śrīcakra teaches us that the avasthās are fluid and interpenetrate to mean different things depending on the āvaraṇa we are in, the context of that āvaraṇa, and most importantly, the level of our discernment and clarity.

For example, suṣupti at the periphery refers to ordinary deep sleep where the conscious mind is absorbed into the darkness of nothingness. Pravṛtti is our ordinary way of operating in the world, where jāgrata or the waking state sucks up our energy into creating and maintaining a self-image. In other words, suṣupti or deep sleep recharges us for jāgrata.

On the other hand, suṣupti at the center is perfect stillness arising from having reabsorbed all the energies of the periphery into the singular goal of liberation, which is the path of Kuṇḍalinī. Here, at the center, the sādhaka is as if sleeping because s/he has absorbed the frenzy of activity into the Self. There is no energy being expended in becoming, and no self-image to upkeep. All activities are occurring within, and yet s/he doesn't act at all. The guṇas and elements rearrange in the sādhaka's experience, nothing going in or out, creation remaining at perfect equilibrium.

The equipoise of suṣupti at the center is one way to think of stithi krama, where the practitioner realizes that zero = infinity.

Although we call it suṣupti, this repose evolves into turya and turyatītā from the withdrawal of energy from becoming at the periphery to being at the center.

The avasthās behave differently at the center and the periphery depending on the fluidity between the subject (Aham) and object (Idam). There is no fluidity between the subject and object at the rim, and the two are distinct and separate in a condition known as *jaḍa*. On the other hand, *ajaḍa* dominates at the center, where the subject and object fluidly flow into each other and Aham and Idam are non-separate.

The jaḍa condition at the periphery (our ordinary state) contributes to avidyā, which colors both suṣupti and jāgrata. Jaḍa suṣupti results in the sleep-like state of ignorance of our true nature and jaḍa jāgrata traps us in the cycles of saṃsāra created by limited desire, knowledge, and action. Suṣupti at the periphery is where we are so profoundly asleep to our true divine nature that the world appears to be very clearly separate from us. These states of jaḍa jāgrata and suṣupti keep us in the mode of seeing the world as something outside of ourselves that we need to protect ourselves from or use for our gain. Even when we are biologically awake, we remain in a state of stupor resulting from avidyā.

Vidyā predominates in the ajaḍa condition at the center, where the avasthās are of Devī. Vidyā resulting in ajaḍa affects suṣupti and jāgrata differently at the Bindu than at the periphery. Here, ajaḍa jāgrata is free of conditioned activity, and ajaḍa suṣupti is deep rest in the light of knowledge. In the repose of ajaḍa, Aham and Idam are one.

In between the jaḍa and ajaḍa states of suṣupti and jāgrata is the *jaḍājaḍa* (mix of jaḍa and ajaḍa) svapna or dream state, where the fluidity between subject and object is intermediate (see Figure 15). Being fluid, it moves in both directions of pravṛtti and nivṛtti. In pravṛtti, jaḍājaḍa svapna avasthā takes us from the ajaḍa suṣupti at the Bindu to the jaḍa jāgrata at the Bhūpura. In this movement, the repose of knowledge of the center becomes condensed and differentiated as limited action at the periphery. In other words, the devolution of the Bindu into the Śrīcakra is the process of ajaḍa suṣupti at the Bindu becoming jaḍa jāgrata at the Bhūpura, which can be seen as the devolution of tattvas, Kuṇḍalinī, vāc and avasthās.

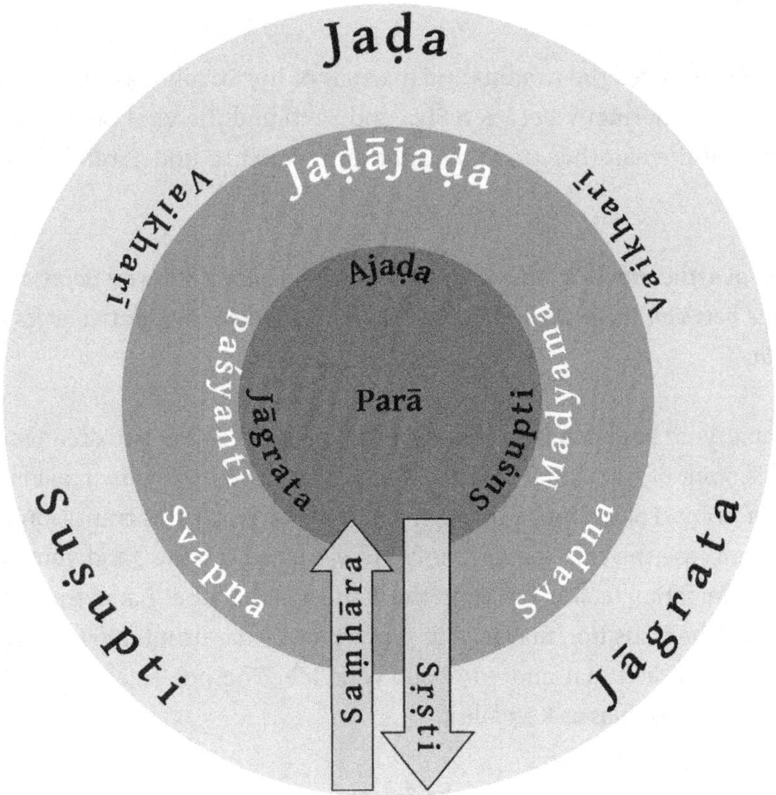

Figure 15. The Krama of the Avasthās in the Śrīcakra

In nivṛtti, jaḍājaḍa svapna avasthā takes us from the avidyā of jaḍa suṣupti at the Bhūpura to the vidyā of ajaḍa jāgrata at the Bindu. This means that the entire saṃhāra krama, be it in the form of ritual, mantra or bhāvanā is the process of moving from the jaḍa avasthās at the periphery to the ajaḍa avasthās at the center. This is the path of reverse engineering which, as we will see, can be viewed through the lens of vāc moving from vaikharī to parāvāk, *Prāṇakuṇḍalinī* to *Parākuṇḍalinī*, *aśuddhādvan* to śuddhādvan, or the Bhūpura to the Bindu. However we conceive this path, it is essentially the progression from becoming to being, or the journey from the periphery to the center.

Avasthās as Sandhis and Marmas

In Chapter 4 we explored the sandhis and marmas of the Śrīcakra as the two- and three-pointed contacts of harmony between Śiva and Śakti and the vital points of prāṇa. Our understanding of the avasthās provides another context to understand these points of confluence.

As one avasthā moves to the next, there is a transitory midway point of confluence between them with the potential for a reversal in jaḍatva or its level of jaḍa.

For example, your body can transition from biological deep sleep to dreams, or you may wake up. This point of transition has the potential to move from jaḍa to ajaḍa depending on the flow of prāṇa. For example, through anugraha or grace, this transition may lead to nivṛtti, in which case the jaḍa suṣupti moves toward ajaḍa jāgrata, and you will wake up in a state of illumination feeling one with the world. On the other hand, through *tirodhāna* or concealment, the transition may lead to pravṛtti and jaḍa suṣupti moves to jaḍa jāgrata, where you wake up as usual and go about your life. The potential for illumination is ever-present in the marmas as Kuṇḍalinī.

The sandhis and the marmas of the Śrīcakra are the transition points of the avasthās that determine our sādhanā through the flow of prāṇa.

The transition points are orgasmic and harmonious conduits for our attention and energy. While the sandhis are two-point contacts of two avasthās, the marmas are the three-point contacts of the avasthās with the addition of the potency that becomes pravṛtti or nivṛtti.

The sandhis and marmas as avasthās determine our moment-to-moment transitions between vidyā and avidyā, bindu and visarga, parā and aparā, nivṛtti and pravṛtti, ajaḍa and jaḍa, and center and periphery (see Table 6). They are the points where Kuṇḍalinī moves between her Parā and Prāṇa forms as both tirodhāna and anugraha.

Table 6. Facets of the Śrīcakra

Attribute	Toward the periphery	Toward the center
Sṛṣṭi/Saṃhāra	Sṛṣṭi	Saṃhāra
Evolution/Involution	Pravṛtti	Nivṛtti
Ha/A	Visarga	Bindu
Gross/Subtle	Jaḍa	Ajaḍa
Knowledge/Ignorance	Avidyā	Vidyā
Kuṇḍalinī	Prāṇakuṇḍalinī	Parākuṇḍalinī
Circle	Periphery/Circumference	Center/Source
Vāk	Vaikharī	Parā
Concealment/Revelation	Tirodhāna	Anugraha
Aham	Ahaṅkāra	Ahambhāva

The Devolution of Devī's Avasthās as Vāc

One of the most esoteric and challenging concepts to understand in classical Tantra is the correlation of language with every other concept. This is because mystical reflections in language become the basis for every concept. Cursorily, we must understand that Sanskrit is highly logical and all-inclusive.

> ***The arrangement of the letters matches the amount of prāṇa that is used in pronouncing each, which becomes supremely significant in mantra sādhanā.***[106]

106 See Prāṇa Nāḍīs, Cakras and Kuṇḍalinī in Chapter 11.

We can then deeply understand the prāṇa-letter correlation of bīja mantras that are often complicated and seem to have no readily apparent meaning. The amount of time it takes to pronounce a letter (mātrā) varies, depending on our stores of prāṇa and level of clarity. Longer mātrās take up more time and energy, occurring when we combine letters of short mātrās.

Not only is there a difference in energy expenditure of the phonemes due to their unique energetic signatures, but their perception also depends on the avasthās. This is because both time and space – the domains in which energy unfolds – are experienced differently in the avasthās. For example, a dream feels longer than its actual duration of a few minutes, and a drive of several hours is "lost" when we are self-absorbed. In both, the avasthā (svapna) influenced the time and energy signature of expression or vāc. This understanding becomes important when we see that phonemes placed at each āvaraṇa correspond to its different elements.

The same phoneme can be found in different āvaraṇas, which can be confusing for Śrīcakra upāsakas. The thing to remember is that the placement of the same phoneme in different āvaraṇas means different things depending on the avasthās. Moreover, the placement of the specific letters in the elements of each āvaraṇa differs according to the text and sampradāya.[107] One way to reconcile this in our understanding is to see them as arising differently depending on the avasthā, the direction of the āvaraṇa (sṛṣṭi or saṃhāra), and the sandhi and marma of the avasthā transition.

107 Whenever there is a discrepancy in the placement of the phonemes in the āvaraṇas between sampradāyas and texts, I have followed my Guru paramparā in this book.

As we delve into its sādhanā, it will us help to remember that the Śrīcakra is the body of Lalitā Devī, and as the power of expression of forms, she is vāc, which varies in the different avasthās. In other words, Devī in her avasthās is vāc, vāc is the Śrīcakra, and Śrīcakra is creation.

When we firmly establish this relationship in our understanding, we come to see the non-separation between mantra and yantra, which is the discipline of Tantra. The yantra is the visual representation of the mantra, both of which are the body of Devī.

Vāc in the Śrīcakra

At the level of parāvāk, the phonemes[108] lie in their *potential* form in the Bindu when Śakti is facing Śiva. When she turns away from him, potential changes to *kinetic* energy and the mass of undifferentiated phonemes differentiate, becoming the matrix of creation. This matrix is known as *Mātṛkā* (little mother) and consists of

108 Distinct units of sound.

the phonemes beginning with *a* and ending with *kṣa*, which will eventually manifest as unique vibrations.

When Śakti turns toward manifestation, the kinetic energy is the state of divine pre-cognition represented by the 16 vowels *(a, ā, i, ī, u, ū, ṛ, ṝ, l, ḹ, e, ai, o, au, aṃ, aḥ)*. The vowels are represented at various levels in the Śrīcakra – the Trikoṇa, Vasukoṇa, Śodaṣadalapadma and Trivṛtta. At each āvaraṇa, however, the significance of the vowels differs according to the avasthā and whether we are in the sṛṣṭi or the saṃhāra krama, which determines whether they are at the paśyantī (Trikoṇa), madhyamā (Vasukoṇa), or vaikharī (other āvaraṇa) levels (see Figure 16).

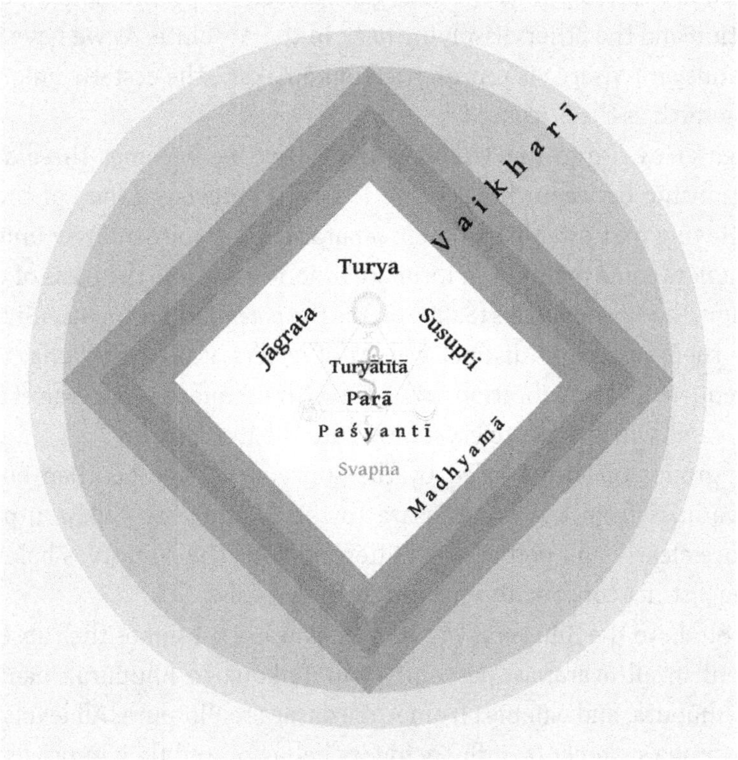

Figure 16. Vāc in the Śrīcakra

The first vowel *a* is known as Anuttara, which is always at the level of Absolute Reality because none of the other phonemes can be pronounced without it. Anuttara is the basis for the matrix. In the Bindu, as Devī turns away from Śiva, Anuttara splits into Prakāśa and Vimarśa or Śiva and Śakti, each containing the potential of the whole. After their seeming separation, they come together as the next vowel, *ā*, which contains a different energetic signature due to its longer mātrā. The remaining vowels unfold in the Bindu at the level of parāvāk, each with its own mātrā and energetic signature. The vowels are the union of the different potencies of Śiva and Śakti.

The last two vowels are *aṃ* and *aḥ*, the anusvāra and visarga. Having gathered all the potencies within herself, Devī is charged as anusvāra, the single point (.) of intense focusing which is emitted out as the visarga represented by two dots (:), one emitting forth as creation and the other dissolving back in the Absolute. As we have seen earlier, the pulse of anusvāra-visarga is represented in Kāmakalā, the ecstatic union of Śiva and Śakti emitting forth as the Śrīcakra.[109]

109 See Kāmakalā in Chapter 4.

The visarga gives rise to the Trikoṇa, where the One becomes three as Śiva, Śakti and the relationship between them. There is now a perceiver (Śiva) of the vāc (Śakti) as paśyantī. Having first established their separation as two seemingly unique entities, Śakti and Śiva now come together in intimate union to become the basis of creation.

In this union, the *kinetic* vowels (Śakti) pierce the *potential* consonants (Śiva) to enliven and organize them into eight distinct groups of letters at the Vasukoṇa. Vāc becomes distinct as frequencies and vibrations charged with uniqueness and variety. This is the level of madhyamā which is yet to crystallize into the tattvas.

The eight groups of letters ruled by the supreme *Vāgdevatās* then burst into the remaining āvaraṇas from the Antardaśara to the Bhūpura as vaikharī, progressively becoming more clearly and perceivably differentiated. The 34 tattvas below Śiva-Śakti arise from the distinct consonants charged by the vowels.

From the Bindu to the Bhūpura, vāc at each āvaraṇa subsumes the subsequent level. Parā is present in all āvaraṇas, paśyantī from Trikoṇa to Bhūpura, madhyamā from Vasukoṇa to Bhūpura, and vaikharī from Antardaśara to Bhūpura. All levels of vāc manifest in the āvaraṇa's elements, influencing its behavior and flow in pravṛtti or nivṛtti. The principle of flow of vāc in the yantra is the basis of mantra sādhanā.

Mantra Sādhanā

Mantra sādhanā is a complex and nuanced topic that lends itself to many iterations of understanding and application. In the context of the Śrīcakra, our understanding of the mantra can take us beyond its simplistic correlation with Devī's body to a deeper dive into the intricacies of vāc and avasthās.

The Pañcadaśī mantra is a sequence of 15 letters arranged in three sections, each with a kūṭa or peak. A detailed analysis of the Pañcadaśī is beyond the scope of this book,[110] but in general, it bestows six arthas or meanings that result in the state of identity between the letters of the mantra and the deities, the sampradāya, Guru, the Śrīcakra, Kuṇḍalinī, and Absolute Reality.

110 See Bhāskararāya's *Varivasya Rahasya* for the different implications and treatments of the Pañcadaśī mantra in the kādi tradition.

The mantra is imparted from the Guru to the śiṣya in dīkṣā that can involve extensive rituals to energize the mantra, mitigate its potential negative effects and empower it. In most cases, the mantra is imparted in vaikharī, through the medium of sound that is in the form of word(s).

> ***Since creation proceeds in the sound-to-word pathway, mantra sādhanā works in the opposite direction, proceeding from the most differentiated word in vaikharī to sound in Parā (see Figure 17).***

For this, the mantra must have the power to swim against Vāmā, the predominant current of creation.

As we saw earlier, Vāmā is the name given to Devī in her paśyantī form as she emits creation from the Trikoṇa. The word Vāmā signifies the force of pravṛtti or extroversion, which is the natural route for our senses. We can't help but be externally turned toward pravṛtti through the function of the ahaṅkāra, which is the function of Vāmā, the predominant current of creation and the force of icchā or will.

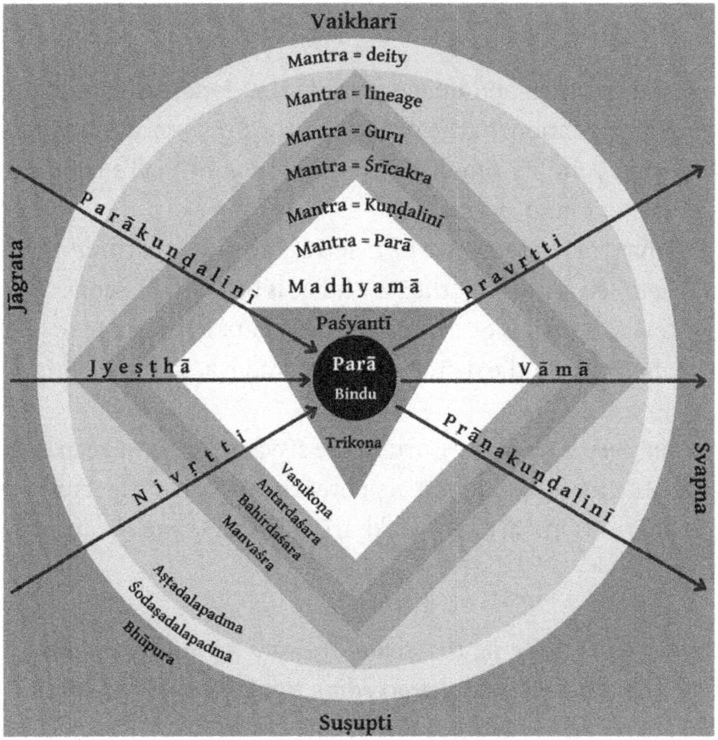

Figure 17. Mantra Sādhanā

Jyeṣṭhā is the name of Devī in her madhyamā state at the Vasukoṇa as the precursor of creation. This "elder" force has the power to overcome the natural direction of Vāmā to take the mind back to its Source in the nivṛtti mārga. Dīkṣā activates this current, which must overcome the powerful flow of Vāmā. Jyeṣṭhā is the current of knowledge or jñāna that is the intermediate stage between icchā and kriyā. The Vasukoṇa at the level of madhyamā vāk is the intermediate stage, which has the potential to turn toward pravṛtti or nivṛtti. The Vāgdevatās rule over this intermediate stage as Jyeṣṭhā. When madhyamā devolves into vaikharī, Raudrī becomes the predominant force.

Raudrī is the name given to Devī as the force of kriyā or action that works in two ways. Once initiated, will and knowledge crystallize as activity. Raudrī is fierce as the personification of kriyā, which is frenzied and relentless in saṃsāra. This force impels us to constantly create karma at the periphery and in the jaḍa avasthās where the icchā and jñāna remain largely hidden. However, as the manifestation of kriyā śakti, Raudrī is also the power of dissolution. When impelled by Jyeṣṭhā, Raudrī becomes the organizing power at the center that results in illumination in the ajaḍa avasthās.

Dīkṣā works on all three currents to enable the word-to-sound pathway. Since it is given in vaikharī, the mantra works on Raudrī's frenzy, providing space and time between action and reaction and slowing down the rate at which we create loops of karma. The kriyā of mantra energization in dīkṣā mitigates jaḍa at the vaikharī level. Through the activation of Jyeṣṭhā, the mantra is infused with the power of knowledge. When Raudrī and Jyeṣṭhā are activated in the nivṛtti direction, the mantra can flow against the powerful Vāmā energy. While Vāmā is the flow of Prāṇakuṇḍalinī, Jyeṣṭhā is the force of Parākuṇḍalinī.

While pravṛtti unfolds in the sound-to-word direction from Parā to vaikharī, the mantra given in vaikharī traverses the many layers from Bhūpura to Antardaśara, dissolving in madhyamā at the Vasukoṇa, paśyantī at the Trikoṇa, and finally in parāvāk at the Bindu.

The Path of Bhukti and Mukti

Śrīvidyā is known as the path that bestows both bhukti or enjoyment and mukti or liberation. Bhukti is enjoyment of sense objects which are naturally externally fixated. Mukti is liberation from the ahaṅkāra. Bhukti and mukti oppose each other and generally reside in separate spheres. Yet, there is a subtle relationship between bhukti and mukti that influences our sādhanā and progress.

Ordinarily, our eṣaṇas keep us entangled in the Vāmā current, seeking out validation, self-worth, and self-image at the periphery in continuous loops of wanting, gain and loss. Our eṣaṇas are hardy, persistent, and all-encompassing, driving our conscious and unconscious behavior, thought and speech. The eṣaṇas don't magically disappear when we embark on a spiritual journey. On the other hand, our spiritual endeavors become the focus of our eṣaṇas. The ahaṅkāra that previously grasped material things to build and sustain a self-image shifts its attention to spiritual paraphernalia. In fact, it's natural to make our sādhanā, rituals and knowledge the focus of our validation seeking where we merely change the garb of the ahaṅkāra. Whether we take ourselves to be materialistic or spiritual, our unfulfilled eṣaṇas drive the need to feel better about ourselves. Donning a spiritual persona does not mitigate the ahaṅkāra. Instead, the spiritual persona with its false self-image becomes the obstacle to mukti.

The problem here is of unfulfilled eṣaṇas that keep us entrenched in the periphery. For example, if our deepest desire is to feel fulfilled and validated in an intimate relationship, turning to spirituality is unlikely to satisfy that itch. We may try to bypass the itch using spiritual concepts but the longing sucks up vital energy. We then find ourselves at an impasse where we can't make progress in sādhanā because of loss of vital energy, or because we are bypassing the eṣaṇa and it remains unfulfilled. This unconscious conflict costs us in upāsanā, where we remain stagnant and stuck without meaningful progress. The primary cause of this conflict is the misunderstanding that mukti can or should be achieved at the cost of bhukti, which bestows neither goal.

As long as our eṣaṇas remain unfulfilled, our natural, externally turned inclination is exceedingly difficult to overcome. This predicament is like trying to feed a hungry, homeless man with spiritual concepts that don't fill his stomach or clothe his back. On the other hand, when our eṣaṇas are fulfilled to a certain extent, we feel sated and content enough to focus on esoteric or higher knowledge. The vital energy leaked in the longing for bhukti is recovered and becomes available for sādhanā. The key here is that our eṣaṇas must be fulfilled and savored before they lose their importance. Prematurely claiming that health, wealth, or validation are unimportant causes greater confusion in our internal landscape and hinders progress.

If we become aware of our eṣaṇas, accept them honestly and work toward fulfilling them without painting them with spiritual concepts, we'd enjoy the validations *and* align with Jyeṣṭhā. For this to occur, we can neither bypass our experience spiritually nor become so attached to specific outcomes that we lose perspective. This is a subtle and nuanced teaching that requires discernment. Working with a Guru can help greatly.

The Śrīvidyā mantra is said to bestow bhukti because it enables the fulfilment of eṣaṇas at the periphery through their right understanding and hastens their attainment.

This is the magic of Raudrī in the mantra as kriyā, who manifests the eṣaṇas so that they can be savored and relinquished in the pravṛtti mārga. As the eṣaṇas are fulfilled, Jyeṣṭhā in the mantra as jñāna enlivens the sandhis and marmas at each āvaraṇa to bestow discernment and dispassion so that we can relinquish the fulfilled eṣaṇas and progress in the nivṛtti mārga. The two forces become the wings of the subtle bird that traverses the intricacies of the Śrīcakra sādhanā, bestowing both delight and wisdom.

Mantra in Aśuddhādvan and Śuddhādvan

When we look at the map of the 36 tattvas, the separation between Aham and Idam occurs at paśyantī, which is at the Trikoṇa level. At madhyamā in the Vasukoṇa, the Māyā tattva with the five kañcukas solidify the separation between the Aham and Idam, which is propagated in vaikharī in the rest of the āvaraṇas. Jaḍa is the basis for our usual way of interacting in the world, where the Aham and Idam are separate and distinct, which is the positionality of the ahaṅkāra. Ajaḍa or the lack of separation between Aham and Idam is the positionality of Ahambhāva.

The mantra moves us from ahaṅkāra to Ahambhāva through understanding the Aham-Idam relationship at the three levels of vāc.

At the periphery, our sense of Aham exists in relation to the objects of the world (Idam) that we wish to possess or dispossess in order to feel fulfilled. This is at the vaikharī level in the jaḍa avasthās, which are situated at the Bhūpura. The mantra progressively takes us through the subtler avasthās of vaikharī from the Ṣodaṣadalapadma to the Antardaśara, where Idam as the objects of the world become increasingly subtler.

At the Vasukoṇa, the Idam is the matrix of vāc, or the subtle objects of the mind. At this madhyamā level, we come to see the Aham in relation to even subtler objects of the mind. Progression to madhyamā occurs only when we have relinquished our eṣaṇas in vaikharī. At this stage, Jyeṣṭhā becomes the predominant current and moves us along to the Trikoṇa where we come to see the Aham at its most purified level.

The path from the Bhūpura to the Trikoṇa is known as aśuddhādvan or the impure path, because of the clear separation between Aham and Idam. With the collapse of the Trikoṇa, the pure path or śuddhādvan begins with increasing non-separation between Aham and Idam.[111] In śuddhādvan, the mantra takes us through the subtle centers within the Bindu.

111 See The Pure Path in Chapter 17.

As we have seen in Chapter 4, AUM is the Absolute Reality without resonance or nāda. The anusvāra of AUM is the nāda that sets creation in process, which becomes the resonance *hrīṃ*. In other words, AUM is parāvāk where Śakti is turned toward Śiva as the Bindu, and hrīṃ is parāvāk where she is turned toward manifestation as the visarga.

While aśuddhādvan is the movement from vaikharī to paśyantī, śuddhādvan is the movement from visarga to bindu or hrīṃ to AUM, which progresses in the nine mystical centers that lie beyond ordinary consciousness.

The hrīṃ of the third kūṭa of the Pañcadaśī dissolves into the Bindu and ascends through eight other increasingly subtle stations (*ardhacandra*, *rodhinī*, *nāda*, *nādānta*, *śakti*, *vyāpika*, *samanā*, and *unmanā*). At nādānta, the resonance of hrīṃ ends and AUM begins, with continued resorption into the next four stages which correspond to the stages of *Śuddha Vidyā*, *Īśvara*, Sadāśiva and finally, Śiva-Śakti where Ahambhāva predominates as Parā.

We must remember that śuddhādvan is out of our reach until we have overcome our insecurities and self-image that keep us in the sphere of becoming at the periphery. For the ascent within the Bindu, our *granthis*[112] must be resolved with an even flow of prāṇa in the sandhis and marmas and no energy being wasted in the other āvaraṇas. This is the path of Kuṇḍalinī which reabsorbs Raudrī, Jyeṣṭhā and Vāmā within herself and shines as Ambikā, the ever auspicious One.

112 See Chapter 11.

Vāc in Sādhanā

Beyond the intricacies of mantra sādhanā, the placement of language in the Śrīcakra is supremely important in understanding its power to create our reality.

> ***When we reflect on our life circumstances from the standpoint of vāc, we see that everything visible in our lives is the solidification of our mind patterns.***

In other words, our outer world (vaikharī) is merely a reflection of our inner landscape (madhyamā).

Whether our life is chaotic and confusing with repeated patterns of suffering and strife or harmony and beauty, it reflects the relationship between the levels of vāc. In addition to mantra sādhanā, the Śrīcakra presents the startling possibility of dynamism, where the playing field of the Bhūpura can be shaped and changed by changing the flow of attention and prāṇa at the Vasukoṇa. This occurs through the systematic process of taming our mind, cultivating the necessary prerequisites, surrendering to the process, and rewiring our brains through discipline, focus and devotion.

Śrīcakra upāsanā gives us alternative ways to interpret our reality, which has profound effects in the manifestation of opportunities, connections, beauty, challenges, and harmony in our external lives.

With this short primer on vāc, we are now ready to embark on the sacred journey of the saṃhāra krama of the Śrīcakra, where all the concepts we have studied will be tested, refined, and applied. We will begin our journey at the Bhūpura where we will meet the deities that rule over the playing field of our moment-to-moment experience.

PART III

THE PRACTICE OF THE ŚRĪCAKRA

जपो जल्पः शिल्पं सकलमपि मुद्राविरचना
गतिः प्रादक्षिण्य-क्रमण-मशनाद्या हुति-विधिः ।
प्रणामः संवेशः सुखमखिल-मात्मार्पण-दृशा
सपर्या पर्याय-स्तव भवतु यन्मे विलसितम् ॥ २७ ॥

japō jalpaḥ śilpaṃ sakalamapi mudrāvirachanā
gatiḥ prādakṣiṇya-kramaṇam-aśanādy-āhuti-vidhiḥ ।
praṇāmas-saṃvēśas-sukhamakhilam-ātmārpaṇa-dṛśā
saparyāparyāyastava bhavatu yanmē vilasitam ॥ 27 ॥

"May my speech be the japa, my work the mudrās, my walking the pradakṣiṇa (circumambulation), my food intake the fire oblation, my sleep the prostration, my enjoyments the offerings; may all my deeds be performed as your worship."
~Saundarya Lahirī, verse 27

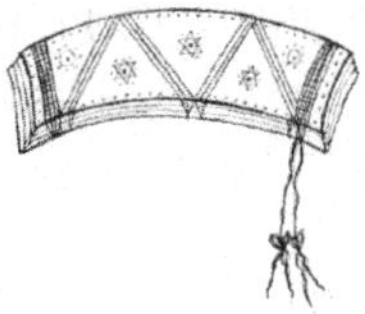

Chapter 7

Bhūpura

नियतिः शृङ्गारादयो नव रसा अणिमादयः
कामक्रोधलोभमोहमदमात्सर्यपुण्यपापमया
ब्राह्म्याद्यष्टशक्तयः ॥ ११ ॥
आधरनवकम् मुद्राशक्तयः ॥ १२ ॥

niyatih śṛṅgārādayo rasā aṇimādayah kāma-krodha-lobha-moha-mada-
mātsarya-puṇya-pāpa-mayā brāhmyadyaṣṭaka-śaktayaḥ || 11 ||
ādhāranavakam mudrāśaktayaḥ || 12 ||

"The ten siddhis including Aṇimā are the ten rasas of niyati, śṛṅgāra etc., while the eight śaktis beginning with Brāhmī are kāma, krodha, lobha, moha, mada, mātsarya, puṇya and papa. The mudrā śaktis are the nine supports."
~ Bhāvanopaniṣad, verses 11-12.

In the previous section, we explored the descent of Śiva-Śakti into all of creation as the Śrīcakra and how this overarching principle of the divine pervades every part of it from the subtle to the gross. In the descent or the sṛṣṭi krama, we went from the Bindu to the Bhūpura. Now we will examine the Śrīcakra in the opposite direction: the saṃhāra krama, which is more relevant to our practice where awareness moves from gross to increasingly subtle objects. Finally, it becomes so subtle that it dissolves in the Bindu.

The outermost āvaraṇa is the Bhūpura (bhū = earth, *pura* = city) or the square base of the Śrīcakra consists of three parallel lines that form four doors or portals pointing to the four cardinal directions (see Figure 18). The significance of these four doors depends on the sampradāya. In general, they can represent the four Vedas and symbolize the four āmnāyas. The eastern gate is ruled by *Bhuvaneśvarī*, the southern by *Dakṣiṇa Kālī*, the western by Kubjikā and the northern by *Guhya Kālī*. Two other gates are not evident in the Śrīcakra design – one above and another below. Each of the six gates represents an āmnāya with its own stream of teachings and practices.[113]

113 See Āmnāya and Sampradāya in Chapter 2.

Entering the Śrīcakra

In some sampradāyas, the gates of the Bhūpura are open to anyone that wishes to enter the Śrīcakra. In others, they are closed and requires dīkṣā and adherence to the rules of the sampradāya. From the perspective of sādhanā, we can enter the Śrīcakra through any of the four gates, which symbolize different starting points in our journey.

The gates also correspond to the four different ways in which we can enter the Śrīcakra – mantras through the eastern, devotion through the southern, ritual through the western, discriminative knowledge or jñāna through the northern, words and logic through the lower, and liberative knowledge through the upper.

The gate we arrive at is highly dependent on the issues that preoccupy us. These are the issues that tether us to the periphery of the circle where our energy is expended. How and why we expend our energy in the periphery is influenced by the layers of conditioning that project onto the ṣaṭcakras. Unfulfilled eṣaṇas and strife involving the ṣaṭcakras that keep us at the periphery comprise the issues of the Bhūpura, including health, loss, money, comfort, relationships, self-worth and self-approval, and a general sense of dissatisfaction. Our issues make up our Bhūpura and create a narrow lens through which we view the world.

Think of it this way. Imagine you're standing at the Bhūpura facing a gate. You can only see this gate because it represents your issues and inclinations. From here, you're going to ascend the Śrīcakra along its steps by following the trail of your issues and inclinations. Your perspective is limited because you aren't privy to the issues and inclinations that might take someone else to any of the other gates. You work on your issues by entering this gate and as you make your way up to the top, you gain a much larger perspective. You see that there are indeed other gates, and each will lead the climber to where you are. The purpose of sādhanā is to gain a holistic vision that includes *all* perspectives from every angle of existence.

The Inquiry

The Bhūpura is known as the *Trailokyamohana* cakra, the one that enchants or infatuates in the three worlds or realms. The Bhūpura consists of three parallel lines and from a three-dimensional standpoint, they are three levels stacked upon each other. There are 28 yoginīs in the Bhūpura known as *Prakaṭa* (fully or explicitly manifest) and they are stationed along the four gates and corners of the three levels (See Figure 18).

From a practical standpoint, the Bhūpura represents our field of gross experiences. This is where our very mundane day-to-day life unfolds in the way we live, work, love, and experience the entire spectrum of sensations, thoughts, and emotions.

It is our field of action, and the Prakaṭa Yoginīs guard the various aspects of this field, being the gatekeepers of both bondage and freedom.

At the Bhūpura, the Divine is fully manifest in the gross material world due to its self-imposed limitations. The yoginīs of the Bhūpura represent the dual aspects of this limitation in time and space – the shadow, where the limitation results in the inevitable cycles of suffering and joy of saṃsāra and the light as the *potential* for freedom.

We can think of the Bhūpura as the field of refinement of the ego. On the spiritual path we tend to be in a rush to transcend the ego which is exceedingly difficult if it isn't well-adjusted to a certain degree. The Bhūpura gives us the opportunity to grow, mature and cultivate a refined ego that can progressively and systematically dissolve in the higher āvaraṇas. Without such cultivation and growth, it's not only exceedingly difficult to ascend to the higher āvaraṇas but attempting to do so can also create varying degrees of psychological, mental, physical, or emotional unpleasantness.

The Bhūpura is the playing field where pravṛtti becomes nivṛtti through the understanding of karma, refinement of action, and the inward turn of the senses that is required in the saṃhāra krama of the Śrīcakra.

We enter the Śrīcakra through the inquiry into our predicament that becomes the stimulus for cultivating awareness.

Figure 18. Bhūpura with Prakaṭa Yoginī

Whatever our unique situation is, it becomes the gate into the Śrīcakra if we wonder *why* we suffer the way we do. As long as we remain in the blaming mode and hold our genes, parents, past, society, family or circumstances responsible for our situation, the Bhūpura remains inaccessible. On the other hand, as soon as we become curious about *our* part in the drama, the gates begin to open.

Prakaṭa Yoginī

The 28 Prakaṭa Yoginīs of the Bhūpura are fully manifest in all their powers of shadow and light (see Figure 19). In her lower right hand, the Prakaṭa Yoginī bears a trident pointing to the three worlds in which the triads of guṇas, language, avasthās and powers manifest, evolve and dissolve. In her lower left hand is a skull that signifies the inevitable destruction of everything that is created, including our fragile self-image. While implements in her lower hands symbolize avidyā, those in her upper hands signify vidyā. The book in her upper left hand beckons us to higher knowledge while the mālā or string of beads in her upper right hand indicates the power of mantra to overcome avidyā.

Figure 19. Prakaṭa Yoginī

As a fully manifest power, the Prakaṭa Yoginī displays the shadow and light of our moment-to-moment experience that has in it the power to bind us in saṃsāra or lead us to nirvāṇa. The prakaṭa yoginīs manifest as three distinct groups in the Bhūpura, each group commanding one of its three levels – the Siddhis in the first, the *Aṣṭa Mātṛkās* in the second, and the Mudrā Devīs in the third.

The Ten Attainments (Siddhis)

The ten yoginīs of the outermost line are known as the *Siddha Devatās* and they symbolize siddhis or attainments (see Table 7). When they bestow their grace, the practitioner attains certain powers. The placement of these yoginīs at the very first level of the Bhūpura is significant when we consider that siddhis are magical powers attained at a very advanced level of practice. In fact, various Tāntrik texts consider the cultivation of siddhis and dominion over the physical world one of the goals of practice. If we were to approach the Śrīcakra in the sṛṣṭi krama, this would indeed be the case, where we would meet the Siddhis in the last stage of devolution.

Table 7. Siddhis of the Bhūpura

Siddhi	Rasa	Bhāvanā
Aṇimā Siddhi (Power to become minute)	Śānta (Tranquility)	Sevā and surrender
Laghimā Siddhi (Power to become light)	Adbhuta (Amazement)	Enjoying the process
Mahimā Siddhi (Power to become large)	Kāruṇya (Compassion)	True generosity of the heart
Īśitva Siddhi (Power to rule over)	Vīrya (Heroism)	Control over mind, speech, and behavior
Vaśitva Siddhi (Power to subjugate)	Hāsya (Mirth)	Seeing past the appearance of solidity
Prākāmya Siddhi (Power to assume any form)	Bībhatsa (Disgust)	Changing physiology at will
Bhukti Siddhi (Power to experience pleasure)	Raudra (Anger)	Understanding the underlying energy of delusion
Icchā Siddhi (Power to desire)	Bhayānaka (Fear)	Clarifying desire and intention
Prāpti Siddhi (Power to become fulfilled)	Śṛṅgāra (Erotic love)	Discerning between subject and objects
Sarvakāma Siddhi (Power to actualize all intentions)	Niyati (Restraint)	Ability to go beyond the confines of conditioning

In the saṃhāra krama that is relevant to our practice, siddhis are the first step of the sādhanā and determine our entry into the Śrīcakra. Here, the siddhis are cultivated through our interaction with the world. In the Bhāvanopaniṣad, Śrī Bhāskararāya makes a correspondence of the siddhis with rasa.

Rasa

Rasa means the nectar or juice of a particular emotion. As we see in sṛṣṭi krama, the Bindu is non-local and pervades the components of the Śrīcakra as the union of Śiva-Śakti in every experience. Rasa is the juice of this union that manifests as the unique flavors and textures of emotions.

Our interaction with the world around us occurs primarily in the realm of emotions. Although logic and reason inform our actions, reactions and responses, our emotions make up the driving force for our moment-to-moment contact with the world. We take in the world via our sense organs and make sense of it in our mind that is *emotionally* conditioned by our past experiences. We then use the intellect to reason and choose based on the social, cultural, and moral norms that shape us, and respond to the situation through verbal or non-verbal expression. Both perception and response are laced with the visceral felt-sense of emotions that influence logic and intellect. In other words, emotion is the primary arising that the intellect tries to reason, resist, accept, validate or justify.

For example, you are at a grocery store minding your own business and run into a good-looking stranger who asks you a perfectly innocent question, "Hi, do you know where I can find coffee filters?" Instantly, your body responds with a flood of neurotransmitters and chemicals of lust – your heart rate increases, your body emits a different odor, and your posture changes unconsciously. Even as your mind registers the spontaneous emotion, your intellect jumps in with the brakes of social and moral conditioning, "I shouldn't feel this way. I'm married. What's wrong with me?" Your response, whatever it is, will be laced with the emotions of lust *and* conflict. Long after you've left the store, you'll carry the flavor of both within. The *emotion* is raw and exciting, but the *logic* adds guilt and self-consciousness.

The Siddhis of the Bhūpura keep us trapped in this mire of confusion. Through their worship, we gain access to the pure rasa of emotions that drive our interactions with the world. Ordinarily, our emotions are chaotic and rapidly shift and change, where we have no access to their purest experience without the involvement of the conditioned mind. Gaining access to the rasa of emotion requires a certain degree of equanimity where we can welcome it with openness and curiosity without becoming entangled in the *story* it may bring up. In our default way of being, emotions incite conflict as we either seek to satisfy them through our actions, or find cultural, social, or moral reasons to not experience them. However, to even enter the Śrīcakra, we must attain the siddhis so that we can play in the material world by fully experiencing its rich and varied spectrum of rasas.

The ten Siddhis are placed on the right side of the four doors and along the corners of the Bhūpura.[114]

114 Garimā Siddhi, the power to become heavy, although traditionally considered a siddhi, is not included in the Bhūpura. In the Dakṣiṇāmūrti sampradāya, she is placed at the trivṛtta, the three concentric circles that separate the gross external world from the internal world.

Aṇimā Siddhi

Aṇu refers to an atom, and *aṇimā* is to become minute like an atom. It's interesting that Aṇimā is the first of the siddhis, and the cornerstone of all attainments. When we think of being small, we may have the idea of having the superpower of being able to navigate tight spaces in the gross world. This may be so, but here, we are examining this siddhi as it refers to humility.

The ability to surrender to a teaching, a teacher, a path, or even to our own process is indeed a superpower. The word "surrender" brings up all kinds of connotations for most of us – especially in the current age of being swindled by those we hold in high authority, including teachers, institutions of learning, corporations we work for, and the politicians that decide our fate. The surrender we are talking about here is not to a person or an institution or a political party, but to the *process* of growth, which is applicable to all areas of life.

If we want to learn anything, the process is most enjoyable and beneficial when we approach it with curiosity and a sense of not knowing along with eagerness to lap up everything that comes our way. When we come to the process empty of pre-conceived notions, we find that a whole new perspective opens. On the other hand, when we come to it with the feeling that we already know, the process slows down or shuts off because our cup is too full and can't be filled any further.

Surrendering to the process comes at a huge cost to the ego, which will find any number of reasons and justifications to do exactly the opposite.

> ***The ego is a conglomeration of thoughts, concepts and ideas that create the self-image. It is the story of me that is maintained through the interactions that occur at the Bhūpura.***

The shadow aspect of Aṇimā Siddhi is the inability to become small for any reason, or to allow the self-image to diminish. Even on the spiritual path, we innocently look at liberation as another thing that might add *to* the self-image, when it is actually freedom *from* it. In this misperception, we hold on steadfastly to the self-image, unable to surrender to the path, the teacher, or the teaching.

We struggle with the idea of surrender because we fundamentally confuse *humility* with *humiliation*. Surrendering feels humiliating to the ego because it already *knows*. When we arrive at a teaching with this attitude, our behavior is laced with cynicism and indignation. Our cup is too full and forcibly trying to surrender is excruciating.

> ***Humiliation is the stuff of the ego whereas humility is the willingness to look past the ego.***

In humiliation, we feel insulted and offended, whereas in humility, we arrive at *śānta*, the rasa of tranquility. There's nothing to defend, and all the challenges thrown up by the teacher or the teaching become opportunities to become even smaller and for the ego to dissolve.

When Aṇimā graces us, our ideas of being special, unique, and significant begin to dissolve as we see that self-image is the ubiquitous play of Māyā. Śānta replaces cynicism with the sense that everything is okay just as it is. Without the need to defend our self-image, our interactions with the world change. We stop looking over our shoulders and put our weapons down. Humility enables us to be of service without the constant vigilance and worry about humiliation.

The importance of humility on the spiritual journey can hardly be overstated, which is symbolized by Aṇimā being the first goddess we encounter in the saṃhāra krama. In many lineages, *sevā* is a central piece of upāsanā, where the śiṣya learns to be of service to the Guru and the *saṅgha*. There are many facets to sevā, but its primary purpose is to find ways to become smaller and invite opportunities to facilitate this change.

Bhāvanā on Aṇimā Siddhi

Sevā is service to the teacher and more broadly, to the path.

Contemplate the meaning of sevā, and where you serve without expectation for anything in return. What is the purpose of your engagement in any work? Do you approach it with a sense of open curiosity to see how you can grow or do you begin with checking what it will do for you?

On a moment-to-moment basis, become aware of your resistance to be small. This can show up in conversations where you might finish the other's sentences (it matters even if this is in our heads), presume what they are thinking, or predict their actions.

Contemplate humiliation versus humility. When in a conversation, discussion or argument, check your stance. Are you defensive and ready to protect your image of who you are? Do you stop the other person to clarify your position and to reiterate your image? What happens if you don't?

Laghimā Siddhi

Laghimā is the power to become light as a feather and be able to float in air. Again, while this can be a gravity-defying magical ability, here we can examine laghimā as an attitude adjustment.

Our usual attitude is one of heaviness and gravity, where we carry the world upon our shoulders. Whatever the causative factors are for the burden that weights us down, the underlying issue is that of *knowing*. Our day-to-day lives are replete with challenges and tough situations, but what makes them more unbearable is the thought that they could have been different. We cement down alternative scenarios that would have, in our imagination, been more desirable. In reality however, there is no way to know if any of those imagined scenarios would have turned out the way we plan them in our minds. The *illusion* of knowing creates a burden and weighs us down. This predicament arises because we remain focused on the results of a particular event, action, or choice, rather than its unpredictable unfolding.

With the burden of knowing, we lose the ability to experience the range of rasas arising from the many facets of a particular circumstance – the pressure or joy of making a choice, the suspense of awaiting the results, the fear, anxiety, or satisfaction of experiencing the fruit of the choice, and most importantly, the wonder and amazement of the unfolding sequence of events. Since we remain focused on whether the fruit of action is desirable or not, we tend to dislike the inevitable unpredictability of events and actions.

> ***Laghimā Siddhi grants us the ability to shrug off the weight of knowing and grants us the rasa of adbhuta or wonder.***

Adbhuta enables us to become light and airy, being entirely focused on doing and choosing purely for the joy of it rather than a pre-specified outcome. With this siddhi, we can be fascinated with the moment-to-moment unfolding of life and open to anything it brings.

Mahimā Siddhi

Mahimā is the ability to become enormous, and here, it refers to becoming magnanimous and cultivating true generosity of the heart.

Ordinarily, our stance is one of obsessive self-centeredness where our self-worth and self-evaluation is dependent on comparison with others. Self-centeredness makes us miserly where we are unable to give – a kind word, a helping hand, a compliment, money, or service – without assessing what's in it for us. In any interaction, our attention remains on our own gain or loss, how it affects us and what it may mean for us. We go about our lives being guarded and self-conscious, feeling conflicted between moral norms of generosity and what that means for our own self.

Our generosity has conditions where it needs to benefit us (or our loved ones) and is laced by a pervasive sense of lack. We fear that in giving, we will incur a loss, as if there is a limited supply of things in the world. We view generosity as a transaction where we guardedly give out just enough so that we can keep more for ourselves.

We are never able to revel in another's success and joy without feeling a tinge of envy or indifference. When we take part in another's loss and grief, our sadness is laced with a sense of relief that it's not happening to us. Even when we are involved in projects to "give back," our attention remains on how this makes *us* feel. We live out our lives gripped in the clutches of smallness, which is the product of self-centeredness.

True generosity is to give without scheming or looking to benefit from it in any way.

The rasa of Mahimā Siddhi is kāruṇya or compassion, which differs from pity.

Ordinarily, what we call compassion is pity, which arises from a stance of superiority. Even when we are sympathizing with others going through rough times, we may subtly rejoice that we are not in the same situation. When we try to uplift others, we may approach the endeavor and the people involved as "projects," focusing on their lack and the satisfaction we derive from our own ability to provide for them. Such an approach is inherently hierarchical, where we come out on top.

Kāruṇya, on the other hand, is the result of magnanimity and true generosity – like the right hand giving to the left. The giving is devoid of any ulterior motive, and Kāruṇya requires us to be free of our own insecurities that make us feel threatened when someone is doing well or pitiful when they aren't.

Mahimā's grace allows us to zoom out of our limited perspectives and see all of life as a free flow of energy that is constantly moving, shifting, and transforming. This energy takes the form of money and resources, health and disease, aging and seasons, pain and joy, loss and gain, and despair and beauty. Everything is in constant flux from us to the world and vice versa. We can't hold on to anything; all we can aspire for is to become spacious and large enough to allow it.

Īśitva Siddhi

Īśitva Siddhi is to gain mastery or dominion, which translates to the ability to control others, but in the context of the Śrīcakra, it is the power to control our own mind, behavior, emotions, and consequently, our own destiny.

Usually, we tend to be the slaves of our own conditioning – the way we have been brought up and the experiences we have accumulated over the course of our lives become ingrained in our neurohormonal pathways. We remain helpless in our ability to be triggered by the world in one way or another, where interacting with the world brings up the same old kinds of reactions. We are so habituated to how we respond to things that our behavior becomes predictable and congealed in certainty. We go about our lives holding everything and everyone else responsible for the way we think, feel, and act.

> ***Īśitva is the ability to gain mastery over our minds and lives so that we lord over our own domain.***

This ability arises from the rasa of *vīrya* or courage, and one who masters vīrya is known as a vīra (feminine: vīrā) or hero.

A vīrā is fearless enough to enter the mind with its maze of confusions, distractions, and temptations. For example, instead of dealing with an emotion by acting it out (as in yelling at someone that they "made" us angry) or reveling in self-deprecation ("it's all my fault; I can't do anything right"), the vīrā chooses to go straight into the emotion, regardless of the intensity of the discomfort. She welcomes and allows the emotion, giving it space. Eventually, she learns to harness the energy of the emotion, transmuting it and directing it to fuel her own sādhanā. The mind loses its grip on her actions and behavior. She changes her destiny.

Vīrya is cultivated through discipline in our lifestyle including diet, habits, and speech. Once we commit to a lifestyle, we keep at it, regardless of logistical challenges. We courageously deal with temptations, training our minds to remain focused. Gradually, because of steadfastness in our discipline, the mind becomes quiet and begins to function in a surrendered role. The world around us evolves in parallel with our inner landscape. Our interactions become streamlined and purposeful, our work becomes more efficient, and our perception of life becomes refined.

As the mind is used willingly to execute tasks and engage with the world at our will, we seem to gain control over time and space. We stop wasting energy in reactionary ways and preserve it through control over thought, feeling, speech and action. This is the gift of Īśitva Siddhi.

Vaśitva Siddhi

Vaśitva is the power to subjugate or influence others. While it is highly sought after in the spiritual arena to control or dominate over others, here the connotation is different.

Ordinarily, we have fixed ideas about how the world should operate and what everyone else must be doing. In our minds, we are constantly trying to rule over the world with our shoulds and shouldn'ts. Since the world doesn't care how we think it should work, we find ourselves frustrated and conflicted.

Our fundamental problem is that we take everything seriously and personally. Even though we have no ability to know how anything "should" turn out, the perceived seriousness of the situation leads to constant anxiety and stress. From our perspective, people and events need to be fixed so they can align with *our* thought. If we could, we would control nature as well, deciding when it "should" rain or shine. Since none of this is possible, stress becomes our default way of being.

When we begin to worship Vaśitva Siddhi, we come to see the ridiculousness of our stance. In the grand analysis, nothing is ever out of place. Every event, no matter how terrible, could not have turned out differently because the way it *did* turn out is the only reality. All shoulds and coulds don't exist except as elaborate plots of the mind.

When the grace of this supreme yoginī begins to flow, we loosen up and all efforts to control anyone drop away. From the dirty dishes in the sink and socks on the floor to world-changing decisions made by political leaders, we allow things to be as they are. Allowing things to be doesn't mean we don't pick up the socks or vote for leaders. We do, but we aren't wedded to the outcome (see Laghimā Siddhi). We can see the mirth of the situation, knowing that in the grand scheme of things, clutter and political decisions don't matter. Our planet is a speck in the cosmos and our time here is inconsequential and fleeting.

The rasa that we get to experience with Vaśitva Siddhi is *hāsya*, which is joy or laughter where we stop taking things seriously and personally. We give up trying to control people and events, learning to become joyfully centered in ourselves. Paradoxically, loosening up and remaining steeped in our own joy results in those around us *wanting* our opinion. Who isn't attracted to self-sustaining joy and laughter? It is exactly when we let go of control that we gain it. This is the magic of Vaśitva Siddhi.

Prākāmya Siddhi

Prākāmya is the ability to attain any form. While this may fascinate us as the siddhi of shapeshifting, here we will examine it from the standpoint of ego refinement.

As we saw earlier with respect to Vaśitva Siddhi, we tend to project solidity to the world around us. This uncompromising stance extends to our life experiences, past events, as well as influences of parents, caregivers, peers, culture, and society. Although our life experiences induce a range of feelings, shame, guilt, and disgust tend to overpower gratitude, love, and joy. If we have been humiliated, abandoned, or ignored or our poor choices have led to challenging long-term outcomes, our story of "me" becomes heavily laced with rage and disgust.

We carry the burden of disgust in the form of either cynicism and arrogance or depression and self-deprecation, all of which make shame and guilt a little more bearable. The problem here is that the rasa of disgust or *bībhatsa* was never experienced in its raw form when it originally arose. When we look at a healthy stress response, there is an acute spike of hormones released to deal with the stimulus. Instantly, the heart rate, blood pressure and blood flow to the skeletal muscle increases, pupils dilate, and we are physiologically prepared to stay and fight the stimulus or quickly exit the situation. This is the classic fight-or-flight response. A tremendous amount of energy is built up to deal with the stressor. Whether we fight or flee, with the completion of a healthy stress response, that energy dissipates.

If we are in situations that bring about the physiologic and energetic response, but we can neither fight nor flee, the stress response remains on a high and the pent-up energy is never completely discharged. Situations that bring about an incomplete stress response include abuse, neglect, and domination by those with more perceived power. When there is no safe way to discharge pent-up energy, it expresses disruptively as a derivative of disgust such as shame, guilt, or depression.

Disgust is a powerful emotion and a challenging one to break through. Although the unconditioned mind is vast and flexible enough to become anything it wishes, disgust keeps us tightly imprisoned in a contracted default stance. Bībhatsa molds us in rigid shapes that become the lens through which we interpret the world and react to it. Our stance arises from a place of touchy defensiveness or volatile anger.

Prākāmya Siddhi graces us with the ability to step back from our minds and take a good, hard look at our patterns. We come to realize that although we were victims of unfortunate circumstances, we don't have to live as victims all our lives.

We have the power to choose another way, and this begins with finding a way to complete the stress response so that the disrupted energy can be safely discharged. With the dissipation of the old and stuck energy, we create space for a new perspective to emerge.

Healing from bībhatsa can take many forms including talk therapy or directed self-inquiry, but all psychological measures work best in the context of lifestyle changes including diet and exercise, which facilitate the release of novel neurotransmitters, hormones, and enzymes.[115]

115 See K. Chinnaiyan, *The Heart of Wellness* (Sfaim Press, 2021).

When we gain control over our own minds, we can willingly change our patterns and assume any form. We are not bound by bībhatsa or its derivatives. At our own will, we can morph into witty, joyful, or compassionate beings merely by bringing about a change in thought that leads to a physiologic change. In this transformation, the rasa of bībhatsa is fully experienced without the stories of victimhood and has become the fuel for change. The mind that was once the enemy becomes our friend, demonstrating its ability for effortless shapeshifting.

Bhukti Siddhi

Bhukti is the ability to enjoy. This siddhi is a tricky one and requires us to know its many paradoxes.[116] As we saw in Introduction, no matter who we are or where we come from, we fundamentally desire permanent happiness. We long for the things we do because we feel they will bring us happiness. And yet when we do get what we want, we don't fully enjoy it because we are afraid of losing it. We never really savor what we have because the disbelief that we have it and the fear of losing it prevent us from sinking our teeth into enjoyment.

116 See also The Path of Bhukti and Mukti in Chapter 6.

Our outward-turned sense organs are naturally enamored by the objects of the world. The predicament of the sense organs is not only that they continually orient toward sense objects – it is that the attachment to the object makes us want to own it. The movement toward ownership begins with an attachment for the object and the desire to have, own, or experience it. The attachment or longing creates an agitation or a feeling of wrath (*raudra*) at the possibility of not owning it. The combination of longing and agitation creates a clouding of the mind; we think back to how life might be without the object and the potential for happiness in the future with it. The resultant deluded state of the mind makes us lose touch with reality.[117]

117 See *Bhagavad Gītā* 2:62-63.

In other words, raudra is the result of (real or imagined) thwarted desire, where we can't or don't get what we want, or fear losing what we have. To be clear, sense objects refer not only to only material things but also to the eṣaṇas of acknowledgment, validation, appreciation, things going our way or the way we think they should, perceived wrong-doing and so on. Even the idea that life should unfold in particular ways, and that the world and others should conform to our thinking are objects that lead to raudra when unfulfilled.

Raudra is fueled by a (often subconscious) memory of having been wronged or slighted. The stress response created in the past becomes activated with this new (real or imagined) threat. Like disgust, the problem with anger is that the stress response has not been completed where the energy is discharged permanently. Instead, it simmers under the surface as the predominant shape of our stance. This undercurrent of anger or agitation prevents us from truly enjoying anything we get.

To deal with anger (see *Māheśvarī*, below), not only do we have to defuse the charge of the old stress response, but also resolve the underlying subconscious issue. This may be accomplished by various approaches that lead to a deep inquiry into the cause of anger. Importantly, examining and reigning in expectations and desires is critical, where the approach is of creating such a broad perspective that the stuck energy of anger is dissipated in its vastness. Peace is cultivated through equanimity and understanding that the fundamental problem we must resolve is the conflict between what should be and what is.

> ***Bhukti Siddhi bestows her grace of the ability to enjoy the rasa of desire toward sense objects without grasping or wanting to own them.***

When we can enjoy the rasa of objects in this radically different way, raudra gives way to ānanda.

Icchā Siddhi

Icchā is intention or will, and this siddhi is the ability to set a clear intention that is bound to yield fruit. As simple as this sounds, it's actually very challenging to even know what we really want. Ordinarily, our wants are in a state of confusion, and we tend to want things that inherently contradict or cancel each other out. This contradictory state of mind becomes particularly challenging on the spiritual path, as it requires us to zero in on a goal to such an extent that we are willing to give up everything else in its favor.

The idea of giving up brings up primal fear (*bhayānaka*) mixed with incredulity, particularly if we have the idea that the householder path is akin to having the cake and eating it too. The sādhanā of Icchā Siddhi gives us the opportunity to clear this misconception.

Normally, the various spheres of the relational world such as our families, jobs, relationships, political and social landscapes with their ever-changing crises keep us intensely occupied in the periphery. Importantly, the content of our own minds keeps us totally enthralled in saṃsāra. When we come to the path of the Śrīcakra, we are catapulted into another way of being and looking at the world, practices that engage our senses, and a community of practitioners with the same interest and investment in it. However, even though our focus in life has begun to shift because of our spiritual inclination, our old ways are so deeply ingrained that they don't magically go away.

As we saw earlier in Chapter 5, there are two broad ways of approaching the Bindu – the path of the renunciate or the path of the householder. Tantra is known as the path of the householder, where there is no need to cut off our ties from society and head to a cave to discover the Bindu. The crucial thing to know here is that whether it is the path of the renunciate or the householder, the "path" is one of unlearning, where we step out of the bounds of our conditioning and social, moral, cultural, political, and countless other norms. Importantly, both the renunciate and the householder must cultivate the dispassion and discernment to pull away from the periphery toward the center.

> ***We must understand at the outset that the householder path isn't exempt from dispassion.***

Both the renunciate and the householder must be willing to give up the periphery in favor of the center. And to make steady progress toward the center, we must fulfill the eṣaṇas at the periphery so that they are permanently relinquished and free up the energy to ascend the Śrīcakra āvaraṇas. The crucial ingredient here is icchā, the intention to progress to the Bindu at *all* costs.

To receive the grace of Icchā Siddhi, we must have the courage and honesty to face our fears – of loss, imagined situations, being small, inconsequential or unremembered. Importantly, we must have the courage to face death. With a gradual relinquishing of fear, we arrive at the willingness to give up everything to make space for vidyā.

Prāpti Siddhi

Prāpti is the ability to be fulfilled, which is arguably the most coveted siddhi. We can have all the other siddhis but without this one, we would continue to be restless for more and not enjoy the ones we possess!

The fundamental obstacle to prāpti is the predicament of looking everywhere else for fulfilment except where it matters – within – or more accurately, a shift from the object to the subject.[118] Let's revisit the ahaṅkāra or the I-maker, which takes the objects of the world and associates them with itself, leading to a confusion between them (objects) and the subject. All the different things we take to be "me" – name, sex and gender, body, accomplishments, ethnicity, religion, nationality and in fact, anything we can possibly think of – is an object. The *story* of I isn't the "I." Every single experience we have had or will have is experienced *by* the "I." The infinite, ever-changing experiences that make up our lives are objects being experienced by the unchanging "I." Our bodies change and age, our minds are constantly shifting, our emotions, opinions, loyalties and beliefs change, but the "I" remains ever-fresh, ageless, and timeless.

118 See also The Conundrum of the Trikoṇa in Chapter 17.

In fact, the countless experiences we have on a moment-to-moment basis are the points of contact between the "I" and the objects of the world. Śiva as the "I" and Śakti as the rich and diverse world of objects are constantly uniting in the rasa of *śṛṅgāra*. The ahaṅkāra misdirects our attention from this union to itself, where instead of knowing ourselves as the subject, we look at ourselves as a collection of objects.[119] Since there is no end to the number of experiences we can have, we never feel fulfilled.

119 Here, experiences are also objects. In fact, everything that is experienced is an object.

Prāpti Siddhi's grace allows us to see through the primary misunderstanding of what the "I" really is.

With this realization, the ahaṅkāra becomes quiescent and we come to experience śṛṅgāra in the mundane, which is the outpouring of contentment and delight in moment-to-moment experience.[120]

120 See 'Transmutation of Desire' in Chapter 12 in K. Chinnaiyan, *Glorious Alchemy* (New Sarum Press, 2020).

Sarvakāma Siddhi

The ability to actualize all our intentions is called *Sarvakāma* Siddhi and is the culmination of all the other siddhis. While we may think of this siddhi as the ability to make any wish come true, the deeper meaning here is to understand the rasa of niyati.

We have previously seen niyati in the context of the five kañcukas, where it is the limitation in space.[121] In other words, niyati is the limitation of our destiny. We don't actualize *all* intentions because our intentions are limited to what we know and what we have previously experienced. Our current experience is the result of our previous experiences and will become the basis for our future ones. Our past experiences leave behind signatures of attractions and aversions, which become the basis for what we want in the future. Although infinite possibilities exist in any given experience, we are not even aware of them – our likes and dislikes seal our fate, and we choose our future accordingly. Even when we feel that our choice is a conscious one, it is still driven by the hope for a certain outcome and rejection of all others.

121 See Kañcukas and Malas in Chapter 9.

Niyati is much more than a psychological construct. It's a physiological one that extends to our DNA – even when we have overcome our likes and dislikes, our bodies are still subject to its codes as karma. Saṃsāra is the cyclical process of death and rebirth, where we come back again and again to live out unfulfilled desires and karmic ties.[122]

Having the grace of Sarvakāma Siddhi is to break through niyati. Psychologically, this is the result of becoming increasingly aware of the limitations we cast upon ourselves in the way we refer to our life experiences and stories. It's a loosening of the ahaṅkāra to go beyond the confines of Māyā through constant self-reflection and opening to Grace.

122 See Kamalatmika in K. Chinnaiyan, *Shakti Rising* (Nonduality Press, 2017).

We now see why the Siddhis are stationed at the outermost layer of the Bhūpura. We meet them in our moment-to-moment interaction with the world, and it is in this messy, confusing arrangement that they can be cultivated.

The entire Śrīcakra is interconnected, where each āvaraṇa is subsumed by the next. This scheme of interconnectedness is bestowed with the highest wisdom, where digging deep into the first layer will inevitably land us in the next and the next until we end up at the Bindu.

Accordingly, when we delve into the Siddhis in the process of inquiry, we come to the underlying energy of the next line of the Bhūpura, which is governed by the formidable Aṣṭa Mātṛkās.

The Eight Mothers

The yoginīs of the middle line are known as the Aṣṭa Mātṛkās and are a group of eight goddesses. The Aṣṭa Mātṛkās have a very long history in Tantra and are steeped in the various aspects of its darśana, including a deep association with the eight groups of the Sanskrit letters. Here in the Bhūpura, however, they play a very significant role that determines our progress in the Śrīcakra.

In the Bhūpura, the Aṣṭa Mātṛkās are associated with eight specific types of "poisons" that inhibit our progress toward the Bindu. Each Mātṛkā symbolizes the poison as well as the nectar that becomes available when the poison is digested. The shadow aspect of each Mātṛkā traps us and trips us up in the quagmire of a particular poison, while her light rescues us from it (see Table 8).

Table 8. Aṣṭa Mātṛkās of the Bhūpura

Aṣṭa Mātṛkā	Manifestation	Bhāvanā
Brāhmī (Trap of desire)	Kāma (Passion)	Cultivation of sexual energy
Maheśvarī (Trap of anger)	Krodha (Anger)	Cultivation of patience
Kaumārī (Trap of covetousness)	Lobha (Greed)	Cultivation of generosity
Vaiṣṇavī (Trap of delusion)	Moha (Delusion)	Cultivation of insight
Vārāhī (Trap of pride)	Mada (Pride)	Cultivation of humility
Māhendrī (Trap of envy)	Mātsarya (Jealousy)	Cultivation of magnanimity
Cāmuṇḍā (Trap of sin)	Pāpa (Sin)	Cultivation of tolerance
Mahālakṣmī (Trap of virtue)	Puṇya (Virtue)	Cultivation of the darśana

Brāhmī

Brāhmī is the Śakti of Brahmā, the creator,[123] and her shadow is lust or kāma. She's the first among the Aṣṭa Mātṛkās because lust for objects is the force that traps us in saṃsāra. Lust keeps us engaged in creating karma with people, past stories, hopes and dreams, and ambition. Thoughts, words, and deeds create ripples that intersect with previous ones, dispersing in ever-expanding circles. Irresistible lust is the glue that binds events that become karma and our destiny.

123 The trinity of creation in Hindu dharma consists of Brahmā the creator, Viṣṇu the sustainer, and Rudra destroyer.

If we were to set aside our preconceptions about lust and understand its importance, we would see why Brāhmī is the first of the Mātṛkās. Biologically speaking, we are driven by the instincts to survive and reproduce. Like all other living organisms, we are wired for self-preservation and propagation of the species. This instinct for self-preservation spills over into the eṣaṇas and is facilitated by lust. Underling the lust for longevity, resources and validation is the longing for self-preservation. Humans are not driven by instinct alone. Instead, we are endowed with the highly developed citta, which confuses biological self-preservation with the psychological need to preserve the self-image.

For example, even though we don't *need* validation to survive, the interaction of the buddhi, ahaṅkāra and manas in the samskāra-laced citta confuses the issue and readjusts our biological responses. Hormonal pathways developed in the hunting-gathering stages of evolution are repurposed for modern times. For example, the hormone oxytocin in mammals fosters attachment to the offspring to ensure their well-being and the instinctual propagation of the species.[124] With the evolution of the human brain, the hormone was associated with attachment to the social structure and groups to ensure survival. The sense of attachment fostered by oxytocin and other hormones becomes the basis for how we view ourselves, for example, as good or bad parents, partners, co-workers, or members of society. Instead of the literal threat to survival thousands of years ago, the focus is now on the figurative survival of the self-image.

124 See 'The Stress Cauldron' in K. Chinnaiyan, *Heart of Wellness* (Sfaim Press 2021) for an understanding of the biological basis for our behaviors.

Ordinarily, most of our prāṇic reserves are spent in acquiring and maintaining the self-image through the acquisition of gross and subtle objects, such as material things, validation in relationships and roles, and justification of our past actions and future aspirations. Importantly, the self-image requires continuous nourishment, which is provided in our moment-to-moment reasoning of our choices and is known as the Brahmā granthi. Self-preservation is the focus of the Brahmā granthi.[125]

125 See Granthis in Chapter 11.

The Brahmā granthi is the most difficult knot to unravel because this is where our unconscious saṃskāras as subconscious vṛttis become conscious actions.[126]

126 See Citta Vṛttis in Chapter 10.

Essentially, our daily prāṇic quota is taken up mostly by the Brahmā granthi in the form of lust, the innate desire to maintain the self-image. The pure, creative energy of lust is distorted, giving rise to all the other poisons such as anger, greed, and pride that rule the second line of the Bhūpura. Lust is the root cause for the hatred and strife we see in the world and in ourselves, where the primary goal is self-preservation. The self-image is strengthened by upholding the views and beliefs that feel good and right, which is why we band with those with similar principles. In this scheme, those that have other views and beliefs become the "other," threatening our self-image.

The power of lust in creating the cascade of poisons that lead to delusion is known as the "ladder of fall,"[127] which begins with desire for an object. The object here can be material (for example, a jacket) or subtle (a relationship) that is taken in by the senses. Our mind, which was undisturbed before we laid eyes on the jacket or the person is now turbulent with the desire to own the object, quickly turning into attachment for it. As desire and attachment thicken and gather momentum, they invoke anxiety and anger if we can't have the object. The energy of anger leads to a temporary memory loss.[128] We forget that before we ever encountered this object, we were doing quite well.

The question we must ask ourselves is, "What triggered this particular cascade of delusion? Why *this* jacket or person?" The answer to this important question lies in the causal body or kāraṇa *śarīra*, which is the storehouse of our samskārās.[129] The subtle psychic impressions of our experience are stored as *unconscious* samskārās in the causal body that reflect as *conscious* likes and dislikes in the subtle body or sūkṣma śarīra. We know we are attracted to that jacket or person, but we don't know exactly *why*. The original event that registered that this design or facial characteristic is desirable is long forgotten but its essence remains as a subtle flavor. *Unconscious* samskārās reflecting as *conscious* likes and dislikes lead to *unconscious* behavior. Our likes and dislikes take us down the ladder of fall, culminating in the loss of the ability to reason, reflecting in our automatic and uncontrollable behavior (see Figure 20). Since vṛttis or likes and dislikes are conscious, this is the sphere we can influence in sādhanā.

127 Famously described in the *Bhagavad Gītā* 2:62-63.

128 For instance, no matter how much we love someone, in a moment of anger, all the reasons we love them vanish and we momentarily lose our bearings of their importance in our life.

129 See the Pañca Kośas in Chapter 11.

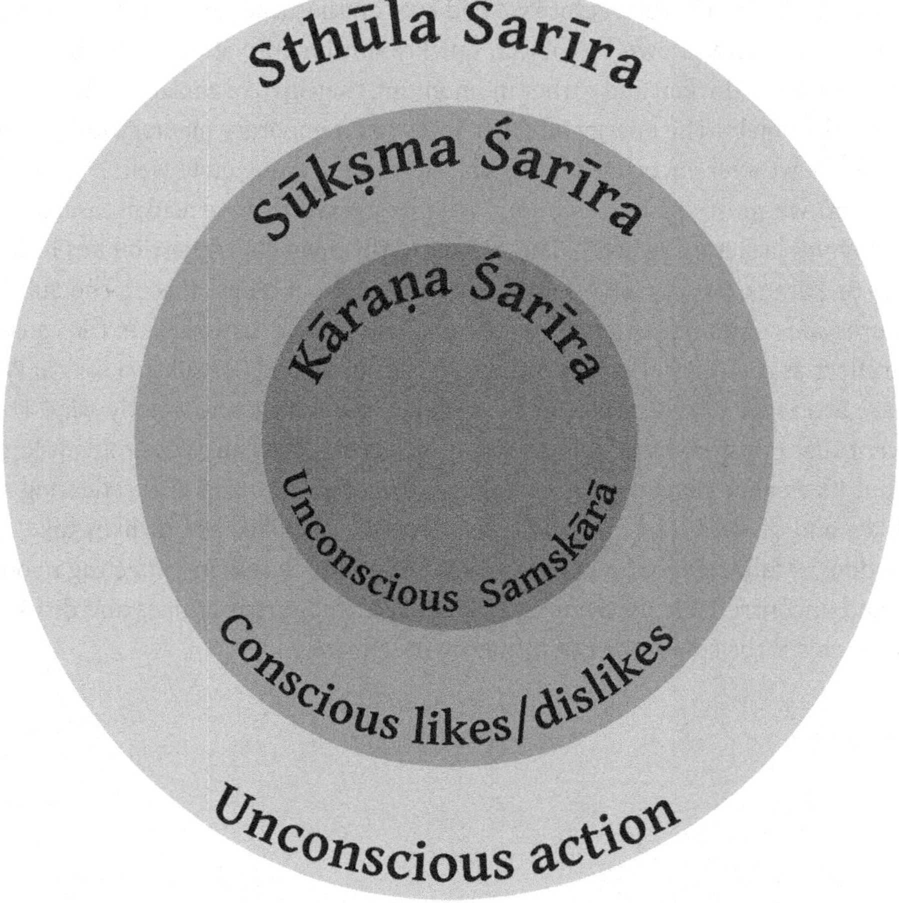

Figure 20. The Śarīras

Discipline is the remedy for lust and all the other vices, which is the purpose of the lifestyle prescribed in sādhanā. A prescribed diet and code of conduct force us to stop expending our prāṇa in chasing sense objects. This is the approach of reverse engineering where we work backwards by bringing awareness to our unconscious behavior, overcome our subconscious vṛttis and eventually erase the unconscious saṃskāras.

Lust is a powerful force when harnessed.

Through discipline, the immense potential of the lust energy is redirected from pravṛtti to nivṛtti, taking us inward and upward into the Śrīcakra.

This kind of discipline that works on redirecting lust energy is known as *brahmācārya*. Although commonly taken as celibacy, the term brahmācārya is much broader in its scope, and implies the cultivation, preservation, and redirection of the primary energy that drives us as embodied beings, which is lust. Within the scope of brahmācārya is the enjoyment of sense pleasures as long as the experience adds to our awareness of our vṛttis and behavior. Ideally, brahmācārya prevents the dispersion of energy into the exhausting business of maintaining the self-image.

If we can understand the workings of lust, we see that all the other poisons are manifestations of its misdirected or chaotic energy (See Figure 21). Lust is the basis for anger, greed, and envy and as we will see below, the resulting delusion is misconstrued as virtue and sin. Unrequited lust is the most common predicament we find ourselves in, since we don't often get what we desire. The natural consequence of thwarted lust is *krodha*, the next poison.

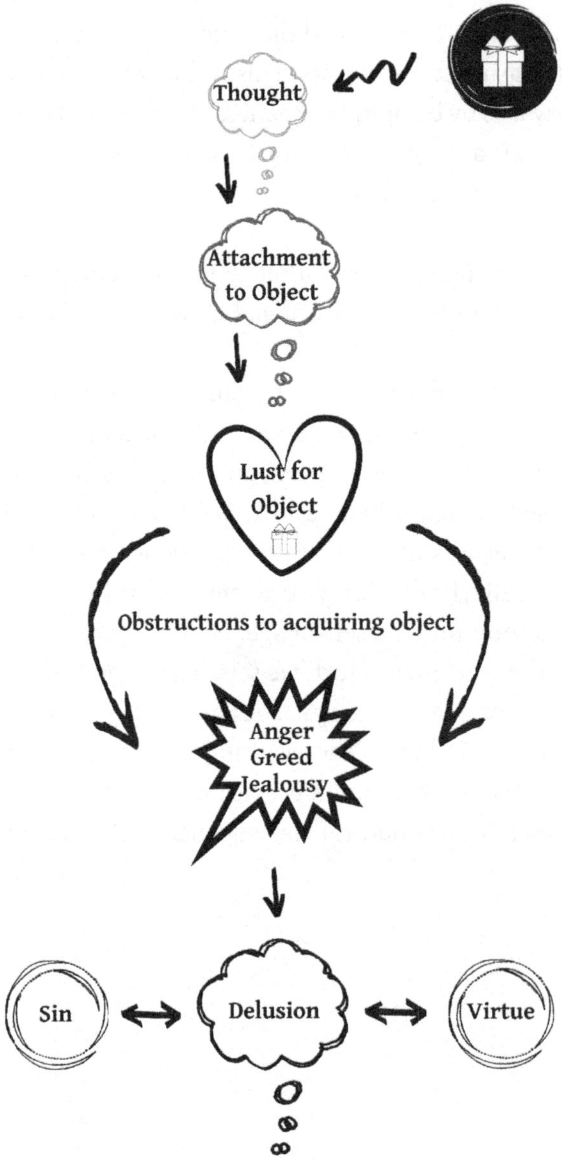

Figure 21. The Shadows of the Aṣṭa Mātṛkās

Māheśvarī

The second of the Mātṛkās, Māheśvarī symbolizes the energy of krodha or anger. When it comes down to it, anger is the result of unfulfilled desire, where an object slips away from our clutches. We don't get what we want, or we get what we don't want, both of which lead to anger.

As we explored above, lust makes us want to own the object of desire. When we acquire the desired object, there is a temporary discharge of the pent-up lust energy and when we don't, it must be released somehow. Anger is an expression of pent-up lust for an object that we can't have or lose after having acquired it. As we will see later, this has to do with the unavailability of all our nāḍīs for the free flow of prāṇa. The lack of discipline, chaotic lifestyles and habitual thought patterns ensure that only certain nāḍīs are consistently available.[130] We lose perspective and with it, the ability to find countless other ways to understand our relationship to desire and sense objects. Anger and its expression in thought, speech and action have deep roots in the chaotic flow of prāṇa in the sūkṣma śarīra. Even when it doesn't result in harm to others, anger is destructive in its expression as depression, panic, anxiety, self-blame, or self-pity.

Like anger, all the other vices are manifestations of misdirected lust energy.

> ***The antidote for anger is patience, cultivation of a deeper understanding of our fundamental desires and patiently unraveling the pathways of our reactions.***

Making a habit of waiting a full minute before responding is one way, where the time is spent in curiously wondering why the energy of anger is arising. Breathing through the contraction before responding allows for space between the stimulus and the reaction, eventually leading to a loosening of the energy and allowing it to flow in new nāḍīs.

130 See Prāṇa Nāḍīs, Cakras and Kuṇḍalinī in Chapter 11.

Kaumārī

Kaumārī represents the energy of covetousness or *lobha*, where we are constantly yearning for more. As with krodha, the origin of lobha or greed is lust leading to wanting more of the desired object. The primary issue here is of wanting to own the object. A glance, a touch, or the sound of a voice of a loved one is enough to stir up desire to own them. As the thought "thickens" through memory and imagination, the desire turns into lobha where we *must* have it. Lobha is the antidote to peace and contentment.

From an energetic standpoint, lobha is the manifestation of being stuck in memory of the past and projection into the future. The object triggers the samskāra of an experience that we have filed away as having been pleasant or resulting in a favorable outcome. The stimulus of the sense object stirs up the unconscious memory and immediately projects to the future – of wanting *more* of that favorable outcome.

The problem with owning the object we desire is that it is bound to lose its freshness after a while. The glance, touch, or sound of the person that was previously enticing can become suffocating or intolerable. Although the sense object has lost its allure, the samskāra is very much alive, and our attention moves on to new objects and experiences to satisfy it. We may feel that it is an entirely new situation when the glance or touch of someone new fulfils the initial itch. Soon, however, lobha kicks in to own more of this new experience... until the newness fades. We keep looking for solutions in sense objects when the problem is much deeper, which is the desire to own and hoard the experience.

> ***If we can enjoy the experience without wanting to own it, lobha gives way to sweetness and the turning of lust to nivṛtti.***

Without expectations or projections, lust becomes a doorway to the joyful exploration of our own dynamic energy. As we will come to see in the upāsanā of the Śrīcakra, *outer* sense objects are experienced in our *inner* landscape. Once we learn this valuable lesson and become inwardly focused on the energy of desire, the need to own sense objects falls away.

The antidote for lobha is to cultivate true generosity of the heart (see Mahimā Siddhi above). When we start to give freely, the energy of greed begins to dissipate and transmute into beauty and harmony.

Vaiṣṇavī

Vaiṣṇavī symbolizes the energy of *moha* or delusion, which arises from a temporary loss of memory as we explored above (see Brāhmī and Figure 21). Memory here refers to the ability to know what to do, or to discern between wholesome and unwholesome action. In the throes of lust, anger, or greed, we forget all the good that has happened in our lives and are inclined to think in extremes of how we *must* have something, how short-changed we are in general, how evil the world, person or situation is, and how we'd like to see them suffer.

Loss of discernment leads to an insanity of sorts, making us behave in immature ways that create more saṃskāras. The most significant way in which we can work on the tendency for moha is through the darśana. The more we study and reflect on the view of the path, the greater the possibility that it will come to our aid when we lose our ability to discern between what is helpful versus what isn't in our upāsanā. Reflection on the darśana gives us progressive insight in our daily activities, which eventually becomes the new lens through which we begin to view the world and our self.

Vārāhī

Vārāhī[131] represents the energy of pride or *mada*, which arises from attachment to our self-image. Our concept of our self is a collection of random bits – memory, acquired notions of right and wrong, slights and challenges, success and achievements, and dreams and hopes, all of which result in a solidified sense of being a unique individual. At its essence, the self-image is the ahaṅkāra.

Being unique brings with it a certain pride, an assurance of being "me" which restricts us from submitting or surrendering to the path, teaching or teacher. Pride makes us take offense at the idea of being small or unimportant, of not knowing, being ignorant or wrong. Mada works hard to preserve the ahaṅkāra and has the shadows of all the Mātṛkās

131 Vārāhī has a very special significance in Śrīvidyā in addition to being one of the Aṣṭa Mātṛkās of the Bhūpura. She is known as the commander-in-chief of Lalitā Devī, and her sādhanā is prescribed at advanced stages when intuition begins to blossom.

in it, which results in the desperate contortion of reality to conform to our self-image. Since the essential mada of the ahaṅkāra is the glue that holds together the shadows of all the Mātṛkās, Vārāhī upāsanā is prescribed at a certain level of practice where the entire structure of the self-image is destroyed in one fell swoop.

> ***One of the greatest gifts of a Guru-śiṣya relationship is the cultivation of humility, which is the antidote to pride.***

When we submit to a Guru, we are forced to give up all the elements that contribute to pride. We come to a place of humility by not taking things personally or as insults, which are obstacles to renouncing the self-image.

Māhendrī

Māhendrī represents the energy of envy or *mātsarya*. As with those of the other Mātṛkās, Māhendrī's shadow is the result of lust. When we are in the throes of desire for an object, the ahaṅkāra prefers to own the anticipated experience. All our malas become activated in the flow of desire, and the māyīya mala that results in the sense of being separate from others kicks into high gear. The desired object must be owned by *me* and nobody else.

Envy arises from feeling as though there are limited resources and if somebody else gets the desired object, it will not be available for us. The desire to own an experience becomes so intense that the thought of someone else having it triggers our inherent sense of lack along with the fear and anxiety around limitation in the supply of blessings. This is the energy of the competitiveness that underscores modern society; we instill insecurity in our children by transmitting the undercurrent of lack where we are unable to revel in the joy, success, or good fortune of others.

The fundamental problem here is that of a stance of poverty. The possibility of objects, experiences, achievements, and good fortune being limited results in wanting to grab all that we can for ourselves. The thought of others having what we can't or don't arises from the poverty mind. The more we envy others, the greater the contraction of poverty. In a vicious cycle, envy and poverty beget each other, standing in the way of abundance.

Magnanimity is the antidote to envy, and this is closely related with generosity of the heart.

Being in a saṅgha of like-minded practitioners is very helpful for the cultivation of magnanimity, where we can see a spectrum of attainment and insight, set aside our feelings of inadequacy, learn from others, and truly appreciate their good fortune.

At its core, Śrīvidyā is the knowledge of Śrī, who is the embodiment of abundance. The more we focus on our own upāsanā without care for the success or failure of others, the greater is the rooting in Śrī.

Bhāvanā on the darśana and the workings of karma loosens the contraction of envy when we realize that each of us is currently reaping what we have sown in the past. When we use this teaching wisely, we refrain from sowing the seeds of envy, which are sure to ripen in the future as a lack of Śrī expressing as inauspiciousness.

Cāmuṇḍā

Cāmuṇḍā is a fierce goddess who appears emaciated and moves among ghosts and ghouls with a corpse as her vehicle. In the Bhūpura, she symbolizes the trap of sin or *pāpa*.

Sin and virtue are made up to maintain the structure of societies, communities, and families. Without a moral compass, our base desires can wreak havoc upon these structures that have been cultivated carefully over centuries of civilization. However, these very concepts that maintain harmony become burdens when they form the lens through which we view the world or ourselves.

In Śrīvidyā, taking our self to be the me-story is the greatest sin.

Śrīcakra upāsanā is the movement from ahaṅkāra to Ahambhāva, where the me-story that obscures the Aham is seen through.[132] When identified with the me-story that is shaped by the concepts of sin and virtue, we never stop to consider that everybody is

132 See Kāmakalā in Chapter 4.

doing their best given their present circumstances and understanding. The me-story is steeped in karma, where our past experience becomes our present behavior that yields future results. As we have seen earlier in this chapter, our unconscious samskārās result in our behavior, which becomes the ground for more samskārās.

In other words, what we classify as sin or virtue is a result of karma. We commit crimes and harm others because we don't know another way. Our samskārās are so dense that they take over the field of action and manifest as wrongdoing to others. As we delve deep into our own process, we come to see the power of our contractions that manifest in the Bhūpura. A deep study of our behavior in the Bhūpura shows us that even when we have cultivated an awareness of our inner landscape, the forces of contraction are so powerful that they result in instantaneous reactions with long-reaching consequences. Long after we have cultivated inner stillness and discernment, the contracted shadows of the Bhūpura Devīs continue to manifest in our lives. What then of those who lack this awareness because they have never had the opportunity to look within?

The idea of sin dissolves when we understand the play of saṃskāras. Evil and good are born of the samskāra seeds that are continually sown from the choices we make, and the speech and actions we employ. When we remain in stark judgment about sin, we create karma with others for their sinful actions. When we judge ourselves for our sins, we remain entrenched in guilt and shame, unable to move past the ghosts that are Cāmuṇḍā's vehicles.

> ***While moral and social norms are needed to function in society, the upāsanā of the Śrīcakra necessarily requires us to internally transcend them if we wish to ascend the āvaraṇas.***

Ideally, the concepts of virtue and sin, like all the other traps of the Bhūpura should become the radii that lead to the center. As long as we remain attached to these concepts, we remain at the periphery, absorbed in avidyā.

Tolerance is the antidote for the contraction of sin, and like the other vices, this is cultivated through the understanding of karma and that we are the product of our circumstances which, in turn, are created by our own choices. When we understand karma, we stop judging others and understand that the greatest sin is to be entrapped in its vicious and unrelenting cycle.

Mahālakṣmī

Mahālakṣmī has numerous symbolic meanings, but here in the Bhūpura, she represents the problematic energy of *puṇya* or virtue. Even though it seems like virtue is beneficial, it does eventually lead to avidyā. In the broad scheme of things, virtue is desirable and must be cultivated through the systematic understanding of our own vices, developing equanimity and higher reasoning along with inner silence.

Virtue here refers to the moral and social conditioning and the rules of civilization. *Puṇya* can only exist as the opposite of pāpa and is always in the context of others. Virtue therefore carries with it the connotations of comparison and judgment and is a vice because it keeps us at the periphery. When it comes to Śrīcakra upāsanā, virtue is a vice because it entraps us in the me-story with its cycles of karma.

However, it is necessary to cultivate virtue through the systematic understanding of the other seven vices. Once it has done its work, virtue is also to be transcended by seeing through its limitation. True virtue bestows the light of the Mātṛkās through the diligent application of vidyā in our day-to-day interactions. If, on the other hand, upāsanā becomes associated with superiority for being on a spiritual path, being compassionate or impartial, or leading a virtuous life, it become the shadow of Mahālakṣmī.

Like sin, understanding karma and the darśana is crucial for transcending the trap of virtue.

> ***Mahālakṣmī's shadow is extremely hardy and difficult to transcend without the guidance of a Guru who can break through the subtle validations of puṇya on the path of upāsanā.***

In studying the outer and middle lines of the Bhūpura, we can deduce how the Siddhis and Mātṛkās are related. If we have cultivated a particular siddhi in the outer line, we won't have to face the shadow of a particular Mātṛkā in the middle line. For example, if we have Aṇimā Siddhi, we have transcended pride, and if we have acquired Mahimā Siddhi, we have overcome greed and envy. If we haven't cultivated the siddhis, we get stuck in the middle line and must work again on all these qualities before moving on to the next line of the Bhūpura, where we meet the Mudrā Devīs.

The Ten Seals

The innermost line of the Bhūpura is guarded by the yoginīs known as the Mudrā Devīs. Mudrā means seal, and these yoginīs direct energy in particular ways. The ten mudrās (appropriately named *daśa* mudrās) are used in ritual worship. These yoginīs also guard over the āvaraṇas of the Śrīcakra. In worship, mudrās formed with hand positions direct and seal energy in particular channels that correspond with an āvaraṇa. Here in the Bhūpura they play a slightly different role, where they make up the transition between the outward orientation that is evident in the first two lines and the internalization that begins in earnest in the Trivṛtta.

Guarding the inner gates of the Bhūpura, the Mudrā Devīs ensure that prāṇa is flowing from the shadow to the light aspects of the Siddhis and Mātṛkās (see Table 9). This line is like a hard stop; even if we carried on with the ritual toward the Bindu, the actualization of realization doesn't occur until the issues of the mundane world are dealt with to a large extent. The magnificent Mudrā Devīs are depicted performing the hand gestures that direct the flow of prāṇa in particular nāḍīs, stimulating the release of corresponding chemicals and hormones and activating the related neural pathways.

The Bhāvanopaniṣad correlates to the Mudrā Devīs with the *ādhāras* (ādhāra = support or foundation), referring to the cakras where Kuṇḍalinī must flow in order to resolve the issues that keep us entrapped in saṃsāra.[133] These are the six cakras (ṣaṭcakra) including the mūlādhāra at the base of the spine, svādhiṣṭāna in the vicinity of the genitals, maṇipura at the navel, anāhatā in the center of the chest, viśuddha at the throat, and ājñā at the center of the forehead. There are three additional cakras including *lambikāgra* at the uvula, kula sahasrāra just below the top of the head, and *akula* sahasrāra at the top of the head. The samaṣṭi ādhāra is the aggregate or sum total of the nine ādhāras, which is the tenth.

133 See The Ṣaṭcakra and the Śrīcakra in Chapter 5.

Table 9. Mudrā Devīs of the Bhūpura

MUDRĀ DEVĪS	MANIFESTATION	BHĀVANĀ
Sarvasankṣobhiṇī (Power to agitate)	Agitation	Equanimity
Sarvavidrāviṇī (Power to drive)	Flight	Steadiness
Sarvākarṣiṇī (Power to attract)	Attraction	Disenchantment with drama
Sarvavaśaṅkarī (Power to subjugate)	Subjugation	Awareness
Sarvonmādinī (Power to intoxicate)	Intoxication	Darśana
Sarvamahāṅkuśā (Power to goad)	Stimulation	Surrender
Sarvakhecarī (Power to roam in space)	Freedom	Witnessing
Sarvabījā (Power over all bījas)	Seed	Grace
Sarvayonī (Power over all yonis)	Source	Grace
Sarvatrikhaṇḍā (Power over the three worlds)	Three Worlds	Grace

We must remember that the association of the Mudrā Devīs with the cakras is not linear. Here at the Bhūpura, the correlation relates to the specific aspects of each cakra that keep us engaged in the periphery that have to do with the flow of prāṇa.[134] Mudrās are external manifestations of internal prāṇic shifts. When we are caught up in sin and virtue, for instance, our prāṇa flows in specific, well-primed nāḍīs conditioned by these concepts. In this instance, prāṇa cannot be forced to flow in other nāḍīs because they aren't available until a shift in perspective occurs. With this, the mudrā seals the energy in the new pathways. What we see here is the harmony of the mind and body that is required to make progress. Our perspective determines the flow of prāṇa, and the mudrās enable continued growth by sealing its new flows.

134 See Prāṇa in Chapter 11.

Another way to understand ādhāra is that it is a necessary shift in perspective that arises through meticulous and correct inquiry in the Bhūpura that is the foundation for the work that is to come in Śrīcakra upāsanā.

Sarvasankṣobhiṇī

She is the all-agitating (*sarva* = all, *sankṣobhaṇa* = agitating) yoginī. Think of the Mudrā Devīs as a group of tough interrogators. They will test you to see if you have indeed worked out your issues in the first two lines of the Bhūpura. They ask difficult questions, pose challenging situations, and observe the flow of prāṇa in your nāḍīs. They bring up circumstances to see if you'll remain on the circumference of saṃsāra or use the opportunity to step onto the radius toward the Bindu. One after another, they polish and hone your *prāṇic* body to keep your focus on the radii. Equanimity is the key to traversing this line, where we notice the temptations of the world with interest but remain disengaged from their drama.

Sarvasankṣobhiṇī agitates the mind, the world, and the cosmos. She creates friction that becomes the energy for the interactions that take place here in the playing field of the Bhūpura. On one hand, agitation creates unrest but on the other, it is the stimulus for growth, evolution, and advances in every field. Without this churning, there is no spiritual path either. She agitates us into finding creative solutions to our limitations through the opening of new nāḍīs; she agitates and disturbs our habitual patterns of thinking and being that are required to traverse this āvaraṇa.

> ***In sādhanā, just when we think we have conquered our habits or mental patterns, she comes along as agitation in the form of interactions, circumstances, relationships, loss, or destruction.***

Often, unrest is a result of churning up old memories and past karma which need to be resolved. When we approach agitation with equanimity and without getting caught up in stories, new ways of thinking and perception become available through the formation of novel neurohormonal pathways. At this point, Sarvasankṣobhiṇī blesses us with her seal that ensures the continued opening of the nāḍīs.

Sarvavidrāviṇī

As the yoginī who places us in flight mode (sarva = all, *vidrāvaṇa* = putting to flight), *Sarvavidrāviṇī* tests us in a different version of agitation – through stress that makes us want to escape. She brings forth the opportunities in daily life where we become so stressed or anxious that it brings forth the cascade of physiological reactions that make us want to flee the situation.

If we can remain steady in these situations by becoming acutely aware of our own internal process, new pathways open, and other choices become available. Her grace enables us to traverse challenging situations in such a way that they become portals to deeper inquiry.

Sarvākarṣiṇī

As the yoginī who attracts all (sarva = all, *ākarṣaṇa* = attracting), *Sarvākarṣiṇī* keeps us fascinated in the drama of the world. We remain so enchanted by our stories that we find it hard to move past them. In fact, we can find our own misery delicious and enticing even when it is painful and perplexing. Just as soon as one problem is solved, another crops up so that our fascination with misery can be satisfied. This juicy entrapment in the stuff of the world is the shadow of Sarvākarṣiṇī.

To rise out of our limitations, we must become disenchanted with their drama and allure. New pathways are created when we examine our problems in a nonjudgmental, curious fashion without entanglement in them.

Sarvavaśaṅkarī

Sarvavaśaṅkarī is the energy of subjugation (sarva = all, *vaśaṅkara* = subjugating). We can see her energy in the subjugating power of Māyā in the macrocosm, and our saṃskāras in the microcosm. Our own stories can take over our being, suppressing our reasoning and clarity where our knowledge and insight become unavailable.

With her grace, our saṃskāra load begins to lessen, and along with the thinning of this veil, we can remain aware during the uprising of our patterns. Through the power of awareness, we create new ways of being with the old stories, where they steadily lose their power and dissipate.

Sarvonmādinī

Sarvonmādinī intoxicates (sarva = all, *mada* = intoxication) and incites passion. She is the power that makes us insane in our longing to own objects and experiences. Like the other Mudrā Devīs, Sarvonmādinī's shadow overpowers our reason, where we can feel like our entire existence depends on acquiring a particular "thing." As we have seen in Figure 21 above, it is this intoxication that drives us into delusion.

The darśana becomes exceedingly important in becoming free of this intoxication. When we understand the basis for our longing, we can stand apart from it and allow its powerful energy to pass through without creating karma and more saṃskāras.

Sarvamahāṅkuśā

The one who goads (sarva = all, mahā = great, *aṅkuśa* = goad), *Sarvamahāṅkuśā* prods us toward limitation or freedom. Turned toward Māyā, she is the power of the outward-turned senses. Turned toward the Bindu, she is the power of the inquiring mind that becomes absorbed in the inward-turned current.

It is her grace that carries us from the circumference into the radius and keeps us moving toward the Bindu.

Sarvakhecarī

Sarvakhecarī is the yoginī who moves freely in space (sarva = all, *kha* = space, *cara* = move/wander). In her shadow aspect, Sarvakhecarī is binding, where we are pinned down by a given thought, feeling, or situation. We are grounded in the muck of existence because we are bound in passing phenomena that are ephemeral. Although subtle and airy, phenomena seem dense and real to us when we are caught up in saṃsāra.

It is only through cultivating witnessing awareness that we come to realize the impermanent and elusive nature of phenomena. Through the grace of this great yoginī, we remain unperturbed amid chaos, where no thought or experience can pin us down. *Khecarī* is an advanced state of practice where one roams about in space in absolute freedom.

Sarvabījā

As the great bīja or seed (sarva = all, bīja = seed), *Sarvabījā* is the seed or root of all of creation. At the macrocosmic level she is the seed of creation, holding within herself the blueprint of all there is and will be. At the individual level she is the seed of our being, our joys and sorrow, our karma, and how, why, and what we do. It is her energy that propels the seeds of our saṃskāras to flower and bear fruit as they do.

It is her grace that burns the saṃskāra seeds to arrive at the great seed of the Source. Being the power of all bīja mantras, she enables the sprouting of novel neurohormonal pathways through their nāda, stretching our capacity beyond our limited minds and blending us into the Bindu.

Sarvayonī

Sarvayonī is the great source (sarva = all, yoni = source or origin) of creation. Yoni refers to the womb or female genital, but in this context, it is the source of all phenomena. From the perspective of the Śrīcakra, Sarvayonī is the source of its entire structure, the Bindu arising, bursting forth and organizing into the various elements. At each level of differentiation, there are immeasurable yonis giving rise to the next level.

On the microcosmic level, our prāṇa is said to pass through innumerable yonis in any given moment. If we can slow down time to an extreme degree, we'd see how thought arises, organizes into one stream, catches another, and passes into a tangent, catches another stream, and becomes yet another tangent, and so on. At the physiologic level, the entire cascade of signaling pathways pass through innumerable yonis, being birthed in gradations and in ever-different chemical and electrical forms.

Sarvayoni's grace bestows the ability to understand the source of the minute movements in our inner landscape. She bestows the power to understand the Śrīcakra. She is thus known as the supreme mudrā, used by devotees everywhere to offer obeisance to Devī.

Sarvatrikhaṇḍā

Ruling over the three parts (sarva = all, *tri* = three, *khaṇḍa* = part), *Sarvatrikhaṇḍā* is the supreme power over the three aspects of reality. The Trikoṇa, which is the primary pramāṇa-prameya-pramatṛ triad is the source of all other triads including icchā-jñāna-kriyā, past-present-future, sattva-rajas-tamas, and the innumerable groupings of the tradition.[135] Sarvatrikhaṇḍā is the energy of these triads that both bind us in Māyā and release us from it.

135 See Chapters 4 and 16.

Sarvatrikhaṇḍa's grace becomes available to us only at the highest level of practice. Here at the Bhūpura, she allows a great insight into our own process that can propel us toward the next āvaraṇa.

Although we have examined the Bhūpura's three lines in a stepwise fashion, this doesn't represent how things may unfold in practice.

> ***Most often, we are faced with the shadows of more than one yoginī, becoming entrapped in their collective energies.***

Both the binding and liberating aspects of these 28 yoginīs can and do manifest together.

Moreover, we must remember that we are examining the Śrīcakra in the saṃhāra krama, with progressive dissolution of the āvaraṇas into the Bindu. Since we continue to live in the world after dissolution in the Bindu, the Bhūpura can also be examined in the opposite direction or the sṛṣṭi krama.

When we return to the sṛṣṭi krama after traversing the āvaraṇas from the Bhūpura to the Bindu, the yoginīs of the Bhūpura express themselves in their liberative aspects, where the Mudrā Devīs represent the free flow of prāṇa without obstructions, the Aṣṭa Mātṛkās are the eight aspects of the liberated mind, and the Siddhis are attainments expressed as physical and subtle powers over phenomena such as the ability to become small, large, light and so on (See Figure 22).[136]

136 See also Chapter 18.

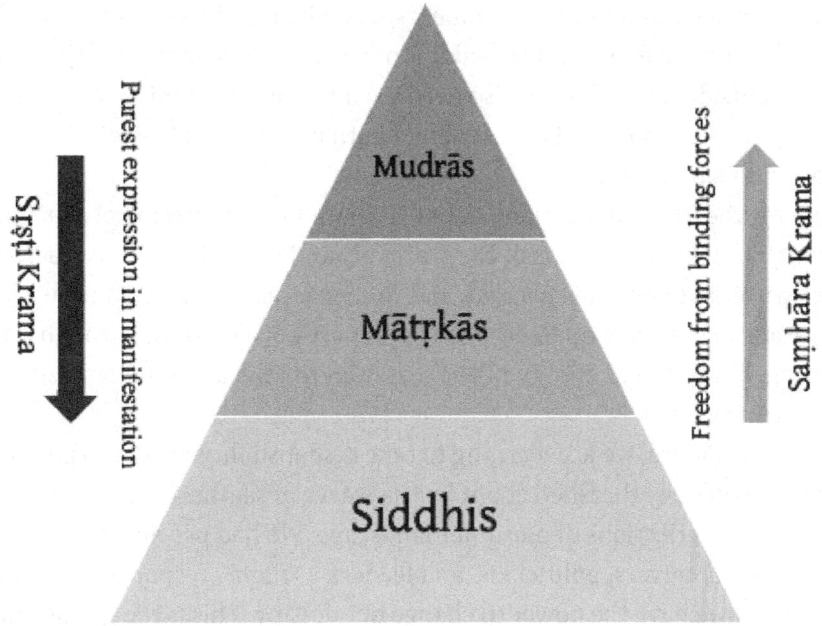

Figure 22. The Bhūpura in the Sṛṣṭi and Saṃhāra Kramas

Cakreśvarī: Tripurā

Ruling over the entire Bhūpura is Tripurā, an emanation of Mahātripurasundarī, who controls the three modes of creation – sṛṣṭi, stithi and saṃhāra or creation, sustenance, and dissolution.

In the saṃhāra krama, Tripurā rules over the incessant creation, sustenance and dissolution of our self-image and the end of its cycle through the grace of the Prakaṭa Yoginīs.

The Prakaṭa Yoginīs point us to the fully manifest world, demonstrating the expression of the Divine in its fully differentiated form. Our interaction with the world becomes the portal for poisons and vices, attainments, and virtues. If there is no outside world, there would be no need or question of siddhis or shadows. It is because of the existence of this manifest outside world that we also need to cultivate the siddhis and the nectar from these poisons. This playing field that is rich in both its potential for poison and nectar is the Trailokyamohana Cakra.

Ruling over the Trailokyamohana Cakra, Tripurā holds the reins of our inner landscape through the manifestations of the world around us as the 28 Prakaṭa Yoginīs. We invoke her with the mantra *am ām sauḥ* and the Sarvasankṣobhiṇī mudrā with the bīja, *drāṃ*. Sarvasankṣobhiṇī, as we saw earlier, is the energy of agitation. Through this mudrā, we invoke the fundamental energy of the agitation to take us in the opposite direction toward the next āvaraṇa.

Here, at the Bhūpura, we are learning to take responsibility for our experience. Until now, we were helplessly thrashed about by the waves of saṃsāra, unable to see that our circumstances are reflections of our inner landscape. We had previously held the world, our parents and caregivers, politicians, and leaders – "them" responsible for our issues. Now, we see that we have the power to change our destiny. This is the gift of Tripurā, the Cakreśvarī of the Bhūpura.

Having paid homage to this āvaraṇa by working tirelessly through the practicalities of this playing field, we are granted access to the next level of the Śrīcakra, the Trivṛtta.

Chapter 8

Trivṛtta

The Trivṛtta (tri = three, *vṛtta* = plane) is made up of three concentric circles (See Figure 23), which are placed in different locations within the Śrīcakra depending on the lineage. They represent various groupings that can depend on the interpretation of the lineage, including the fire, moon, and sun, the three guṇas, the three avasthās, the three puruṣārthas (dharma, artha and kāma) or the groups of the Sanskrit alphabets. The Trivṛtta is not ritually invoked in all sampradāyas and is assumed to be the important transition between the āvaraṇas. Here, we will examine the Trivṛtta from the standpoint of the puruṣārthas and vāc.

Puruṣārthas

Puruṣārtha means a goal of human existence that is universal. Whoever we are and wherever we come from, and whether we are on the spiritual path or not, the puruṣārthas apply to us. All our dreams and aspirations can be classified into one of four puruṣārthas: dharma, artha, kāma and *mokṣa*.

We have previously examined dharma as a function of harmony.[137] On an individual level, dharma is the aspiration for a meaningful life that drives us to live and thrive. Biologically speaking, dharma is about leaving a legacy or to feel like our life was worth something. The need for a meaningful life is so significant that the possibility that our life means nothing can lead to depression and despair. Population studies have shown that a sense of purpose is strongly associated with a longer lifespan. We *need* a sense of purpose, which is highly individual and dependent on our samskārās and upbringing. When we reach the end of our life, dharma is the puruṣārtha that gives us the fulfilment for having lived a meaningful life or a general sense of dissatisfaction if we have regrets.

Dharma innately contains within it the need to live and let live, without impinging on others' freedom or causing suffering for ourselves or others. When we align with dharma,

137 See The Structure of the Śrīcakra in Chapter 4.

the natural order of harmony, our aspiration of purpose can be fulfilled without creating internal or external conflict. Dharma is also highly individual, where we must first identify and then pursue what is true for our own inclinations that add to the harmony of the larger unit (family, community, country, and world). For example, if your natural inclination is to be a concert pianist but you end up training to be a busy electrician, thoughts of "what if" will continue to afflict you. Similarly, if you are naturally inclined toward being a husband and father but go off to the caves because your spiritual ideal renounced the world, the lifestyle of a monk will become suffocating. Both examples highlight the importance of *svadharma* (dharma pertaining to the self) compared to *paradharma* (dharma pertaining to others).

When misaligned with our natural inclination, a deep internal rift is birthed with associated psychological, emotional, mental, and physical ailments. Dharma extinguishes itself when it is fulfilled without creating conflict, at which point we move from the rim to the radius. However, this requires a high level of viveka and vairāgya, since our clouded buddhi can misinterpret this universal drive to mean getting ahead or fulfilling desires at all costs.

The second puruṣārtha is artha, which is the universal aspiration to have our needs meet. The thing about artha is that there tends to be a fine line between needs and wants or eṣaṇas.[138] As a puruṣārtha, the need for resources is universal and most fulfilling when aligned with our dharma.

138 See The Eṣaṇas in Chapter 5.

The third puruṣārtha is kāma, which is the need to fulfill sense pleasures with art, music, romantic relationships, sexual experiences, and so on. Since our senses are naturally turned outward and impelled by the centrifugal force of Vāmā, kāma takes us in ever-expanding circles toward the periphery. Ideally, kāma is enjoyed and used in sādhanā where its energy becomes the fuel for our journey to the Bindu.

Usually, a fourth puruṣārtha is added to this list, which is mokṣa or liberation from saṃsāra. However, to even arrive at a point where we can focus on mokṣa, the first three puruṣārthas must be fulfilled to a certain degree. Since mokṣa requires a turning back of attention upon itself, we need to feel sated that our life has been at least somewhat meaningful, we have been adequately nourished with resources, and have enjoyed sense objects. Bhukti is the sense of fulfilment of the puruṣārthas, which naturally turns the mind inward toward mokṣa.[139] As long as the puruṣārthas are unfulfilled, we remain caught up in the periphery.

139 See The Path of Bhukti and Mukti, Chapter 6.

The inclusion of the first three in the Trivṛtta is of great significance. They make up the boundary between the playing field of the Bhūpura where they can be fulfilled, and the subtler āvaraṇas that take us toward the center.

Vāc in the Trivṛtta

The Trivṛtta contains the Sanskrit phonemes in its three concentric circles, representing vāc at the intermediate level of manifestation. As we saw in Chapter 6, the Bhūpura and the Trivṛtta are at the vaikharī level. Yet, there is a subtle difference between them, represented by the placement of the phonemes in the Trivṛtta between the sthūla manifestation at the Bhūpura and the sūkṣma that begins at the Śodaṣadalapadma (see Figure 23).

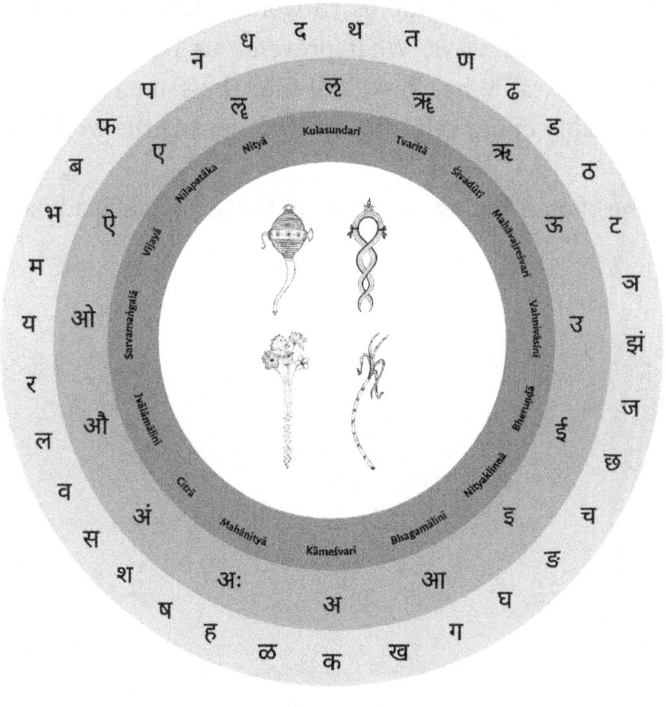

Figure 23. Trivṛtta

The consonants are placed in the outermost circle and the vowels in the middle circle, representing the subtle planes of the tattvas. The Nityā Devīs guard the innermost circle as the unfolding of the vowels in time and space. As we saw earlier, the consonants are inert and activated by the piercing of the vowels. The vowels are associated with the Nityā Devīs who symbolize the phases of the moon that represent the limitation of the timeless and spaceless Divine in time and space.[140] In the unfolding and resorption of the vowels in time and space, the tattvas represented by the consonants evolve and change in the cycles symbolized by the moon phases.

140 See Nityā Devīs in Chapter 16.

The Trivṛtta is the transition between the gross or fully manifest plane of the Bhūpura and the subtle plane that begins in the Śodaṣadalapadma. At this level we gradually become aware of our internal landscape, the vāc that shapes it and its projection onto the Bhūpura. Self-awareness here is one of curiosity and empowerment that the world is but a projection of our internal vāc.

The Trivṛtta makes it possible for us to wonder why we are driven to interact with the world in particular ways. What prevents us from achieving the nectar of the Trailokyamohana cakra? Why do we fall into the same circumstances again and again? What is the quality of our self-talk? Are we viewing the world as a threat? Or an opportunity?

Through this line of questioning, we arrive at the Śodaṣadalapadma.

Chapter 9

Śodaṣadalapadma

पृथिव्यप्तेजोवाय्वाकाशश्रोत्रत्वक्चक्षुर्जिह्वाघ्राणवाक्पाणिपादपायूपस्थ
मनोविकाराः कामाकर्षिण्यादि षोडष शक्तयः ॥ १३ ॥

Pṛthvaptejo-vāyvākāśa-śrotra-tvak-cakṣur-jihvā-ghrāṇavāk-pāṇipāda-
pāyūpasthāni-manovikārāh kāmākarṣiṇyādi-ṣoḍaśa śaktyaḥ || 13 ||

"The sixteen śaktis including Kāmākarṣiṇī are the five great elements (earth, water, fire, air and space), the five sense organs (ears, skin, eyes, tongue and nose), the five organs of action (tongue for speech, hands for grasping, legs for walking, anus for excretion, and genitals for procreation)."
~ Bhāvanopaniṣad, verse 13.

The Bhūpura is the demonstration of the eternal unlimited Divine becoming limited by putting on the armor-like kañcukas. Creation inherently involves limitation which is evident in both the macrocosmic and microcosmic spheres. Say you want to create something such as a piece of art. At this point, all possibilities exist on the blank canvas. However, with every stroke of the brush, you eliminate all *other* possibilities except the one emerging in your creative thought. A similar process occurs at the macrocosmic level.

The Kañcukas and the Malas

Devī's descent into creation involves the donning of a sequence of armors through which her true nature is effectively veiled. These armors are known as kañcukas, which she puts on by the power of her own absolute freedom or svātantrya śakti. The first three of the five kañcukas are contractions of tattvas 3-5, which are icchā, jñāna and kriyā śakti (see Figure 24). Icchā becomes limited as rāga, jñāna as vidyā, and kriyā as kalā.

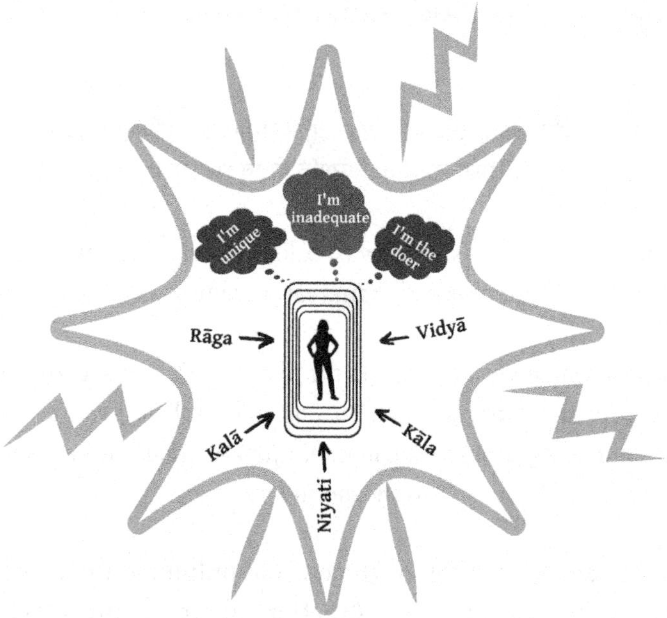

Figure 24. The Kañcukas and Malas

While Devī's icchā, jñāna and kriyā are unconditioned, rāga, vidyā and kalā are conditioned by samskārās. The conditioning of samskārās applies to both the macrocosm and the microcosm. For example, the solar system is conditioned and shaped by the history of the universe; similarly, a chemical or electrical reaction is the result of countless other upstream ones.

Our past experiences become the source of kañcukas as well, creating an inherent sense of lack in the process. If you take something very large and stuff it into a very tight space, it's bound to create a sense of lack. The general feeling would be, "I feel small and limited when I am much bigger and greater than this." This inherent sense of lack is the very nature of creation. In becoming you and me, the Divine willingly becomes associated with our limited identities and stories. And yet, we have a sneaking suspicion that something is missing. No matter what we do to resolve this inherent sense of lack, it never goes away, and persists no matter how successful or happy we are or how much we have attained by way of fame and fortune. This universal sense of lack is known as āṇava mala.

Mala means impurity. The root of āṇava is *aṇu*, which means tiny particle. The āṇava mala is the feeling of smallness which arises from the me-story that is created in time and space. It starts at birth and ends with death with a large collection of experiences in between, each adding to the me-story and yet leaving us with the sense that there must be more to life than the string of stories. The sense of me creates a separation from others, which is known as the *māyīya* mala. To resolve the inherent sense of lack from the āṇava mala, we collect more experiences and since they differ from everyone else's, we feel unique and separate. To overcome the fundamental sense of lack, we compare ourselves with others and try to get ahead by trying to own our experience in time (kāla) and space (kalā). As soon as we own an experience, a sense of volition sets in – this is the *kārma* mala.

Rāga means passion and it is a contraction of icchā; it is closely related to all three malas. Passion here refers to strong likes and dislikes, which make us feel unique and different from everyone else. Feeling small and limited, and owning my actions and consequences makes me the hero of *my* story centered around *my* attractions and aversions.

My passions drive me toward resolving the inherent sense of lack arising from the āṇava mala. Since rāga limits me to my story, my knowledge (vidyā) and sphere of action (kalā) will also be limited, arising from what I've learned in the past and how I would like to influence my future. In other words, my saṃskāras bind me in linear time, which is the next kañcuka (kāla).

Being bound in time and space, feeling inadequate, unique, and taking myself to be the doer subjects me to the cause-and-effect rule of karma, which is the fifth kañcuka (niyati). If the outcome of my action is what I had desired, I'm happy and this results in more attractions. If not, it creates aversion through disappointment. Either way, more saṃskāras are collected, becoming seeds for future actions. This is the cycle of karma (see Figure 25).

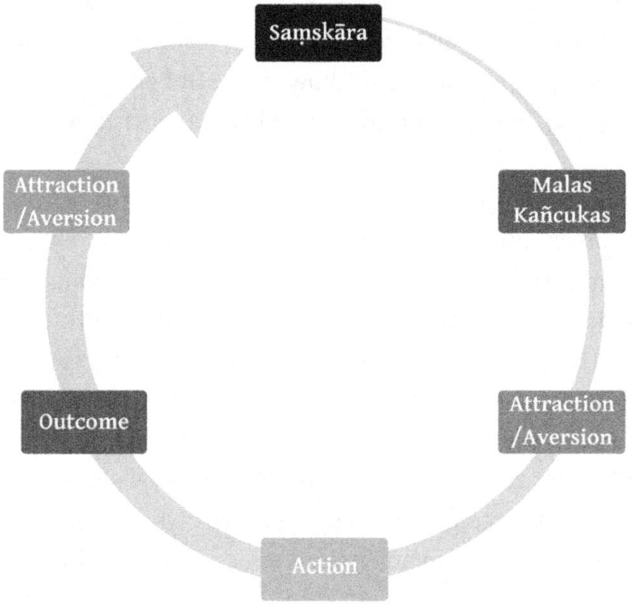

Figure 25. The Cycle of Karma

Limitation is the very nature of existence, and it is in this mode that we operate in the world, which is at the Bhūpura.

> ***My ordinary way of being is that of my story of me interacting with my story of you, where neither is the real story.***

Although our attractions and aversions propel us to act in particular ways, the outcome is never guaranteed. We hardly pause to consider why we do what we do; our buddhi is clouded by our saṃskāras, resulting in lack of clarity. The way we see the world through this clouded lens of the buddhi is what determines how we will interact with the world. Our saṃskāras arise from our attractions and aversions and keep us bound in saṃsāra through the cycles of karma.[141]

141 See 'Kamalatmika' in K. Chinnaiyan, *Shakti Rising* (Nonduality Press, 2017).

Since the Bhūpura is where we create karma, we can get stuck there if we don't ask the right questions. When our inquiry goes deeper and we wonder what it is that makes us interact the way we do, we move into the next āvaraṇa, the Śodaṣadalapadma.

The Inquiry

The Śodaṣadalapadma (*śodaṣa* = sixteen, *dala* = petal, *padma* = lotus) is known as the *Sarvāśāparipūraka* (sarva = all, *āśā* = desire, *paripūraka* = fulfilling) cakra. The yoginīs of this āvaraṇa have names ending with ākarṣiṇī, which means she who attracts.

Recall that all the yoginīs of the Śrīcakra have opposing forces – they can either entrap us in saṃsāra or liberate us from it. Each yoginī of the sixteen petals (see Figure 26) is an ākarṣiṇī or attractor because she can either ensnare us in saṃskāras or liberate us from them. Aversion is implied in attraction, since not liking or wanting something is always in reference to something else that we want or desire.

When we refer to this āvaraṇa as the one that fulfils all desires (Sarvāśāparipūraka cakrā), it doesn't mean that all our desires will be granted. The yoginīs of this āvaraṇa are secret (*Gupta*), since they show us that the real secret of fulfilling all our wishes and attain enduring contentment is to tap into the *energy* of desire.

The Gupta Yoginīs are worshiped in an anti-clockwise direction beginning at the eastern gate with *Kāmākarṣiṇī* (see Table 10).

Figure 26. Śodaṣadalapadma with Gupta Yoginī

Table 10. Yoginīs of the Śodaṣadalapadma

Yoginī	Attraction	Nityā Devī	Alphabet	Bhāvanā
Kāmākarṣiṇī	Desire	Kāmeśvarī	a	Ownership
Buddhyākarṣiṇī	Intellect	Bhagamālinī	ā	Knowledge
Ahaṅkārākarṣiṇī	Ego	Nityaklinnā	i	Self/me-story
Śabdākarṣiṇī	Sound	Bheruṇḍā	ī	Sound
Sparśākarṣiṇī	Touch	Vahnivāsinī	u	Touch
Rūpākarṣiṇī	Form	Mahāvajresvarī	ū	Form
Rasākarṣiṇī	Taste	Śivadūtī	ṛ	Taste
Gandhākarṣiṇī	Smell	Tvaritā	ṝ	Smell
Cittākarṣiṇī	Mind	Kulasundarī	ḷ	Sense registration
Dhairyākarṣiṇī	Courage	Nityā	ī	Resilience
Smṛtyākarṣiṇī	Memory	Nīlapatāka	e	Memory
Nāmākarṣiṇī	Name	Vijayā	ai	Labeling
Bījākarṣiṇī	Seed	Sarvamaṅgalā	o	Decluttering
Ātmākarṣiṇī	Soul	Jvālāmālinī	au	Attention
Amṛtākarṣiṇī	Immortality	Citrā	am	Impermanence
Śarīrākarṣiṇī	Body	Mahānityā	ah	Body

Gupta Yoginī

The Nityā Devīs take the position of the Gupta Yoginīs here at the Śodaṣadalapadma (see Figure 27). While at the Trikoṇa, the Nityās manifest in their complete and unique splendorous forms, here they are situated as the group of ākarṣiṇīs.

The Gupta Yoginī is regal in her posture, bearing sword, shield, bow and arrow in her four hands. With the bow and arrow in her upper hands, she ensures the outward flow of the senses in the continuous arising of attraction and aversion to sense objects. Her sword cuts through the cycles of karma created through the senses and her shield grants the wisdom of discernment.

Figure 27. Gupta Yoginī

Kāmākarṣiṇī

Kāma is wanting or longing, and Kāmākarṣiṇī as the allure of desire is the first Gupta Yoginī because yearning is the primordial attractor. From an understanding of Māyā with the kañcukas and malas, we can deduce that desire is inbuilt in creation. All living creatures have the fundamental desire to survive and reproduce and Kāma arises as the biological instinct to propagate the species. It is a powerful force and when cultivated appropriately (see Brāhmī in the Bhūpura), it becomes the fuel for sādhanā and to traverse the higher āvaraṇas.

The energy of lust is the creative fuel for all our endeavors, advancement in all fields, evolution, learning and growth – it is the driving force of eṣaṇas. This creative desire is necessary and on an individual level, it turns out to be a problem when it manifests as rāga or passion. Rāga, as we have seen above, limits knowledge and action because we expect a specific outcome. Lust, which we explored in the Bhūpura, is a problem when it is associated with a desire to own an experience. Unbridled lust that focuses on owning a person or experience creates karma and keeps us bound in saṃsāra.

> ***When misdirected towards owning the experience rather than enjoying it, the delicious, potent, and creative energy of kāma binds us in Māyā.***

Kāmākarṣiṇī's grace enables the right cultivation of kāma. Through this grace we find the resources and ability to fulfill our eṣaṇas and turn inward. In her liberative aspect, Kāmākarṣiṇī makes it possible for us to be absorbed in the creative energy without concern about the outcome.

Bhāvanā on Kāmākarṣiṇī

Kāma or desire is the very juice of life. Kāma becomes a trap and a problem when we confuse it with ownership and needing to attain very specific outcomes.

Learn to feel into the pure energy of desire without imagining how it can be fulfilled. Focus on how the desire feels now, relinquishing thoughts about how you will feel in the future when it is satisfied.

Consider a simple desire, such as that for coffee or chocolate. Typically, the desire leads to an automatic action such as fixing a cup of coffee or reaching for a piece of chocolate. The powerful energy of desire remains unexplored.

Pause. Feel into the *feeling* of wanting. Let go of the object of desire (coffee or chocolate). Slow down your breath and drop into your body. Allow the delicious feeling of desire to wash over you. Allow the feeling to grow. Realize that the satisfaction of desire is already within you, hidden in the energy of desire. Opening to the energy of desire is the secret worship of Kāmākarṣiṇī.

Buddhyākarṣiṇī

Buddhyākarṣiṇī is the attraction of the intellect. On the spiritual journey, we have many mystical experiences and insights. Buddhyākarṣiṇī facilitates attachment to such experiences.

When we become attached to our insights and to our own intellectual abilities, we remain in the transactional world and cannot traverse the nivṛtti mārga.

> ***The experiences and insights become portals of lokeṣaṇā, where they validate the ego and keep us in the realm of Māyā.***

Like all phenomena, experiences and insights are impermanent and even when they are profound or spectacular when they occur, they become dormant memories if they don't goad us deeper on our path.

Two types of knowledge are required on this path – *baudha* jñāna and *pauruṣa* jñāna. Baudha jñāna refers to intellectual knowledge acquired through the study of texts, discussions, and oral transmission. Pauruṣa jñāna is experiential knowledge that is acquired through the steady application of what is learned through study. Without relentless application of the knowledge in moment-to-moment practice, we can become burdened by intellectual knowledge, which ends up being the most difficult and hardy veil to pierce because of its great allure to the āṇava mala.

Knowing *about* something is not the same as embodying it. If you go to law school, you don't become the law. Your relationship with law remains transactional, where you know *about* it. On the spiritual path, pauruṣa jñāna is not knowledge *about* the Divine but to know yourself *as* the Divine. This is known as Self-knowledge. The transactional knowledge of baudha jñāna is the allure symbolized by Buddhyākarṣiṇī.

Humility is the antidote to Buddhyākarṣiṇī's Māyā, where we approach this vidyā and the teacher with the willingness to leave behind everything we know. Surrender is the secret to her grace. When we surrender to the teaching, we can be molded and the kañcukas can be loosened.

Ahaṅkārākarṣiṇī

The attraction of the ego, *Ahaṅkārākarṣiṇī* is the allure of the me-story, which is juicy and endlessly interesting. As far as Ahaṅkārākarṣiṇī is concerned, the storyline is unimportant. Whether we take ourselves to be good, bad, generous, caring, cruel or sweet is quite irrelevant. When it comes down to it, it is merely the *content* of the me-story that differs among the seven plus billion of us who share this planet. We are all enchanted with ourselves. Even self-loathing comes from this enchantment with the me-story and being totally identified with it.

Through Ahaṅkārākarṣiṇī's grace, we understand that what we think we are is a misplacement of identity. The Ahaṅkāra tattva lies in the realm of Prakṛti and is an object of the Puruṣa or Self. Yet, it takes other objects in the sphere of Prakṛti and makes them objects of itself.

> ***Essentially, the me-story is the predicament of an object pretending to be the subject (see Figure 28).***

The allure of the world of objects (Prakṛti) fuels the ahaṅkāra, which is the Māyā of Ahaṅkārākarṣiṇī. She binds us in this misidentification of self and influences all the other ākarṣiṇīs of this āvaraṇa.

PURUṢA (THE INDIVIDUAL I)

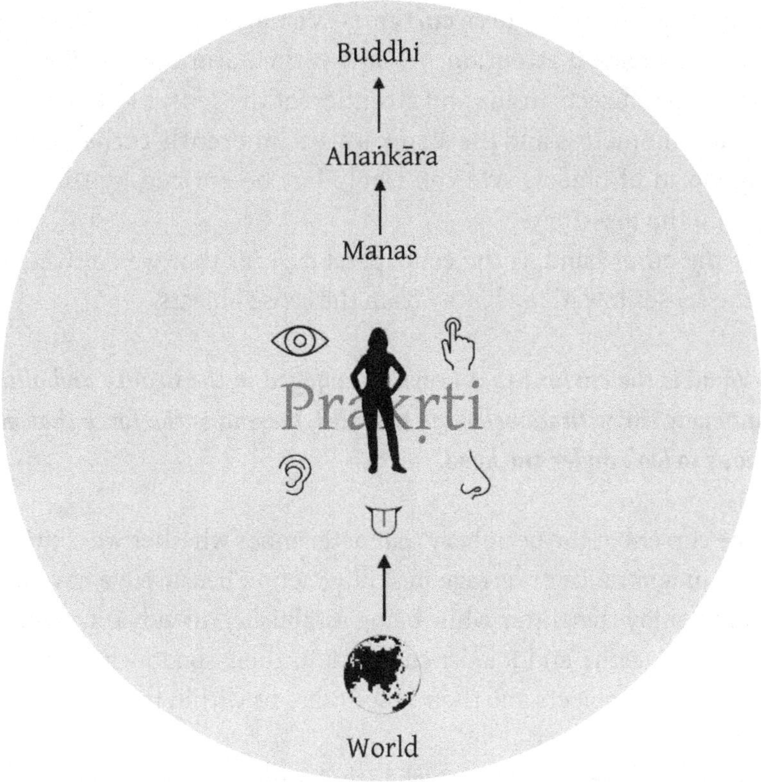

Figure 28. Puruṣa and Prakṛti

The Sense Ākarṣiṇīs

Sound, texture, form, flavor, and smell make up the five tanmātras, the subtle elements that make it possible for the sense organs to experience the external world. The tanmātras enable the ear to hear, skin to feel, eyes to see, tongue to taste and nose to smell.

The ākarṣiṇīs corresponding with the tanmātras turn our senses outward into the world of objects, without which they would hold no allure for us and the ahaṅkāra would not be able to keep up the ongoing weaving of the me-story.

Recall the discussion on the three currents – Vāmā, Jyeṣṭhā and Raudrī, that determine the flow of prāṇa and attention.[142] Vāmā is the naturally dominant centrifugal force of creation that directs prāṇa and attention of the senses to the external world. The sense organs, tanmātras and the ahaṅkāra are inherently turned toward the rich and engaging world of objects. We can't help but be enticed by them and borrow them to make up the me-story!

142 See Mantra Sādhana in Chapter 6.

Jyeṣṭhā, on the other hand, is the centripetal current that we cultivate in upāsanā, which turns the senses inward and away from the sense objects.

While Vāmā is the current that keeps us engaged in the beauty and allure of the shiny new car with its bells and whistles, Jyeṣṭhā is the force that makes us curious to look under the hood.

Raudrī is the current at the periphery that determines whether we continue to create waves of karma in ignorance or engage in skillful action because we have looked under the hood and can enjoy the glitter while being established in vidyā. The sense ākarṣiṇīs embody the Vāmā, Jyeṣṭhā and Raudrī currents; in their shadow aspect, they keep us engaged in the world of objects and their grace takes us within to discover the workings of the tanmātras.

Śabdākarṣiṇī is the allure of sound, which includes not only the external world but also of the bits and fragments that arise as thought, feeling and memory, the constant chatter of self-talk, self-evaluation and self-judgment, the snippets of dreams as well as the voice of reason or intuition.

Sound is transmitted in the mahābhūta of space and registered by the ear, enticed by Śabdākarṣiṇī.

The allure of the sound carried by the world of objects is so great that it obscures the inherent inner silence of the mind and the soft voice of reason or intuition. The allure of sound is why it is hard for us to meditate in noisy environments. It is also the allure of Śabdākarṣiṇī that keeps us engaged in thought, which most often occurs as subtle sound in the form of a monologue.

Sparśākarṣiṇī is the attraction of touch. Of all the senses, touch is a fundamental need in mammals. From the grooming activities in apes and monkeys to cuddling with a lover or child in humans, the tanmātra of *sparśa* connects us intimately to others. In primates, social touch establishes hierarchy, access to mates and food, and provides comfort in an uncertain world. Babies thrive on touch and even well-fed and otherwise cared-for infants can wither without it or have physical and psychological ailments as adults. We bond through touch, which is the most sensual of the tanmātras, enticing us through texture and temperature. Sparśa is transmitted in the mahābhūta of air and registered through the skin as texture, temperature, pressure, and pain.

Of all the senses, sparśa is unique in that when we touch ourselves, the sensations of both touching and being touched are pleasurable. Sparśa is deeply associated with emotions and influences the way we perceive the world. Touch that is comforting or safe shapes us toward seeing the world as being friendly and non-threatening, whereas unwanted touch traumatizes us. Sparśākarṣiṇī keeps us bound in Māyā through her allure of touch, where it becomes an integral part of the me-story.

Rūpākarṣiṇī is the attraction of form, which tends to be the dominant sense for most of us who associate beauty with form, be it in the colors of a sunset or the face of the beloved. Rūpākarṣiṇī is the enticement of form, which is transmitted through the mahābhūta of fire and registered by the eyes as shapes and colors. Vision is such an important aspect of who we take ourselves to be that it becomes the portal for our memories, thoughts, and emotions. Memories often exist as images which become an essential aspect of our identity. Our self-image is often associated with how we look in mirrors or photographs.

> ***Form is so predominant in our psyche that we use this tanmātra to create images of God in our own likeness.***

Rūpa ensnares us in the judgments we make about skin color or racial characteristics that are purely functional and biological. This tanmātra has entrapped us in ideals of beauty and form to enable genocide, world wars, slavery, and discrimination. Even when we don't subscribe to any of these views, Rūpākarṣiṇī's presence becomes evident every time we judge something to be beautiful or ugly.

Rasākarṣiṇī is the allure of taste that is transmitted through the mahābhūta of water and registered in the tongue. We can see her in action in our slavery to the tongue and the taste buds. Rasa or taste drives culture and is an exceedingly hardy samskāra. Most diseases are a result of this samskāra, especially in modern societies. The food industry capitalizes on this samskāra, understanding that our addiction to rasa supersedes our self-control. Very often, we quit spiritual paths whose diets don't agree with our taste buds. When it comes to taste, we find innumerable ways to justify our choices – intolerance, culture, habit, lack of self-control, and so on.

The human experience revolves so much around the tanmātra of taste that we celebrate and mourn with food and drink. It is because of this nearly impossible-to-break addiction to the tongue that most spiritual paths have a prescription of diet and fasting. Until this addiction is overcome, it is impossible to make big strides on the inner journey.

Gandhākarṣiṇī is the attraction of smell, which is the most primitive of the senses. It is carried by the mahābhūta of earth and registered in the nose. *Gandha* or smell has the power to evoke even subconscious memories associated with specific emotions and if we can tap into this, we can inhabit the psyche of a particular age. For example, the smell of rain can instantly bring about a sense of lightness and happiness, and the memories of dancing in the rain as in childhood. For a moment, we become that child internally, with the thoughts and feelings that occupied our mind at that age.

Gandha is closely associated with rasa or taste, adding to our sensory experience of food. Like rasa, it entices us in saṃsāra, making up the experiences that become our identity.

The sense ākarṣiṇīs show us that the tanmātra is pure and unconditioned on its own with no ability to associate with the objects of the world. The association of the sense with the objects arises from our conditioning. The many impressions we form about the senses such as good or bad sound, form, touch, taste, or smell are a matter of preference or previous experience of pleasure or pain.

When we work with sense ākarṣiṇīs through bhāvanā, we can learn to dissociate the object from the tanmātra. For example, what is it like to have a slice of pizza in front of you and not eat it? Can you appreciate its form and smell without grasping? Can you differentiate between the memory of the taste that impels you to bite into it and the freshness of this moment where it is just a sense object?

Cittākarṣiṇī

Citta here is the mind, the field in which the sense organs are registered and recalled. It's not enough to have sense organs or the sense perceptions; they must be registered somewhere to be functional. For example, we can have eyes (organ) but be blind (lack of sight perception), but even with eyes and sight, we must be able to make sense of what we see. The eyes register a form by the photoreceptors and the signal is sent to the brain, where the image is created. However, the citta is where we make *sense* of the image. The citta gives meaning to sense perception, where they become absorbed as being desirable, undesirable, or irrelevant.

Cittākarṣiṇī is the allure of the citta, which holds us captive so that entirely innocent and neutral sense perceptions become the ground for our attractions and aversions, spilling out into the world through our behavior. Remnants of our past collect in the citta as samskārās, clouding and obscuring the buddhi and influencing the way we perceive incoming new sensory inputs, which in turn drives our conduct. In her shadow aspect, Cittākarṣiṇī traps us in this cycle of unconscious samskārās driving our jñānendriyas and karmendriyas.

On the other hand, Cittākarṣiṇī is a portal to freedom if we can learn to stand apart from the sense registrations where they can be enjoyed fully without becoming the motivations for continued avidyā.

Dhairyākarṣiṇī

Dhairya is courage, which is inherent in living. It takes courage to leave the comfort of the womb and the familiarity of breathing through the placenta to take the first breath. It takes courage to roll over, explore the world around us, and to put ourselves into increasingly risky situations that life naturally calls for. The fact that we go to sleep at night without knowing if we will wake up in the morning is an act of courage. It takes courage to leave the house or turn on a stove, and to engage with life on a moment-to-moment basis.

Dhairyākarṣiṇī in her shadow aspect manifests on a spectrum with anxiety and panic with ordinary situations on one end, and brash and obnoxious behavior on the other. Across the spectrum, lacking or misinterpreting courage is the problem.

Lack of resilience, where minor daily events throw us out of balance, arises as a shadow of all the ākarṣiṇīs. We have a highly contracted and narrow definition of how things should be, and when they don't fit into this tight sphere, we have a physio-psychological response. Our stress level remains on high alert, poised to release hormones and chemicals to avert potential threats.

On the other hand, brash or rebellious behavior that looks brave on the surface isn't necessarily a reflection of inner courage. When rebellious behavior arises from the shadows of the Aṣṭa Mātṛkās in the Bhūpura, it reflects Dhairyākarṣiṇī in her Māyā aspect. In this situation, our reactions are in response to an externally imposed standard, and in the brashness, we seek validation and maintenance of a self-image. When Dhairyākarṣiṇī bestows her light, we become naturally courageous from being aligned with what is, requiring no validation or upkeep of a self-image.

Smṛtyākarṣiṇī

Smṛti is memory, which refers not only to our conscious recollections but also to the subconscious, wordless samskārās that drive our moment-to-moment behavior. *Smṛtyākarṣiṇī* is the attraction to memory that's largely automatic and can't be helped. In many ways, our current life is a product of our memories. We design our lives and our minds to be congruent with what we have filed away as good and bad memories, steadfastly avoiding situations that may recreate the latter and actively searching for ways to reinvent the former.

We are so excessively attached to our memories that long after an event, we continue to harbor grudges and longings in equal measure. Memory is so sticky that the impression formed at the first contact with someone or something becomes the basis for how we continue to interact with them.

Smṛtyākarṣiṇī influences our behavior based on memory, where we are unable to show up in innocence and guilelessness in our daily interactions.

Memory is required to create and maintain the self-image. It impels us to seek experiences that are congruent with the memory, so that the image can be upheld and nourished. For example, as parents, we have a very difficult time when our children grow up and leave home or choose to live drastically different lives. The memory of our child as an infant or toddler overshadows their reality of being grown-up or troubled.

Smṛtyākarṣiṇī overpowers our ability to see things the way they are by how they used to be. When she bestows her grace, we can savor the memory, understanding its place in the past and disallowing it to color the present.

Nāmākarṣiṇī

Nāma is name and *Nāmākarṣiṇī* is the irresistible tendency to name or label experience. Ordinarily, we have no ability to experience an object without immediately labeling it. For example, the moment our eyes land on a tree, the mind has already concluded that it is a tree. The word "tree" has become so well-associated with the object "tree," that in our experience, they appear to be the same. Powered by memory, the object and the word referring to it become inexorably entwined, where we can't separate them.[143]

When the label and object become one, we lose the ability to experience an object *as is*, where it can be known as a fresh experience in every interaction. As soon as we think tree, we have lost the ability to experience a tree. Although literally correct, the referential nature of labeling creates a barrier between us and the experience – the label stands in the way of knowing an object.[144]

143 See Vāc in Practice in Chapter 14.

144 See 'Mātaṅgī' in K. Chinnaiyan, *Shakti Rising* (Nonduality Press, 2017).

Nāmākarṣiṇī's boon is freedom from referential language, where we lose the attachment to labeling.

This has profound implications for the self-image, which is a conglomeration of labels. The bhāvanā poses the question, "If I'm not any of my labels, what am I?" This line of questioning has the potential to bring down the entire house of cards that is built by the ahaṅkāra.

Bījākarṣiṇī

145 André Padoux, (Translated by Jacques Gontier), *Vāc. The Concept of the Word in Selected Hindu Tantras* (Delhi: Sri Satguru Publications, 1992).

Bīja, which means seed, refers to the primordial seed of creation. The Śākta tradition tells us that the Absolute Reality emanates as the triad of bindu, bīja and nāda,[145] which then bursts forth as manifestation. Like a seed that holds a tree in it, bīja holds the pattern of the cosmos in it, which unfolds as the intricate pattern of the Śrīcakra.

The bīja is the hidden blueprint of the microcosm, which spills over into the way we think, act, speak and feel. Even though it is hidden, the allure of the bīja manifests in the way we become entrenched in saṃsāra in the constant struggle to find validation, protect what is ours, and acquire what we think we need. *Bījākarṣiṇī* is the inherent longing to spill out what is in our specific blueprint. At the highest level, the bīja is the purest map of reality. Our ignorance obscures this knowledge, where instead of the highest reality, our samskārās become the map of our lived reality. Even though Bījākarṣiṇī continuously beckons us to the highest reality, we get caught in the many detours framed by our samskārās.

Bīja also refers to reproductive fluid, which contains the entire blueprint of a human being. Bījākarṣiṇī is the allure of this potential that is accompanied by the yearning for procreation, which is the drive of all sentient beings. The allure of Bījākarṣiṇī becomes displaced and fragmented into the energies of validation seeking, maintaining inauthentic relationships and repression of the primal yearning of the bīja. The sādhanā of this magnificent yoginī is to redirect our energies to the bīja through constant reflection and decluttering of our lives, our relationships, and our aspirations. When this primal energy can be accessed, it opens us to the primordial bīja, the map of the ultimate reality.

Ātmākarṣiṇī

Ātma refers to the eternal, unchanging Self at the individual level.[146] As we saw earlier, the āṇava mala is the universal sense of being limited, which gives us the vague sense that there is something more to us than what meets the eye and keeps us on the search for completion. *Ātmākarṣiṇī* is the allure of the Self that keeps us on the path of constant seeking for itself.

The allure of the ātma keeps us going, deliciously entrapping us through desire (Kāmākarṣiṇī), intellect (Buddhyākarṣiṇī) and ego (Ahaṅkārākarṣiṇī) in the realm of the senses (sense ākarṣiṇīs) that are registered in the citta (Cittākarṣiṇī), becoming memory (Smṛtyākarṣiṇī) infused with courage (Dhairyākarṣiṇī). It's the allure of the ātma that results in taking the word for the object (Nāmākarṣiṇī) that is transmitted in the form of the bīja (Bījākarṣiṇī).

Ātmākarṣiṇī is the irresistible draw of the Self that holds the previous attractions together and keep us entrapped in saṃsāra. Although we sense the inherent longing for *something*, we lack the clarity about *what* that something is, and search for it in all the wrong places. If we can understand this fundamental longing, the entire game of hide-and-seek becomes clear, and we can then engage in the Bhūpura with a different stance – that of joy, curiosity, and spontaneity.

The sādhanā of Ātmākarṣiṇī results in the very significant turning around of attention, where we realize that although *what* we are seeking is the Self, *where* we are seeking it is the problem. She bestows the vidyā of knowing whether we are on the periphery or the radius, which is an important step in upāsanā.

146 The definition and understanding of Ātma differs according to text and tradition. In some, it is the Puruṣa at the individual level.

Amṛtākarṣiṇī

Amṛta is the nectar of immortality and our fundamental goal, and *Amṛtākarṣiṇī* is the irresistible attraction to the idea of living forever. From the moment we are born, death hangs over our heads like an uninvited, persistent guest. Even when things are going well and we are in our element, the possibility of death is never too far away. It drives the primordial need of all creatures to reproduce, which ensures that a part of us lives on.

The puruṣārthas and eṣaṇas give us the framework to understand this primary longing for immortality, which arises as the need to leave a legacy and to be remembered. Even criminals crave recognition for their heinous crimes in the desire to leave a legacy!

From another perspective, the inherent sense of there being more to the story than being born, living in a limited time-space fractal, and dying also brings with it the vague sense of being immortal. At some level, we have a sense of incredulousness that life seems transient and fleeting with very little ultimate meaning. We try to find meaning and immortality in the context of our fleeting lives, hanging onto the occasional spark or glimpse we are given in moments of inexplicable beauty and wonder.

The allure of Amṛtākarṣiṇī makes us yearn for a long life and good health. The fear of death makes us fearful of aging and decay, and the allure of immortality drives us to do something meaningful. Amṛtākarṣiṇī's shadow keeps us at the periphery and in the linear time-space continuum of becoming, where no level of attainment can grant immortality. As we saw above in Ātmākarṣiṇī, this is because we are looking in the wrong place; everything associated with the ahaṅkāra is necessarily in the sphere of Prakṛti, which is temporary and fleeting. With the boon of this yoginī, we come to see that no objects of the world can bestow immortality. Her vidyā grants us the ability to see that immortality is our essential nature as the Ahambhāva, propelling us from the circumference to the radius.

Śarīrākarṣiṇī

Śarīra is the body, and *Śarīrākarṣiṇī* is the ubiquitous attraction of the body. Even though we may not overtly identify with our bodies (and feel that the "me" is somewhere inside our body), we cling to the image of the body as being an important facet of who we are. Attributes of the body, such as skin color, race and sex become *our* attributes. Health and disease become extremely personal, where we become survivors of this or that disease. Our bellies and pant sizes cause pride or shame, and our self-expression is heavily influenced by how we dress or groom ourselves. Śarīrākarṣiṇī's shadow as the obsession with the body is particularly evident in the age of social media, where our bodies are the vehicles for lokeṣaṇā and validation-seeking.

Śarīrākarṣiṇī's light changes our perspective about our body, where it is seen as the exquisite vehicle for transformation, and the perfect replica of the macrocosm.

Cakreśvarī: Tripureśī

The Śodaṣadalapadma is known as the Sarvāśāparipūraka or the wish-fulfilling cakra, because this āvaraṇa holds the key to understanding the mechanism of desire and tapping into its underlying energy. Understanding the energy of desire opens the portal to its origin, where the longing for objects is transmuted and whether we acquire them or not becomes irrelevant – our wishes are self-fulfilled. The yoginīs of this āvaraṇa are known as Gupta (secret) because of this subtlety. Their vidyā shows us the mechanisms for our interactions in the Bhūpura.

When we worship the yoginīs in any āvaraṇa, they bestow specific gifts that become double-edged swords. For instance, Kāmākarṣiṇī bestows the boon of becoming irresistibly attractive, where you are desired by everyone around you. Similarly, Buddhyākarṣiṇī gives you the ability to attract people through your intellect. If these gifts fulfill our unmet eṣaṇas and propel us onward to the next āvaraṇa, they become great boons of liberation. On the other hand, if they create cascades of desire for more, they trap us in the periphery.[147] Moreover, no gift comes without a consequence and a sacrifice of some kind. In the above example, becoming desirable to everyone around you may mean the loss of treasured and meaningful relationships.

147 When discussing this aspect with my Guru he said, "Ask only for Devī in the Bindu! If you ask for other things, the yoginīs will trap you and won't let you progress."

Tripureśī is the Cakreśvarī of the Śodaṣadalapadma and she rules over the Sarvāśāparipūraka cakra. She is invoked with the mantra *aiṃ klīṃ sauḥ* and the mudrā bīja *drīṃ* corresponding with Sarvavidrāviṇī, the power of diffusion and flow. Through this āvaraṇa, she diffuses the energy of the higher āvaraṇas into the playing field of the Bhūpura. Through this mudrā we invoke this power of diffusion and to reverse the flow of attention, where we become curious about our own process.

We are now learning to look in the right direction, understanding that there is an expansive, maze-like backstage for the movie that is played out at the Bhūpura. The way we behave onscreen is driven by the ākarṣiṇīs, who keep us entrapped in the push and pull of the mind and senses. Awareness of our grasping is the gift of Tripureśī, who impels us to take another step backstage with self-inquiry.

What drives the energies of these attractions? Why are we so deliciously entrenched in the elements of this āvaraṇa? When we engage in bhāvanā through these questions, we are pushed along to the next āvaraṇa, the Aṣṭadalapadma.

Chapter 10

Aṣṭadalapadma

वचनादानगमनविसर्गानन्दहानोपादानोपेक्षाख्य- बुद्धयोऽनङ्गकुसुमादिशक्तयोऽष्टौ ॥ १४ ॥

Vacana-ādāna-gamana-visarga-ānanda-hāna-upādāna-
upekṣākhya-buddhay-anaṅgakusumādyaṣṭau || 14 ||

"The eight śaktis including Anaṅga Kusumā are the five functions of speech, reception, locomotion, excretion, and happiness, and the three intellect divisions of rejection, attention, and indifference."
~ Bhāvanopaniṣad, verse 14

Thus far in the scheme of the Śrīcakra, we began the inward journey in the Bhūpura by becoming aware of our moment-to-moment interactions and inquiring into the fundamental discontent that brought us to the Śodaṣadalapadma. Between the two, we came across the Trivṛtta, which is the bridge between the gross outer world of the Bhūpura and its internalization through the sixteen attractions of the Śodaṣadalapadma. In traversing the Śodaṣadalapadma, we concluded that contentment is the secret to fulfilling all desires. Unless we have some semblance of contentment, we cannot progress on the inward journey since the drama of the interactions in the Bhūpura will continue to entice us.

The Inquiry

In the Śodaṣadalapadma, we encountered the sixteen attractions that in their shadow aspect entrap us in the objects of the world. The constant grasping resulting from discontent leads us to behave the way we do in the playing field of the Bhūpura. When we examine the nature of grasping, we come to realize that the fulfilment of our wishes doesn't lie in the playing field at all – it lies in the turning around of the senses from the world of objects to the energy of the attractions. In this turning around, we become fulfilled, where we see that contentment cannot lie in the world of objects.

Now we begin to sense the movement of energy that lies prior to the ākarṣiṇīs and the inquiry here is, "What is the origin of discontent? What drives the grasping of the 16 elements of the Śodaṣadalapadma?"

This inquiry brings us to the Aṣṭadalapadma, the eight-petaled lotus.

The All-Agitating Cakra

The Aṣṭadalapadma (*aṣṭa* = eight, dala = petal, padma = lotus) is known as *Sarvasankṣobhaṇa* (sarva = all, sankṣobhaṇa = agitating) cakra. We arrive here because the objects of the world that had previously held our attention have now become a burden, where we would like to understand why they fascinate us and make us restless. When we had no awareness of this restlessness, we assumed that our restlessness arose from not having what we want. Through our journey so far, we realize that we want certain things *because* of our restlessness – this is a tremendous turnaround!

When we apply ourselves to self-inquiry or bhāvanā, we come to see that although we take in the world, the container that receives it is already quite full. Our past experiences that make up the container determine the way we interpret our current ones. The citta (here to mean the combination of the buddhi, manas, and ahaṅkāra) is this container, where every sense perception coming in from the outside is interpreted, weighed, and stored away to become yet another part of the me-story. Events and circumstances that are completely random and impersonal become personal and intimate through the container of the citta, which is why an earthquake, or a pandemic elicits totally different reactions from everyone experiencing it.

The citta with its smattering of past impressions is the battlefield we prepare for at the beginning of the day. On this battlefield, we receive the world with its unpredictable events. We will internally slay those that threaten our dearly held ideals and protect those that nourish them. We encounter the world in a contracted way because of prefilled content of the citta.

Citta Vṛttis

The citta "space" is made up of five types of thoughts or impressions that result in vṛttis or mental modifications: *pramāṇa, viparya, vikalpa, nidrā,* and *smṛti* (see Figure 29).[148] Vṛttis prevent us from seeing things as they are and influence the way we process sense perceptions and interact with the world.

148 From the *Yoga Sūtras* of Patañjalī, 1:6.

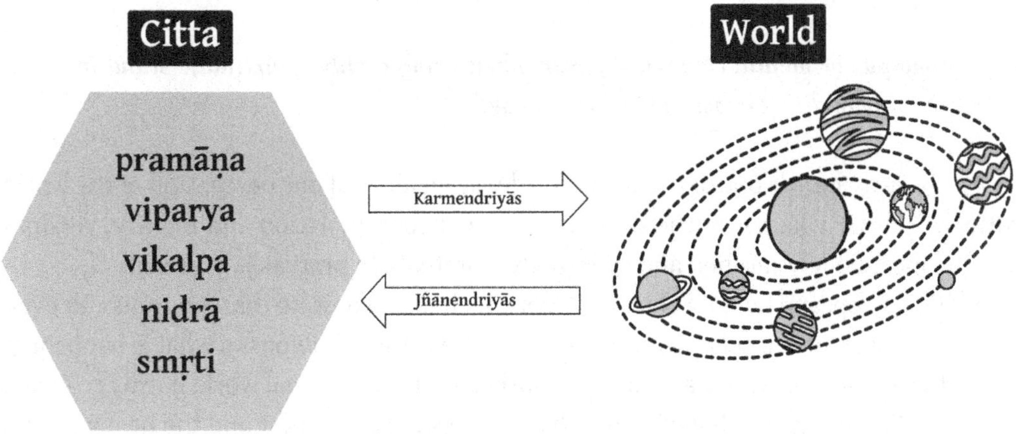

Figure 29. Citta Vṛtti

Pramāṇa is right knowledge, which is based in logic and reason, and is devoid of emotional swaying. It is neutral and factual, like thinking the sky is blue because blue light scatters more of the sunlight passing through the atmosphere. Pramāṇa is supported through direct evidence (*pratyakṣa*), inference (*anumāna*) or authority (*āgama*).[149] When it comes to understanding our internal landscape, the darśana helps us cultivate pramāṇa, where we learn to see things as they are without emotional coloring. The inward path of the Śrīcakra is the path of correct knowledge, which begins in āgama and moves on to anumāna and eventually, pratyakṣa pramāṇa.

149 From the *Yoga Sūtras* of Patanjali 1:7.

Viparya is incorrect knowledge, where the thought is based on misperception of a fact, like in the telephone game. In the process of its dissemination, a fact becomes distorted by mainstream and social media, confused with opinions, and obscured by fears, hopes, rage and envy. Viparya is the antithesis of pramāṇa, and not based in direct experience, inference, or authority. The cultivation of pramāṇa is the solution for viparya.

Vikalpa is a mental construct that is created in the mind with the acquisition of information. Most of our learning is based on cultivating mental constructs and concepts where we create mental images and scenarios to understand the world around us. In sādhanā too, learning is inevitably accompanied by mental constructs that are imaginative and often in the mystical realms based in fantasy.

Vikalpas or mental constructs, even when being highly "spiritual," stand in the way of direct experiential knowledge.

The remedy here is one of replacing the dense vikalpas of our perception of the world with the subtler vikalpas of the darśana. Through contemplation and inquiry, vikalpas become increasingly rarefied and eventually culminate in pratyakṣa pramāṇa.

Nidrā is sleep, and here it refers to either the dream-like state that is our default even in waking hours, or the deep sleep-like state where we are oblivious to what is happening around us. In either case, we are so self-absorbed that the external world hardly registers or not at all. Through the hyperactive, distractive state of the first and the heavy inertia of the second, nidrā clouds and dulls our perception. The remedy for nidrā is mindfulness and the cultivation of single-pointedness.

Smṛti, as we have seen in the context of the Śodaṣadalapadma, is memory, and it compounds the other four types of vṛttis. Smṛti can be used to our advantage through the constant remembrance of the darśana, the goal, the practice, and the teaching.

The citta with its vṛttis is the originator of agitation. Vṛttis originate from samskārās and create more samskārās in a vicious cycle. Thought patterns and mental modifications originating from samskārās in this cyclical fashion eventually become our habits that shape our destiny.

Aṣṭadalapadma

The yoginīs of the eight-petaled āvaraṇa, the Aṣṭadalapadma are known as the *anaṅga* (*an* = without, *aṅga* = body) devatās (see Figure 30). Like the vṛttis, they don't have a reality rooted in materiality, but control our perception, thought, emotion, speech, and behavior through their power over the Śodaṣadalapadma. They create the agitations that ripple through the lower āvaraṇas.

Depending on the text, these yoginīs are interpreted differently; often, the same commentator of two different texts on the subject might give entirely varied meanings to them. One common interpretation is the association of these deities with the different forms of Eros, specifically related to the vidyā of *Kāmadeva*, an important aspect of Śrīvidyā.[150] Another interpretation is to equate the eight yoginīs of this āvaraṇa to the *puryaṣṭaka*.[151] Here, we will examine them as described in the Bhāvanopaniṣad, which assigns specific psychophysiological attributes to each of the yoginīs that contribute to the citta vṛttis (Table 11).

150 See Chapter 1, K. Chinnaiyan, *Glorious Alchemy: Living the Lalitā Sahasranāma* (New Sarum Press, January 2020).

151 Puryaṣṭaka means the city of eight, and comprises the jñānendriyas, the karmendriyas, the citta, the prāṇa vāyus, the mahābhūtas, rāga, karma, and avidyā (see N356-N362 of the *Lalitā Sahasranāma*).

Figure 30. Aṣṭadalapadma with Guptatara Yoginī

In the Bhāvanopaniṣad model, the yoginīs correspond with the five organs of action or karmendriyas and three types of intellect, all of which contribute to the citta vṛttis.

Table 11. Yoginīs of the Aṣṭadalapadma

Yoginī	Direction	Alphabet	Manifestation	Bhāvanā
Anaṅga Kusumā	East	k, kh, g, gh, ṅ	Vacana (Speech)	Darśana
Anaṅga Mekhalā	South	c, ch, j, jh, ñ	Ādāna (Reception)	Pratyāhāra
Anaṅga Madanā	West	ṭ, ṭh, ḍ, ḍh, ṇ	Gamana (Locomotion)	Uncoloring
Anaṅga Madanāturā	North	t, th, d, dh, n	Visarjana (Elimination)	Mindfulness
Anaṅga Rekhā	Southeast	p, ph, b, bh, m	Ānanda (Pleasure)	Presence
Anaṅga Veginī	Southwest	y, r, l, v	Hāna (Rejection)	Pratyāhāra
Anaṅga Aṅkuśā	Northwest	ś, ṣ s, h	Upādāna (Attention)	Sense control
Anaṅga Mālinī	Northeast	l, kṣ	Upekṣa (Indifference)	Uncoloring

Guptatara Yoginī

The yoginīs of the Aṣṭadalapadma are called *Guptatara* or very secret since they are more hidden and obscure than the Gupta Yoginīs of the Śodaṣadalapadma.

The Guptatara Yoginī (see Figure 31) bears a sugarcane bow and a flower arrow in her lower two hands while the upper ones hold a blue lotus and a ball of flowers. The flower arrow and the sugarcane bow represent the hooking of the mind on sense objects through the tanmātras, while the blue lotus is the symbol of victory over the senses. The ball of flowers is reminiscent of the diffuseness of vidyā and avidyā in the citta that is enriched by the function of the tanmātras.

Unlike the other āvaraṇas, the yoginīs of the Aṣṭadalapadma are not worshiped in sequential petals. The first four are placed in the four cardinal directions beginning at the petal facing west in a clockwise direction (west, north, east, south). The next four are situated in the petals facing the northwest, northeast, southeast and southwest directions.

Figure 31. Guptatara Yoginī

Anaṅga Kusumā

Anaṅga Kusumā symbolizes the flowering of agitation by way of expression. She holds the key to agitation, which is rooted in *vacana* or speech. In Chapter 6, we explored vāc, which is significant in the understanding of the Śrīcakra. Vāc is the Divine in manifestation, where creation is her expression, her voice, and her words.

As we saw in the Śodaṣadalapadma, the tanmātras bridge the external world to the mind through the sense organs. By itself, a tanmātra is pure, unconditioned, and untainted. However, what is taken in by the tanmātra becomes corrupted by the *citta vṛttis*. The way in which the sensory input of the tanmātras is expressed results in the types of citta vṛttis that are created. Without the expression of the vṛttis, we would remain unaffected by the world of objects. Expression here doesn't apply only to words; it includes fragments of images, sounds, and other impressions that result in the immediate recognition and filing away of objects in categories of good/bad, desirable/undesirable, and so on.

When we take in of the world through the tanmātras, we register the experience by way of language or expression, which creates vṛttis. Even what we think is *the* truth is a mental construct that is created and sustained through expression in the citta. These mental constructs that are vague and as if without a defined body (anaṅga) shape the way we view the world and interact with it. If *my* truth is different from yours, I'll have an issue with you, and either try to convince you to see the light or hold you in subtle or gross contempt. My samskārās are so blinding that I fail to see that my truth is just a mental construct that is created through bits and pieces of language. This is the incredible power of Anaṅga Kusumā, where there is a continuous flowering of impressions in the mind that result in both our internal and external experience.

It's at the Aṣṭadalapadma where we can start to discern the subtleties of how we perceive objects through the process known as *pratyāhāra*, which is the process of withdrawal from the senses.

> ***In pratyāhāra, we go to the source of the flowering of the vṛttis, by withdrawing our attention from the object itself and focusing on the subtle energies that it evokes.***

When Anaṅga Kusumā bestows her grace, we can identify the vikalpas or the mental constructs that masquerade as the experience. With this discernment, we can learn to relinquish the vikalpa in favor of the lived experience.

Bhāvanā on Anaṅga Kusumā

Say you are watching a movie and come to a violent scene that triggers a very strong reaction. Ordinarily, your vṛttis around that situation come to the surface and you may flinch, feel a sense of rage, powerlessness, pity or a host of other emotions. Your mind comes up with thoughts that express these emotions to yourself or others while your body reacts by increasing heart rate and blood pressure, and the release of hormones and chemicals. After a while, the mind-body reactions subside and the vṛttis go back to their dormant state... until the next time.

Pratyāhāra can be practiced here by withdrawing from the stimulus and paying attention to the internal landscape with nonjudgmental awareness.

Notice the arising of the vṛttis of the mind and the reactions of the body with curiosity and openness. Recall the darśana of the Śrīcakra. What is the source of the vṛttis? Without grasping at the mental and emotional turbulence, place your attention to the inner space in which it arises. Observe the contents of the mind as they ebb and flow while placing your attention on the stillness in which they arise.

With continued work in this inward direction, the energy of the arising takes a 180-degree turn into its source where it dissolves into radiant silence. To learn to surf the energy of a vṛtti takes skill and practice but is worth the effort. This is the secret worship of Anaṅga Kusumā which turns the expression of agitation to that of peace and joy.

Anaṅga Mekhalā

Mekhalā means girdle, referring to the agitation of reception that creates an illusionary boundary, or a "belting in" of an experience that eliminates all other possibilities. In this function, *Anaṅga Mekhalā* corresponds to the function of *ādāna* or reception. In receiving a part and belting it in as the truth, we close off to the whole. The problem is not that our truth is not the truth; it's that our truth isn't the *whole* truth. Part-truth is given credibility through expression when it becomes a vṛtti.

> ***The characteristic of a vṛtti is that as soon as it is given an expression, it can only manifest in one way, eliminating and canceling all other possibilities.***

This is the shadow of Anaṅga Mekhalā. For example, as soon as we decide that violence is "bad," we close ourselves off to all other possibilities.

Propelled by Anaṅga Kusumā, Anaṅga Mekhalā creates an invisible boundary around the experience. The idea that violence is bad or evil creates a vikalpa that stands in direct contradiction to life. In reality, violence is the very foundation of life. As any woman who has given birth knows, creation is an extremely violent event. Life is sustained through death and destruction. The explosion of massive old stars into supernovas or creation of black holes are violent events that move the universe in evolutionary ways. Growing food, building homes, and creating consumer products are violent events, resulting in destruction at various levels. Nature is violent and having a specific idea of how it *should be* makes it impossible to see what *is.*

The totality of existence is the fundamental concept of the Śrīcakra and its sādhanā is to rise above the dualities of saṃsāra and nirvāṇa to see that both exist in the moment-to-moment arising of experience. What we see and how we perceive it determine whether we are entrapped in saṃsāra or are free from it. The practice here is to learn to receive sensory input without coloring it with our own misperceptions, which is the purpose of bhāvanā.

Anaṅga Madanā

Madanā refers to intoxication which results in *gamana* or movement. The flowering of the vṛtti through language and its entrapment in a particular directionality results in a sort of intoxication. We become overwhelmed and overpowered by the directionality, which is like being intoxicated and inebriated. In the immediate neurohormonal cascade powered by the expression of the vṛtti, our movements become disjointed and fall out of harmony with our environment. In the heat of the moment, even our loved ones take a verbal, mental or literal beating. Our actions become hateful and fearful when we project pain triggered by a vṛtti. Crimes of passion are the most extreme example of this principle in action.

On a subtler scale, if I am triggered by a situation, the way I interact with it is peppered with agitation. For example, if someone calls me a name, it will trigger a vṛtti and my interaction with them instantly shifts including the way I look at them when speaking, my posture and stance. Even the way I walk away from it will display my discontent and agitation. My breathing and heartbeat will change, taking time to return to normal. This is the power of intoxication exerted by *Anaṅga Madanā.*

Once the vṛtti is triggered, its course is set and bound to culminate in specific ways. Uncoloring our samskārās is the antidote to this tendency, which is to allow them to arise without any reaction and observing the force of their emotional signature. With ongoing practice, the samskāra loses its ability to trigger an emotional response or the intoxication.

Anaṅga Madanāturā

Madanāturā refers to the urgency of intoxication, which results in the reflex of *visarjana* or elimination. At the level of the body, agitation affects our elimination, with an increase in urination and disorders of defection (diarrhea or constipation). Elimination is a process of throwing out waste or end-products of metabolism, and agitation leads to disordered metabolism, which shows up as urgency.

Anaṅga Madanāturā manifests also in the uncontrollable urgency of thought and speech when a vṛtti is triggered, both of which are end-products of the internal cooking of the vṛtti. There is a build-up of pressure, rushing out as the stream of thought that stands in judgment of a situation. Even when we are externally calm, the urgency is unmistakable in the cascade of physiological reactions that are driven by it.

The way we work with this energy is through mindfulness and pausing when there is an uncontrollable need to speak or react.[152]

152 Note that trying to control a natural urge like defecation, urination, sneezing, coughing, and other reflexes is not the same as controlling the need to react mentally or verbally to a situation. Natural urges of the body should not be suppressed as this can lead to problematic issues and diseases.

Anaṅga Rekhā

Rekhā is line, and *Anaṅga Rekha* is the yoginī who creates the line of agitation related to ānanda or pleasure. We don't tend to associate agitation with pleasure, but if we think about it, we can see how pleasure initially leads to a sense of enjoyment and relaxation, but immediately creates the craving for more and/or the fear of loss.

Addictions are the most telling example of this yoginī's shadow. The first cigarette can be neutral or repulsive. With the next and the next, it becomes pleasurable, and soon, the pleasure is the source of agitation. Not having it results in all kinds of triggers. Conversely, the triggering of vṛttis becomes the excuse to indulge in pleasure, as it often happens when we are trying to quit a habit. As soon as we feel the arising of stress, the very thing we are trying to give up becomes the anchor. Anaṅga Rekha draws the line of agitation in pleasure through the possibility of loss or not having more of it.

Working with this energy requires the cultivation of stillness and presence, which is achieved through mindfulness, pratyāhāra, and a disciplined lifestyle.

Anaṅga Veginī

Veginī is the yoginī of speed and refers to the agitation of *hāna* or rejection, which is a function of projecting our own vṛttis on to the world. We constantly project our own stuff onto the other in relationships, assuming we know what they are thinking or experiencing. In the process, we operate from a stance that is entirely self-centered.

This shadow also shows up in the way we mistake projection for compassion. When we see somebody going through a rough patch, we project *our* ideas and thoughts on how *we* would be impacted with a similar situation, approaching them from this space of "knowing." In the assumed knowing, the shadows of all the Anaṅga devatās instantly come into play, leading to an almost instantaneous reaction to the other person's situation. The rapidity provides no space to understand that there is no possible way for us to know what anyone else experiences. In this suffocating stance, we reject the other person's authentic experience and replace it with our own projected one.

The practice of pratyāhāra allows us to slow down and see that whether we are rejecting others or are feeling rejected by them, the underlying issue is that of our own vṛttis. In the end-analysis, rejection has nothing to do with anyone else except our own self. Even when someone tells us that they are rejecting us, how we take it becomes a function of our own citta vṛttis. When we understand that the way we see the world is the result of our own vṛttis, we lose the ability to take anything personally; we see that their behavior has nothing to do with us but has everything to do with the contents of their own citta. This is the light of *Anaṅga Veginī*, which is hāna or rejection of the false and the illusory in favor of direct experience illuminated by sattarka.

Anaṅga Aṅkuśā

Aṅkuśa means goad, and here, the word refers to the yoginī who brings about an agitation of *upādāna* or attention resulting in distraction, which tends to be our default. Our attention is in a constant state of agitation due to the arising of vṛttis in response to the continuous stream of sensory input in the waking and dream states. In the waking state, we are continually processing the contents of our conscious mind and in the dream state, we are agitated by the subconscious mind that is active in its limitless capabilities.[153] It's as if our attention is goaded in countless directions all at once.

153 See Avasthās: States of Consciousness in Chapter 6.

We can hardly pay attention in a conversation without it being filtered through the contents of our own citta resulting in agitation. In this agitation, we lose the ability to experience the world in an uncorrupted fashion. When engaged in a conversation, agitation presents as the inability to listen. When the other person is talking, our ability to listen is hampered by the plot of how to respond and put forth *our* ideas.

One of the greatest accomplishments of sādhanā is the cultivation of a quiet mind.[154] When the citta vṛttis come to rest, our attention is steady and free of agitations. The power of *Anaṅga Aṅkuśā's* goad becomes available to direct awareness where we want it to go. While previously we were slaves of the mind, Anaṅga Aṅkuśā makes us its master through the gift of upādāna.

154 See 'Baglamukhi' in K. Chinnaiyan, *Shakti Rising* (Nonduality Press, 2017).

Anaṅga Mālinī

Mālinī refers to the yoginī with the garland, and here, she is the agitation of *upekṣa* or indifference. At the outset, we must distinguish indifference that is problematic, from dispassion, which is a desirable quality. In dispassion, we can relinquish our own dearly held beliefs because we are not attached to them. The vṛtti is neither suppressed nor repressed but extinguished altogether. Indifference, on the other hand, is a quality of not caring or being unmoved by an experience because it's irrelevant to us. We just don't want to "go there" and prefer to not react at all. It's the response to a situation that doesn't trigger a vṛtti because it is effectively suppressed or repressed, yet it continues to have the *potential* to trigger the vṛtti, which is laced with agitation. One example of indifference is to say, "It is what it is," when "it" really is a case of sour grapes and marked by resignation.

Resignation comes from a place of resistance, where we don't *really* want the experience to be the way it is. The unpleasantness of the situation is too much to bear and feel, and indifference is the best reaction to it. The vṛtti is very much alive in its subtle expression but is not allowed an external reaction. Dispassion, on the other hand, is the result of absolute and total acceptance. The vṛtti is met head-on every time it arises with fearless nonjudgmental awareness. We ride its energy to understand its source and where it dissolves, which is why there is no agitation with dispassion. Sensory input occurs but even the *potential* for it to cause a disturbance has been erased. With dispassion, we can meet situations with fresh perspectives and pragmatic solutions uncolored by our past experiences. This is the gift of upekṣa.

Anaṅga Mālinī's grace allows us to understand the power of our vṛttis to keep us entrapped in the sphere of becoming. She grants us the awareness to see the garland of citta vṛttis that define our identity, that are reflected onto the attractions and aversions of the Śodaṣadalapadma, and the way we interact with the world in the Bhūpura.

Cakreśvarī: Tripurasundarī

To even arrive at the Aṣṭadalapadma from the Bhūpura is an accomplishment that is propelled by grace and dedicated upāsanā. Even though we have examined each yoginī individually, they arise together when propelled by a citta vṛtti. Anaṅga Kusumā flowers the process of expression, while the other yoginīs simultaneously cast their spells of belting the experience, agitation, intoxication, and the urgent psychophysiological response.

The vṛtti brings up agitation of pleasure or rejection, both resulting in the wavering of our attention. Even when we have worked through these agitations on a gross level to arrive at indifference, there is an underlying agitation contained in it from the persistence of the vṛtti (see Figure 32).

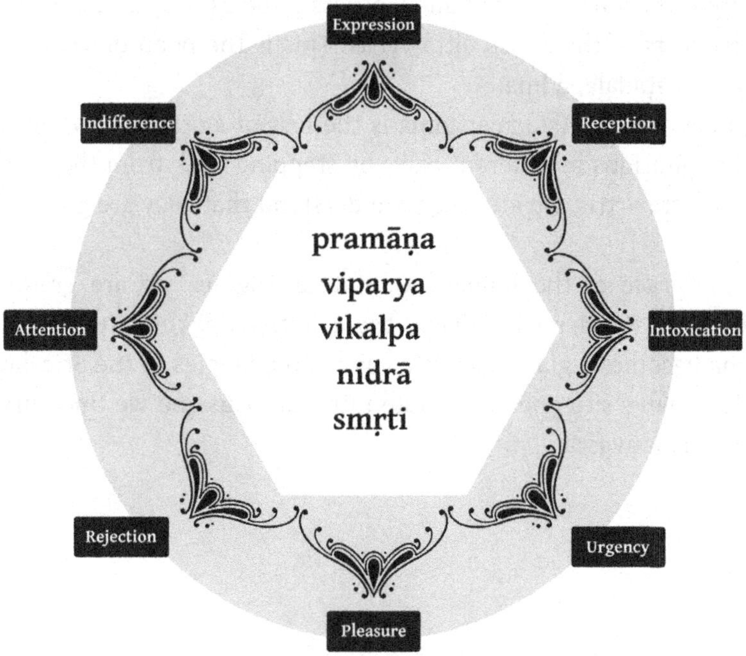

Figure 32. Citta Vṛttis in the Aṣṭadalapadma

Tripurasundarī, an emanation of Mahātripurasundarī, is the Cakreśvarī that reigns over this Sarvasankṣobhaṇa cakra of agitations. She is invoked through the mantra *hrīṃ klīṃ sauḥ* with the mudrā bīja *klīṃ* and the corresponding mudrā, Sarvākarṣiṇī, the power of attraction.[155] Here in this āvaraṇa, we see the juiciness of the agitations that keep us bound in our habitual ways. They are the driving force of our attractions and aversions in the Śodaṣadalapadma. We now see, for example, how the vṛttis of viparya, nidrā and smṛti result in the push and pull of liking this and disliking that. We are beginning to realize the power of vikalpas, the mental constructs that we take to be real and true.

155 See Sarvākarṣiṇī in Chapter 7.

Our spiritual quest begins to change when we realize that everyone is a product of their citta vṛttis; people of similar vṛttis band together to create a collective vikalpa that becomes a religion, sect, political party, or faction. The world is driven by these great yoginīs, and nothing escapes them! A deep understanding of our own mind becomes the basis for compassion, where we can allow others to be as they are, realizing that they, like us, are products of their own citta vṛttis. This is the boon of Tripurasundarī, the Cakreśvarī of the Aṣṭadalapadma.

The attainment of the Aṣṭadalapadma is the loss of agitations. When we can work with our eight agitations in different ways by stepping back from the sense input and working on the citta vṛttis, we are able to understand that they are gateways to deeper insight.

Through the grace of the limbless Guptatara Yoginīs, we are granted the right inquiry, which is to wonder what drives the agitations of the citta. At this point, the Aṣṭadalapadma becomes a giant leap into the main triangles of the Śrīcakra where the whole equation changes to one of absolute internal focus and we find ourselves in the next āvaraṇa, the Manvaśra.

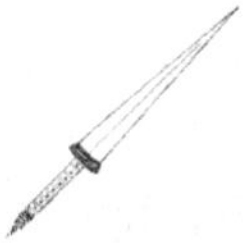

Chapter 11

Manvaśra

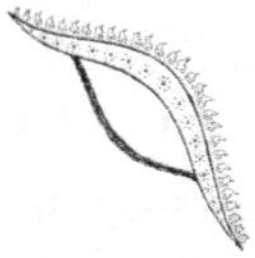

अलम्बुसा कुहूर्विश्वोदरी वारणा हस्तिजिह्वा यशोवती पयस्विनी
गान्धारी पूषा शङ्खिनी ईडा पिङ्गला सुषुम्ना चेति चतुर्दश नाड्यः ।
सर्वसंक्षोभिण्यादिचतुर्दश शक्तयः ॥ १५ ॥

alambusā-kuhūr-viśvodharā vāraṇā hastijihvā yaśovatī payasvinī
gāndharī pūṣā śaṅkhanī īḍa piṅgala suṣumnā ceti caturdaśa
nāḍyāh Sarvasankṣobhiṇyādi-caturdaśa śaktyaḥ || 15 ||

"The fourteen śaktis including Sarvasankṣobhiṇī, etc. are the fourteen nāḍīs, which are alambusā, kuhū, viśvodharā, vāraṇā hastijihvā, yaśovatī, payasvinī, gāndharī, pūṣā, śaṅkhanī, īḍa, piṅgala, and suṣumnā."
~ Bhāvanopaniṣad, verse 15.

On the journey into the Śrīcakra, we began at the Bhūpura, where we encountered our limitations as the shadows of the Siddhis, the Aṣṭa Mātṛkās, and the Mudrā Devīs. Through the correct inquiry, we arrived at the Śodaṣadalapadma, where we examined the grasping nature of the mind as the sixteen attractions or fascinations that drive our interactions in the Bhūpura. By the grace of the yoginīs of this āvaraṇa, we realized the fundamental nature of discontent, which brought us to the Aṣṭadalapadma, where we met the eight types of agitations that drive our attractions and aversions.

The Inquiry

One of the essential insights of the Aṣṭadalapadma is that of the powerful pull of sense objects, where they determine our entire experience. This outward turning of the senses can drive even our engagement in sādhanā, where we use it to act and react to external circumstances. The Anaṅga devatās show us how our citta vṛttis drive us to manipulate our experience to land at a desirable goal.

Manipulation shows up as the subtle need for approval from others or a constant movement toward self-validation or self-justification. It's as if there is an internal observer that keeps score of how we need to experience spiritual practice. This observer requires constant reassurance that we are on the right track and that our sādhanā is progressing along nicely. We reassure ourselves when we feel good and berate ourselves when we don't, with a constant flow of energy into self-approval. This movement keeps us entrapped at the Aṣṭadalapadma and in the realm of agitation, which in turn leads to the grasping of the Śodaṣadalapadma and the contracted nature of our interactions in the Bhūpura.

The sādhanā of the Sarvasankṣobhaṇa cakra brings us face-to-face with our self-deception and shows us the nature of our agitations. At this point, we lose interest in self-validation or the need for approval. Sādhanā loses the energy of posturing or pleasing the observer and becomes deeply authentic. We are in it for its own sake, removed from how it looks to anyone else, free of superstition and the need to make an impression upon others or ourselves.

At this point, we can make the significant leap from the Aṣṭadalapadma to the Manvaśra. The inquiry here is, "What is the source of agitation?"

In some sampradāyas, the first three āvaraṇas - Bhūpura, Śodaṣadalapadma and Aṣṭadalapadma - are omitted and the Śrīcakra begins with the Manvaśra. This is to say that an upāsaka of the Śrīcakra is mature enough where the senses are turned inward through the preparatory practices of the first three āvaraṇas. The earliest depictions of the Śrīcakra consisted of the āvaraṇas of the triangles, and the other elements were added later.

The Manvaśra is where the understanding of non-duality begins in earnest through the understanding of prāṇa.

Prāṇa

Prāṇa is the energy of consciousness. As we saw in Chapter 4, Śiva is the transcendent and immutable and Śakti is the immanent and mutable. As Śiva's creative energy, Śakti is dynamic and constantly changing, becoming time and space, and unfolding as the universe, and as you and me. As this primordial creator, she is known as *Mahāśakti.* A small portion of Mahāśakti becomes *Prāṇaśakti*, the animating force of creation.

Prāṇaśakti pervades creation and permeates every plane of existence. Without prāṇa, there is no life, buddhi, ahaṅkāra, manas, or any of the tattvas. Breath is the gross sign of prāṇa, which drives the process of breathing, the intake of oxygen, its exchange in the lungs, and the release of carbon dioxide. Prāṇa drives the functions of all the organs and organ systems in the body, and yet it is unseen and cannot be directly measured. In nondual traditions, prāṇa is said to reside in the *prāṇamaya kośa*, one of the five sheaths that make up the body-mind.

The Pañca Kośas

We can think of the *pañca kośas* (pañca = five, *kośa* = sheath) as being nested within each other (see Figure 33). In Vedānta, the *annamaya kośa* is the physical body that is nourished by food (*anna*), which is animated by the *prāṇamaya kośa*, the sheath in which prāṇa flows. The mind with its many facets is mapped to the *manomaya kośa*, while the intellect is said to be in the *vijñānamaya kośa*. The fifth and final sheath is the *ānandamaya kośa*, the seat of bliss. It's important to note that all five of the kośas in this model belong to the category of Prakṛti, as in, there is a subject or individual self that is the witness of the sheaths (Puruṣa). The Self is not included in this model, and we arrive at it through a systematic inquiry of the kośas.[156]

156 See Brahmānandavalli in the *Taittirīya Upaniṣad*.

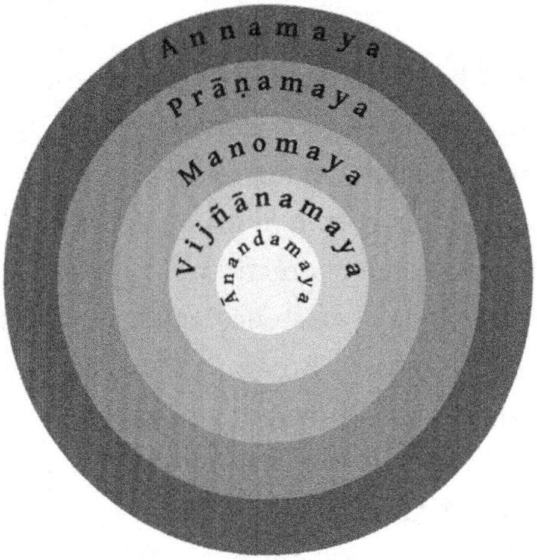

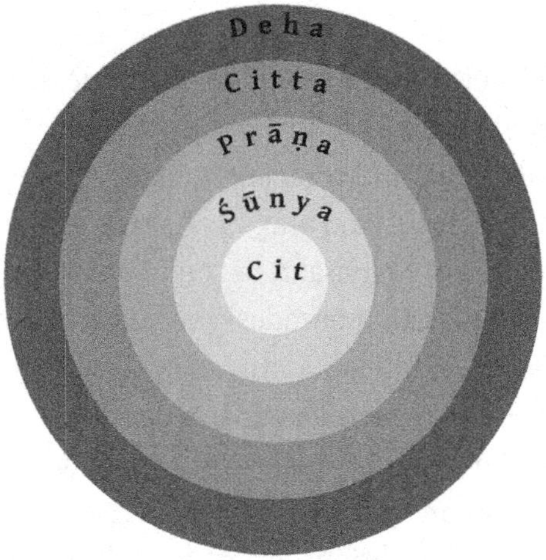

Figure 33. Pañca Kośa

In the Tāntrik model of the pañca kośas, the annamaya kośa remains the same, and is subsumed by the citta, which as we have seen is the internal landscape of thoughts and emotions that registers sensory input. Prāṇa is further upstream, driving the functions of the body and mind. Beyond prāṇa is the void or *śūnya*, a state beyond the mind where emptiness is paradoxically fullness or wholeness.[157] Beyond the void is *cit*, the Self or Supreme Consciousness.

157 Śūnya here is different from the emptiness of Buddhism, and refers to the state beyond the tattvas, where nothing is being created or destroyed.

From a practical standpoint, the pañca kośas are a brilliant way of understanding sādhanā. Ordinarily, we identify with the outer kośas and take them to be who we are, including the body, the mind, or a combination of the two. This misapprehension is a result of scattering of prāṇa and its erratic flow, which results in chaotic mind states. If we can understand the pathways of prāṇa and work on harmonizing its flow, our sādhanā becomes streamlined and meaningful.

The sheaths can be grouped into three śarīras or bodies – the sthūla or gross body is made of the annamaya kośa or deha (physical body), the sūkṣma or subtle body is the combination of the prāṇamaya, manomaya and vijñānamaya kośas, and the kāraṇa or causal body is the ānandamaya kośa, which is the reservoir of samskārās. The kāraṇa śarīra reflects on the sūkṣma śarīra, which influences the sthūla śarīra (see Figure 34).

Figure 34. The Śarīrās in Manifestation

Prāṇa Nāḍīs, Cakras and Kuṇḍalinī

As we saw in Chapter 4, there are three fundamental attributes or guṇas of Prakṛti – tamas, rajas and sattva, which permeate all manifestations including our body-minds. The flow of prāṇa in the nāḍīs is determined by the samskārās of the kāraṇa śarīra.

When we are in a tāmasik state, the flow of prāṇa is sluggish, the mind is clouded, and we lack the ability to understand the subtler aspects of the Śrīcakra. In this state, the Śrīcakra becomes an object that is viewed for its worldly attributes. We may wish to own one for good fortune or fear owning one out of superstition.

When we are in the rajāsik state, the flow of prāṇa is erratic and constantly shifting. Our attention shifts rapidly from lower to higher knowledge and results in confusion. The predominant rasas of anxiety, restlessness, anger, envy, greed, and passion predominate with not enough patience, deliberation or stillness required for the nivṛtti mārga. Our passions keep us on the circumference, and we can't dip deep enough into the radius.

In the sāttvik state prāṇa flows steadily through the nāḍīs, with an increase in our attention span and ability to be still. The flow of prāṇa is even and harmonious, and the mind naturally flows back to its source. Cultivation of sattva occurs through the combination of a disciplined lifestyle, the right view, practices aligned with the view, and most importantly, by the grace of the Guru. This is one of the characteristics of Kuṇḍalinī sādhanā.

Kuṇḍalinī and cakras are concepts fundamental to the understanding of Śrīcakra upāsanā. In this tradition, prāṇa is upstream to the citta and flows in channels known as nāḍīs, which are neither arteries nor nerves but subtle channels that represent the phenomenon through which prāṇa becomes limited in time and space. Of the countless nāḍīs, fourteen of the most important are considered here in the Manvaśra, each corresponding to a small triangle of this āvaraṇa. Of the fourteen, three are significant – the *iḍa*, *piṅgala* and *suṣumnā*, which run along the spine. The suṣumnā in the center is flanked by the īḍa on the left and piṅgala on the right, which intertwine at various points like the caduceus.

The nāḍīs are loosely divided into two types – *prāṇavahā* and *manovahā*. The prāṇavahā nāḍīs are conduits for prāṇa that drive physiological processes, while the manovahā nāḍīs are conduits for the activity of the inner landscape (the mind, including thought and feeling).

At this point, we need to know that the description of the nāḍīs differs widely among texts, including their number,[158] their function, and their course. While some texts describe the nāḍīs as arising from a common point known as the *kanda*, which is said to be below the navel in the subtle body, others locate the origin of particularly the important ones from the heart/chest area. In this chapter, we will explore the fourteen main nāḍīs as described in the Bhāvanopaniṣad.[159]

The nāḍīs converge at various points throughout the prāṇic body and these foci are known as cakras. In this tradition, six cakras are considered important and are mapped along the spine starting at the base and ending at the third-eye center.[160] The cakras can be seen as the rooting points of the five great elements: earth (mūlādhāra), water (svādhiṣṭāna), fire (maṇipura), air (anāhatā), and space (viśuddha). Ājñā, the last of the six cakras corresponds to the mind, which is beyond the five elements.

Prāṇaśakti begins her work of creation at the highest level of Absolute Reality, devolving to the five great elements (see the Tattva Map in Chapter 4) and ending in pṛthvī or earth, the last of the thirty-six tattvas. At the microcosmic level, she completes her work and comes to rest in mūlādhāra cakra at the base of the spine, which corresponds to the earth element.

158 The *Śiva Saṃhita* states that are 350,000 nāḍīs whereas the classical yoga texts such as the *Haṭha Yoga Pradīpika* and the *Gorakṣa Saṃhita* declare that there are 72,000. Other texts describe varied numbers of nāḍīs.

159 Ramachandra S.K. Rao, *The Tantra of Sri-Chakra (Bhavanopanishat)* (Delhi: Sri Satguru Publications, 2008).

160 See Chapter 7 in K. Chinnaiyan, *Glorious Alchemy: Living the Lalitā Sahasranāma* (New Sarum Press, 2020).

However, this outward flow of Śakti alternates with her inward flow. When she is in union with Śiva, yet to burst forth as manifestation, she is known as *Śaktikuṇḍalinī*. When she turns towards manifestation as Prāṇakuṇḍalinī, she seemingly forgets Śiva and when she turns toward Śiva as Parākuṇḍalinī, she forgets creation. When she opens her eyes the world manifests and when she closes her eyes, she is absorbed in Śiva and the world ceases to exist.[161] The universe flows between these two movements, which is known as spanda. Kuṇḍalinī is the power of consciousness, which is cit or Self (see Figure 33). As the subtlest or parā form of Śakti, Kuṇḍalinī is as if hidden in plain sight. She is the source of prāṇa that animates the Śrīcakra in the sṛṣṭi-stithi-saṃhāra and the saṃhāra-stithi-sṛṣṭi directions.

161 See nāma 281 of the *Lalitā Sahasranāma*: unmeṣa nimiṣotpanna vipanna bhuvanāvaḷiḥ.

In the microcosm we encounter Kuṇḍalinī at her various levels of manifestation, which become relevant in upāsanā.

Upāya means the remedy or means of attaining a goal.

The specific upāyas prescribed for a practitioner depends on the expression of Kuṇḍalinī in their life, mind and upāsanā. Going back to the circle analogy, for a practitioner whose prāṇa is expended primarily in the concerns of the periphery, a practice of the inner radius or the center will be ineffective. The ideal practice at the periphery engages the upāsaka so that s/he becomes naturally inclined toward the center. On the other hand, in an upāsaka who is ripe for higher practices, Kuṇḍalinī rests at a different level and upāya must be tailored accordingly. Accordingly, three levels of practice are prescribed depending on the manifestation of Kuṇḍalinī (see Figure 35).

Figure 35. Kuṇḍalinī and the Upāyas

Prāṇakuṇḍalinī is Śakti's most obvious expression in the microcosm, where we can easily experience prāṇa in the breath and body movements. This obvious manifestation of Kuṇḍalinī is at the level of kriyā śakti, where our internal state has already manifested in the actions of the breath and body. From the standpoint of vāc, this is at vaikharī, and viewed from the perspective of the sheaths, at the annamaya and prāṇamaya kośas. At this level, we can engage with practices such as prāṇāyāma or regulation and extension of the breath, *āsana* or posture, diet, and lifestyle. These practices are grouped as *āṇavopāya* (āṇava = minute, here referring to limitations of body/world, upāya = means). In

Śrīcakra upāsanā, āṇavopāya applies to the practice of the āvaraṇas from the Bhūpura to the Vasukoṇa.

At the subtle level of the mind, Kuṇḍalinī is known as Śaktikuṇḍalinī, where she is the activity of the citta including thought, emotion, and vṛttis.[162] Śaktikuṇḍalinī is at the level of jñāna śakti, where the intention has evolved into knowledge but has not yet manifested in the body; it is at the level of madhyamā vāk and the manomaya kośa. It is at this level that we practice bhāvanā, replacing dense vikalpas by the finer, rarefied ones of the darśana. Practices at this subtler level also include mantra and meditation, and are categorized as *śāktopāya* (śakti = power, upāya = means), and in the purest sense, they are prescribed at the level of the Vasukoṇa.

162 See Citta Vṛttis in Chapter 10.

Even subtler than the mind is the clear and discerning buddhi, where Kuṇḍalinī is known as *Jñānakuṇḍalinī* at the level of icchā śakti, paśyantī vāk and the vijñānamaya and ānandamaya kośas. The upāsaka is able to reside at this level through the subtlest change in stance from object or Idam to subject or Aham. Due to the upāsaka's highly developed viveka, s/he can abide in the highest āvaraṇa with the subtlest effort. S/he identifies with the world as the self, and contemplation here is to attain unbroken abidance in the highest reality or Śiva.[163] This practice falls under the category of *śāmbhavopāya* (*śāmbhava* = relating to Śiva, upāya = means), which is at the Trikoṇa and Bindu, treading the pure path or śuddhādvan.

163 It must be remembered here that whenever we say Śiva, Śakti is implied, and vice versa.

Here, we must note that the hierarchy of the upāyas must not be confused with techniques. The same technique can be applied in any of the three upāyas. For example, mantra sādhana can fall under āṇavopāya, śāktopāya or śāmbhavopāya depending on where we are – the periphery, the radius or the center.

Within the scope of each upāya, the same technique yields different results.[164]

164 My Guru Sumitji says, "Advanced techniques don't make an advanced practitioner!"

A fourth upāya known as *anupāya* (*an* = no, upāya = means), refers to the spontaneous liberation conferred upon a practitioner merely through the Guru's grace, which is an exceedingly rare phenomenon. When we examine anupāya through the lens of karma, we see that what appears to be spontaneous is in fact a culmination of effort. The practitioner may not have exerted much effort in *this* lifetime, but the ripening has occurred through plenty of practice in previous unseen births.

The essential thing to remember is that all upāyas manipulate prāṇa in the nāḍīs. The scheme of the cakras, granthis and nāḍīs is to help us understand the flow of awareness, which is far more important than the specifics of a cakra or granthi. In fact, one of the signs of maturity in upāsanā is a loss of interest in levels except to assess whether one is progressing along the radius or is caught up in the periphery.

In the microcosm, Śiva is said to reside at the sahasrāra cakra, which is beyond the mind at the crown. The ordinary state of being is the play of Prāṇakuṇḍalinī, of the one becoming many. At the microcosmic level, the play of Prāṇakuṇḍalinī is seen in the outward turning of prāṇa where we are entirely caught up in the world of objects and saṃsāra at the Bhūpura. The *potential* for turning inward is known simply as Kuṇḍalinī, which lies dormant at the base of the spine.

In coming to rest at the mūlādhāra, it is as if Śakti forgets Śiva and becomes entirely engrossed in the world, which is reflected in the flow of prāṇa in the subtle body, especially in the three main nāḍīs. Ordinarily, prāṇa flows in the īḍa or the piṅgala, periodically switching from one to the other. During the transition phase of switching from one to the other, prāṇa flows briefly in the suṣumnā. The īḍa and piṅgala, as we will see below, symbolize the dualistic way of being, or our engagement in the periphery. The potential to turn to the radius appears when prāṇa flows in the suṣumnā. However, this is brief and unnoticed due to the erratic flow of prāṇa in all the nāḍīs, which is influenced by the rajas and tamas in our psyche.

The significance of the cakras and what they represent depends on the lineage and tradition. Practically speaking, the cakras are neither good nor bad but more of a gauge of where our prāṇa is expended. Normally, we are allocated 21,600 breaths per day (about 15 per minute). This number may not refer exactly to the number of breaths, but more to units of prāṇa, where it is distributed over the number of breaths we take, which depends on our physiology and state of mind.

Various texts and traditions describe the general expenditure of prāṇa in the cakras (Table 12), or the allotment of prāṇa and the amount of time spent in each cakra. Here, we must understand that some cakras do the heavy lifting of running the machinery of the body and require more prāṇa.

Table 12. Daily Distribution of Prāṇa

Cakra	Number of breaths (prāṇa)	Time (hour:minute:sec)
Mūlādhāra	600	00:40:00
Svādhiṣṭāna	6000	06:40:00
Maṇipura	6000	06:40:00
Anāhatā	6000	06:40:00
Viśuddha	1000	01:06:40
Ājñā	1000	01:06:40
Sahasrāra	1000	01:06:40
Total	**21,600**	**24 hours**

Although this scheme can differ according to lineage, what is important here from the standpoint of sādhanā is the conservation of prāṇa. As we noted earlier,[165] we normally exist on the periphery, where most of the prāṇa is expended.

165 See The Ṣaṭcakra and the Śrīcakra in Chapter 5.

In general, the first three cakras are outward turned, which is to say that the issues of the mūlādhāra, svādhiṣṭāna and maṇipura cakras keep us engaged in the periphery through the need for sense gratification and eṣaṇā fulfilment. The anāhatā is the point of turning inward, where the fascination with the external world has abated and we are on the radius. The viśuddha and ājñā come into play as we progress on the radius and have nothing to do with the issues of the periphery. Since the understanding of the cakras is so highly nuanced, it is easier to think of sādhanā in terms of the granthis.

Granthis

Granthi means knot, and the word here refers to the tangle of issues that are associated with cakras. The granthis represent obstructions in the flow of prāṇa, which in turn arise from the samskārās of the kāraṇa śarīra and constitute important milestones in sādhanā and can be used in self-assessment.

The granthis are named after the deities of creation (Brahmā), sustenance (Viṣṇu) and dissolution (Rudra), corresponding to creation, sustenance, and dissolution of the

Aham-Idam separation. In Śrīcakra upāsanā, we can loosely correlate the granthis with the sṛṣṭi, stithi and saṃhāra cakras (see Figure 10 in Chapter 4). At the Brahmā granthi (sṛṣṭi cakra), vāc is fully manifest as vaikharī, and our vision is toward *becoming* at the periphery. Here, we are in the mode of upkeeping our self-image in the upasarga direction (see Figure 12 in Chapter 5) at the sṛṣṭi cakra of the lower three āvaraṇas. As we make our way up the Śrīcakra in the saṃhāra krama, we turn from pravṛtti to nivṛtti, arriving at the Viṣṇu granthi corresponding to the stithi cakra. Here, we are not competing or struggling with the world because we can see that it (Idam) arises *within* us (Aham). At the Rudra granthi analogous to the saṃhāra cakra, the vestiges of separation are resolved and Idam *is* Aham; there is no other and all is I. Here, vāc has evolved from madhyamā in the Vasukoṇa to paśyantī in the Trikoṇa, and to Parā in the Bindu.

The Brahmā granthi is the most difficult knot to untie because of its density. In other words, the bulk of our samskārās relate to this granthi, which is a combination of the issues of the first three cakras. From the table above, we see that most of our prāṇa is expended in the business of the Brahmā granthi, which involves the three puruṣārthas and the eṣaṇas.[166] Our attention is turned outward in the maintenance of our identity and individuality, and constant self-validation.

166 See Puruṣārthas in Chapter 8 and Eṣaṇas in Chapter 5.

The Brahmā granthi is at the level of the mūlādhāra cakra, while the Viṣṇu granthi is at the maṇipura, and the Rudra granthi at the ājñā. As we will see in the Bahirdaśara, conservation of prāṇa is of critical importance if more is to be made available for higher transmutation. And for this, the untying of the Brahmā granthi is crucial. It is only with the resolution of the Brahmā granthi that we can even begin to turn inward with increasing focus and freedom from self-validation and self-deception. The higher esoteric concepts and experiences are not even accessible until this happens. With the resolution of the Brahmā granthi, we stop caring about physical comforts, gratification of sense pleasures, validation or approval from others, or the need to control events and people. There is a sense of peace with the outer world, where everything appears perfect even in its chaotic state. Even when engaged with the world, attention flows inward easily and freely, with delightful curiosity about the nuts and bolts of the process of experience rather than its content. We lose interest in owning anything in the world of objects, but the rasa of their experience increases by leaps and bounds. Emotions like anxiety, anger, fear, envy, and greed are resolved, and we relinquish the need to compare ourselves with others or judge them. Our internal moment-to-moment sādhanā becomes our preoccupation.

Kuṇḍalinī, which lies dormant at the mūlādhāra, pierces the Brahmā granthi when activated, resulting in extensive changes in our lives, perception, focus, and priorities.[167] Until the untying of the Brahmā granthi occurs, these changes can be reversible and unstable, where there remains the potential to vacillate between saṃsāra and nirvāṇa. It is only after this granthi is resolved that our fickleness comes to a total rest whereupon we arrive at the Viṣṇu granthi. The Rudra granthi is yet a distant concept at this point because it is there that the final vestiges of Māyā and dualities dissolve.

167 See Section 3 in K. Chinnaiyan, *Glorious Alchemy: Living the Lalitā Sahasranāma* (New Sarum Press, 2020): N99-N104.

The most important first step is the untying of the Brahmā granthi, which results in being rebirthed into a mature practitioner. This is the level of the Manvaśra.

Manvaśra

The Manvaśra (fourteen-triangled) is also known as the *Caturdaśara*. The word Manvaśra refers to the triangles of the worlds, which are said to be 14 in number,[168] and it is the āvaraṇa that represents the fourteen main nāḍīs that determine the functions of the sense organs, the organs of action, the mind, intellect, and ego. The fourteen triangles represent the fourteen nāḍīs that drive the functioning of these elements, and this āvaraṇa is known as *Sarvasaubhāgyadāyaka* (sarva = all, *saubhāgya* = auspicious, *dāyaka* = bestower) cakra, or the cakra that bestows all auspiciousness (see Figure 36).

168 In Hinduism, there are seven higher worlds and seven lower worlds.

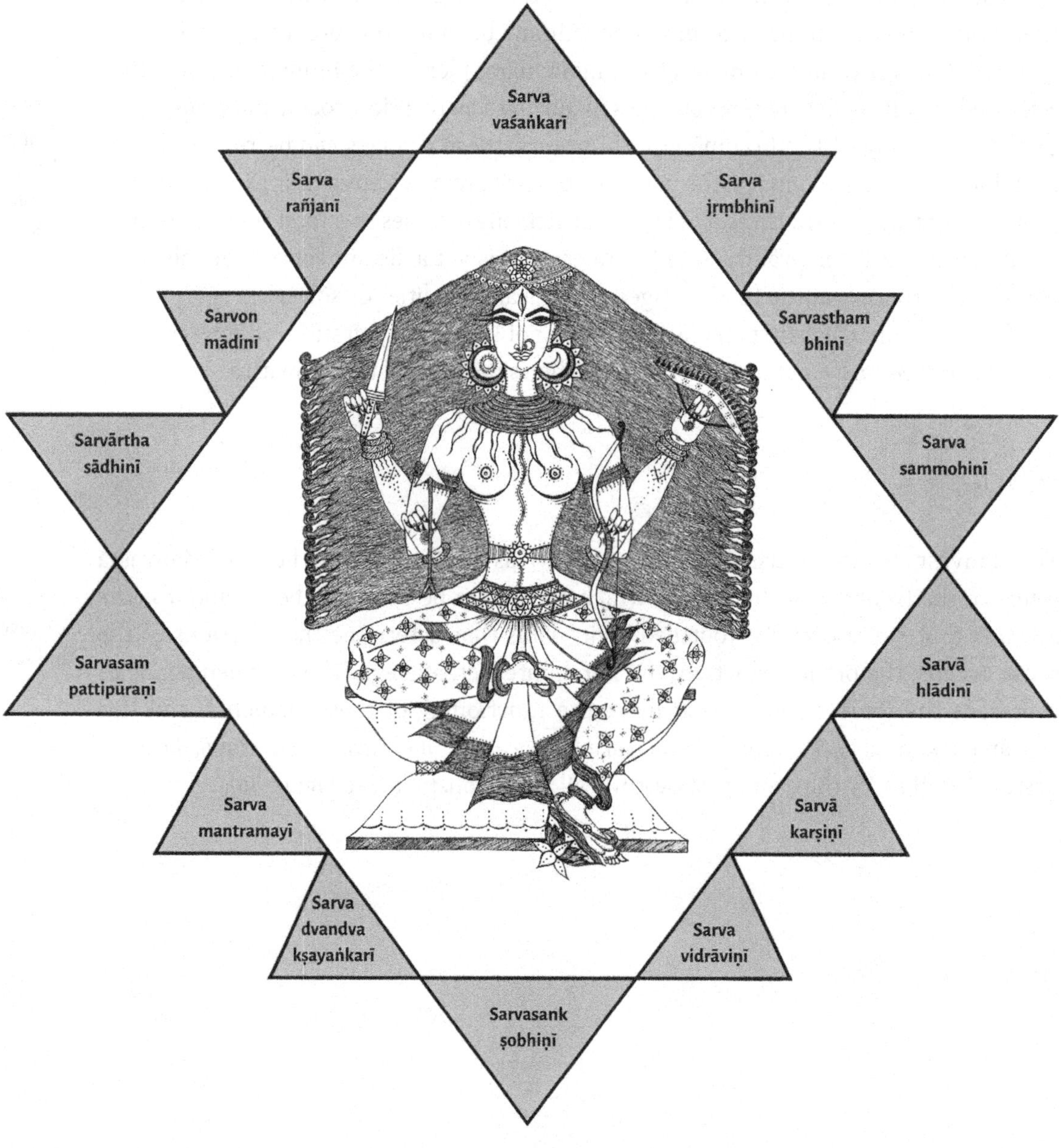

Figure 36. Manvaśra with Sampradāya Yoginī

Auspiciousness here refers to the opening that occurs when attention turns upon itself. Here at the Manvaśra, we come to see that prāṇa is, in reality, the flow of awareness in the citta. Conditioning is the repeated flow of awareness in certain nāḍīs because of which all the other nāḍīs become closed off and unavailable. Obstruction to the flow of prāṇa is the root cause of illness of the body or mind.

When we become deeply aware of our agitations in the Aṣṭadalapadma and inquire into their source, we start to acquaint ourselves with our nāḍīs. Even though we often don't have direct access to our samskārās, the agitations of the Aṣṭadalapadma, the grasping of the Śodaṣadalapadma and interactions in the Bhūpura give us indirect knowledge of our conditioning. In this growing awareness, our samskārās start to dissolve and the nāḍīs that were previously closed off become increasingly available for the flow of prāṇa.

The deities of this āvaraṇa are known as Sampradāya Yoginīs (Table 13).

> ***Sampradāya means tradition; turning inward at this level results in the spontaneous cultivation of the qualities that are traditionally desired in all paths, such as tolerance, honesty, and generosity.***

While they are forced or pointedly cultivated in the Bhūpura, here they arise naturally because of a natural broadening of perspective. The yoginīs are situated in an anti-clockwise fashion beginning at the east portal.

Table 13. Yoginīs of the Manvaśra

Yoginī	Psychophysiological	Nāḍī	Alphabet	Bhāvanā
Sarvasankṣobhiṇī	All-agitating	Alambuṣā (anus to mouth)	k	Fasting
Sarvavidrāviṇī	All-diffusing	Kuhu (throat to genital)	kh	Sublimating sexual energy
Sarvākarṣiṇī	All-attracting	Viśvodharā (stomach)	g	Digesting experience
Sarvāhlādinī	All-gladdening	Vāraṇā (diffuse)	gh	Delighting in experience
Sarvasammohinī	All-deluding	Hastijihvā (right eye to left toe)	ṅ	Higher reasoning
Sarvasthambhinī	All-arresting	Yaśasvinī (right big toe to left ear)	c	Higher reasoning
Sarvajṛmbhinī	All-releasing	Payasvinī (right eye, right toe)	ch	Releasing non-serving patterns
Sarvavaśaṅkarī	All-subjugating	Gāndhārī (left eye to left foot)	j	Subjugating lower impulses
Sarvarañjanī	All-delighting	Pūṣā (left big toe to right ear)	jh	Openness
Sarvonmādinī	All-maddening	Śaṅkhanī (throat to anus)	ñ	Aligning with darśana
Sarvārthasādhinī	Provider of all desires	Sarasvatī (tongue)	ṭ	Refining expression
Sarvasampattipūraṇī	Provider of all wealth	Īḍa (left side of spine to left nostril)	ṭh	Allowing what is
Sarvamantramayī	Made up of mantras	Piṅgala (right side of spine to right nostril)	ḍ	Cultivating viveka and vairāgya
Sarvadvandvakṣayaṅkarī	Dispeller of dualities	Suṣumnā (central channel to crown)	ḍh	Opening to Grace

Sampradāya Yoginī

The Sampradāya Yoginī is red-hued and four-armed (see Figure 37). In her lower hands, she carries a bow and arrow, symbolizing the allure of the tanmātras that maintains the restricted flow of prāṇa. Conditioning arising from attachment to sense objects ensures that prāṇa flows in familiar nāḍīs, nourishing circular patterns of thinking and feeling that create more samskārās and keep us entrapped at the periphery.

In her upper hands, the Sampradāya Yoginī bears a knife and a shield of fire. The knife cuts away the cords of attachment to the sense objects, opening new nāḍīs for prāṇa. The fiery shield protects the inner landscape from falling into the old trap of conditioning. The opening of new nāḍīs creates novel neural and hormonal pathways, creating fresh perspectives and spontaneous action.

Figure 37. Sampradāya Yoginī

Sarvasankṣobhiṇī

The first of the yoginīs of this āvaraṇa, Sarvasankṣobhiṇī is the one who agitates all.

Here in the Manvaśra, she reigns over the nāḍī known as *alambuṣā*, which carries prāṇa to the anus and connects it to the mouth.

While we can understand the agitating health effects of dysfunctional elimination such as constipation or diarrhea, the significance of this nāḍī is greater. From its position here in the Manvaśra and our understanding of prāṇa, we can relate this to the stuckness occurring at the Brahmā granthi.

> ***We spend a large proportion of our time being preoccupied with the body, its upkeep, the signs of wellness or health, validation from others and self about its appearance, loathing its various aspects, how and what to eat, grooming, and on and on.***

We remain in the sphere of the body, fearing disease, death, disability, and loss - of our own bodies or of those we love. Our life revolves around hunger and its satiation, where we work, make a living, and pay our bills to "put food on the table."

Hunger and thirst are the primordial drives of all life forms. This basic and obsessive focus on the body is represented by the nāḍī that courses between the mouth and the anus. It is because of our slavery to the tongue that elimination becomes problematic. We can go so far as to say that all our interactions in the playing field of life are centered around this nāḍī.

Our inability to eliminate the waste products of our past experiences, hurts, slights, memories, and me-stories result in the obstruction of this nāḍī. An obstructed nāḍī is the source of agitation and ill-heath.

There are many ways to work with nāḍīs, including kriyās and yogic exercises, breathing techniques and postural yoga. Fasting is a wonderful technique for this nāḍī. Fasting doesn't refer to food only, but also to senses, speech, and other stimuli. Having a strict diet and discipline that are followed at all costs is immensely beneficial for resetting the neurohormonal pathways and streamlining the mind by relinquishing our taste preferences. Through the relentless focus on doing what is needed and eliminating what isn't, our life begins to change in drastic ways. Even without directly focusing on the elimination of the samskārās that obstruct this nāḍī, they become attenuated and gradually dissolve. With the unobstructed flow of prāṇa in this nāḍī, we begin to experience taste like never before. Our own inward focus stimulates us and fills us with joy.

Sarvavidrāviṇī

Vidrāvaṇa means to flow or diffuse and Sarvavidrāviṇī (all-diffusing) rules over the *kuhu* nāḍī, which bridges prāṇa between the genital organs and the throat. Sublimation and transmutation of sexual energy is a central practice in Tantra, where it is absorbed and directed upward. When it changes direction to the higher centers from its habitual course that is downward, we gain pure knowledge (viśuddha), which is devoid of its usual entrapments such as lust driven by the senses. Lust energy becomes the fuel for transformation.

Sarvākarṣiṇī

Ākarṣaṇa is to attract, and Sarvākarṣiṇī corresponds to the *viśvodharī* nāḍi, which runs between the kuhu and *hastijihvā* nāḍīs in the vicinity of the navel. It allows the flow of prāṇa towards the process of digestion of not just food but also of our sense perception and past experiences. This nāḍī is said to distribute the flow of prāṇa through the suṣumnā.

Sarvāhlādinī

Hlādhana is the quality of refreshment and *Sarvāhlādinī* corresponds to the *vāruṇī* nāḍī, which is said to flow between the *yaśasvinī* and the kuhu nāḍīs. This nāḍī distributes prāṇa throughout the lower belly in some systems, and in others, it is said to supply prāṇa to the entire body through the circulatory system. The distribution here is what confers delight, where the flow of prāṇa is associated with vitality and excretion of waste, leading to freshness.

Sarvasammohinī

Sammohana is the one that causes bewilderment, and *Sarvasammohinī* corresponds to the *nādi* known as hastijihvā, which runs between the right eye and the left big toe.

Translated as "elephant tongue," hastijihvā is said to be the conduit for mystical experiences and abstractions as well as non-linear thought, which are registered in the right hemisphere of the brain. Abstractions and esoterism without the complementary limb of logic and higher reasoning can result in bewilderment, fascination, and digressions into avidyā.

Sarvasthambhinī

Sthambaṇa is the one who arrests, and *Sarvasthambhinī* corresponds to the nāḍi known as yaśasvinī, which runs between the right big toe and the left ear. The flow of prāṇa in this splendid (*yaśasvin* = splendid or celebrated) nāḍī facilitates higher thought, sattarka or higher reasoning, and balances the mystical and esoteric experiences in sādhanā. Higher reasoning arrests the story-making tendencies of mystical experiences and results in their correct assimilation, which results in progress along the path of vidyā.

Sarvajṛmbhinī

Jṛmbhana refers to expansion, and *Sarvajṛmbhinī* corresponds with the *payasvinī* nāḍī, which flows between the *pūṣā* and *sarasvatī* nāḍīs, terminating in the right ear lobe. This nāḍī is one of release or expansion, which is why the earlobes are pierced in some traditions. Expansiveness here refers to the ability to retain what is useful and release all that isn't.

Sarvavaśaṅkarī

Vaśaṅkara is to subjugate, and Sarvavaśaṅkarī corresponds to the nāḍī known as *gāndhārī*, which flows between the left eye and the left big toe. It is said to carry prāṇa from the lower part of the body toward the ājñā cakra, subjugating the "lower" impulses of avidyā in favor of vidyā.

Sarvarañjanī

Rañjana is to please, and *Sarvarañjanī* corresponds to the pūṣā nāḍī, which flows between the left big toe and the right side of the right eye. Pūṣā is the nourishing nāḍī, and is said to complement the yaśasvinī, being open, sweet, and expansive.

Sarvonmādinī

Mādana is to intoxicate, and Sarvonmādinī corresponds with the *śaṅkhanī* nāḍī, which flows between the sarasvatī and gāndhārī from the throat to the anus. Śaṅkhanī, which means the mother-of-pearl, is said to carry the prāṇa that purifies the blood. Becoming increasingly established in vidyā is intoxicating, because of the sweetness of the nectar arising from aligning with the right view.

Sarvārthasādhinī

Arthasādhanā is to accomplish goals or objectives, and *Sarvārthasādhinī* corresponds to the supreme sarasvatī nāḍī, which flows between the kanda and the tongue. Sarasvatī is the goddess of speech/expression, and this nāḍī bestows this ability. As we saw in Chapter 6, manifestation is an expression of vāc, and as this nāḍī becomes purified through sādhanā, our expression becomes fluent, clear, and refined.

Sarvasampattipūraṇī

Sampatti refers to wealth and *pūraṇa* is completion, and *Sarvasampattipūraṇī* corresponds to the īḍa nādi, one of the three principal nāḍīs that lies on the left of the suṣumnā. Along with the piṅgala, the īḍa nāḍī wraps around the suṣumnā, with the three coalescing at the cakras.

The īḍa is known as the moon/candra or the cool nāḍī, and ends in the left nostril, carrying prāṇa to the right side of the brain.

It is passive and expansive, associated with allowing, tolerance and patience. One of the gifts of being open and inclusive is that all wishes are automatically fulfilled. If we can allow what is, without being bogged down by what should be, we find that it is challenging to wish for something else. Paradoxically, it is when we stop wishing for other than what is that the whole universe seems to open for us, bringing to fruition all we ever wanted.

Sarvamantramayī

Mantramaya is to be replete and proficient in all mantras, and *Sarvamantramayī* corresponds to the piṅgala nādi. Complementing the īḍa nāḍī, the piṅgala sun/sūrya or the hot nāḍī traverses the other side of the suṣumnā, ending in the right nostril and perfusing the left side of the brain.

Mantra siddhi is attained through dedicated practice and an ever-deepening understanding of the mantra's many aspects, which requires the cultivation of discernment, dispassion, and perception, all of which are promoted by the opening of the piṅgala.

> ***Through the systematic control over breath and prāṇa, the īḍa and piṅgala harmonize the complementary aspects of the brain.***

It is only through such harmonization that we can look beyond the limitations of saṃsāra.

Sarvadvandvakṣayaṅkarī

Dvandva refers to opposites or duality, *akṣaya* means undecaying, and *Sarvadvandvakṣayaṅkarī* refers to the goddess who dissolves all dualities into the undecaying, corresponding to the suṣumnā nāḍī. This has to do with the "awakening" of the potential known as Kuṇḍalinī.

As we saw earlier in this chapter, we can think of Śakti as the energy of manifestation, where she comes to rest in the earth element or the mūlādhāra, as if hidden in plain sight. In the microcosm, Prāṇakuṇḍalinī turned toward manifestation is the experience of duality where prāṇa moves alternately in the īḍa and piṅgala throughout the day, switching between hot and cold, reasoning and surrender, and contraction and expansion. In between these two polarities, we remain entrapped in saṃsāra, shifting endlessly between attractions and aversions, beauty and disdain, and joy and pain. This is because Parākuṇḍalinī (or simply, Kuṇḍalinī), the *potential* for transcending saṃsāra, is said to be asleep.

Kuṇḍalinī is said to lie dormant at the mūlādhāra cakra, which grounds us in the world of objects, coiled around a psychic Śiva *liṅga* (phallus-like symbol of infinity or awareness) three and a half times with her head blocking the entrance to the suṣumnā (see below). Prāṇa needed for psycho-physiological functions flows primarily through the īḍa and piṅgala, keeping us grounded in the world of objects or the playing field of the Bhūpura from the point of view of the Śrīcakra.

Throughout the day, prāṇa switches back and forth between the īḍa and piṅgala, reflected in the breath becoming predominant in the right or the left nostril. When the īḍa is active, for instance, the left nostril is "open," breath flows more freely on the left, and the right nostril is slightly constricted. Prāṇa is said to switch between the two sides approximately every ninety minutes. During the transition phases, prāṇa briefly enters the suṣumnā when the breath flows equally in both nostrils. When we develop keen awareness of the flow of prāṇa and cultivate sensitivity to our breath patterns, we can notice subtle but distinct differences in how we feel, think, and perceive depending on which nostril is active.

There are many aspects to Kuṇḍalinī "awakening," which results in changes in not just our mental or emotional spheres but also in our physiology, perception, priorities, and objectives. If we think of Kuṇḍalinī as the potential for transcending the dualities of saṃsāra, we can understand awakening as the conversion of this potential to kinetic energy. What was previously dormant "wakes up," dynamically changing every aspect of our lives.

> ***The ignition for this change from potential to kinetic can be any number of things, including dīkṣā or initiation, a traumatic life event, or deep depression or despair.***

It can also occur spontaneously. However it occurs, this event is a descent of divine grace, as it will result in extensive housecleaning and eventually lead to resolution of dualistic tendencies.

Kuṇḍalinī and Nāda

Kuṇḍalinī being coiled 3.5 times around a Śiva liṅga has deep significance. As we saw in Chapter 1, the whole Śrīcakra can be seen as the devolution of the sound-to-word pathway from the Bindu to the Bhūpura in the sṛṣṭi krama, and the evolution from word to sound in the opposite direction with the eventual dissolution of sound in the saṃhāra krama. The understanding of Kāmakalā in Chapter 4 is crucial when it comes to Kuṇḍalinī, particularly as it relates to the Śrīcakra. Kāmakalā depicts the process by which the potential energy becomes kinetic energy, where AUM, the potential of Absolute Reality with the 3.5 mātrā or measure becomes hrīṃ, the kinetic energy that devolves into creation.

The potential energy of Absolute Reality is symbolized by the syllable AUM (ॐ), which has a measure (mātrā) of 3.5 units. AUM is known as the praṇava or primordial sound. A, U and M constitute the first three mātrās, representing the triads of creation including the three avasthās, worlds, and primary śaktis of the Trikoṇa. The bindu or dot with the half-moon makes up the remaining 0.5 mātrā of AUM, which is the fourth and the fifth principle.

The first three mātrās of AUM are without nāda or vibration, being the integral of all vibrations in creation and subsuming them all. The dot or anusvāra is the primordial nāda, which becomes the Īm or hrīṃ of Kāmakalā and is Prāṇakuṇḍalinī. AUM is Parā at the level of Absolute Reality where Śiva and Śakti are merged in quiescence, with no nāda or perceivable vibration. Hrīṃ is Parā turned toward manifestation as the nāda of AUM, represented by the 0.5 mātrā.

In the microcosm, the dormant Kuṇḍalinī is coiled 3.5 times around the Śiva liṅga symbolizing the obscuration of Absolute Reality in the din of saṃsāra. The kinetic energy of Kuṇḍalinī śakti is wrapped around the potential, hidden in earth, the last and densest tattva. Earth has all five attributes (sound, touch, form, taste, and smell), denoting the most differentiated form of vāc, vaikharī.

The purest form of nāda that begins in the Kāmakalā as hrīṃ (or Īm) becomes obscured in successive stages of differentiation from parā turned toward manifestation in the Bindu to paśyantī in the Trikoṇa, madhyamā in the Vasukoṇa and vaikharī in the rest of the Śrīcakra. Vaikharī becomes increasingly dense and differentiated, coming to rest at pṛthvī or earth, the last tattva. In this process, hrīṃ, the purest undifferentiated kinetic energy becomes concealed and inaccessible in the manifest world even though it is the driving force of manifestation.

The purpose of Śrīcakra upāsanā is to first access the pure and undifferentiated nāda of hrīṃ, which will then lead to the AUM of Absolute Reality in the final stages of ascent in the Bindu through the nine stations of mantra.

Kuṇḍalinī is described as a snake coiled 3.5 times around the Śiva liṅga with her tail in her mouth and blocking the entrance to the suṣumnā (see Figure 38). Here, the kinetic energy of creation or Prāṇakuṇḍalinī is so dominant that Parākuṇḍalinī is obscured and hibernates as the potential for the reverse engineering process of awakening. Prāṇakuṇḍalinī being centrifugal as Vāmā drives our attention and activity to the periphery and the radius remains hidden.

The process of awakening results in the conversion of the potential energy of Parākuṇḍalinī into kinetic energy that will need to overcome the naturally outward directed Vāmā force and align with the centripetal Jyeṣṭhā.

At this point, Kuṇḍalinī śakti that lay asleep begins to uncoil like a snake and enters the suṣumnā. Her hiss is the Śakti prāṇava hrīṃ, which must integrate the scattered and differentiated vibrations of vaikharī at the periphery into the progressively subtler ones of madhyamā and paśyantī on the radius to dissolve in the supreme undifferentiated nāda of AUM as hrīṃ. The progression of Kuṇḍalinī occurs through the resolution of all dualities of the ṣaṭcakras and the three granthis, facilitated by the opening of nāḍīs to allow the free flow of prāṇa. The suṣumnā becomes the primary conduit of prāṇa, resolving the dualities and ascending beyond the turbulence of the periphery. The sandhis and marmas of the Śrīcakra are points of confluence and flow of Kuṇḍalinī śakti as she integrates the parts of our fragmented awareness into an unbroken whole.

> ***As sādhanā progresses, Kuṇḍalinī śakti rises awareness through the stations of the mantra where the nāda of hrīṃ dissolves or ends (nādānta), and the upāsaka is absorbed into the Absolute Reality, AUM.***

Here, the fire and moon of the Kāmakalā resolve into the Mahābindu.

Kuṇḍalinī awakening, if smooth and uneventful, results in the steady and progressive movement of attention from artha and śabda to turn upon itself as the subject. The varied problems of Kuṇḍalinī awakening have many causes that are out of the scope of this book. Some of the psychophysiological issues are the result of premature or forced Kuṇḍalinī awakening, when its massive energy of housecleaning is short-circuited by the very high voltage energy violently entering unprepared contracted nāḍīs. Without the right lifestyle, perspective and guidance, these symptoms can be problematic and dangerous. This is a significant reason for the characteristics of Śrīcakra upāsanā, including the Guru-śiṣya relationship, the need for mantra dīkṣā, the secrecy around practices, and the emphasis on the sampradāya.

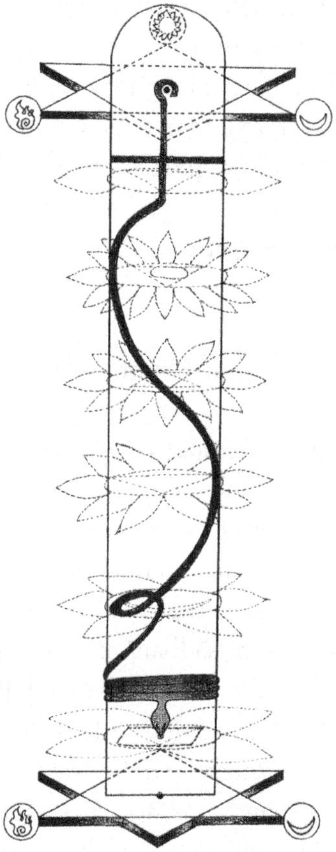

Figure 38. Kuṇḍalinī

The suṣumnā integrates and subsumes the triad of the sun, moon, and fire, and encloses two other nāḍīs – *citriṇī* and Brahmā. The citriṇī nāḍī is the seat of AUM and the Brahmā nāḍī which is the subtlest of all is the pathway to Brahman and the source of nectar or amṛta. Kuṇḍalinī entering the suṣumnā is a significant occurrence, where she systematically cleanses the buddhi and purges samskārās, often violently. Nonserving patterns are set right with no concern for our comfort or the ego's posturing. If we are unprepared for this massive event, the inherent conflict of this force with the ego's desire for eṣaṇā fulfilment can be a struggle.

When Kuṇḍalinī becomes active, awakening becomes the top priority, and all of life is poured into the process. A colossal house cleaning occurs where prāṇa begins to flow into the contracted nāḍīs, converting shadow to light and transcending both. Sarvadvandvakṣayaṅkarī goes to work to resolve our linear and dualistic perspective and grants us the holistic, nonlinear vision of nonduality. The nāḍīs begin to open progressively and the energy that was previously exhausted in maintaining facades through validations, justifications and mind stories is freed up for higher transmutation.

Cakreśvarī: Tripuravāsinī

The Sampradāya Yoginīs of the Manvaśra lead us through their shadows to light, where we understand the implications of obstructed nāḍīs and the expansiveness in the psychophysiology with their opening. While there are many techniques involving the breath, *bandhas* (locks), mudrās (seals) and postures, and various cleansing procedures (*ṣaṭkarmas*) that work on releasing obstructions in nāḍīs, the most important aspect of Kuṇḍalinī sādhanā is self-inquiry under the guidance of a Guru. The importance of a strict discipline in diet and lifestyle cannot be overstated. To even understand the flow of prāṇa, we must establish a routine that is free of chaos and is aligned with the cycles of day/night and the seasons.[169]

169 K. Chinnaiyan, *The Heart of Wellness* (Sfaim Press, 2021).

Tripuravāsinī, an emanation of Mahātripurasundarī rules over the Sarvasaubhāgyadāyaka cakra of auspiciousness. Tripuravāsinī is invoked by the mantra *haiṃ hkliṃ hsauḥ* with the mudrā bīja *blūṃ* and the corresponding all-subjugating mudrā, Sarvavaśaṅkarī. Constant contemplation of the darśana and cultivating a perspective that is more aligned with it allows us to free up the nāḍīs and gain control over the flow of prāṇa. Attainment of the Manvaśra is to have access over the flow of prāṇa, and to be able to direct it at will.

Ultimately, "nāḍī" is closely related to "nāda," which means to flow. Being aligned with the darśana gradually dissolves the samskārās obstructing the flow of prāṇa in the nāḍīs, opening us to the grace of the Sampradāya Yoginīs. Pleased with our devotion and dedication, they propel us to the next āvaraṇa, the Bahirdaśara.

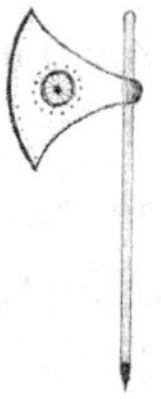

Chapter 12

Bahirdaśara

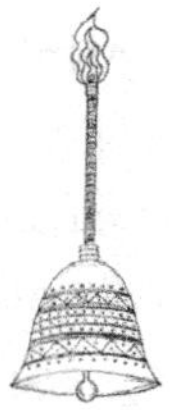

प्राणापानव्यानोदानसमाननागकूर्मकृकरदेवदत्तधनञ्जया दश वायवः ।
सर्वसिद्धिप्रदादि बहिर्दशारगा देवताः ॥ १६ ॥

Prāṇa-apāna-vyānodāna-samāna-nāga-kūrma-kṛkara-devadatta-dhanañjaya
daśa vāyvah sarvasiddhipradādi-bahirsdaśāragā devatāḥ || 16 ||

"Prāṇa, apāna, vyāna, udāna, samāna, nāga, kūrma, kṛkara, devadatta, and dhanañjaya, which are the ten vāyus are Sarvasiddhipradā, etc. in the outer ten triangles."
~ Bhāvanopaniṣad, verse 16.

As we make our way up the Śrīcakra, we pause to re-evaluate our journey which began at the Bhūpura, the playing field of saṃsāra. Here, we encountered the Siddhis, the Aṣṭa Mātṛkās and the Mudrā Devīs who in their shadow aspect bound us in the contractions of saṃsāra, and in their benevolent aspect, granted us access to skillful engagement in the world and propelled us to the Śodaṣadalapadma. Here, we met the sixteen ākarṣiṇīs who were the driving forces of the drama of the Bhūpura. With their grace, we were thrust onto the Aṣṭadalapadma, where the Anaṅga Devatās revealed the fundamental agitations of the citta that flowered into the attractions of the Śodaṣadalapadma. As we continued to inquire into their source, we were led to the Manvaśra and the Sampradāya Yoginīs who granted us the knowledge of the flow of prāṇa in the nāḍīs.

The Inquiry

At the Manvaśra, we took stock of our energy and re-evaluated our expenditure of prāṇa, seeing that most of it is used up in the Brahmā granthi centered around self-preservation.

The Sampradāya Yoginīs revealed the obstructions to the flow of prāṇa in the nāḍīs, which keep us bound in our contracted patterns of thinking, feeling and being.

When we gain a deeper understanding of the flow of prāṇa through discipline, focus, surrender, and a committed practice, we begin to dig further. At this point, we have left behind the need for external validation or maintaining a self-image. Concerns about our body and its maintenance have abated and we are no longer slaves to our tongue, and hunger, thirst and sexual impulse are internal energetic impulses that are utilized in upāsanā. External objects are enjoyed without ownership, and our interactions in the world are free of contractions and flow in spontaneity and generosity.

Our inquiry now naturally shifts to the workings of prāṇa, which takes us to the Bahirdaśara. The inquiry here is, "What is the driving force of prāṇa in the nāḍīs? Why does it flow as it does?"

Vāyu

If we look at the whole process of creation, its fundamental property is *dynamism*. Creation *flows* – first as the movement of self-recognition in Absolute Reality that results in Śiva as Prakāśa and Śakti as Vimarśa (see Tattva Map in Chapter 4). Icchā or divine will is the orgasmic movement of the desire to create, unfolding as Prāṇakuṇḍalinī all the way down to pṛthvī. Vāyu[170] is the impelling principle of dynamism that starts creation, maintains it, and eventually dissolves it. Vāyu as this force is subtler than the air element among the pañca mahābhūtas without which there would be no creation.

When we look at this process in terms of the Kāmakalā, the movement of the red and white bindus interpenetrating each other to create the mixed bindu is facilitated by vāyu. The resultant nāda, which is the resonance of the flow of creation is the very root of dynamism. Śakti turning toward Śiva to collapse into the anusvāra or looking away from him as the visarga is catalyzed by vāyu as is the process where parā becomes paśyantī, madhyamā and vaikharī, and subtle thought is vocalized into speech.

Life flows as the breath, the unceasing beating of the heart, the movement of electrical signals across neurons, the flow of chemicals and enzymes flawlessly upkeeping the body's exquisite machinery, the movement of the tectonic plates, earthquakes and

170 In this book, vāyu as the principle of movement is spelled with a lower-case v to differentiate the word referring to the god of wind or air.

tsunamis, the unbroken spin of the heavenly bodies around their axes and each other, and the hide-and-seek of the moon through its phases. Dynamism is the very essence of aliveness, which is the function of vāyu. One way we can conceptualize this is through the understanding of Śakti in different ways. At the highest level, she is known as Mahaśakti, containing within herself all energy as the potential. A tiny fraction of this potential becomes kinetic energy through the function of agni, the transformative power, and is known as Prāṇaśakti. We can think of vāyu as being the dynamism of Prāṇaśakti, who goes by the other name of Prāṇakuṇḍalinī.

From a very broad perspective, moving from one component of an āvaraṇa to another throughout the entire upāsanā of the Śrīcakra is the play of vāyu and agni. We will examine the importance of agni in the next chapter, but for now, let's explore the experience of vāyu in the microcosm.

Prāṇa Vāyus

Thus far, we have explored vāyu from a very broad macrocosmic perspective. To understand it from the standpoint of the microcosm that is particularly relevant for us in the Śrīcakra upāsanā, we need to go back to the Tattva Map to the level of Puruṣa and Prakṛti. As we have seen in Chapter 4, Puruṣa is individual consciousness or subjectivity, and Prakṛti is materiality or the world of objects, which arise from her three inherent qualities or guṇas – sattva, rajas and tamas.[171]

171 See The Tattvas in Chapter 4.

Sattva means essence and it is the guṇa of clarity and intelligence, rajas is movement, and tamas is heaviness. Sattva and tamas are static whereas rajas is dynamic. Rajas combines with sattva and tamas giving rise to the jñānendriyas, the karmendriyas, the tanmātras and the pañca mahābhūtas. The pañca mahābhūtas combine in specific ways giving rise to the three *doṣas*.

Doṣa means flaw or fault, referring to the fundamental process of creation that disturbs wholeness to introduce apparent divisions in it. Wholeness is static and nondual, while creation results in dynamism that leads to awe-inspiring drama based in duality. Doṣas are the primary properties of the manifest universe – *vāta*, which is the blend of air and space is the property of movement; *pitta*, the mixing of fire and water is the principle of transformation, and *kapha*, the combination of water and earth is the principle of structure.

Being applicable to everything in creation, the doṣas are seen in all of nature. Vāyu becomes vāta as the principle of dynamism in nature and is seen in everything that involves movement, pitta in all change and transformation (seasons, aging, evolution, and digestion), and kapha in the structure of the macrocosm and microcosm (think planets, bones, cells and so on).

> ***At the macrocosmic level, vāyu is diffuse and without direction, and propels creation as a whole.***

At the level of the microcosm, the directionality of the flow of vāyu becomes channelized as the prāṇa nāḍīs that we explored in the previous chapter. Within the framework of this directionality, we can think of vāyu as manifesting in ten different ways. These ten "types" of vāyu are known as the prāṇa vāyus, symbolized by the triangles of the Bahirdaśara.

Bahirdaśara

The Bahirdaśara (*bahir* = outer, and *daśara* = comprising of ten) is the outer ten-triangled āvaraṇa where each represents one of the ten prāṇa vāyus (see Figure 39). This āvaraṇa is called the *Sarvārthasādhaka* (sarva = all, artha = aims, sādhaka = fulfilling) cakra, or the cakra that fulfils all aims or desires.

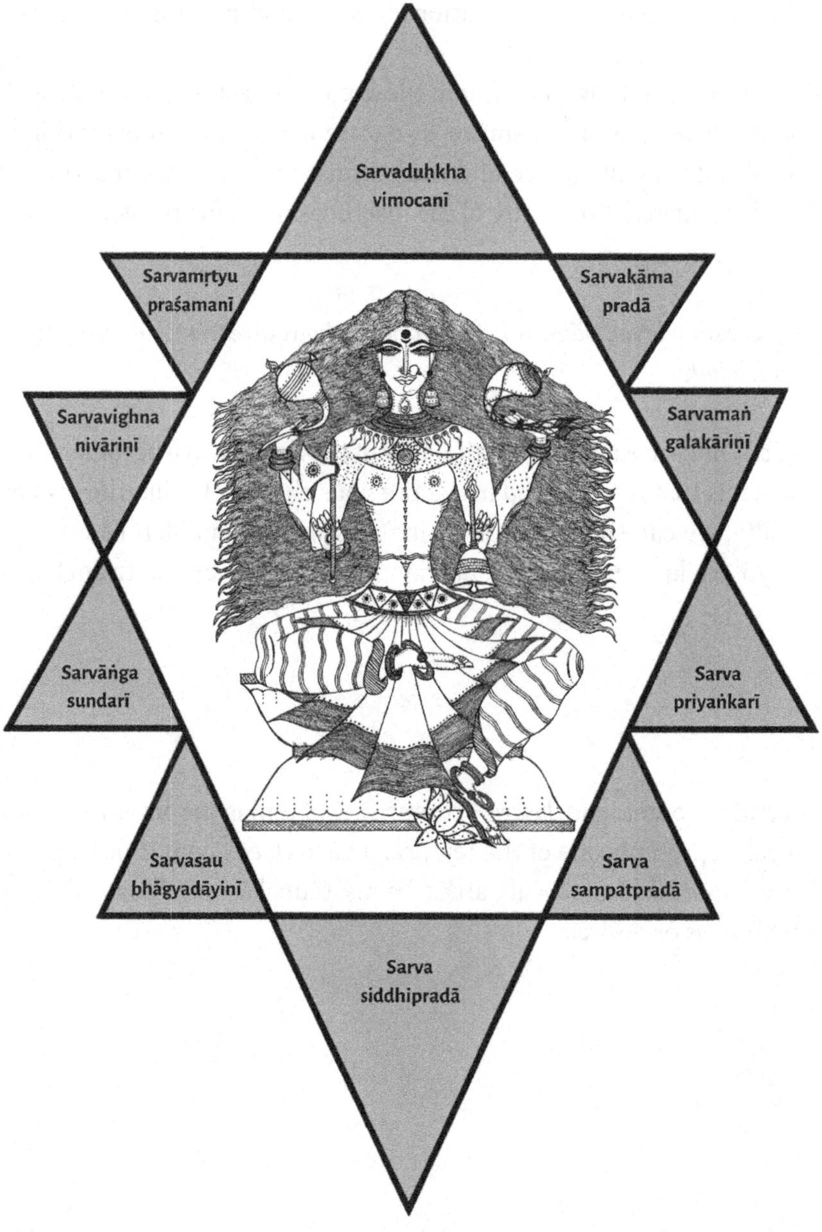

Figure 39. Bahirdaśara with Kulottīrṇa Yoginī

Remember how we ended up here? From the drama of the playing field that is the Bhūpura, we began to take progressive backward steps, realizing the essential nature of our desires, restlessness and insecurities that drove how we interacted with others and our own selves. At some point of reaching the required level of ripeness, we were catapulted into the Śodaṣadalapadma, where we saw the drivers of our neuroses and through the grace of the ākarṣiṇīs, we were propelled onto the Aṣṭadalapadma where we came face-to-face with the agitations behind the attractions, arriving at the Sarvasaubhāgyadāyaka cakra to see how the functioning of the fourteen nāḍīs influence our behavior by creating agitations and attractions.

As we saw earlier in the Śodaṣadalapadma, our angst and restlessness arise from the āṇava mala, our fundamental sense of lack. Ordinarily, our externally turned senses look for all kinds of "things" to allay this sense of lack – material goods, relationships, validation by way of fame or notoriety or simply a sense of belonging somewhere, justifications for our past and current behaviors and misfortunes, and so on.

The whole idea of the spiritual path is to "turn back" upon the disquiet to find its root cause.

The trick here is to ask the right questions. Without these said questions, we remain entrapped in the *stories* of the angst and restlessness.

For example, if we find ourselves agitated in a relationship, our inquiry can proceed in two broad ways even though the question is the same, which is, "What is the source of this conflict?" In the first, we dig into the history of the relationship to its origins. We recall how things were in the beginning of the relationship, and progress through its unfolding of who did and said what that has brought it to its current predicament. In the second, the kind of inquiry we are discussing here results in a "turning back upon itself" of the question. The source of the conflict is traced to our own expectation of the outcome in the relationship and what the other person must say or do. This expectation comes from our own desire, which in turn is fueled by our own agitation. The agitation in turn arises from dysfunctioning nāḍīs. Same question, two outcomes – in one we remain entrapped in the drama of the world and in the other, we are progressing toward the Bindu. Overanalysis at the level of the conflict leads us to more conflict at the periphery, whereas the right analysis leads us toward freedom at the Bindu.

As long as we remain entrapped in conflict, we find ourselves lacking and incomplete. In the process of turning back from arising experience, all our wishes become fulfilled (Sarvārthasādhaka) in the process of understanding that we were never incomplete in the first place. Fulfilment of all desires comes from seeing that who we are is and has always been unbroken and whole.

The yoginīs of this āvaraṇa are called *Kulottīrṇa* (kula = clan or family, *uttīrṇa* = to traverse). They help us traverse the kula, which in this instance refers to the grouping or the clan of the prāṇa vāyus that are conditioned to flow in specific ways in the nāḍīs. They are situated in an anti-clockwise direction beginning at the east portal (see Table 14).

Table 14. Yoginīs of the Bahirdaśara

Yoginī	Psychophysiological	Prāṇa Vāyu	Alphabet	Bhāvanā
Sarvasiddhipradā	Bestowing all attainments	Prāṇa	ṇ	Mindfulness
Sarvasampatpradā	Bestowing all wealth	Apāna	t	Unlearning
Sarvapriyaṅkarī	Bestowing all desirability	Vyāna	th	Darśana
Sarvamaṅgalakāriṇī	Bestowing all prosperity	Udāna	d	Other vāyus
Sarvakāmapradā	Bestowing all desires	Samāna	dh	Digesting experience
Sarvaduḥkhavimocanī	Removing all suffering	Nāga	n	Darśana
Sarvamṛtyupraśamanī	Countering all death	Kūrma	p	Resilience
Sarvavighnanivāriṇī	Removing all obstacles	Devadatta	ph	Single-pointedness
Sarvāṅgasundarī	Beauty of all limbs	Krikala	b	Cultivating steadiness
Sarvasaubhāgyadāyinī	Bestowing all auspiciousness	Dhanañjaya	bh	Cultivating steadfastness

Kulottīrṇa Yoginī

The four-armed Kulottīrṇa Yoginī is brilliant and colorless like quartz (see Figure 40). The mace and noose in her upper hands direct the flow of vāyu to create the countless kulas or groupings of the cosmos. With the axe in her lower right hand, she cuts through the kulas that keep us in saṃsāra, and the sound of the bell in lower left beckons us to the primordial kula of the Trikoṇa.

The Bhāvanopaniṣad, which we are following here, doesn't correlate each of the yoginīs specifically with the prāṇa vāyus (such as *Sarvasiddhipradā* with prāṇa vāyu and so on). By broadly stating that this āvaraṇa corresponds to the ten sub-types of vāyu, the text leaves it to the practitioner to find the holistic correlation. In the ultimate analysis, it's less important to adhere to specific correlations of the yoginīs with various elements and tattvas since they tend to be highly varied between texts. In the grand scheme of things, making our way to the ground of all being – the Bindu – is the most important goal.

In this chapter, the specific correlations between the yoginīs and the prāṇa vāyus are from my upāsanā and understanding. Your own correlations may differ, and I hope that any differences in our understanding will only help deepen your upāsanā.

Figure 40. KulottīrṇaYoginī

Sarvasiddhipradā

The first of the Kulottīrṇa Yoginīs, Sarvasiddhipradā bestows all attainments (sarva = all, siddhi = attainment, *pradā* = bestower) and represents the prāṇa vāyu.

Prāṇa vāyu is the first of the ten sub-types. It controls all the others and refers to the specific *direction* of prāṇa.[172] Prāṇa vāyu is the inward direction of prāṇa, being responsible for the intake of breath, food, water, sense perception, knowledge, inspiration – anything that flows in from the outside.

172 As opposed to prāṇa, which is the generic term used for the vital creative force that we explored in the previous chapter.

On the path of sādhanā, prāṇa vāyu facilitates the flow of the teaching from the teacher to the student. Through this vāyu we find the perfect teacher at every point of our journey. Even when the teacher turns out to not be right for us, the learning from the interaction can result in immense growth and progress. However, as we will see below, if we hold onto such interactions with bitterness and resentment, no growth is possible even with the "right" teacher.

Prāṇa vāyu brings in knowledge in every moment of life. Most often, this remains unknown to us because we remain oblivious or closed off to its flow, remaining entrapped in the linear mind. Our samskārās arising from our past experiences and aspirations for the future influence what we can take in or process. The past and the future keep us so engrossed in the linearity of cause and effect that we remain closed to the influx of vidyā that tends to be non-linear and without cause or effect. In every second, nearly 11 million bits of information are sent to the brain. However, the conscious mind can process only about 50 bits per second of these impulses, mostly based on the information we have previously accumulated.

In other words, even though prāṇa vāyu works unceasingly, bringing in more than what we want or need, we are aware of only a fraction of its gifts. If, on the other hand, our capacity to receive can be expanded by purging all that is accumulated, we would attain all siddhis or perfections.

Bhāvanā on Sarvasiddhipradā

Mindfulness is the moment-to-moment awareness of our internal landscape in a *nonjudgmental* fashion.

Ordinarily, we are aware of our internal landscape, but this is colored by anxiety and judgment about its contents. We get caught up in the content or the stories associated with it.

In the practice of mindfulness, we learn to observe the arising without reacting to the content. Observation of the arising, when laced with curiosity, strips it of anxiety or grasping. Humor is extremely helpful as well ("Ah, here comes *this* story again!").

Mindfulness in moment-to-moment application is greatly enhanced by its seated practice. Spend 10-20 minutes twice a day being quietly aware of the breath. Simply notice the movement of the breath. Whenever a thought, emotion or sensation arises, notice it, acknowledge it, and return to the breath. Cultivate stillness.

Carry this practice into your daily activities. Slow down the mind's process by returning to the breath, noticing and acknowledging an arising, and returning to the breath. This is the internal worship of Sarvasiddhipradā.

Sarvasampatpradā

Sarvasampatpradā (sarva = all, *sampata* = wealth, pradā = bestower) is the yoginī that bestows all wealth, corresponding with the *apāna* vāyu, which is the downward direction of prāṇa. Apāna governs all downward movements such as elimination, urination, ovulation, childbirth, menstruation and sexual activity. In addition, apāna is responsible for the subtle elimination of unlearning.

Here, we may wonder how elimination is related to acquiring wealth. When it comes to regulation of the vāyus, apāna is the most important. None of the other vāyus can function well without an optimal apāna. For example, if our elimination is weak, no amount of "good" or nutritious food will be useful. Digestion (*samāna*) and assimilation (*vyāna*) don't function at their optimal levels without a strong apāna. We may keep taking in what we think is nutritious food, but nutrients remain unabsorbed and eventually become poison. Growth is stunted due to inadequate or dysfunctional apāna vāyu.

So too on the inner journey – without letting go of our past experiences, hurts, slights, gripes, resentments and erroneous perceptions – no teaching, however elevated or sublime, can be digested or assimilated.

> ***The path of the Śrīcakra is one of prolonged, relentless unlearning, where everything that we think we know must be relinquished, which is the function of the apāna vāyu.***

With constant unlearning and relinquishing of our ideas, ideals, beliefs, and social, moral, and cultural norms, vidyā begins to take hold of us at a cellular level. With a strong apāna, more of what is taken in through prāṇa vāyu becomes available for transformation and transmutation through the *udāna* because of optimal functioning of samāna and vyāna.

We become replete with wealth (Sarvasampatpradā) by systematically letting go of everything we hoard!

Sarvapriyaṅkarī

Sarvapriyaṅkarī (sarva = all, *priyaṅkarī* = desirability or amiability) bestows all desirability and corresponds to vyāna vāyu.

Vyāna vāyu is centrifugal in direction, moving outward and becoming diffuse in the process. It governs circulation, nerve impulses, joint and muscle movement as well as mental activity. On the inner journey, vyāna vāyu governs assimilation of what is ingested and digested by way of knowledge and practice.

Very often on the spiritual path, it's not that we don't have theoretical understanding – we do, but it remains out of our reach because it isn't assimilated through the correct application of a teaching or concept in our day-to-day life. This lack of assimilation is the result of a weak vyāna vāyu, which as we saw previously, is highly dependent on the strength of the apāna vāyu.

Think about someone you find amiable or desirable. What is the secret of their attractiveness? Beyond good looks or charm, it is their aura of magnetism, which arises from the ability to interact in a centrifugal way that moves outward, touching those with whom they interact. Attractiveness lies in the ability to take in the world through the senses, make wholesome interpretations about it and reflect it back to the world. This power is the gift of a strong vyāna vāyu, where we become *sarvapriyaṅkara* or all-desirable.

Sarvamaṅgalakāriṇī

Sarvamaṅgalakāriṇī (*sarva* = all, *maṅgala* = prosperity, kāraṇa = causing) is the yoginī who confers all prosperity and corresponds to the udāna vāyu.

Udāna vāyu flows in the upward direction and governs expression through speech, memory, growth, effort, inner strength, and resolve. Importantly, it is responsible for transmutation of Kuṇḍalinī awakening.

As we have been exploring here, the optimal functioning of all the aspects of vāyu is important for spiritual progress and transmutation. Especially when it comes to the udāna vāyu, transmutation is stunted or obstructed when the other four main vāyus are out of balance or chaotic. We may want spiritual growth, but it often conflicts with our other wants that keep the vāyus functioning in disorderly ways, keeping us on the periphery. We want the mystical experiences but are unable to let go of our attachment to the mundane. We want the most advanced teacher or teaching but can never settle down and call off the search, restlessly moving from one to the next. We are fascinated with the idea of freedom but don't want to move past our social and moral conditioning.

In this inner conflict, the vāyus remain chaotic with little, if any, available for meaningful transmutation. Even when Kuṇḍalinī "awakens," the flow of prāṇa is erratic and tears through nāḍīs that are unprepared, leading to discomfort and the physical, psychological, mental, and emotional untoward effects that many of us experience. This is the conflict between the impulse to traverse the radius and the habitual way of staying in the circumference. This conflict that is deep-rooted in the mind is caused by suboptimally functioning prāṇa vāyus.

When the udāna vāyu is strengthened through the optimal functioning of the other prāṇa vāyus (especially apāna), transmutation occurs at a rapid rate in the mind and body, leading to deep insights that are not merely intellectual; they are also experiential. These insights change our perception and take us to higher realms. Even while being in the world, we begin to experience the mystical by engaging in the mundane. Auspiciousness abounds in all areas of life, and we come to experience *sarvamaṅgala* or all-encompassing prosperity.

Sarvakāmapradā

Sarvakāmapradā (sarva = all, kāma = desires, pradā = giver) is the yoginī who fulfils all our desires and corresponds to the samāna vāyu.

Samāna means to equalize, and this vāyu has a centripetal direction, governing over digestion. Here, digestion refers to not just the breakdown of food but also of sense perception, emotional states, thoughts and ideas, beliefs, and life experiences. On the spiritual journey, samāna governs the ability to digest teachings and concepts to make it available for assimilation by vyāna.

A common phenomenon in modern spirituality is the pattern of incessant seeking. We skip from one teacher, teaching, practice, and tradition to the next without ever spending the time and effort to digest any of them. Impatience takes over when we aren't given the next "advanced" teaching or if the practice doesn't immediately yield its fruit. We become frustrated and angry with teachers who keep coming back to the basics of discipline and effort, feeling slighted that somehow we are being held back from progress. While there are plenty of examples of spiteful and charlatan teachers, here we will focus on authentic ones.

The most basic teaching becomes advanced through its consistent application and digestion, which depends on the state of our vāyus. One mantra is enough, as is one technique, if we have the discipline to follow through by systematically eliminating everything that doesn't serve our path or goal. The problem arises when instead of focusing on the practice given to us, we fall into the trap of comparing ourselves with others, believing we are capable of more when we aren't, berating ourselves for failing, judging the teacher for their failings, and so on.

A comparable issue when it comes to the samāna vāyu is that of diet – often, we focus exclusively on what we must eat or consume for health and well-being without an understanding of our own capability to digest it. We obsess about the nutritional value of this or that, failing to see that we may lack the ability to extract the said nutrition from the food. Nutrition fanatics keep adding more and more varieties of foods and supplements to their diet with very little return, not because the food doesn't have value but because they lack the ability to extract the food's value.

So too on the spiritual journey. We would do well to trust that the teaching or practice given to us is enough, and as our samāna vāyu becomes stronger, more will come our way. It is strengthened through the systematic letting go of our baggage through the apāna vāyu and skillfully digesting our experiences, emotions, and mind contents without them leaving traces of samskārās.

In fact, as samāna comes into balance along with all the other vāyus, all our wishes are fulfilled. One of the main obstacles to a wish being fulfilled is that there is no space for it in our internal landscape. Our ideas about how the wish must be fulfilled occupy so much space that there is none left for it to manifest as it will. As we cultivate the ability to digest our experiences, we create room for more.

Skillful digestion means that we hold no grudges or expectations of how life should turn out; we are open to life as it is.

When we become open, we are graced by Sarvakāmapradā, and are granted the ability to fulfill all our wishes.

Sarvaduḥkhavimocanī

Sarvaduḥkhavimocanī (sarva = all, *duḥkha* = suffering, *vimocana* = deliverance) is the yoginī who frees or delivers us from all suffering and corresponds to the *nāga* vāyu.

Nāga is one of the minor prāṇa vāyus and governs the function of burping or belching, hiccups, and flatulence, all of which in excess are signs of indigestion, swallowing excessive amounts of air through various modes such as carbonated drinks, chewing gum, fermented foods, talking while eating, and so on, or gases released by undigested food in the gut. In Āyurveda, it is said that a good indication to stop eating is the experience of the first burp. For this, we need to be aware and mindful of our body and its processes.

How can this minor process be a cause of suffering as implied by the name of the corresponding yoginī? Excessive belching is a sign of a "suffering" gastrointestinal process, including the dysfunctional digestion of subtle food – sense impressions, interactions with others, memories of past experiences, perception of our life circumstances – all of which lead to suffering.

Through the Guru's grace, this vāyu becomes stronger, eliminating suffering by creating new ways of experiencing and perceiving the world and ourselves.

Sarvamṛtyupraśamanī

Sarvamṛtyupraśamanī (sarva = all, *mṛtyu* = death, *praśamana* = pacifying, healing, or curing) is the yoginī who cures all death and corresponds to the *kṛkara* vāyu.

Kṛkara vāyu is a minor vāyu that is responsible for sneezing and coughing. Sneezing is an automatic expulsion of air from the nose and mouth and is usually caused by irritation of the nasal mucous membranes. Coughing is a semi-automatic expulsion of air from the large respiratory passages, usually occurring as a protective mechanism to clear them from irritants.

Sneezing and coughing are common signs of serious infections that have fatal consequences including death. Irritations and infections that lead to these impulses often have to do with suboptimal immunity, where the body is unable to mount an adequate response to the said irritant or infectious agent. On the other hand, the irritant or infection can overwhelm the body's immune system, even if it is strong and well-functioning, leading to mṛtyu or death.

From the standpoint of sādhanā, we can think of this vāyu as being responsible for how we deal with irritants in our internal landscape, and immunity as it refers to resilience. We can be on the spiritual path for years, being dedicated to our practice and devoted to the teachings, and yet have low resilience. Our fundamental view has remained unchanged (due to a weak udāna vāyu) and the most minor thing can bring about a violent and automatic internal reaction, much like a sneeze or cough.

We need perfect conditions to meditate or contemplate, where the slightest disturbance throws us off. Everything must be just so, or we feel derailed. In essence, the spiritual practice has replaced our daily habits without touching the underlying neurosis. We can spend hours, days or weeks in solitude feeling elevated with our own insight and wisdom, and generally feel like we are "enlightened." When we come out of isolation and begin interacting with people, all our vṛttis return in full force resulting in violent outbursts. Even if we don't behave violently, a thought form embedded with it is enough to dissipate our elevated insight. With the merest inconvenience, the merit accumulated through practice instantly vanishes or dies.

This gracious yoginī blesses us with a cure for all deaths through the cultivation of resilience, which occurs through the strengthening of the kṛkara vāyu. One of the most profound realizations we can have at this stage is that of impermanence and to see that all phenomena, including death, are temporary. The mind becomes still in this insight and immune to external or internal irritants or infections, resulting in the healing of all death.

Sarvavighnanivāriṇī

Sarvavighnanivāriṇī (sarva = all, *vighna* = obstacles, *nivaraṇa* = to refute) is the yoginī who refutes obstacles to dissolve them and corresponds to the *devadatta* vāyu.

Devadatta vāyu governs and regulates the experience of hunger and thirst as well as the function of yawning, which is the involuntary and reflexive inhalation of air along with a stretching of the eardrums, following by exhalation. Yawning is associated with tiredness, sleep, boredom, and stress, all of which are obstacles to the alertness that is required in sādhanā. Yawning is in fact thought to be a signal for pack animals to stay alert or to synchronize their sleep/wake times.

On the spiritual path, however, yawning is a sign of the many obstacles that stand in the way of absorbing, digesting, assimilating and transmuting vidyā.

We often think of obstacles on the spiritual path to refer to the external disturbances of family, work, lack of time, and so on. We never stop to consider that the fundamental vighna may be (as it always is) internal.

> ***Fatigue is often the result of not knowing how to conserve our prāṇa, which is wasted in unnecessary and draining activities and mental/emotional processes.***

We tend to lack the ability to be focused and single-pointed, and instead our attention is diffuse and scattered. The constant back-and-forth of this scatteredness is associated with chaotic neurohormonal pathways which affect the whole body and result in fatigue and sleepiness, boredom, and the general inability to take in knowledge in a meaningful way.

External situations that are viewed as obstacles are (always) opportunities for practice. Usually, we make these situations obstacles to sādhanā because we lack the skill to navigate them or the resolve to practice despite them.

When we arrive at the feet of this majestic yoginī, she graces us with the right perspective and resolve where obstacles are no longer seen as problems or hindrances, but as opportunities to refine practice.

Sarvāṅgasundarī

Sarvāṅgasundarī (sarva = all, aṅga = limbs, sundara = beauty) is the yoginī who bestows beauty of all limbs and corresponds to the *kūrma* vāyu.

Kūrma vāyu regulates eye blinking, which is an automatic movement designed to protect the eyes by keeping them moist and constantly cleansing them of any impurities. Some studies have demonstrated a correlation between blinking and brain activity, switching on certain pathways and turning off others with each reflexive closing of the eyelids.

In general, two networks in the brain are important from the standpoint of sādhanā: the task-positive and the default mode.[173] Each network is associated with a particular "type" of thought. Functional thoughts arise from the task-positive network and are associated with tasks requiring focus such as planning, writing, talking and so on, and are action-oriented. Non-functional thoughts, on the other hand, arise from the default mode network and arise when we are not actively engaged in tasks. These thoughts have no purpose and result in daydreaming, ruminating over the past, imagining the future, and are associated with regret, anxiety, stress, and stagnation. They revolve around validation and justification of choices and events, self-worth, and judgment and comparison with others.

173 See 'Bagalamukhi' in K. Chinnaiyan, *Shakti Rising* (Nonduality Press, 2017).

In the fraction of a second (usually about 150 milliseconds) that it takes to blink, the brain switches from the task-positive network to the default mode network. The mind switches back and forth, momentarily losing focus and regaining it. This is not to say that daydreaming doesn't happen with the eyes open – as we know from our own experience, when we are deep in thought, we blink less. The point here is that even when engaged in a task, there is a constant switching of attention, demonstrating the lack of steadiness that is of paramount importance in sādhanā.

Other studies have shown that long-term meditators blink less often, a sign of finer regulation of the kūrma vāyu. The increased frequency of switching between networks and the differences in brain activity require excessive prāṇa. Expending prāṇa results in the loss of health and beauty of the body, while retaining it results in radiance and vitality.

Sarvāṅgasundarī steadies our gaze by conserving prāṇa, bestowing beauty of all the limbs.

Sarvasaubhāgyadāyinī

Sarvasaubhāgyadāyinī (sarva = all, saubhāgya = auspiciousness, *dāyinī* = grantor) is the yoginī who grants all auspiciousness and correlates with *dhanañjaya* vāyu.

Dhanañjaya vāyu regulates aging and decomposition as well as the function of the heart, particularly the opening and closing of the heart valves. It remains functional even after death, resulting in decomposition of the body. A dysfunctional dhanañjaya vāyu facilitates diseases of the heart muscle and the valves as well as rhythm disorders. Importantly, decay and decomposition can begin in life through the process of disease and aging, resulting in inauspiciousness from the standpoint of the inability to continue sādhanā.

At the subtle level, dhanañjaya vāyu maintains freshness that comes from lack of decay and stagnation, which fuel our restlessness in sādhanā, where we keep jumping from one thing to the next. Stagnation feels like dead weight that we have no ability to rid ourselves of, and to escape it, we keep searching for the next new thing. In other words, our entire life can be seen as a search for freshness and an escape from the drudgery of decay. In this process, we fail to realize the auspiciousness of life in its infinite colors and shapes.

Our quest for freshness in sādhanā confers the inability to gain much from any of it, keeping us squarely on the circumference even when we fool ourselves into believing we are on the radius. All our attention remains in the Bhūpura, but we deceive ourselves into thinking we are at the Bahirdaśara! As a result, we don't gain meaningful insights from either āvaraṇa. This is the greatest form of inauspiciousness.

When we arrive at the feet of Sarvasaubhāgyadāyinī, she confers the cultivation of a balanced dhanañjaya vāyu and the gift of auspiciousness where every aspect of the routine of sādhanā is bathed in freshness and vibrancy. Through her grace, stagnation and decay of linearity dissolve, giving way to non-linearity where everything arises and dissolves in the eternal now.

The Vāyus in Practice

Even though we have examined the vāyus individually, they are not distinguishable from each other as separate entities. They function as a whole, as do the yoginīs of any given āvaraṇa. If we were to examine the prāṇa vāyus together, we see that whatever is outside is taken in through the action of prāṇa, and that which is taken in is digested through samāna. The digested material is then assimilated through vyāna while the undigested mass is eliminated via apāna. The assimilated material is then transmuted and transformed into speech, memory, intelligence, and insight via udāna.

We can see the effect of the prāṇa vāyus in sādhanā if we look at them together (Figure 41). Here, we begin with our bank of samskārās which are comprised of undigested experiences, ideals and learning that prevent vidyā from being absorbed through prāṇa vāyu. This is because samāna is weak and unable to digest the samskāra mass, vyāna is not strong enough to assimilate the digested material and apāna is unable to eliminate the waste. The samskāra mass manifests through the action of nāga as suffering because of its dysfunctional digestion, lack of resilience via kṛkara, obstacles to transformation via devadatta, excessive prāṇa expenditure via kūrma, and decay and stagnation via dhanañjaya. The samskāra mass weighs on the inner landscape and therefore, little growth and transmutation can occur through the udāna.

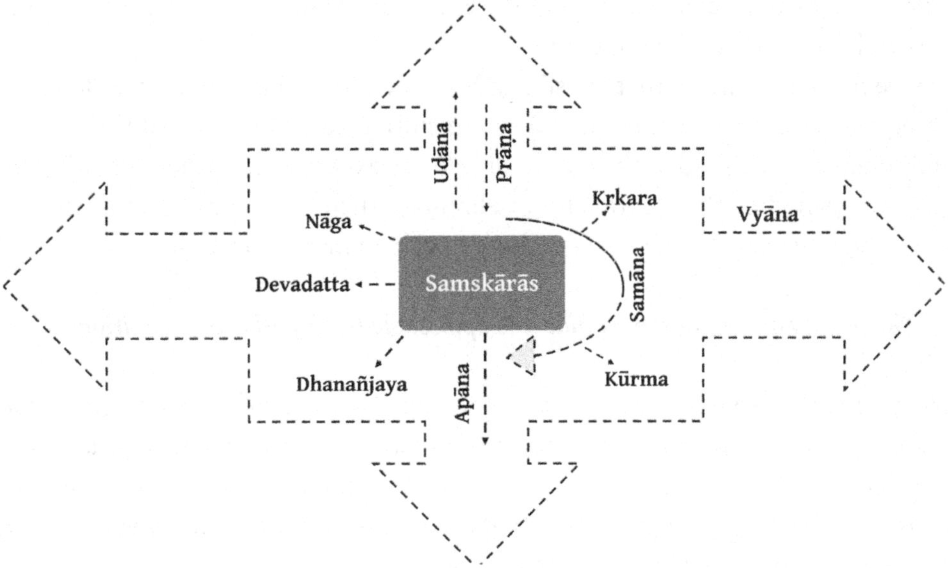

Figure 41. Prāṇa Vāyus

Let's examine this concept further through the lens of the Śrīcakra. The world we take in via prāṇa is used to create citta vṛttis, which in turn is based on our previously accumulated samskāra mass. The vṛttis that make up our world view determine *what* and *how much* of the world we can take in, severely limiting our ability to open to everything that is available to us. Furthermore, our ability to digest our experience depends on past knowledge, which means that we interpret our experience according to our vikalpas. In other words, the waste products of our past experience clog up our ability to take in things as they are. If our apāna is functioning at an optimal level, no samskārās or vṛttis are formed since they are instantly digested, eliminated, assimilated, and transmuted.

So, we have the prāṇa vāyus at the Bahirdaśara that control the flow of prāṇa in the nāḍīs at the Manvaśra, which are obstructed by citta vṛttis arising from deep-rooted samskārās that result in the agitations at the Aṣṭadalapadma. The agitations at this level driven by the prāṇa vāyus far up in the Bahirdaśara become further contracted into the dualities of attractions and aversions at the Śodaṣadalapadma, playing out in our interactions with the world at the Bhūpura.

We see from this pattern that the strength and quality of our prāṇa vāyus determines our progress on the spiritual path. If they are cultivated and harnessed through long-term discipline, samāna vāyu fires up to digest our experiences without creating more samskārās, apāna functions optimally to eliminate them, vyāna assimilates them and turns poison to nectar, and udāna uses them to gain higher realizations.

The beauty of this system is that it is applicable to all paths and traditions.

Whether we are Śrīvidyā upāsakas or not, we need optimally functioning prāṇa vāyus if we want to progress. Essentially, all spiritual practices - breath, mantra, ritual, meditation, self-inquiry, lifestyle practices - are designed to manipulate the prāṇa vāyus. Since prāṇa is the most palpable manifestation of the Divine, this understanding of the vāyus helps us become grounded in the purpose of sādhanā.

Cakreśvarī: Tripurāśrī

The Kulottīrṇa Yoginīs of the Bahirdaśara show us both their shadow and light aspects through the dysfunctional and optimal functioning of the ten prāṇa vāyus. As we saw in the previous chapter, the most important practice for bringing the vāyus into balance is a disciplined lifestyle that honors the circadian rhythm where we eat and sleep on time, a diet that favors digestion through the choice of light and nutritious foods while avoiding those that are inflammatory or cause chaotic a flow of impulses, and a daily practice of quiet and contemplation.

Tripurāśrī, an emanation of Mahātripurasundarī rules over the Sarvārthasādhaka cakra that fulfils all wishes through the grace of the supreme Vāyu. She is invoked through the mantra *hsaim hsklīṃ hssauḥ* and the mudrā bīja *saḥ* that corresponds with Sarvonmādinī, the all-intoxicating one. Willingness to relinquish our slights and stance in favor of transmutation allows us to adhere to discipline and align with prāṇa as it begins to flow freely through the nāḍīs. This free-flowing stance is fortified by intoxicating and alluring forays into the higher realms as more and more prāṇa becomes available for transmutation.

The grace of the Kulottīrṇa Yoginīs catapults us out of the limitations of kula and into the next āvaraṇa, the Antardaśara.

Chapter 13

Antardaśara

एता दश वह्निकलाः सर्वज्ञाद्या अन्तर्दशारगा देवताः ॥ १९ ॥
Etā daśa vahnikalāh sarvajñādyā antardaśāragā devatāh || 19 ||

"Sarvajñā, etc. are the ten digits of fire in the inner ten-triangles."
~ Bhāvanopaniṣad, verse 19

It has been a long and arduous journey up until now, and progression from one āvaraṇa to the next is a leap in understanding and insight. We have arrived here at the Antardaśara from the Bahirdaśara where we encountered the Kulottīrṇa Yoginīs who create turbulence through the prāṇa vāyus and free us from unrest through their unlimited grace.

The prāṇa vāyus exert their influence upon the nāḍīs of the Manvaśra, which are reflected in the agitations of the citta at the Aṣṭadalapadma. Our hardy vṛttis create the push and pull of the senses at the Śodaṣadalapadma, fully manifesting at the Bhūpura as the shadows of the Prakaṭa Yoginīs where our neuroses become evident in the ways we interact with the world.

The Inquiry

From the Bhūpura to the Bahirdaśara, our journey was propelled by deep contemplation and inquiry, where we bravely investigated the causative factor of each manifestation. At the Bahirdaśara, we become intimately familiar with the prāṇa vāyus, which are the driving forces of our stuckness and lack of progress. Through committed discipline and establishment of a regulated lifestyle, we can begin to bring the vāyus into balance.

At this point in our upāsanā, we can assume that our attention is fixed on the radius with less and less energy wasted in seeking out validation, keeping up appearances, and maintaining a self-image, which were the primary drivers of our interactions in the Bhūpura. When we were able to put our self-interest aside and delve deep into our patterns, we arrived at the understanding of the shadows of the Siddhis, Aṣṭa Mātṛkās and the Mudrā Devīs. Through their grace, we were able to traverse the Bhūpura and arrived at the Śodaṣadalapadma where we discovered the driving forces of our behavior in the world.

When we surrendered at the feet of the Gupta Yoginīs, we transcended the dualistic nature of attractions and aversions, and were propelled to the Aṣṭadalapadma. Here, we came face-to-face with our agitations arising from the citta vṛttis, and submitting to the Guptatara Yoginīs, we arrived at the Manvaśra where we realized how the flow of prāṇa in the nāḍīs gives rise to the vṛttis. Through the grace of the Sampradāya Yoginīs, we were called to look further upstream, and we discovered the prāṇa vāyus in the Bahirdaśara, which drive the flow of prāṇa in the nāḍīs of the Manvaśra.

The Kulottīrṇa Yoginīs grace us with the ability to delve further into our inner landscape and now we arrive at the next inquiry, "What is the driving force of the prāṇa vāyus? What makes them behave the way they do?" With this inquiry, we arrive at the Antardaśara.

Agni

Agni means fire, but as we will see, it is much more than one of the five great elements. As we saw in the last chapter, Mahāśakti is the supreme potential power and Prāṇaśakti is a tiny fraction of it, which when mobilized manifests as creation. The conversion of potential to kinetic energy is catalyzed by agni, which is the power of transformation.[174]

If the Bahirdaśara taught us that movement is the sign of life, here in the Antardaśara, we will discover that movement and transformation go together. One necessarily accompanies the other – movement implies a before and an after, point zero to point infinity, a here and a there. Any movement implies directionality in time and space, which occurs because of transformation. This moment arose from the digestion of the previous one. Day becomes night through the continuum of transformation. When we go from point A to point B, transformation occurs in infinite ways – cells die and new ones are stimulated, nerve impulses are digested along their linear pathways, chemicals and enzymes are

174 In this book, agni as the principle of transformation is spelled with a lower-case 'a' to differentiate the word referring to the god of fire.

cycled through continuous loops of production-release-breakdown-resorption, thought arises and subsides... all while the earth is spinning around the sun and the solar system swings around the center of the galaxy, continuously propelling evolution, creation, and destruction.

When we look deeply, we see that transformation *drives* movement. If there is no transformation, there is no movement and stagnation results, which is known as *āma.* Everything we associate with life undergoes change, indicating that agni is the fundamental property of creation, including time, which is the transformation of one moment into the next.

Ordinarily, we associate agni with digestion and the processing of food. In *Āyurveda*, digestion occurs in sequence across seven dhātus, or tissues, where each is powered by its own agni. Digestion starts at the rasa dhātu (plasma), where its agni extracts the appropriate nutrients and moves the substrate to the subsequent dhātus – *rakta* (blood), *māṃsa* (muscle), *meda* (fat), *asti* (bone), *majjā* (marrow), and *śukra* (reproductive fluid). At each dhātu, digestion becomes more refined, with the elimination of increasingly subtle wastes. The end-product of digestion is the most refined substance known as *ojas*, which is responsible for immunity, longevity, and contentment.

If we were to examine this process against the backdrop of our knowledge of the Bahirdaśara, we see that the agni inherent within each of the prāṇa vāyus is responsible for its action. The transformative power of samāna is its agni, while the eliminative power of apāna is its agni, and so on. The "weakness" of a particular prāṇa vāyu points to its weak agni, where the movement of the prāṇa vāyu is inhibited by the lack of transformative power, resulting in stagnation. At a subtle level, this stagnation results in a backlog of samskārās, creating both inertia (tamas) and agitation (rajas), both of which result in a tight identification with the ego and its concerns, percolating from the Antardaśara all the way down to the Bhūpura.

Let's revisit the Tattva Map in Chapter 4. The premise of the darśana here is that the formless Śiva-Śakti becomes all forms of creation. The transformation of the formless to form is catalyzed by agni and vāyu. Each of the tattvas has its own agni, which pervades the guṇas and elements of Prakṛti, giving each its form and function.

Agni is the fundamental intelligence in all forms of creation.

Homa

A homa is a fire ritual that brings together the entire scope of upāsanā and is centered around Agni.[175] Ordinarily, a homa is performed to propitiate a given deity in the medium of fire for a given goal, such as health, material benefits, or spiritual upliftment. Typically, the ritual is performed in a space created by an enclosure of bricks, or a copper utensil made for this purpose. After purificatory rituals, Agni is invoked into the space by pouring various offerings such as clarified butter (*ghee*), grains, and aromatic herbs into the fire. Known as *āhuti*, these offerings become invocations of Agni. Mantras are chanted with each offering, ending with svāhā.[176]

175 Homa is a "small-scale" fire ritual performed by and for smaller groups of people whereas a yagña is a larger community ritual. In practice, the two are alike to onlookers.

176 Svāhā is the śakti (wife) of Agni, who empowers him.

Agni is the mediator between our desires and their fructification and is idolized as a magnificent being with three faces, four arms and seven "tongues" of fire emanating from his body. He carries our desires to the other deities and brings back their blessings to us through the medium of fire. Homas are exceptionally purifying rituals that engage all the five senses, require exquisite attention to detail, diligence, and mental sharpness. With every āhuti, we pour a little of ourselves into Agni's dancing flames. Bit by bit, Agni demands and digests more and more of our dullness, stubbornness, meanness, pettiness, contractions, disappointments, fears, and hopes. As the eyes focus on Agni's dynamic form, the ears dwell on the sound of mantras, the nose and tongue smell and taste the smoke and the skin absorbs his warmth, we find ourselves being transformed by him.

Although homa is commonly known as an external ritual, for those of us on the contemplative inner journey, every aspect of sādhanā is a fire ritual. We recognize agni in moment-to-moment existence as the intelligence of the tanmātras, jñānendriyas and karmendriyas that make up the bridge between our inner landscape and the world as thought, emotion, speech, and action. Agni is the intelligence of the prāṇa vāyus as well as the nāḍīs that manifest in our inner and outer worlds. It is also the transformative power of the karma we create through the workings of this intricate machinery that is the microcosm, which becomes a part of the macrocosm. Agni, then, is the intermediary between the microcosm and the macrocosm, and pervades both.

Antardaśara

The Antardaśara is the inner ten-triangled āvaraṇa where each triangle represents an aspect of agni. This āvaraṇa is known as the *Sarvarakṣākara* (sarva = all, *rakṣākara* = protecting) cakra that is all-protective (see Figure 42).

Protection means different things at different stages of sādhanā. When we start out on the path, we may need to invoke protection from external forces, such as invisible entities, distractions, interruptions, relationship issues, worries and anxieties, memories, and dreams. However, as we dive deeper into our inner workings, we come to see that the enemy is not "out there," but "in here" as the fundamental misapprehension of our true nature. Here at the Antardaśara, we come to see that the convoluted workings of our inner landscape have their origins in this central misunderstanding. Here, we seek protection from this misunderstanding.

From any one āvaraṇa to the next is a huge leap with respect to perception and lasting insight. However, the leap to the Antardaśara is especially significant since after this āvaraṇa, nothing in our experience will be the same. When we call upon this cakra for protection, we invoke the highest vidyā to come to our aid to remove the veils of Māyā, which is why the yoginīs of this āvaraṇa are known as *Nigarbha*, which means hidden (ni = within, *garbha* = womb). Like a fetus in the womb that must mature and "cook" until ready to be birthed, we find ourselves here only when we have done the work in the previous āvaraṇas and must now cook in the fire of knowledge if we wish to transcend saṃsāra.

It is in this āvaraṇa that we contemplate upon the nature of separation between the world out there and the me in here, and where the chasm between the two begins to dissolve. The concept of protection arises only in the context of "me" versus "not me." We fear, covet, or stand in comparison or competition of what is "not me." Through the grace of the Nigarbha Yoginīs, we come to see that we have always been protected, and that our previous sense of vulnerability arose from feeling separate from everything else.

> ***Fear and hope can arise only when there is something outside of ourselves or an external source that can threaten our existence or allay our shortcomings.***

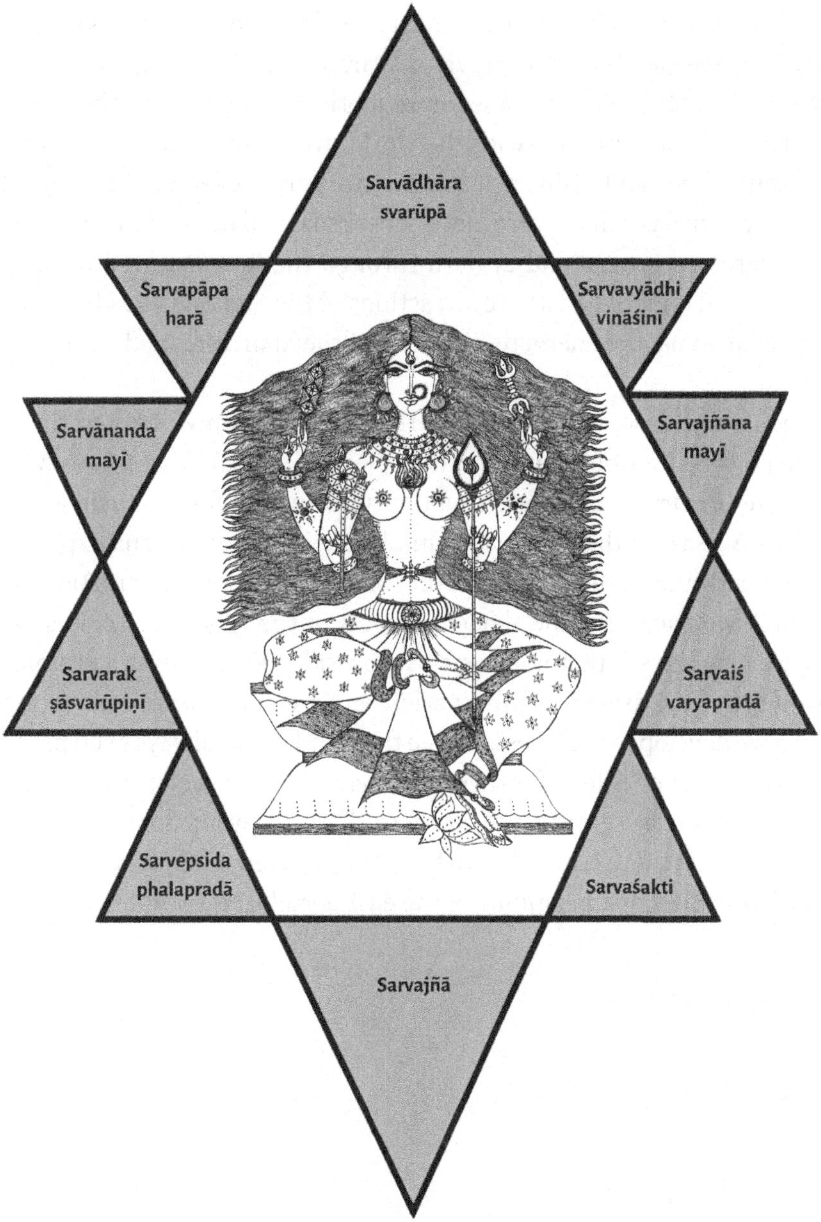

Figure 42. Antardaśara with Nigarbha Yoginī

As we have seen in Chapter 9, the māyīya mala is the progenitor of the sense of separation that is seen across all the previous āvaraṇas. At each progressive level of sādhanā, the experience of the malas becomes more subtle. At the Bhūpura, the malas were overtly expressed in our interactions with the world, where our attention was focused on the needs, wants, likes and dislikes of the me-story. However, at that stage, they weren't seen clearly as malas, which were more conceptual and not real in our direct experience. As we progressed inward and upward through the āvaraṇas, the malas became more acutely felt and understood as the attractions of the Śodaṣadalapadma, the agitations of the Aṣṭadalapadma, the energetic channels of the Manvaśra, and the prāṇa vāyus of the Bahirdaśara.

At the Bahirdaśara, we came to see that the dichotomy between the world and me is created by the flow of the prāṇa vāyus. Here at the Antardaśara, we will see that the prāṇa vāyus are driven by an even subtler fundamental force – their subtle intelligence as agni. As we saw in the sṛṣṭi krama in Chapter 4, the Vasukoṇa explodes as creation, beginning with the Antardaśara. In other words, this is where creation begins to manifest. When we transcend the shadow aspects of the Nigarbha Yoginīs in the saṃhāra krama, we come to see that nothing exists outside of me. This is a profound realization that results in fearlessness – if all experiences arise in me, what is there to fear?

When we develop fearlessness, we see that our life has always been protected; there is nothing to protect or defend for there is no *here* versus *there*. The Nigarbha Yoginīs dispel the idea that there are entities outside of us that will swoop down to protect us; instead, they show us that there is no other to fear. They are ten in number and are situated in an anti-clockwise direction beginning at the east portal (see Table 15).

Table 15. Yoginīs of the Antardaśara

Yoginī	Psychophysiological	Agni	Agni Kalā	Alphabet	Bhāvanā
Sarvajñā	Omniscience	Recaka (eliminating)	Dhūmrārci	m	Karma
Sarvaśakti	All powers	Pācaka (digesting)	Uṣmā	y	Digesting experience
Sarvaiśvaryapradā	Bestowing all wealth	Śoṣaṇa (drying)	Jvalinī	r	Action
Sarvajñānamayī	All knowledge	Dāhaka (burning)	Jvālinī	l	Sacrificing knowledge
Sarvavyādhivināśinī	Destroying all ailments	Plāvaka (leaping)	Visphuliṅginī	v	Darśana
Sarvādhārasvarūpā	All forms of support	Kṣāraka (pouring)	Suśrī	ś	Groundedness
Sarvapāpaharā	Destroying all sins	Kṣobhaka (agitating)	Surūpā	ṣ	Transcending norms
Sarvānandamayī	All happiness	Udgrāhaka (receiving)	Kapilā	s	Opening
Sarvarakṣāsvarūpiṇī	All forms of protection	Jhṛmbhaka (assimilating)	Havyavāhinī	h	Assimilating experience
Sarvepsidaphalapradā	Bestowing all desires	Mohaka (attracting)	Kavyavāhinī	kṣ	Sacrificing selfhood

Nigarbha Yoginī

The four-armed, pearly white Nigarbha Yoginī bears a thunderbolt and a spear in her upper hands, symbolizing her power of transformation. The thunderbolt contains the heat of transformation that is propelled into action by her spear. Her lower hands hold a discus and a javelin, signifying her swift grace that cuts through the dense stagnation of āma to facilitate the clarity of the buddhi. (see Figure 43).

There are numerous correlations between the Nigarbha Yoginīs and psychophysiological processes. Some texts correlate them with the five sense organs and the five tanmātras. However, at this level (as opposed to the same correlations at the Aṣṭadalapadma, for example), the correlation of the sense organs and the tanmātras is with the agni or their driving force. In other words, even though the same elements are included in different āvaraṇas, the correspondence at each level is with the attribute of that āvaraṇa. The sense organs are examined with respect to agitation in the Aṣṭadalapadma, the prāṇa nāḍīs at the Manvaśra and their transformational power at the Antardaśara.

The Nigarbha Yoginīs are also correlated to the ten digestive fires and the ten kalās of agni. Kalā means digit; sūrya or the sun has 12 kalās, soma or the moon has 16 kalās and agni or fire has ten kalās. One way to look at the relationship between the digestive fires and the agni kalās is to examine them as the process and the result. This is the approach I have taken in the exploration of this āvaraṇa. You may find other correlations. The most important thing to realize is that the Antardaśara represents the end of stithi; saṃhāra begins at the next āvaraṇa, where all traces of identification will be progressively erased.

Figure 43. Nigarbha Yoginī

Sarvajñā

Sarvajñā means omniscience, and refers to the first of the Nigarbha Yoginīs, corresponding with *recaka* agni and the kalā *dhūmrārci* (*dhūmra* = smoke, *arci* = flame). Recaka refers to the power of purging or eliminating, and this process of releasing identification with the me-story results in omniscience.

Let's revisit the kañcukas, the five coverings of Māyā.[177] As you'll recall, the kañcukas bind the unbound Absolute Reality by creating limitations in desire (rāga), knowledge (vidyā), action (kalā), time (kāla), and space (niyati). Omniscience or all-encompassing knowledge can be attained only by discarding the kañcuka of vidyā. For this, we must examine the process of limitation of knowledge where the divine jñāna śakti becomes vidyā.

177 See Kañcukas and Malas in Chapter 9.

Recall the difference between the pure and impure paths, which are demarcated by the Māyā tattva.[178] Above the Māyā tattva, Aham (me) and Idam (that) are non-separate, whereas below the Māyā tattva, they become distinct and separate. In other words, the kañcukas create the illusion of me and the other when it doesn't exist.

178 See Mantra in Aśuddhādvan and Śuddhādvan in Chapter 6.

Jñāna śakti being above the Māyā tattva is diffuse and smoke-like, pervading space and time. Importantly, it is unconditioned and not primed by a history or story. It is unbound by the grooves of conditioning that create the impure path, and this knowledge is all-pervading. All possibilities exist at this level because there is no memory or emotional imprint of how things "should" be.

On the other hand, vidyā (the kañcuka) creates the illusion of separation between Aham and Idam and is conditioned by experience. It is the product of karma, where the accumulation of emotional, mental, and psychic imprint from previous experience colors the present and determines the future. Our knowledge is necessarily limited because we lose the potential of all possibilities in karmic loops.

> ***When the burden of karma is eliminated through recaka, its rigid and pre-determined path disintegrates, giving rise to dhūmrārci, the smoke-like essence that diffuses across the boundaries of time and space.***

Omniscience is the power of knowing things that occur beyond the limited reach of the senses.

As karma is dissolved, we routinely find that we "know" without knowing *how* we know. Synchronicities become common, along with a deepening alignment with reality. Our thought process becomes expansive and all-encompassing.

Bhāvanā on Sarvajñā

Karma is an extremely insidious phenomenon that occurs as soon as the ahaṅkāra gets entangled with a person or situation, where it adds to the bank of samskārās.

For example, you don't see eye-to-eye with a co-worker. You have felt slighted and humiliated on several occasions, and every time you think about him, you have a visceral reaction. Unfortunately, you need to continue to work with him and every time you discuss an issue, you assume he's out to get you and prepare for it.

Your reaction and response to him is crystallized by what you know from your experience, which prevents you from seeing that there are countless other possibilities in any interaction.

He may just be doing his job and has no interest in insulting you. He may have a disorder that prevents him from communicating the way you think he should, and he may like you! Your way of communicating may be stressful for him.

The (mostly) unconscious samskārās you carry about him determines your behavior, which in turn adds to the samskārā bank. In other words, your karma with him fixes your path, creating perpetual loops of reactions and outcomes.

Becoming acutely aware of your assumptions, hurts and resentments, see if you can choose to behave differently. Treat every interaction as a stand-alone situation that is not primed by the past ones. Allow the past interactions to go up in smoke. This is a challenging sādhana, but the most practical way to worship Sarvajñā.

Sarvaśakti

Sarvaśakti (sarva = all, śakti = power) embodies all powers and correlates with *pācaka* agni and the kalā *uṣmā* (heat). Pācaka is the power of digestion, and the process of cooking results in the gift of uṣmā.

At this point, we must explore the difference between digesting and spiritually bypassing when it comes to experience. Often, we think we are eliminating (see recaka above) when we are actually avoiding or bypassing the issue. In the above example, you may feel that being on the spiritual path mandates that you *shouldn't* be angry or upset with your co-worker. You may use concepts such as "he is Śiva-Śakti" or "everything is always perfect" to avoid confronting your own discomfort. While the concepts are correct, they are not useful here because your direct experience is discomfort – you don't perceive his divinity and things aren't perfect in your inner landscape.

Pācaka occurs when we face our discomfort and the messy mass of sensations and emotions head-on.

> ***Bypassing is trying to get to the Bindu directly from the Bhūpura without doing the work of the intervening āvaraṇas, where knowledge remains conceptual and not experiential.***

When we meet our pain, fears, aggressions, hopes and anxieties directly, we progress along the āvaraṇas. It is like following a trail of breadcrumbs, where each of our inner contractions is digested through the correct view, practice, perspective, and application.

This is the path of Kuṇḍalinī, where tremendous heat (uṣmā) is generated in the process of digestion and used for transformation and transmutation. Power is the result of this constant transmutation. Ordinarily, we think of power as the ability to lord over the world or having authority or influence over others. However, most displays of power are manifestations of deep-rooted insecurity and powerlessness, where we resort to finding completion through others' submission.

The highest powers arise from conquering the greatest foes – our own demons. When we conquer our own limitations through their systematic digestion, we come to our natural state that is replete with all powers (Sarvaśakti). Through pācaka mediated by the grace of this yoginī, we come to see that there is no other to subjugate.

Sarvaiśvaryapradā

Sarvaiśvaryapradā (sarva = all, *aiśvarya* = wealth, pradā = bestower) is the giver of all wealth and auspiciousness and corresponds to *śoṣana* agni and the kalā *jvalinī* (glow). *Śoṣana* is the power of drying.

As we saw earlier in this chapter, āma is the antithesis of agni and is the word used for the experience of stagnation. There are many signs and symptoms of āma, including weight gain, sluggishness, and most importantly, manifestations of inflammation. Āma accumulates when agni is dull or imbalanced, resulting in a loss of *tejas* (radiance or glow). It is described as a substance that is the opposite of ojas, the finest end-product of digestion that confers contentment, longevity, and immunity. While ojas is a golden nectar that is clear and flows freely, āma is sticky and foul.

In our psyche, āma manifests as tamas, the heavy, stubborn inertia that holds us back from fulfilling our potential. While tamas in the macrocosm is the guṇa of heaviness that gives structure and shape to the universe, it manifests in the microcosm as the dense veiling of Māyā resulting in a tight identification with the me-story. Tamas is like a whirlpool that sucks us in, tightly binding us to our stories, emotions, and thoughts. Like āma, tamas is sticky and foul in the psyche and results in the loss of radiance. It makes us dull, sluggish, and lethargic, afflicting us with a "brain fog" that prevents us from absorbing vidyā.

Āma needs to be dried out by agni's śakti of śoṣana. Grace descends as this power, melting tamas and mobilizing our stuck energy first to rajas and then to sattva. As āma begins to dry up, we are infused with the glow of agni's kalā jvalinī. Radiance is the result of embodying tejas, the subtle essence of agni, which imparts lustre to the skin and keeps us warm. As we turn inward and progress along the radius, we become radiantly auspicious, emitting it to the world around us.

Āma prevents us from realizing the wealth of our potential. With its melting, we come to realize that all possibilities are available for us. Śoṣana unlocks our creativity, where we find delightful ways to fulfill our intentions and experience the eṣaṇas. Aiśvarya is this wealth of joy and enthusiasm that is obscured by āma. Sarvaiśvaryapradā graces us with this priceless wealth that propels us towards the Bindu.

Sarvajñānamayī

Sarvajñānamayī (sarva = all, jñāna = knowledge, mayī = replete) makes us sated with knowledge and corresponds to *dāhaka* agni and the kalā *jvālinī* (flame).

Dāhaka is to burn, and when we think of knowledge, it is vibrant – like a burning flame. Unlike knowledge, ignorance is dull and sluggish. Knowledge here doesn't refer only to transactional knowledge, where our lack of understanding of a topic is mitigated by gaining information about it. Transactional knowledge drives most of our lives and careers, where we collect increasing information about the world around us to overcome the lack of understanding in various areas. However, there will never be a limit to the knowledge we can collect this way, and there will always be something we don't know!

Self-knowledge, unlike the transactional type, is the understanding of the subject in relation to objects, which include our own thoughts, emotions, perceptions, and the me-story. Self-knowledge transcends transactional knowledge in that it isn't information acquired to fill in a gap. Instead, it is the knowing of the *knower*. While transactional knowledge remains at the circumference, Self-knowledge is at the center, the Bindu.

> ***On the inner journey, Self-knowledge requires the sacrifice of transactional knowledge.***[179]

179 See 'Bhuvaneshwari' in K. Chinnaiyan, *Shakti Rising* (Nonduality Press 2017).

From the standpoint of vidyā, transactional knowledge is avidyā or ignorance. As we progress along the radius to the center, we will need to relinquish the circumference. This includes all the knowledge we have collected through reading texts, discussing concepts, and collecting ideas and practices. Jvālinī is the kalā of agni that accepts this sacrifice, growing bigger and stronger as it is fed and yielding its proportional fruit.

Dāhaka burns away avidyā with increasing insight into the nature of the Self. Transactional knowledge makes us feel good and validates us by filling in the gaps created by our insecurities. Paradoxically, the more we dive into Self-knowledge, the lesser the need for validation. As the flame is sustained by the constant sacrifice of transactional knowledge, we become indifferent to praise and blame. Self-knowledge makes us see that there is no other upon whom we can confer praise or blame.

Sarvajñānamayī blesses us with the grace of all knowledge – both transactional and Self-knowledge – that leads us steadily toward vidyā by burning away the mass of avidyā or ignorance.

Sarvavyādhivināśinī

Sarvavyādhivināśinī (sarva = all, *vyādhi* = ailment, *vināśinī* = destroyer) destroys all ailments and corresponds to *plāvaka* agni and the kalā of *visphuliṅginī* (sparks). Plāvaka is the power of leaping.

As we will see in the next chapter, ignorance of our true nature is the fundamental ailment or sickness. At the level of the body-mind, disease is the result of āma and tamas, the properties of stagnation. As the flames of agni leap up to devour the āma, we experience an incredible lightness in the mind and body. Sparks of joy, tolerance, and sweetness light up our being and we are healed even if we are not cured.

While the grace of this yoginī can and does cure disease and illness, we would benefit greatly from a subtler understanding of healing within the context of the darśana, which describes disease as the result of karma. As we saw earlier, karma is the sum total of all our previous actions spanning across lifetimes. It manifests as our DNA and genetic material that unfolds in this life as our traits and predilections. If I have a family history of cancer and carry a gene for it, it is the result of past karma. Nothing is accidental, and nothing happens "to" us. Creation, including our life, is the constant interaction of Prakṛti's three guṇas.

Our current situation can be viewed as the snowball effect of every little thing we have ever done. The snowball gathers mass and momentum as it moves down the cliff, consuming and destroying things in its path. So too with karma – it fructifies in the countless good and bad things that pop up in our day-to-day life.

At the end of the day, we have nobody and nothing else to blame other than our own karma, which is the result of our own choices over time.

Agni's plāvaka śakti sparks this higher understanding, resulting in the lifting of heaviness and healing all ailments.

Sarvādhārasvarūpā

Sarvādhārasvarūpā (sarva = all, ādhāra = support, svarūpa = form) is the all-supporting yoginī and corresponds with *kṣāraka* agni and the kalā known as *suśrī* (splendid). Kṣāraka is essence, or the property of pouring forth.

Loss of groundedness is one of the biggest problems on the inward journey. Without being firmly grounded in the world, the Bhūpura, we can become heady with concepts and ideals that remain intellectual and impractical. Without grounding, we lose the essence of the teaching even if we know it well from an academic or bookish standpoint. This ungroundedness is the result of a dysfunctional agni, which has not transformed conceptual understanding into a lived one.

Tāntrik sādhanā of the householders is designed to avoid ungrounding.

We set out on the spiritual path while being fully engaged in the joy and muck of day-to-day life with jobs, families, relationships, and other complications.

In this approach, we are required to apply the vidyā through the cultivation of moment-to-moment awareness. We are forced out of dreamy contemplations into the nitty-gritties of work and play while also finding the time and inspiration for continued and advancing practice and study.

Through constant application of the teachings, we discover the ever-auspicious form of Devī in all of existence. By becoming firmly grounded in the mundane, the essence of vidyā begins to reveal itself as suśrī – the splendid auspiciousness underlying both the strife and ecstasy of life.

Sarvapāpaharā

Sarvapāpaharā (sarva = all, pāpa = sins, *harā* = she who destroys) who destroys all sins and corresponds to *kṣobhaka* agni and the kalā of *surūpa* (whole).

Kṣobhaka is the power of agitation or disruption. We can easily relate to the disruptive power of agni, which destroys everything in its wake without consideration for its worth or use. Pāpa, or sin, makes sense only from the standpoint of puṇya or virtue. As we explored in the Bhūpura, sin and virtue keep us bound in karma and the cycles of saṃsāra. When caught up in the worldly sphere or the circumference, we remain within the bounds of sin and virtue that are arranged by society, family, culture, and prevailing moral norms. What is sin within a particular set of norms isn't in another. While these boundaries are needed to maintain societal harmony and peace, they are not inherent as rules in the structure of creation.

Importantly, even when we remain within the norms, we are internally agitated since we are always looking for validation for being virtuous or feeling shame and guilt for sinning. This push and pull of sin and virtue is our default stance when our gaze is externally focused.

When we turn to the nivṛtti mārga, we lose the agitation arising from seeking external validation or judgment. The concepts of sin and virtue stop making sense as norms and instead, beauty and auspiciousness pervade our experience. We are naturally inclined toward dharma instead of being forced to adhere to rules. Our energy becomes whole, and the agitation of fragmentation is replaced by the agitation of longing for wholeness (surūpā).

Sarvānandamayī

Sarvānandamayī (sarva = all, ānanda = bliss, mayī = replete) confers the satisfaction of happiness or bliss and corresponds to *udgrāhaka* agni and the kalā of *kapilā* (golden).

Ānanda is a word that is translated as happiness or enjoyment. In practice however, it is the quality of contentment, the lack of which keeps us on the path of seeking. Ānanda tends to be elusive not because we don't have opportunities to experience happiness but because we can't derive contentment even when we are happy.

Udgrāhaka is the attribute of reception. Agni receives whatever we offer to him without discrimination. Ghee in the context of a sacred ritual is as easily received as flesh and bones in an incinerator. Agni's udgrāhaka śakti is the key to its transformative power, which we must cultivate for ānanda. Usually, when something goes well for us we don't allow ourselves to completely receive the blessing. Instead, we look for potential obstacles such as the fear of losing it, false humility, comparison with others who have "more," and so on. Joy or happiness never seem to permeate us fully where we can soak in it.

If we can learn to fully receive joy, we would touch upon contentment. Each of us stumbles upon ānanda by accident when it takes us entirely by surprise. For me, it was the birth of my second child; I held her in my arms and felt completely sated. I had known delight with my firstborn, of course, but because I had envisioned my family to consist of two children, the search was still on for fulfilment. With the fulfilment of this eṣaṇā, my mind had called off that search and the joy sunk in. I surrendered to it so fully that the ānanda permeated my bones and I basked in its golden light.

The characteristic of ānanda is that it becomes available to us in all states if we surrender to it. In addition to joy, we never fully receive pain, grief, anger, envy, and other agitations. If we can be fully open and allowing of them, we touch upon ānanda as the underlying rasa or taste of experience. Udgrāhaka makes us replete with all bliss (*sarvānandamaya*), bathing us in kapilā, the warm golden light of contentment.

Sarvarakṣāsvarūpiṇī

Sarvarakṣāsvarūpiṇī (sarva = all, *rakṣa* = protection, svarupiṇī = form) is all-protecting, and corresponds with *jhṛmbhaka* agni and the kalā *havyavāhinī* (oblation-bearer). Jhṛmbhaka is the power of assimilation.

Like udgrāhaka, jhṛmbhaka has to do with the internalization of experience. Ordinarily, our experience is not fully internalized or assimilated because of the phenomenon of secondary and tertiary experiences. Let's examine this with an example. You are helping your seven-year-old child with math homework and he's not getting it despite your best efforts. As he continues to make the same mistake again and again, your patience starts to run thin and you feel anger boiling up. The energy rises and you feel like smacking your son. Suddenly, you remember that you're on the spiritual path and "should not" be angry. With this, a secondary emotion comes in – guilt. How could you possibly want to hit your child in anger? What is the point of waking up at 5 AM every day to meditate? Your mind spins with the self-flagellation. And then you remember that you're supposed to allow things to be without trying to manipulate experience. A tertiary emotion comes in – self-pity. You can't even remember the teaching! Mind you, the energy of anger hasn't gone away. It has become contaminated by the energies of guilt and self-pity, and when you finally calm yourself through the convoluted process of "remembering" the teaching, the energy dissipates. However, it hasn't left you, and will rise again the next time an opportunity arises.

On the other hand, if you can assimilate the energy of anger fully without corrupting it (through secondary and tertiary arisings) or acting on it (smacking your child), it does indeed move through you. Importantly, the charge of anger dissipates, and the energy becomes available for transmutation. It morphs into orgasmic energy, opening infinite possibilities for creative thought. You may recall or create a totally different way of explaining things to your son where he immediately gets it, or you remember that you know an excellent math tutor whose services you can avail.

Havyavāhinī refers to the kalā of agni that carries offerings or oblations for which he is revered in fire rituals. In a homa ritual, ghee is the most important offering, and is mixed with all other substances that go into the fire. Like ojas, ghee is a highly refined substance and is the purest essence of milk. For its various medicinal and spiritual properties, ghee is an elixir that refines everything that is mixed with it and makes its essence available to agni. In addition to being the fuel for fire, it amplifies the *vāhaka* or carrier attribute of fire. Agni consumes the ghee, assimilating the offerings that are mixed with it, and carries it to the deity being invoked in the homa.

When we invoke this yoginī of the Antardaśara, she graces us with the ability to assimilate experience. We cultivate the ability to imbibe the essence of an experience, making it available for higher transmutation. We are protected against avidyā in the form of the conditioning that blocks its assimilation. Gradually, we begin to recognize the difference between energy and thought. In the above example, the energy of anger is raw and pure whereas the thought about its sin or virtue corrupts it. If we can stay with the energy, we are protected against both sin and virtue.

Devotion to energy gives us the insight that nothing exists outside of us. Nobody can "make" us angry, fearful, anxious, or hurt. Instead, we come to see them as stimuli for the arising of the energy that is already within us. With this shift in perspective, we come to see that we are always protected.

Sarvepsidaphalapradā

Sarvepsidaphalapradā (sarva = all, *īpsita* = wished for, *phala* = fruit, pradā = bestower) gives us all our desired fruits and corresponds to *mohaka* agni and the kalā *kavyavāhinī* (carrier of the sacrifice).

One of the greatest gifts of the homa ritual is the cultivation of dispassion. In other types of rituals, the offerings are symbolic – we offer food, clothing, jewelry and other valuables as a symbolic gesture and partake of them as the blessed residuum (*prasāda*). In a homa ritual, on the other hand, all offerings are poured into the fire. Here, the very real consumption of the offering by Agni is symbolic for our inner process. We must pour all our inner conflict, the good and the bad into the fire of transformation. Nothing can be held back to enjoy later as the prasāda. The transformation and transmutation *are* the prasāda. For this, we must be ready to pour ourselves into the fire.[180] After all, that's why we are treading this path!

Mohaka is the attribute of attraction. Fire is inherently attractive for its light, warmth, and the possibilities it brings for civilization. Being one of the primary forces of creation, it is the organizing principle for its five functions of sṛṣṭi, stithi, saṃhāra, tirodhāna and anugraha. It is agni's mohaka śakti that makes these functions possible. Tirodhāna is the power of concealment manifesting as Māyā, where we are so deluded by what appears to be an objective world that we entirely forget the subject. It is mohaka that keeps us engrossed in the circumference even when we think we are treading the radius.

As we have explored in the Bhūpura, being caught up in the world of objects creates the desire to own them and brings strife when we can't. When we approach the Śrīcakra with this frame of reference, we hope that this yoginī will fulfill all our wishes

180 See Chapter 1 in K. Chinnaiyan, *Glorious Alchemy: Living the Lalitā Sahasranāma* (New Sarum Press, 2020) for a brief retelling of the Lalitopākhyāna. Lalitā Devī manifests in the Devās' homa fire when they start sacrificing themselves into it, which is why she is called cidagni kuṇḍasambhūtā (N4, born in the fire-pit of consciousness).

and make it possible to own more objects of the world. This may happen, but as we have seen throughout this book, every yoginī has a shadow and a light side. In her shadow aspect Sarvepsidaphalapradā will grant our wishes but keep us entrapped in saṃsāra. The mohaka śakti remains externally focused as tirodhāna.

On the other hand, when she grants her grace (anugraha), the mohaka is transmuted into the attraction for nothing other than the Bindu. We are finally on the radius, and willing to sacrifice ourselves into the fire. Mohaka makes us dispassionate towards everything else, where all offerings are readily thrown into the fire for kavyavāhinī to devour. We are content with the subtle prasāda of the upāsanā.

The Agni Kalās in Practice

Tapas is the sādhanā of the entire Śrīcakra, but especially of the Antardaśara. Homa is the practice of this āvaraṇa, where every arising is sacrificed into agni, the internal fire.

> ***Thoughts, emotions, cravings, judgments, contractions, memories, hopes, and fears are sacrificed into the flames of awareness.***

At this point, it is essential that we have cultivated the two critical attributes of viveka (discernment) and vairāgya (dispassion) along with higher reasoning (sattarka).[181] Viveka is the ability to discern between the fire and the objects that must be sacrificed into it. This is not easy to do without the cultivation of sattarka. Higher or perfected reasoning can only be cultivated when we have disengaged from the drama of the me-story to a certain extent and can apply the teaching of the darśana. It requires us to relinquish emotionality in favor of logic and pragmatism, and to understand (at least intellectually) how and why things unfold as they do. It is sattarka that enables the rise of dispassion where we can willingly and joyfully throw everything into the fire.

181 See Bhāvanā in Chapter 5.

Agni here is the fire of consciousness, the supreme subject that is untouched by all objects. Recall that the ahaṅkāra is the I-maker that takes objects (Prakṛti) and "makes" them the subject.[182] The true I is the attributeless witnessing awareness (Puruṣa) that

182 See Tattvas in Chapter 4.

cannot be experienced. Everything that is experienced is an object whereas the subject is the experienc*er*. To arrive at this level of viveka, we must have traversed through all the previous āvaraṇas, refining our ability to reason without the clouding of the me-story.

With this background, we take on the sādhanā of the Antardaśara, where we have constant awareness of the distinction between the subject and object. This awareness allows us to relinquish the object in favor of the subject. Remaining grounded in our daily activities, we continuously burn through āma and tamas by returning again and again to the subject, which is indescribable.

This may start out as awareness of awareness (the subject) where we notice that we are aware of being aware. In this practice, we return again and again to the process of being aware, relinquishing the *content* of awareness. For example, if we are caught up in a memory, instead of becoming enamored by its story (the content), we realize that it is a temporary arising in awareness as a memory-thought. This pragmatic approach takes us from transactional knowledge to Self-knowledge. Dispassion allows us to extricate from the *content* of thought into the *process* of thinking and eventually to the *thinker*. It's important to state here that eventually, even spiritual concepts and ideas are thrown into the fire without a second thought. Everything that stands in the way of Self-knowledge must go, including spiritual thoughts and concepts of virtue and good karma.

Every aspect of our upāsanā is mediated by agni. Upāsanā, in essence, is one long process of surrender, where we constantly empty ourselves by pouring things into agni's dynamic flames, which reorganizes the prāṇa vāyus in the Bahirdaśara. Agni's influence is far-reaching; the reorganization of the prāṇa vāyus stimulates the opening of previously closed nāḍīs at the Manvaśra. In other words, new neurohormonal pathways are forged; agitations in the Aṣṭadalapadma settle down and our interactions at the Bhūpura become more harmonious because of the resolution of attractions and aversions at the Śodaṣadalapadma.

If we make it to the Antardaśara, we are close to Self-knowledge because it was a great leap to this āvaraṇa, from the Bahirdaśara. However, the leap to the Vasukoṇa, the next āvaraṇa is even more momentous. This doesn't even happen until we have paid the most appropriate and reverential dues to agni at this āvaraṇa.

Cakreśvarī: Tripuramālinī

The Nigarbha Yoginīs of the Antardaśara are extremely hard to please, or even encounter. As with the yoginīs of the other āvaraṇas, they have shadow and light aspects that determine whether we are bound in saṃsāra or are progressing toward liberation from it.

Tripuramālinī, an emanation of Mahātripurasundarī, rules over the Sarvarakṣākara cakra that protects us by granting us the realization of the power of agni. The yoginīs and Cakreśvarī of this āvaraṇa are invoked through the mantra hrīṃ *klīṃ bleṃ* and the mudrā bīja *kroṃ* corresponding with Sarvamahāṅkuśā, the all-stimulating one. Surrender of objects in favor of the supreme subject is the stance that allows us to traverse this āvaraṇa, which will in turn influence the prāṇa vāyus and the opening of nāḍīs. The stance we arrive at here is one of self-confidence, where we see that nothing exists outside of our own experience. At this point the nivṛtti mārga begins in earnest, and transmutation speeds up.

The grace of the Nigarbha Yoginīs wakes us up from the traps of duality and pushes us to the next āvaraṇa, the Vasukoṇa.

Chapter 14

Vasukoṇa

शीतोष्णसुखदुःखेच्छा सत्त्वं रजस्तमो वशिन्यादि शक्तयोऽष्टौ ॥ २० ॥

Śītoṣṇa-sukha-duḥkhecchāh sattvam rajastamo vaśinyādi śaktyoṣṭau || 20 ||

"Cold, heat, happiness, misery, sattva, rajas and tamas are the eight śaktis including Vaśinī, etc."
~ Bhāvanopaniṣad, verse 20

As captivating and challenging as the journey has been up until the Antardaśara, we have now arrived at another critical juncture. Recall that we have been exploring the Śrīcakra in the saṃhāra krama of dissolution, moving from the gross to the subtle with every āvaraṇa.

The grouping of the nine āvaraṇas in the three groups of three corresponding with the sṛṣṭi, stithi and saṃhāra kramas that we explored earlier will now begin to make sense.[183] We now know from our upāsanā that the first group (Bhūpura, Śodaṣadalapadma and Aṣṭadalapadma) comprised the sṛṣṭi krama because the objects of the world, body and mind are fully manifest as the gross and subtle elements influencing each other. We also traversed the middle group (Manvaśra, Bahirdaśara and Antardaśara), which makes up the stithi krama because it sustains the elements of the first group via the nāḍīs, vāyus and agni kalās. We now arrive at the final group (Vasukoṇa, Trikoṇa and Bindu) of saṃhāra krama where everything that was created in the first and sustained in the second will dissolve.

183 See The Krama of the Āvaraṇas in Chapter 4.

Although the transition from any one āvaraṇa to the next is significant, the leap from one group to another tends to be momentous. This is because the line of inquiry at these critical junctures takes a significant turn and requires exponential stillness, sattarka, viveka and vairāgya.[184] Take, for instance, the transition to the Manvaśra. While the inquiry in the Bhūpura, Śodaṣadalapadma and Aṣṭadalapadma involved the world, the

184 See Bhāvanā in Chapter 5.

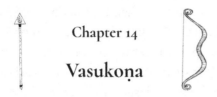

body and the mind and the analysis of their interaction, here we had to shift the contemplation to the flow of the nāḍīs. Our bhāvanā needed to proceed in the right direction, where we weren't caught up in the periphery but proceeded on the radius. We had to become willing to dig deep instead of rearranging the debris at the rim.

From the Manvaśra to the Antardaśara, we kept up the excavation that revealed the logarithmic unfolding of our inner process. Through constant contemplation and steady application of the insights we gained at the feet of each Nigarbha Yoginī, we came to see our infinite modes of self-deception that keep us locked in saṃsāra. When you think about it, landing at the agni kalās from the objects of the world is a near-impossible task without the systematic and highly logical organization of the Śrīcakra. From here, our inquiry needs to be precise, sharp, and clear if we are to arrive at the Vasukoṇa.

The Inquiry

At the Antardaśara, we encountered the inner intelligence of the flow of prāṇa in the form of agni, the great transformer. We came to see how this inner fire that blazes as the life force and intelligence of creation creates a misapprehension because of the veils of Māyā. The separation between me and the world creates the dichotomous predicament, giving rise to fear and hope, expectations and grief, anger and envy, and validation and disappointment.

The Nigarbha Yoginīs showed us how their shadow aspects entangle us in misapprehension and lit our way to vidyā through the cultivation of single-pointed devotion to the path, dispassion, discernment, and importantly, higher reasoning. As these qualities replace our default way of being such as emotional reactivity, ungroundedness, mind noise and rumination over the past and future, a remarkable change begins to take place in the body-mind.

Stillness of the mind and body become the new default with an inability to engage in obsessive thought. Emotional reactivity is replaced by equanimity, where choices and decisions are made without consideration of past history or future expectations. Productivity and creativity increase exponentially because no energy is wasted in activities that don't confer joy or benefit to all. With the grace of the agni kalās, the body becomes radiant and clear as novel neurohormonal pathways are forged and new chemicals are released. There is no lethargy or fogginess and the need for sleep is reduced greatly. The mind is sharp, clear, focused, and quiescent. This is the state of sattva.

At this point we begin to turn toward the Vasukoṇa with the questions, "What is the organizing principle of agni's transformative power that drives the flow of prāṇa manifesting as myself and the world? What is the intermediary between the formless Śiva-Śakti and the subtle form of Agni? How does the formless crystallize into form?"

This contemplation in the context of a sāttvik buddhi catapults us out of the circumference altogether and brings us to the door of the Vasukoṇa.

Vasukoṇa

The Vasukoṇa is the eight-triangled āvaraṇa (*vasu* = eight, *koṇa* = angle) representing aspects of vāc.[185] The triangles are presided by the supreme Vāgdevatās (deities presiding over vāc), who are known as *Rahasya* (secret) Yoginīs (see Figure 44). This āvaraṇa is known as the *Sarvarogahara* (sarva = all, *roga* = sickness, *hara* = destroyer) cakra.

185 See Chapter 6.

The Vasukoṇa is the primordial expansion of the Bindu and the Trikoṇa, and the entire Śrīcakra is its expression in manifestation.

In other words, the Vasukoṇa is the primordial cause of manifestation that organizes into the rest of the Śrīcakra, beginning with the Antardaśara. In the saṃhāra krama, we arrive here from the Antardaśara through the grace of the Nigarbha Yoginīs. To arrive at the Antardaśara is a tremendous gift of grace, symbolic of the significant cleansing of the buddhi that has already taken place through the work done in the other āvaraṇas. To be propelled to the Vasukoṇa is nothing short of miraculous grace, for here we will be stripped of the last bit of karma that keeps us bound in saṃsāra.

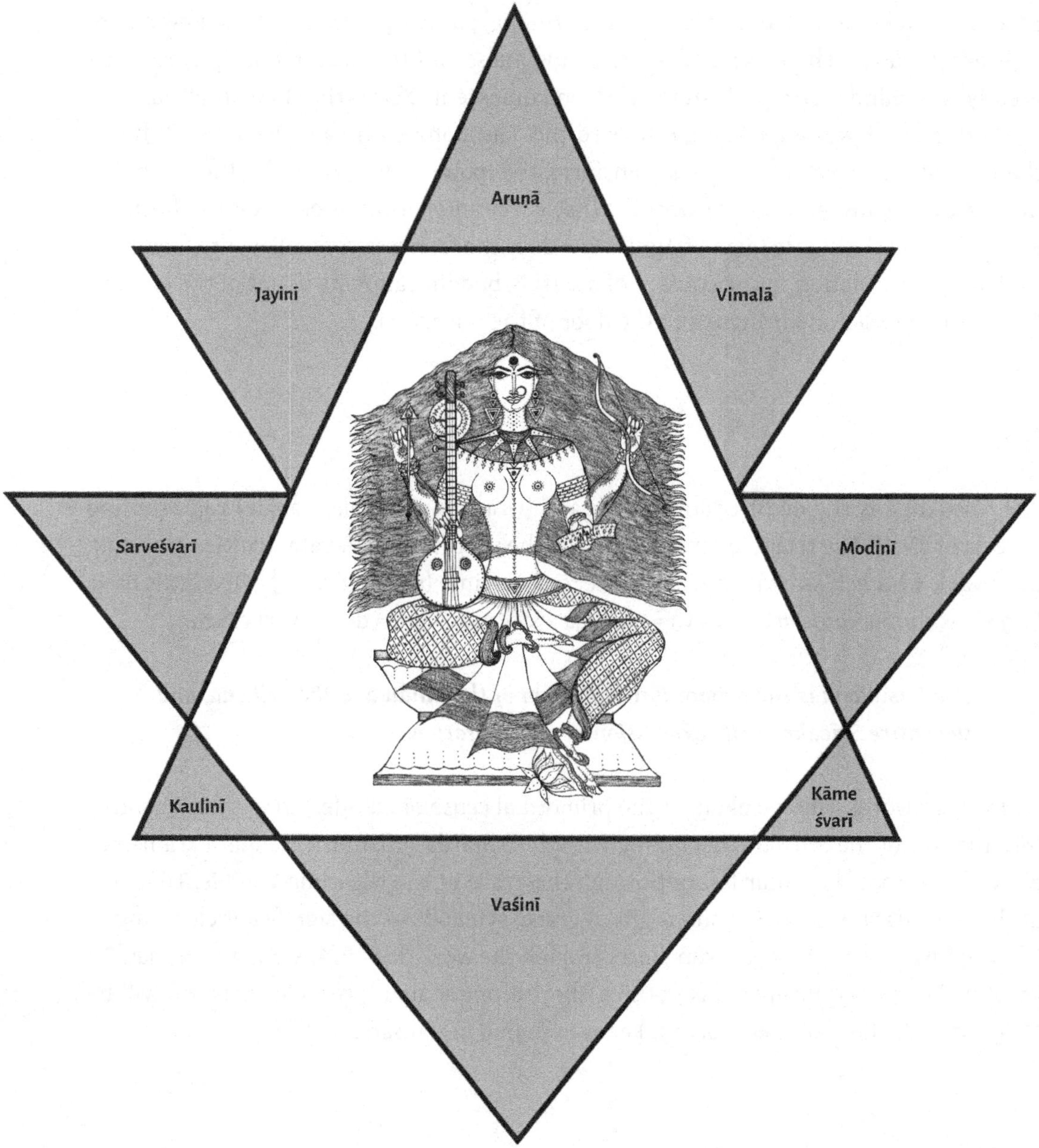

Figure 44. Vasukoṇa with Rahasya Yoginī

The fundamental ailment that we suffer from is that of a mistaken identity. Our problems begin with the separation of Aham and Idam – I and That – precipitated by Māyā with her kañcukas and malas. At the highest level of creation, Śiva (subject) looks in the mirror and recognizes Śakti (object) as himself. When covered by Māyā, Śiva looks at Śakti and sees her as the other. This subtle separation that occurs at the Trikoṇa is crystallized at the level of the Vasukoṇa. Another way of looking at this split is through the lens of language or vāc.

From the standpoint of language, we have seen the split occurring between śabda and artha, or sound and its meaning.[186] At the level of Absolute Reality, śabda and artha are non-separate. With the seeming separation of Śiva-Śakti at the Trikoṇa, śabda and artha also separate. Śabda devolves into language and artha into the world to which language refers. Śabda, artha, and the relationship between them explodes as creation as the eight aspects represented by the Rahasya yoginīs (see Figure 45).

186 See Kāmakalā in Chapter 6.

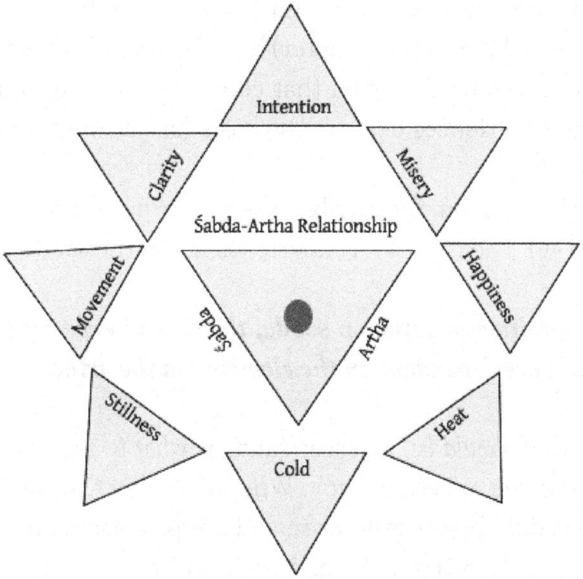

Figure 45. Vasukoṇa in Manifestation

Śabda and Artha

Think of śabda as the unconditioned, pure arising and artha as the meaning assigned to it through learning and conditioning. For example, the word "table" points to a specific object made of legs and a surface. When dismantled, it is no longer a table but its parts. When broken down further, it is the material (wood, glass, etc.) making up the pieces. With further dissection, it is a particular molecular structure (which is given the name of wood or glass). In essence, the table is a collection of atoms organized in specific ways. The issue here is that we take the word "table" to be śabda when it is artha. Its śabda is the arising of an object that is nameless, but the artha assigned to it makes it appear to be real and true.

The artha of table is derived from all the structures coming together and being assigned with a meaning. This principle applies to everything in existence, including the contents of our inner landscape that we take to be absolutely and irrevocably true. Slights, insults, and trauma arise as pieces and fragments of guṇas interacting with each other as śabda (see *Jayanī*, later in this chapter) but when woven together by our learning of good and bad, they become the artha that congeals onto our buddhi. The artha we assign to random life experiences become the basis for karma, creating samskārās and manifesting as our reality.

The artha superimposes on the śabda, where the pure essence of the arising is obscured (see Figure 46). The rasa of an experience lies in the śabda sphere.

> ***In the superimposition of artha on śabda, the rasa of experience is lost, and our joy and pain are dependent on the elements in the artha sphere.***

Artha results in what *should be*, whereas śabda is *what is*. During times when *what is* matches *what should be*, we experience joy. When they don't, we feel misery. Cycles of *sukha* (happiness) and duḥkha (misery) arise and are propagated in the artha sphere of saṃsāra, which is linear. Nirvāṇa and freedom from karma lie in the sphere of śabda, which is non-linear. Śrīcakra upāsanā takes us from artha to śabda here at the Vasukoṇa.

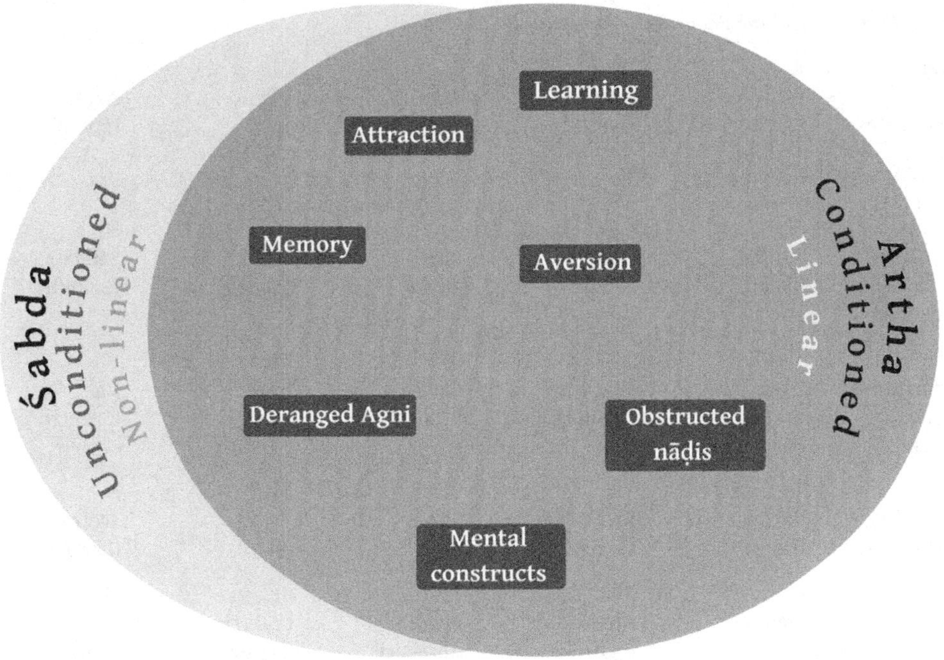

Figure 46. The Superimposition of Artha on Śabda

At the Vasukoṇa, śabda and artha become differentiated into the eight groups of the Sanskrit phonemes, each correlating with a particular attribute that binds us in the separation between Aham and Idam. The phonemes crystallize the formless into form through decreasing levels of subtlety from Parā to vaikharī, becoming the 36 tattvas (see Table 16 below). Sanskrit is unique in that nearly every possible sound is included in its scope in its eight phonetic groups – vowels, semivowels, sibilants, aspirates, and the guttural, palatal, cerebral dental, and labial consonants.[187] It is also unique in its logic and organization, where most sounds and their variations are included in this algorithmic scheme, which is the secret of the eternal Veda.

187 The eight phonetic groups are also correlated with the Aṣṭa Mātṛkās in some classification systems. From the standpoint of the Śrīcakra, where they are situated in the Bhūpura, the correlation would be at the level of vaikharī, whereas that of the Rahasya Yoginīs in the Vasukoṇa would be at the level of madhyamā.

Table 16. Correlation of the Phoneme Groups with the Tattvas

Kavarga Pañca Mahābhūtas (Great elements)	K Kśiti (Earth)	Kh Apaḥ (Water)	G Agni (Fire)	Gh Vāyu (Air)	Ṅ Ākāśa (Space)
Cavarga Tanmātras (Sense perception)	C Gandha (Smell)	Ch Rasa (Taste)	J Rūpa (Form)	Jh Sparśa (Touch)	Ñ Śabda (Sound)
Ṭavarga Karmendriyas (Organs of action)	Ṭ Pāyu (Anus)	Ṭh Upastha (Genitals)	Ḍ Hasta (Hands)	Ḍh Pāda (Legs)	Ṇ Vāk (Speech)
Tavarga Jñānendriyas (Sense organs)	T Ghrāṇa (Nose)	Th Rasana (Tongue)	D Cakṣu (Eyes)	Dh Tvak (Skin)	N Srotra (Ears)
Pavarga (The empirical I)	P Manas (Mind)	Ph Ahaṅkāra (Ego)	B Buddhi (Intellect)	Bh Prakṛti (Nature)	M Puruṣa (Self)
Semivowels Kañcukas (Coverings)	Y Rāga (Passion)	R Vidyā (Knowing)	L Kalā (Space)	V Kāla (Time)	Ḷ Niyati (Causation)
Sibilants Śuddhādvan (Reality)	Ś Kriyā (Action)	Ṣ Jñāna (Knowledge)	S Icchā (Intention)	H Śakti	Kṣ Śiva

Just as an atom in its infinite permutations and combinations gives rise to the known elements in the Periodic Table, the algorithm of Sanskrit provides the basic structure for the arising, maintenance, and dissolution of the universe. At this āvaraṇa, we come to understand the correlations between the phonemes and the structure of the universe. The phonemes make up the subtle thought of the Divine that solidifies as you, me, and countless other forms.

Vāk is vibration, which is the source of agni. By vibration, we mean the subtlest, tiniest ripple in the great stillness of Absolute Reality that results in the initial separation of Śiva and Śakti. This disturbance gathers force and explodes into infinite vibrations of differing frequencies – from Śiva all the way down to pṛthvī. In the Antardaśara, we saw that every element has its own agni. At the Vasukoṇa, we will see that the unique facets of agni are the result of the different ways in which it is expressed. The power of agni's differing expressions is derived from the Rahasya Yoginīs. Dāhaka agni differs from pācaka agni because of the subtle difference in its *expression,* or vāk. The Antardaśara is the āvaraṇa where form becomes perceptible as agni, but the *structure* and *function* of that form is provided by the imperceptible vāk.

The supremacy of śabda or vibration that gives rise to form is the basis for mantra *śāstra* or the science of mantra. Since śabda is the basis of form, we resort to it in its specific vibrations as mantra to return to the formless. The mystical and mysterious Vāgdevatās control the power of mantra, which enables us to traverse the final group of the three āvaraṇas.

Rahasya Yoginī

The Rahasya Yoginīs (Vāgdevatās) grace us with the discernment and clarity to traverse this āvaraṇa.

The regal Rahasya Yoginī is red-hued and four-armed and bears a bow and arrow in her upper hands. In stringing the bow with the arrow, she binds śabda with artha, propagating the tattvas from the Antardaśara to the Bhūpura. The *vīṇa* (a stringed instrument) in her right lower hand is the source of śabda and artha, the one we must follow on our journey back to her. The *pustaka* (book) in her left lower hand is the source of all knowledge (see Figure 47).

Figure 47. Rahasya Yoginī

The eight Vāgdevatās situated in the Vasukoṇa are considered in an anti-clockwise direction beginning at the east portal (see Figure 44). The Bhāvanopaniṣad correlates the yoginīs with several groups of eight.[188] From the cosmic and psychophysiological perspective, they are associated with the five great elements and the three guṇas. They are also correlated with the seven dhātus and the seven goddesses that preside over the cakras.[189], The *eighth* is the integral of all the others. They also correspond with the puryaṣṭaka (meaning, eight constituent parts) consisting of the jñānendriyas, the karmendriyas, the citta,[190] the prāṇa vāyus, the mahābhūtas, rāga, karma, and avidyā. Importantly, they correlate with the eight groups of phonemes, establishing their presence in all tattvas.

When we refer specifically to the great elements with respect to the Vāgdevatās, we must remember that the associations between the phonemes and tattvas occur at various levels. For instance, *Vaśinī* is correlated to water, but the water element or mahābhūta is associated with the *kavarga* (the phoneme *Kh*) in Table 16, which is assigned to *Kāmeśvarī* in Table 17. To avoid confusion, it is easier to think in terms of general principles rather than the specifics. In the above example, the *attribute* of water is correlated with Vaśinī whereas the element or mahābhūta of water with the kavarga. Remember that the same principle occurs at all levels of the Śrīcakra – it's just that our perception of it changes and evolves as we ascend the āvaraṇas.

The correlations of the Rahasya Yoginīs with the guṇas and psychophysiological processes such as cold, heat, happiness, misery, intention, clarity, movement, and stillness may seem like a stretch. However, this important teaching points to our dualistic perception that binds us in saṃsāra since cold and heat, and happiness and misery don't exist without the other of the pair. Intention is the mass of desires that form the basis of duality, and the guṇas are the unconditioned forces that give birth to conditioned opposites.

The conclusions we can draw from the associations between the phonemes and the psychophysiological processes will be unique to our sādhanā and how we interpret the teaching based on our Guru paramparā. What follows is a loose description based on my understanding of this teaching, which may inform yours. How this will unfold for you will be entirely up to the Vāgdevatās!

188 See Ramachandra S.K. Rao, *The Tantra of Sri-Chakra (Bhavanopanishat)* (Delhi: Sri Satguru Publications, 2008).

189 Dākinī, Rākiṇī, Lākinī, Kākinī, Sākinī, Hākinī and Yākinī.

190 Citta is also known as antaḥkaraṇa and made up of the mind, intellect and ahaṅkāra.

Table 17. Yoginīs of the Vasukoṇa

Vāgdevatā Yoginī	Phoneme Group	Phonemes	Psychophysiological	Tattvas	Bhāvanā
Vaśinī	Vowels	a ā i ī u ū ṛ, ṝ ḷ, ḹ e, o, ai, au, aṃ, aḥ	Cold (Water)	Absolute Reality	Adaptability
Kāmeśvarī	Kavarga	ka kha ga gha ṅa	Heat (Fire)	Pañca Mahābhūtas	Equanimity
Modinī	Cavarga	ca cha ja jha ña	Happiness	Tanmātras	Contentment
Vimalā	Ṭavarga	ṭa ṭha ḍa ḍha ṇa	Misery	Karmendriyas	Mindfulness
Aruṇā	Tavarga	ta tha da dha na	Intention	Jñānendriyas	Pratyāhāra
Jayanī	Pavarga	pa pha ba bha ma	Clarity (sattva)	Empirical I	Suchness
Sarveśvarī	Semi-vowels	ya ra la va	Movement (rajas)	Kañcukas	Surrender
Kaulinī	Sibilants	śa ṣa sa ha kśa	Stillness (tamas)	Śuddhādvan	Insight

Vaśinī

The first of the Vāgdevatās, Vaśinī (the one who subjugates), presides over the vowels and is correlated with the water and cold.

Vowels are the most important elements of the Sanskrit alphabet because the consonants cannot be pronounced without them. Vowels are the śakti of the consonants, giving them life and direction; they allow the movement of *expression* of the consonants. On the other hand, consonants provide the container for the vowels to be expressed in specific ways. In the Śākta tradition, vowels are given the place of Śakti, and consonants are Śiva.[191] Vaśinī rules over the vowels or the infinite ways in which consonants can be expressed. If the consonants are the tattvas, the vowels provide direction and energy for their expression, which is like the flow of water.

191 Note that in some Śaiva traditions, it is the other way around – vowels are Śiva and consonants Śakti.

Water, like vowels, has its own structure, power, and energy. However, it also has the property of providing structure, power, and energy to anything that contains it. It makes up nearly 70 percent of our body and is the medium of expression for electrical and chemical impulses that drive the physical, mental, and psychological processes that make up what we take to be I. There is no life without water, which is the driving force of evolution and civilization. Water can be soft and gentle, like a serene mountain lake, or ferocious and destructive like a tsunami. In all its forms, it is inherently cold, agile, refreshing, and life-giving.

Water is a great subjugator. It takes on the shape of its container and becomes the vehicle for nourishment or destruction. It embodies the guṇas of sattva and rajas by being inherently clear and dynamic.

Physiologically, we are warm-blooded and designed to operate within a narrow range of temperature, where the extremes of cold and heat result in discomfort or illness. Vaśinī subjugates our physiology by limiting its functional parameters and making it vulnerable to the experience of cold. These parameters limit flow and expression, where tamas weighs down upon the clarity of sattva and the exuberance of rajas.

The most significant attribute of water is its adaptability, which is the function of its sattva and rajas. When limited by tamas, it loses its adaptability. In us, the stagnation of the water element inhibits the flow of the vowels and limits them to our conditioned way of being. The supreme vowels become dull and unable to charge the consonants, which are our senses, perceptions, and the objects of the world. We are unable to see the beauty of existence because of stagnation at this level, where we become creatures of habit, and everything must be just so for us to thrive or even exist. Rigidity and lack of adaptability result in stress and anxiety when things don't go as planned.

> ***When we surrender to this great yoginī, she graces us with the power of water, where we are infused with the ability to flow and adapt, and to align with reality as it unfolds.***

She grants us with the power of subjugation, which is not the product of brute force, but of boundless softness and malleability.

Bhāvanā on Vaśinī

Rigidity of being is a significant obstruction in sādhanā. We tend to hold on steadfastly to our habits, upbringing, beliefs, ideas, shoulds and should nots. The path of the Śrīcakra is a continuous letting go.

Question every single one of your ideas and beliefs.

Realize that all ideas and beliefs arise out of learning. Anything you perceive as wrong is right in someone else's sphere of social, cultural and moral conditioning. Recall the darśana, particularly that of Māyā which projects the illusion of right and wrong, and me and the other.

Ask yourself if you'd rather be right or happy.

Train yourself to focus on the Bindu, which is free of all constrictions.

Learn to flow with life, holding no grudges or hang-ups internally, even when living life according to your social and cultural norms.

Kāmeśvarī

Kāmeśvarī (kāma = desire, *īśvarī* = sovereign) rules over the desire for expression, presiding over the kavarga (consonants in the group beginning with *ka*), corresponding to the fire element and heat.

Kāma, or desire, is the driving force of creation, and manifestation begins with it. Kāmeśvarī in the Vasukoṇa rules over desire, which originates as a subtle ripple in stillness (Parā) and gains momentum and urgency as it descends into paśyantī and madhyamā to become fully manifest as vaikharī. When desire arises at the subtlest level, it contains all possibilities in it for manifestation. Let's examine this with an example. When the desire arose for me to write this book, it was vague and undefined. It was a longing for a creative outlet. As I sat with it, allowing it to percolate, *thoughts* began to arise from the *feeling* of longing. My Gurus' blessings and guidance infused the thought with power, and the ideas for the content, layout, and emphasis began to take shape. The process of writing crystallized the initial desire into words and sentences, eventually becoming the book you hold in your hands. Everything that is manifested in your life underwent this process as well, beginning with desire and ending in the seemingly solid end-product.

This process of condensation from desire to result is catalyzed by agni, as we saw in the Antardaśara, which is set in motion at the Vasukoṇa as expression. The kavarga (class of consonants beginning with K) corresponds to the pañca mahābhūtas or the great elements, which are the most obvious manifestation of the Divine that is available for us to experience through our senses (see Table 16 above).

> ***The mahābhūtas that are fully expressed as vaikharī began as an idea or kāma in the mind of the Vāgdevatā Kāmeśvarī.***

The earth that supports us, the water that nourishes us, the fire that warms us, the air that enlivens us, and the space that holds it all – the five great elements are continuously born, sustained, and dissolved by this great yoginī.

Without her grace, our desire finds no expressive outlet. We can have many ideas but none or few of them come to fruition because the fundamental attribute of heat that is required for creative expression is dull or missing. The ability to even perceive the subtle ripple of desire and give it room for full expression is the gift of this yoginī. All the great inventions of the ages are catalyzed by her through the medium of human expression. When we become devoted to her, she clarifies our perception through the subtle principle of heat, burning away the dullness and stagnation that obscures it.

While the quality of coldness relates to stagnation and lack of adaptability, heat is the quality of aggression and ruthlessness. When desire is tainted by rigidity, we set ourselves up for disappointment. If the arising of desire incites a specific outcome because of lack of flexibility, the expression is stunted by fear and hope. On the other hand, when the desire becomes mingled with ambition, fear gives way to ruthlessness where we will do "whatever it takes" to manifest the desire. Instead, if we can be in the flow of desire, its heat opens us up to the joy of the creative process, which becomes the end goal.

With her grace, desires become manifest because we can tune into those that will bring joy and benefit to the world. This can only happen if we can transcend the dualities of heat and cold, where we rise above what will solely benefit us at the cost of others. However, we must remember that arriving at this point of equanimity is not the result of moral norms or externally enforced values. We arrive here because we have *transcended* duality altogether where loss and gain, fame and insult, and happiness and misery have stopped making sense.

Modinī

Modinī (the one that delights) rules over joy, presiding over the *cavarga* and corresponding to happiness.

The cavarga rules over the tanmātras, or the subtle elements that bridge the mahābhūtas to the sense organs – smell, taste, form, touch, and sound. Ordinarily, we pay no attention to the tanmātras because the external world enchants us.[192] The tanmātras are the sense perceptions that make it possible for us to experience the world. However, the phenomena of the world collide with our conditioning to produce our habitual way of interacting with it, where we push away what doesn't resonate with us and grasp at things that do.

192 See Citta Vṛttis in Chapter 10.

Our default way of being is determined by the allure of the external world and colored by our own conditioning. The *process* of perceiving is ignored in favor of the *objects* that are perceived. The objects of the world are so attractive that we forget the process that enables us to experience them. Even when we are experiencing inner sights and sounds, there is a fascination with them rather than the tanmātra that makes it possible.

The subtle tanmātras are the pure and unconditioned doorways to perception. The *sense* of form or sound is delightful regardless of the *object* that is seen or heard, which is the difference between śabda and artha. However, objects are necessary substrates for the tanmātras and if we can learn to use sense objects as stimuli for enjoying the corresponding tanmātra, the process becomes delightful.

For example, you are walking along on a busy street, taking in the crowd, the noise, the smells, and the touch of people brushing against you. Ordinarily, you may have a host of reactions to this potpourri of senses, with your likes and dislikes making you tolerate some stimuli and bristle against others. On the other hand, if you are graced by Modinī, you delight in the process of sense perception where each stimulus opens the gateway to your own inner experience. Every sense perception becomes an orgasmic experience, where you are delighting in your own inner process. This happens through the higher understanding that all sense perceptions are registered and interpreted in your own mind, and no external world exists other than this. This higher understanding allows you to transcend your likes and dislikes, where it doesn't matter *what* the stimulus is – the *process* is always delightful.

Modinī graces us with happiness, but this is beyond the dualistic experience of joy and sorrow. The happiness at this level is one of total contentment where we lack nothing, and the world becomes a playground to experience the range of human potential. We stop shielding ourselves against the other or using them to further our own agendas. It is the state of delightful aloneness, where the whole world is included in our sense of I or Aham.

Vimalā

Vimalā (the one who is stainless) rules over misery and presides over the *ṭavarga*, corresponding to purity.

The ṭavarga rules over the karmendriyas or the organs of action, including the anus, genitals, hands, feet, and speech. These are the hard-working tattvas that enable us to interact with the external world. Through the karmendriyas, our internal landscape is expressed in the outer world.

Like the tanmātras, the karmendriyas are unconditioned and pure, manifesting what comes through them via our intention and knowledge. A sharp object like a knife becomes an instrument for healing at the hands of a surgeon or harm at those of a killer. The *hands* are untainted in their structure and function, as are the other organs of action.

Misery befalls us when the karmendriyas become the medium for acting out our contractions. Take, for example, the genitals, which are significant topics of shame, guilt, and power dynamics. Societal structures are built and maintained on the concept of virtue centered around the genitals. Economic strategies are created based on exploiting others' (or our own) genitals. From the standpoint of physiology alone, the genitals are no different than any other organ, made up of tissue, nerves, skin and mucus membrane and are the medium for reproduction. However, long-standing conditioning around this function brings up social, cultural, and moral judgments and dictions that corrupt their purity.

> ***When stripped of all conditioning, the functioning of the karmendriyas is ecstatic and joyful.***

The pure experience of walking, grasping, speaking, eliminating, or procreating is obscured and unavailable when the karmendriya is tainted by our conditioning. The process of washing dishes, for instance, can be ecstatic and joyful if we can experience the pure sensations of water, the texture of the dish, the subtle movements in our hands, and the contact between the various elements. Instead of śabda, our attention remains on the artha, where we rush through the task with the intent of getting it done and moving on to the next thing.

Every action can become a portal to the pure experience of life, when our default stance is one of stillness and paying exquisite attention to its details. This is the essence of mindfulness, which opens us to Vimalā's grace of untainted action.

Aruṇā

Aruṇā (the one who is ruby-like) rules over intention and presides over the *tavarga.*

Longing is an important component of sādhanā. Without longing for the Truth, it is impossible to muster up the perseverance needed to progress. However, longing is a double-edged sword which can (and does) lead us down blind alleys and diversions. In its crude aspect, it keeps us in the mode of seeking, where we have trouble committing to a path, teacher, or practice.

We go from path to path and teacher to teacher because they don't fulfill our eṣaṇas. Due to a fundamental confusion and misapprehension, we don't realize two crucial points related to desire. The first is not understanding that what we *really* want is to feel validated and the second is that the path to liberation is to be free of the *need* for validation. We approach the teacher or path to be free of the bonds of saṃsāra but expect them to pacify the ego through validation. When they don't fulfill this eṣaṇā, we move on to the next teacher or path. The two diametrically opposing desires keep us engaged on the circumference and the radius remains out of reach.

The jñānendriyas correspond with the tavarga and consist of the sense organs that are, by default, externally directed. This is the natural way of being since the senses are meant to allow us to experience the world. Longing is the habitual mode of the senses, where they hungrily consume the world and feed the ahaṅkāra, which then creates the I out of it. Recall that the āṇava mala is the fundamental sense of lack that drives us to seek completion through objects.[193] Instead of looking inward to find the source of lack, we have the irresistible desire to find wholeness in objects. Ordinarily, the jñānendriyas and the karmendriyas are rajāsik in nature, and driven by the desire for more, they innocuously lead us to believe that accumulating objects and sense experiences will fill the vacuum created by the āṇava mala.

193 See Kañcukas and Malas in Chapter 9.

Longing is the manifestation of rajas or dynamism, which is traditionally depicted as a reddish hue, the color of passion. While passion is a necessary ingredient in sādhanā, it can and does have the shadow aspect of becoming ungrounded in lacking stillness. When laced by sattva, however, longing becomes the arrow that is pointed toward the goal without any distractions. The mass of intentions becomes clarified where we don't have conflicting desires. For example, we are clear about needing time for sādhanā without also wanting to spend time with friends. Paradoxically, when we become clear and focused about what we want and where we want to be, everything in life falls into place to make it happen.

The most common reason for not making progress in sādhanā is the issue of conflicting desires where we want to have the cake and eat it too.

A common misunderstanding of the Tāntrik sādhanā being a life-affirming path is to think that we can have liberation *in addition to* all the other sense objects and experiences. This statement tends to make us think that liberation is an experience that can be owned, like a car or a purse. In this misperception, we place liberation in the linear field of artha, where nothing needs to be given up and liberation can simply be added to the box of experience.

There's nothing further from the truth. Liberation requires the ability to relinquish ownership of experience in the artha sphere. As long as we hanker after sense objects, we have no access to the śabda sphere of pure and unconditioned experience. It is only when longing turns upon itself that we realize the source of wholeness, which lies within. At this point of renunciation of experience, the path becomes life-affirming. This is the great paradox. In giving up the effort to *own* an experience, we get to enjoy it to the fullest.

> ***The affirmation of life in Tāntrik sādhanā is the nonlinear enjoyment of the world, which occurs only when we realize the unbroken wholeness in which the subject and object arise as one.***

Aruṇā's grace enables the refinement of desire and longing, where the jñānendriyas turn inward. Sense objects become the stimuli to recognize their experience, which is always internal. This 180-degree turn becomes the gateway to joyful exploration of the sense perception, catalyzed by the longing now directed toward the source of the āṇava mala.

Jayanī

Jayanī (the one who is victorious) rules over the sattva guṇa, presiding over the *pavarga* and symbolizing victory over the other guṇas.

As we explored earlier in this chapter, to even arrive at the Vasukoṇa takes immense clarity of mind and a sāttvik buddhi.[194] By this, we understand that the buddhi must be largely clear of rajāsik and tāmasik samskārās. Increasingly, on our way here, we have lost interest in the drama around us. This manifests as thoughts that are no longer about how good or bad the world is, or we are. The mind's gossip has died down, and it is polished to such an extent that it works at our command. We don't daydream, ruminating over the past or the future. When thoughts about the past or the future arise, we are not caught up in their content. Instead, we turn to them with curiosity about their origin – from where does thought arise and into what does it dissolve? Following this line of inquiry, we arrive at the silent gaps in between thoughts, which becomes our default way of being.

194 See The Tattvas in Chapter 4.

Recall that the three guṇas are Prakṛti's primordial forces (see the Tattva Map in Chapter 4). Sattva, rajas and tamas are the foundational attributes of everything in existence from the macrocosm to the microcosm. They combine in specific ways to give rise to all the tattvas below Prakṛti, including the buddhi, ahaṅkāra and manas, the tanmātras, karmendriyas, jñānendriyās, and the pañca mahābhūtas. What this means is that the flow of events contained within time and space is nothing but the guṇas in action, combining and unfolding in specific ways.[195] The guṇas that make up the individual interact with the guṇas that make up the world to create the continuous stream of karma, which is also made up of guṇas.

195 See *Bhagavad Gītā*, 3.28 and 3.29.

The pavarga corresponds to the empirical I, made up of the manas, ahaṅkāra, buddhi, Prakṛti and Puruṣa, the essence of which is sattva (see Table 16 above). Except for Puruṣa, the fundamental quality of each of these elements is clarity (Puruṣa is the subject and entirely devoid of guṇas). It's just that the interaction of the guṇas creates confusion of icchā, jñāna and kriyā. Our intentions (icchā) become clouded by the mass of samskārās that becomes our limited base of knowledge (jñāna), giving rise to actions and behavior (kriyā) that remain within the confines of conditioning. The *content* of the manas that reflects the ahaṅkāra is influenced by the samskārās that veil the buddhi (see Figure 48).

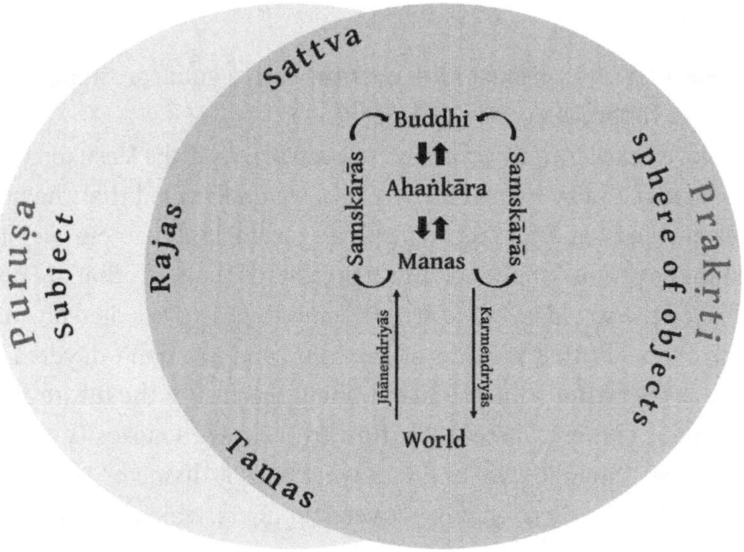

Figure 48. The Guṇas of Prakṛti

Jayanī graces us with victory over sattva. Up until here, we were cultivating sattva preferentially over rajas and tamas through discipline, surrender, and self-inquiry. Until now, the knowledge we had of the guṇas was at the relative level, where we understood sattva as calmness in relation to the hyperactivity of rajas or the torpor of tamas. Here at the Vasukoṇa, however, we will imbibe the fundamental essence of each guṇa which will take us beyond the framework of the guṇas to the next āvaraṇa.

The sattva we had cultivated to arrive here was defined by calmness, clarity, and the lack of turbulence of rajas or the sluggishness of tamas, which occurred after a large chunk of our karma was dissipated through the cultivation of viveka, vairāgya and sattarka.[196] The buddhi has become so clear that the ahaṅkāra is largely inactive. It has lost the habit of I-making, which reflects upon the manas as a quiet mind. Sattva in this context is like a calm mountain lake in relation to the rapids of rajas or the stagnant marsh of tamas. However, we now move beyond the comparative mode of the guṇas to their very essence.

196 See Bhāvanā in Chapter 5.

Sattva, at the Absolute level, is the essential sap of creation. It is what "is" or the suchness of experience beyond concepts or ideas.

> ***Suchness transcends the mind and is not something we can arrive at through analysis. It is the inherent quality of even the mind, but to know this, the mind must be transcended.***

Here, the victory over the mind is so great that no event or circumstance – war, pandemic, or mass destruction – is a problem. Instead, there is a joyful acceptance of the totality of life because we are in its flow. The totality is within us, where nothing is out of place, wrong or resisted even when fully engaged in what externally appears as strife. Here, we have tapped into the essence of sattva, with unshakeable peace and steadiness becoming our new default.

Catalyzed by the grace of Jayanī, we understand the suchness of the empirical I, which naturally rests the mind in its unconditioned state of Puruṣa or subjectivity.[197] While previously we took ourselves to be the objects that the ahaṅkāra took from Prakṛti, we now see the extremely subtle difference between the two. We previously shrugged off the idea of taking ourselves to be our body, name, gender, or history, but a subtle sense of the *objective* I remained – we could still *experience* the I. Anything that is experienc*ed* requires a subject that experienc*es*. Jayanī gives us victory over this remnant of the objective I, where we stop taking ourselves to be anything that we can experience or know. By understanding the essence of sattva, we come to know our own essence as the knower of experience. The difference between the subjective I and I as an object is at the subtlest and finest śabda-artha split and requires the transcendence of guṇas altogether, which is the gift of Jayanī.

197 Here, subjectivity at the level of Puruṣa is only at the individual level. It is only with piercing of the Māyā tattva above Puruṣa that subjectivity encompasses the other within the subjectivity, where Idam = Aham. See the discussion in Bindu, Chapter 17.

Sarveśvarī

Sarveśvarī (sarva = all, īśvarī = sovereign) rules over rajas and in presiding over the semi-vowels, she exerts lordship and control over creation.

The semi-vowels correspond to the kañcukas of Māyā, which are the dynamic veils that obscure Absolute Reality. The kañcukas are not static, stagnant tattvas, but highly active and volatile, adapting, changing, and evolving from moment to moment based on the samskārās that come up to manifest in our thought and action. For example, when you are meditating, you may have great clarity about not being the body or seeing how much more benevolent and generous you could be. When you are at a parent-teacher conference later that afternoon and the teacher tells you that your child is misbehaving in school, your clarity and benevolence dissolve. In their place arises a fierce protectiveness of your child, defensiveness about his behavior, self-doubt that you are not doing your job as a parent, and anger at the teacher for her assessment.

Instantly, the five kañcukas have clouded reality. You have a passionate sense of ownership (rāga) over your child and your knowledge about your child is limited by your observations and interactions with him (vidyā). Your vidyā about your child exists in time (kāla) and space (kalā) because you have no knowledge of who he was before he became your son or the time when he will no longer be your child. Your assessment of him is further limited by cause-and-effect (niyati), where his behavior is shaped by his own karma as well as your upbringing. The kañcukas, which didn't exist when you were meditating, have now manifested as a very real problem.

Rajas is movement, and its essence is dynamism, which is the primordial principle of life. Without rajas, there would be no kañcukas. We usually think of the guṇas as being below Māyā in Prakṛti; here, however, we are examining the lifeblood of rajas, which is embedded in the very first movement of separation of Śiva and Śakti giving rise to the cascade of the tattvas. Sarveśvarī is the principle that brings together agni and vāyu as the very first movement of creation. The process by which the three guṇas combine and interact is driven by rajas as Sarveśvarī, who rules over creation.

Her grace enables us to tap into the driving principle of rajas, which can only happen when we are entirely aligned with her flow. While Aruṇā gifts us with the refinement of rajāsik longing, Sarveśvarī takes us "behind the scenes" of rajas. This absolute alignment with the flow of rajas is the secret of siddhi attainment, where we transcend the kañcukas.

> ***Paradoxically, the ability to "rule over" elements of creation is granted when we are fully surrendered to its flow.***

Ordinarily, we have many siddhis that arise from being totally in the flow. When you are tired, for example, you don't need to *do* anything to fall asleep, which is an act of total surrender. No matter how bad your day has been or how much grief you are experiencing, you give in to sleep when it arrives. This is a siddhi, and anyone with chronic insomnia will agree with this statement! In dream and deep sleep, we become one with their flow and are in a state of surrender. The ability to make it rain is similar, where we are so surrendered to the elements of water and sky that we become one with the very essence of rajas. This oneness doesn't differentiate between my body here and rain there – the two don't exist as separate objects. Defying gravity, walking on water, turning water into wine, and other historical examples are not myths – they are examples of a practitioner aligned with rajas and operating under the grace of Sarveśvarī.

She breaks us free from the chains of rajas in the artha sphere, and in this freedom, we gain lordship over this guṇa.

Kaulinī

Kaulinī (the one that is of the kula) rules over tamas, presiding over the sibilants that correspond to the pure tattvas above Māyā. She is the supreme enjoyer of creation.

Above the Māyā tattva with its kañcukas are the pure elements of icchā, jñāna and kriyā, along with Śakti and Śiva. At this point, we may wonder how tamas can be associated with the highest tattvas when we have been discussing it as stagnation. Like many seeming contradictions, this is an issue of levels – at the Absolute level, tamas refers to its essence, and at the relative level, its manifestations.

The essence of tamas is structure; it provides the framework or the container for creation to seed, sprout, grow and change. The five highest tattvas are the primary kula, which translates as family or clan.[198] Kula refers to various types of grouping – for example, the phonemes in each *varga* or class, the yoginīs of a particular āvaraṇa, the tattvas at each level, practitioners of a saṅgha, a Guru paramparā, a sampradāya, and so on. Creation can be considered a kula since it arises from the same source.

Kaulinī[199] rules over the expression of tamas in the highest tattvas, which make up the fabric of the universe. From the farthest unseen reaches of space and the mass of astral

198 See Kulottīrṇa Yoginī in Chapter 12.

199 See N94 in K. Chinnaiyan, *Glorious Alchemy: Living the Lalitā Sahasranāma* (New Sarum Press, 2020).

bodies down to the minutest subatomic particle, everything is made up of Śiva-Śakti and the fundamental forces of icchā, jñāna and kriyā. Nothing escapes this kula including all realms and states of consciousness. Creation is saturated with the essence of this kula being expressed in the moment-to-moment unfolding of the body-mind in the greater context and rhythm of the planet, solar system, and universe. It is upon this great fabric of tamas that rajas and sattva play out their expressions of movement and clarity.

Arriving at the source of tamas occurs at a very advanced level of sādhanā. Here, the practitioner has left behind the circumference in the artha sphere altogether and is close to being consumed by the center. As we now know, the kañcukas create the separation of Aham and Idam. Once the Māyā tattva is transcended, the practitioner experiences increasing levels of oneness with the world. The final dissolution of this separation will occur at the Trikoṇa, but here, blessed by the Vāgdevatās, we pierce through the very fabric of creation that is permeated by the subject-object differentiation.

Kaulinī, the final Vāgdevatā of the Vasukoṇa graces us with the ability to recognize the primary kula in all other kulas. At this stage, we are unable to see the other as such, recognizing all we experience as aspects of ourselves. Moment-to-moment experience is nonlinear and orgasmic.

> ***The recognition of the other in the I is the source of supreme enjoyment, where the dualities of joy and sorrow don't exist and instead, there is the ecstatic blooming of ānanda.***

Vāc in Practice

Arriving at the Vasukoṇa requires a very high level of discernment and the ability to differentiate between increasingly subtle objects. This is especially important when we consider the way the ahaṅkāra works, which is to take the objects of Prakṛti and superimpose them upon the Puruṣa, where this superimposition is taken to be the I (see Figure 28 in Chapter 9 and Figure 48 above). Everything we identify with – name, gender, roles, family, culture, history, personality traits, hopes, and fears – is an object. By the time we arrive at the Vasukoṇa, this differentiation is quite clear, and we no longer take gross objects such as name, gender, and roles to be the I. However, subtler objects still make up the identity, facilitated by expression, or vāc.

Two teachings that may help us understand the intricacies of expression are those of *nāmarūpa* and *padārtha*. Nāmarūpa (nāma = name, rūpa = form) refers to the association between name and form. Take an example of a tree. As soon as you hear the word tree, the image of one comes up. If you've never seen one because you were born blind, you will still have an image based on what you've *heard* about a tree. Remember that the senses are the gateways to the citta, and one way or the other, the world will enter it. So here we have a tree, which is an object with form (rūpa) and the word that refers to it (nāma), which is also an object. Neither is the *subject*, which is the important insight here. Both the nāma and rūpa are apprehended by the subject that is independent of them.

Another way to understand the śabda-artha concept is through the word padārtha (pada = object, artha = meaning). Everything arising from Prakṛti is a padārtha, as in an object with a meaning where the meaning is also an object. Take the tree, our object of contemplation. The word refers to the object, which is a combination of trunk, bark, branches, and leaves. The word "tree" is referring to this combination of objects, but can the word refer to the tree*ness*? The tree*ness* of the tree is its *subjective* experience, which the word cannot capture. A tree stripped of its leaves, branches, bark, and trunk is no longer a tree from our perspective, but its essence, the tree*ness* that is undefined, cannot be destroyed.

Nāma and rūpa, or pada and artha are the primary divisions of expression arising from parāvāk. The three-way split into the subject and two objects that seem like one results in paśyantī, the receiving or reflective level. Here, the sole subject (Puruṣa) is witnessing both objects (Prakṛti) superimposed as one. At madhyamā, this superimposition becomes denser, settling in the citta as the truth. At vaikharī, this superimposition is complete, and the word tree is superimposed upon the tree*ness* that is undefinable.

When we apply the same concept to the I, we can see the infinite combinations of nāmarūpa that superimpose the I-ness or subject that is undefinable. We take ourselves to be the combination of the name and form, or the word and its meaning. If you identify with your role as a mother, for instance, the label of mother becomes associated with the role, both of which are taken on to mean *you*. You become the mother, when, both the word and its association are objects. What you are is not a mother but the one that perceives both the word and the object to which it refers.[200] By identifying with the word mother, your role entraps you to think, act and react in particular ways.

200 See 'Mātaṅgī' in K. Chinnaiyan, *Shakti Rising* (Nonduality Press, 2017).

The superimposition of nāmarūpa upon the subject that is your I-ness is the fundamental roga or disease.

Starting in early childhood, we start to collect the mass of names of forms that will become our identity, such as our given name, our abilities and disabilities, talents and weaknesses, and specific traits related to gender, social, cultural, and moral norms. Our superiority or inferiority complexes, and the way we interact with the world are informed and driven by the nāmarūpa mass. Importantly, the nāma of each rūpa is taken as the empirical truth, which then becomes another aspect of our identity. Take the word "shy" for example, which refers to the attribute of being reserved or timid amidst others. However, the attribute or rūpa of shyness can't be found in the word or nāma. Both are objects that point to each other, but together, they are mistakenly taken to refer to the I, and we conclude, "I am shy." In reality, the I is pure, unconditioned and without any attributes – it transcends nāmarūpa. However, with repeated association between the name and form, the identification with it becomes increasingly dense and "real."

Taking objects to be our subjective reality shapes how we interact with the world. Our interactions are the predicament of *objects that make up the I* interacting with *objects that make up the other.* In other words, when I say that I love, hate, admire, or loathe you, it is the interaction of my story of me with my story of you. The important thing to note here is that despite the phenomenon of objects interacting with objects, there is no real objectivity in the interaction! Recall from the Antardaśara that nothing exists outside of us, which means that the other is a collection of objective characteristics of others, which are our *own* interpretations and projections. In the example of the tree, we may assign treeness to it based on our experience of it, but only the tree can experience its tree*ness.* We can never truly know another until we know our own true nature. Only then can we see that the essence of our true nature is identical and continuous with all that exists.

It is at the Vasukoṇa that we begin to understand the enormity of vāc in the creative process at both the macrocosmic and microcosmic levels.

Each of the Vāgdevatās in her shadow aspect obscures the subtleties of expression and entraps us in Māyā, while her light leads us to its source. The mapping of these yoginīs with the Sanskrit phonemes and the tattvas allows us to delve into their source by transcending dualities such as cold and hot or happiness and misery, and eventually to understand the basis of nāmarūpa.

Cakreśvarī: Tripurāsiddhā

The Rahasya Yoginīs of the Vasukoṇa are the initial emanations of Lalitā Devī from the Bindu and are the secret codes of Reality. The Vasukoṇa subsumes and permeates all the subsequent āvaraṇas as their expression. Only when we have been graced by the yoginīs of the previous āvaraṇas can we arrive at their feet.

The Vāgdevatās are celebrated as the composers of the Lalitā Sahasranāma, which contains the secrets of creation. The Vāgdevatās composing this secret (rahasya) Sahasranāma are of great importance, where they cloak Reality within the nāmarūpa of the hymn. Understanding the Sahasranāma is a sādhanā that spans lifetimes, where eventually the names and forms encased in it give way to their subtle essence to bring us to their composers. From the brief understanding of this āvaraṇa here, we can conclude that the Vāgdevatās are the composers of Reality, which is encased in the Sahasranāma. Their sādhanā heals us of the fundamental disease or *roga* that keeps us in saṃsāra, rendering us fit for our ongoing journey to the next āvaraṇa, the Trikoṇa.

Tripurāsiddhā, an emanation of Mahātripurasundarī rules over the Sarvarogahara cakra. Through the sādhanā of this cakra, we become befitting of her blessing of the attainment or siddhi over the triads. She is invoked by the mantra *hrīṃ śrīṃ sauḥ* and mudrā bīja *hskhphrem* corresponding to Sarvakhecarī, the goddess who bestows the ability to roam freely in space. Freedom from nāmarūpa removes the vestiges of bondage in the material world and we are now free to roam in space.[201]

201 See Sarvakhecarī in The Ten Seals, Chapter 7.

Propelled by the grace of the Vasukoṇa, we are now inching toward Devī, but first we must meet her *āyudhas* or implements that await us between the Vasukoṇa and the Trikoṇa.

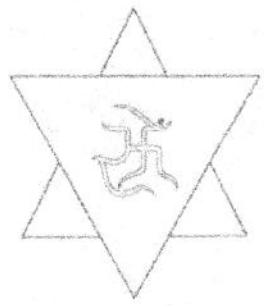

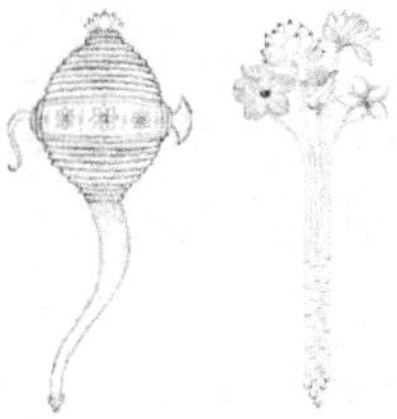

Chapter 15

Devī's Āyudhas

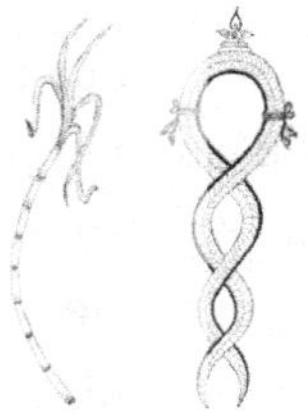

शब्दादि तन्मात्राः पञ्चपुष्पबाणाः ॥ २१ ॥
मन इक्षुधनुः ॥ २२ ॥
रागः पाशः ॥ २३ ॥
द्वेषोऽङ्कुशः ॥ २४ ॥

Śabdāditanmātrāḥ pañca puṣpabāṇāḥ || 21 ||
Mana ikṣudhanuḥ || 22 ||
Rāgaḥ pāśaḥ || 23 ||
Dveṣoṅkuśaḥ || 24 ||

"Śabda and the other tanmātras are the five flower arrows.
The mind is the sugarcane bow.
Rāga is the noose.
Hatred is the goad."
~ Bhāvanopaniṣad, verses 21-24

What a journey it has been! We have arrived here, at the periphery of the Trikoṇa, and we are about to be consumed by Devī's presence in the Bindu. At this point in our journey, it's hard to remember starting out at the Bhūpura and making our way up the āvaraṇas and out of our limitation.

A contracted way of being defined our existence at the Bhūpura, where the Prakaṭa Yoginīs schooled us with deep insights about our tightly held patterns and beliefs. At the Śodaṣadalapadma, the Gupta Yoginīs showed us our attractions and aversions that reflected in our behavior. The Guptatara Yoginīs at the Aṣṭadalapadma granted us the knowledge of the agitations that reflected upon the Śodaṣadalapadma as our attractions and aversions. As we continued to make our way up the Śrīcakra, we were embraced by the Sampradāya Yoginīs at the Manvaśra, who taught us how the agitations flowed in the prāṇa nāḍīs and propelled us to the Bahirdaśara and the Kulottīrṇa Yoginīs. Here, we discovered the source of the nāḍīs – the prāṇa vāyus, and then we arrived at the Antardaśara, where the Nigarbha Yoginīs introduced us to agni, the force of transformation. When we finally arrived at the Vasukoṇa, the magnificent Vāgdevatās graced us with the knowledge of the very source of creation – vāc.

Only when we have been graced by the Rahasya Yoginīs can we venture into the space between the Vasukoṇa and Trikoṇa. This space is permeated by sacredness of monumental proportions, for here reside Lalitā Devī's implements – her five flower arrows, sugarcane bow, noose, and goad. They surround the Trikoṇa and reside around the Trikoṇa. If you are sitting at the east portal with the apex of the Trikoṇa facing you, the flower arrows are to your left, the sugarcane bow to your right, and the noose and the goad along the straight line of the triangle (see Figure 49).

Devī's implements are her modes of action, which means that in this space, we come face-to-face with the way creation works. These modes, or her powers, are also yoginīs – *Bāṇinī* (flower arrows), *Cāpinī* (sugarcane bow), *Pāśinī* (noose) and Aṅkuśinī (goad). Lalitā Devī, in one of her popular four-armed anthropomorphic forms, holds the flower arrows and the sugarcane bow in her right and left lower hands, and the goad and noose in the right and left upper hands, respectively.

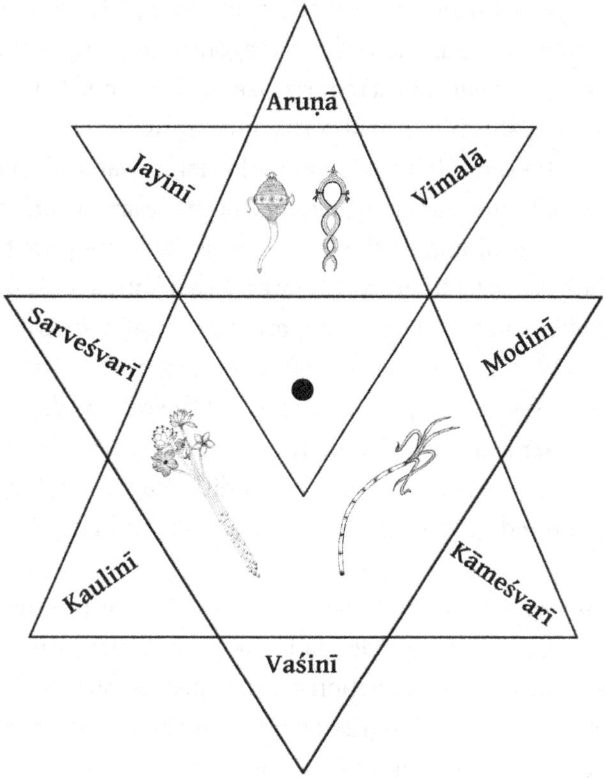

Figure 49. Devī's Implements

Bāṇinī and Cāpinī

Bāṇa is arrow and *cāpa* is bow; Bāṇinī and Cāpinī are the personifications of the five flower arrows and sugarcane bow in Devī's lower hands, corresponding to kriyā śakti.

Devī's bow and arrows are her mode of action. They are also the modes of action of Kāmadeva,[202] who is the mind-born son of Brahmā, the creator. Brahmā's meditation on creation gives birth to the handsome and charming Kāmadeva equipped with the sugarcane bow and flower arrows, and he is assigned the task of agitating minds through the power of desire. Also known as *Manmatha* (*man* = mind, *matha* = agitate), Kāmadeva is the

202 Also known as Manmatha. See Chapter 1 in K. Chinnaiyan, *Glorious Alchemy: Living the Lalitā Sahasranāma* (New Sarum Press, 2020).

primary driver of creation and an important deity in Śrīvidyā. His bīja *klīṃ* is incorporated into the central Śrīvidyā mantras. He is the protagonist and villain of the *Lalitopākhyāna* as Kāmadeva who becomes *Bhaṇḍāsura* to terrorize the *Devās* and bring about the descent of Lalitā Devī who annihilates him and absorbs him within herself.

The five arrows are flowers – lotus, red lotus, blue lotus, water lily and the mango blossom, while the bow is made up of a sugarcane stalk. Both the arrows and the bow have three forms – sthūla, sūkṣma and kāraṇa. At the sthūla (gross) level, they are the obvious flowers and sugarcane. At the sūkṣma (subtle) level, they are bīja mantras packed with power, and at the kāraṇa (transcendent or causal) level, they are the five tanmātras and the mind.

We may wonder how it is that the tanmātras represented at the other āvaraṇas are also placed here. As we saw earlier, the placement of the tattvas depends on the context of an āvaraṇa. The higher āvaraṇas contain the tattvas in their subtler or more undifferentiated states, becoming increasingly free of conditioning. Here, Bāṇinī and Cāpinī are Devī's tanmātras and mind at their purest and highest level and are entirely devoid of conditioning.

In addition to the tanmātras, the flower arrows represent the five different ways in which creation takes place – excitement, maddening, confusion, stimulation, and fading. Being unconditioned, these modes of action are not specific, but are the subtle variations of vāc or expression. They are the ingredients that when mixed together and let loose, collide, repel, and combine to become everything from Māyā to pṛthvī. They are released from the sugarcane bow, Devī's deliciously sweet mind that is intoxicating and attracting for all creation. Even though creation springs out of her arrows and seems to do its own thing, it is bound to her mind.

At the microcosmic level, we have seen the allure of the tanmātras, but here we become aware that no matter what we are seeking, we are always seeking Devī, for she is the primordial *principle* of seeking as the kriyā śakti.

We become engrossed in the energy of kriyā śakti at this level of sādhanā because the content of conditioning has been erased.

Having overcome the kañcukas of Māyā, we are aligning with Devī's mind and tanmātras, becoming increasingly aware of the macrocosmic principles of action. Having relinquished personal gain and strife, we are able to understand the universal force of action.

Here outside the Trikoṇa, we are able to see in wholes, understanding how the flutter of a butterfly's wings moves an entire galaxy. Paradoxically, we can see that nothing is ever happening the way it appears. While in the lower āvaraṇas the world seemed to be separate and "outside" of us, here, all action is seen to occur within us. We have expanded in our subjectivity to include the world and now see that action anywhere by anyone at any time is occurring as my action here and now.

Pāśinī

Devī holds the *pāśa* (noose) in her upper left hand, which is personified as Pāśinī, corresponding to icchā śakti. When we look at the Tattva Map in Chapter 4, icchā śakti is the third tattva that follows the initial separation of Śiva and Śakti, signifying the role of Divine intention as the primordial force of creation. Even though intention is placed third in the Tattva Map, it is the driver of the initial stir in Absolute Reality, which is the desire of the One to become Many. The difference between the two "flavors" of intention is that within Absolute Reality, it is in its purest form and non-binding, saturated by svātantrya śakti or Absolute Freedom, which is *within* the Trikoṇa at the Bindu.

After the separation of Śiva-Śakti, icchā becomes a noose that binds creation. With the original separation, the cascade of creation is inevitable and devoid of Absolute Freedom, which is why the implements are placed *outside* the Trikoṇa. They are the bridge between the Trikoṇa and the Vasukoṇa, where Divine will, knowledge and action begin to crystallize as vāc, which will explode into the rest of the Śrīcakra.

Unconditioned intention is a difficult concept for the conditioned mind. Ordinarily, we have a specific desire and outcome, and based on what we know about it, we plan our course of action to attain it. If there is no idea of an outcome, we wouldn't know how or where to direct our action.

Remember that the implements are beyond the Māyā tattva and are undefined forces of creation.

Pāśinī is the pure energy of intention who lassos creation through her unconditioned power of wanting, which is free of what (kriyā śakti) and how (jñāna śakti).

Icchā śakti is the finest vibration of separation, and to be aligned with it is an advanced level of practice. Here, the upāsanā requires the subtle understanding between Aham and Idam; it involves the slightest shift of stance from Idam to Aham.

Aṅkuśinī

Aṅkuśa means hook, or the elephant goad that Devī holds in her upper right hand, becoming personified as Aṅkuśinī and symbolizing jñāna śakti.

In the Lalitā Sahasranāma, the aṅkuśa is called the goad of wrath.[203] Some temples of India have elephant stables, where these magnificent animals are worshiped and participate in the worship of the temple deities. On special occasions, the elephants participate in temple processions through the town or village and a mahout is assigned to watch over them. As they amble along, the elephants become distracted by the sights and smells of the town, their trunks restlessly exploring the various objects along the way. The goad is used to redirect and restrain the elephants so they keep up with the procession.[204]

203 N9: krodhākārāṅkuśojjvalā.

204 In no way is this description meant to condone violence to elephants or other animals.

The goad in Devī's hand is the power of knowledge. Krodha, which is anger or wrath is a descriptive word used for the power of driving intention. Aṅkuśinī drives the expansion of creation through time and space by directing icchā śakti.

Jñāna is the subtle condensation of icchā as the know-how to turn will into action.

For this, the subtlest, most undifferentiated energy of icchā must be given direction, which will then leave Devī's hands as the flowery arrows of kriyā śakti.

The Implements in Practice

While the four implements at this level between the Vasukoṇa and Trikoṇa represent the purest reflections of intention, knowledge, and action, they permeate all the other āvaraṇas as their primary modes of action. At every āvaraṇa, there is a proliferation of the icchā, jñāna and kriyā arising from those of the previous āvaraṇa.

Let's take a real-life example. You are invited to a party at a friend's home. Although you have been friends for many years, you haven't seen each other in a while. When you arrive at her home, you can barely recognize it because she has renovated the space and it is beautiful! As she gives you a tour and talks about the renovation process, a vague desire begins to shape in your mind – you can renovate your home too. The thought had never previously risen in your mind, but now it takes over. As you drive home, this desire proliferates into a vision. You'll take down that wall, move the counter around, open the patio, and on and on. Soon, the vision becomes more concrete, and you obtain measurements, calculate costs, and hire a contractor. Within months, you have a renovated home.

In the process of repairs, you discover that the roof needs to be replaced and the plumbing is outdated and leaky, and the basement is infested with mice. You hire a roofer, a plumber, and an exterminator. Each contractor's work is driven by the desire for a specific outcome, the knowledge of that desire, and acting upon it. In the process, you forged new relationships with people and objects, which brought out many of your traits. Those traits crystallized your communication as well as the final product, your renovated home.

In the process of redecorating, you decide to create a small wine cellar for the few bottles that came your way in the past few years. In the process of organizing them you look up the wines and become fascinated by the scope of winemaking and wish to procure more for your cellar. Accordingly, you book a wine-tasting tour where you make new friends who introduce you to the art of cheesemaking.

You get the point. At every step in the creation process, icchā, jñāna and kriyā create countless streams, begetting more icchā, jñāna and kriyā. With every action, we create more desires that demand fruition. Unlike Devī's implements, however, the icchā, jñāna and kriyā at all other āvaraṇas are conditioned and couched in Māyā. We are bound by the noose of desire that arises from our own samskārās and icchā becomes rāga. The goad at the conditioned level thrusts us about in our likes and dislikes where knowledge of our desire is also colored by our samskārās, becoming vidyā. This limits our action in time (kāla), space (kalā), and causality (niyati). We act (cheesemaking) because of something (winemaking), which arises from something else (renovation) that started as an innocent encounter with a friend.

At every step of the way, our choices arising from our desires crystallize into what becomes our life. If we take a good look at our life and circumstances, we will see they are reflections of our own minds. In other words, we have nobody else to blame for anything that happens in our life. When we arrive at Devī's implements that transcend time and space, this fact becomes our reality where we see the continuity of time across lives. We see how karma continues from one lifetime to another, where everything that happened "to" us is a continuity of the choices we made at some point.

Devī's implements are also the modes of upāsanā, where our icchā becomes refined through continuous reflection, the arrows directed solely toward the Bindu where all our desires coalesce into this single desire. Her noose becomes the lasso that drags us there, and her goad drives away the samskārās that can otherwise deflect the arrows.

Having prostrated to Devī's implements, we are granted access to the next āvaraṇa, the Trikoṇa.

Chapter 16

Trikoṇa

अव्यक्त महदहङ्कारा: कामेश्वरी-वज्रेश्वरी-भगमालिन्योऽन्तस्त्रिकोणगा देवताः ॥ २५ ॥

Avyakta-mahad-ahaṅkārāh kameśvari-vajreśvcarī-
bhagamalinyontas-trikoṇagā devataḥ || 25 ||

"Avyakta, mahat and ahaṅkāra are Kāmeśvarī, Vajreśvarī, Bhagamālinī in the Trikoṇa."
~Bhāvanopaniṣad, verse 25.

Getting here to the Trikoṇa has been the upāsanā of many lifetimes. The worries that plagued us in the Bhūpura, and the internal conflict that marked the remaining āvaraṇas have resolved. Our vision is solely on the Bindu. Graced by Devī's implements, we have our attention fixed on the Bindu, but before we get there, we must traverse the Trikoṇa.

It's important to understand here that the journey through the āvaraṇas is tricky. When we say we move from one āvaraṇa to the next in the saṃhāra krama, it means that the issues associated with it are largely resolved. Our samskārās at each subsequent level become increasingly transparent through the cultivation of sattva. As the buddhi becomes more sāttvik, samskārās loosen their grip and our icchā, jñāna, and kriyā become increasingly free, joyful, and orgasmic.

We can sometimes feel like we have made great progress, only to discover samskārās that were previously hidden. Very often, a single samskāra takes *years* of work because it arises again and again in varied contexts.

As long as we keep resisting a particular samskāra, it repeatedly crops up in familiar patterns and life circumstances.

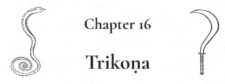

Unwittingly, we blame the world, our families, upbringing, or fate for the rut that we find ourselves in, not understanding that the manifestation of a samskāra in our life in the Bhūpura has its roots all the way up in the Vasukoṇa.

It is only when we surrender to the vidyā and fully accept the samskāra where we can examine it without emotional coloring that it starts to unravel. We know that a particular samskāra has dissolved when it is a non-issue. We face situations that would previously have brought up all kinds of vṛttis without batting an eyelid. It is through the application of vidyā in the very real and sticky circumstances of our life that the samskārās dissolve, leading us gradually through the āvaraṇas.

This journey of the saṃhāra krama can be examined through the lens of classical Tantra, once again using the tattvas as the focal point.

The Ascent of Sādhanā

Let's revisit the process of sādhanā from the perspective of the Śrīcakra. The Tattva Map in Chapter 4 provides a comprehensive framework for both the descent of Absolute Reality into creation as well as the ascent of sādhanā from the standpoint of the individual. Recall the three malas – the āṇava mala, which is the fundamental sense of lack, the māyīya mala, which results in the sense of separation, and the kārma mala, which is the sense of doership.[205]

205 See Kañcukas and Malas in Chapter 9.

The ascent of sādhanā is divided into aśuddhādvan and śuddhādvan, or the impure and pure paths. This division is based on the perceived separation between Aham, the subject and Idam, the object. The Māyā tattva casts this veil of separation, where below it, Aham and Idam remain separate and above this tattva, they are non-separate.

The kañcukas and malas are the separators of Aham and Idam. Among the malas, the āṇava mala is the hardiest and the last to dissolve above the Māyā tattva with its kañcukas. The māyīya and kārma malas dissolve at the level of the Māyā tattva. The malas that determine our perception become the basis for another way of classifying sādhanā.

Sakala

At the most differentiated level (vaikharī), all three malas are functional. This means that we perceive the world to be "out there" and the I is "in here" where both are separate and unique entities. This state of perception is known as *sakala*, which spans the twenty-five tattvas from buddhi to pṛthvī. In Śrīcakra upāsanā, the three malas persist all the way from the Bhūpura to the Antardaśara (see Figure 50).

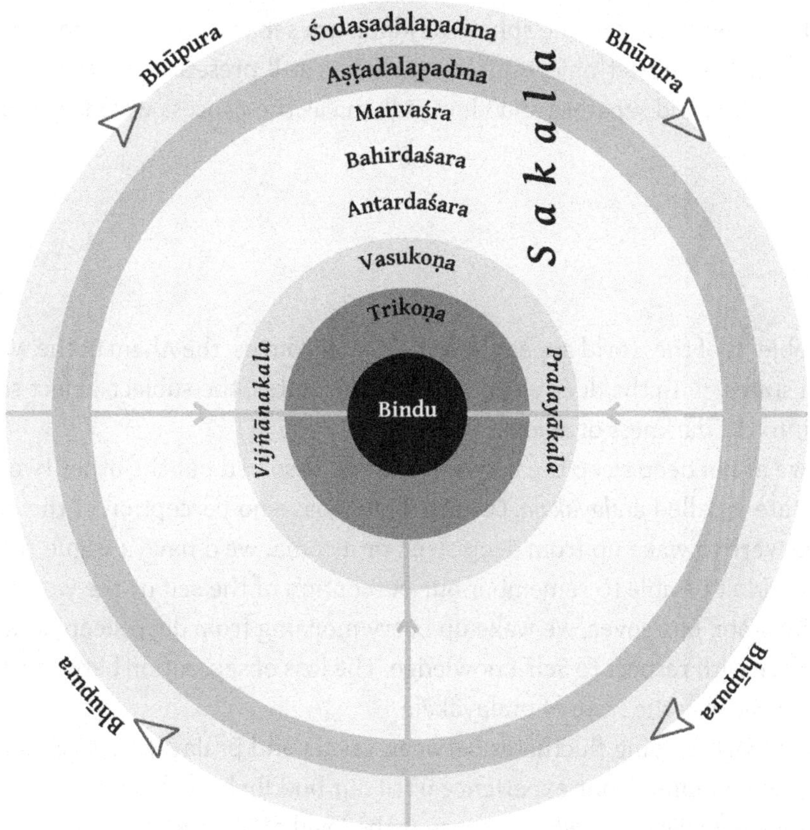

Figure 50. The Levels of Perception in the Śrīcakra

Throughout this book, we have seen that discernment is needed to know whether we are on the circumference or the radius. We don't enter the radius until we have left behind the continuous upkeep of a self-image. Through the painstaking journey of surrender and inquiry, we make gradual progress across the first six āvaraṇas that bring us to the manas, ahaṅkāra and buddhi tattvas. And through progressive clarity of the buddhi, we can discern the increasingly subtle forces such as vāyu and agni. Along the way, our buddhi has discarded the tāmasik and rajāsik samskārās to become increasingly sāttvik, and the bulk of the malas have been purified. Yet, the malas operate here at the subtle level where the progressively subtle forces of likes/dislikes, agitations, nāḍīs, prāṇa and agni, which are in the sphere of Idam, are separate and unique in relation to the I or Aham. The subject-object differentiation is still present with all the malas. We feel we are unique and separate and view sādhanā as the process we engage in through our own volition.

Pralayākala

In sakala, objects of the world appear to be separate from us, the Aham in the waking and the dream states. [206] In the deep sleep or comatose states, the subject-object separation dissolves into the darkness of avidyā.

206 See Avasthās in Chapter 6.

When we are in deep sleep the kārma mala has dissolved but the other two are present. This state is called *pralayākala.* Ordinarily, we have no perception of the deep sleep state. If we were to wake up from deep sleep or a coma, we'd have a vague recollection of it but wouldn't be able to remember our perception of the self or the world when we were in that state. Moreover, we wake up every morning from deep sleep no wiser than the day before with respect to Self-knowledge. The loss of separation between Aham and Idam in deep sleep is the state of pralayākala.

Our usual way of being fluctuates between sakala and pralayākala, the two states of perception that dominate our experience until our buddhi becomes clarified enough for the next stage of *vijñānakalā*, which occurs at the level of Puruṣa.

Vijñānakalā

At the level of the Māyā tattva, the state of perception is known as vijñānakalā, where the dissolution of the subject-object differentiation occurs in deep meditative states known as *samādhi*. Unlike the state of deep sleep where the dissolution is into avidyā, the meditative absorption in vijñānakalā is the result of vidyā. Here, both the māyīya and kārma mala have disappeared and only the āṇava mala remains. However, this is not a stable state. When the absorption or samādhi ends, the malas return to varying degrees.

In Śrīcakra upāsanā, both pralayākala and vijñānakalā occur at the Vasukoṇa, which is at the level of the Māyā tattva. The difference between them is the collapse of the Aham-Idam separation into avidyā in pralayākala and into vidyā in vijñānakalā. Both states of perception are enabled by the Rahasya Yoginīs, and it is their grace that propels us from pralayākala to vijñānakalā.

Above the Māyā tattva is the pure path or śuddhādvan, where increasing stabilization in vidyā results in progressive and permanent dissolution of the malas.[207]

207 See Mantra in Aśuddhādvan and Śuddhādvan in Chapter 6.

The Inquiry

Even though we have examined the line of inquiry that takes us from one āvaraṇa to the next in the saṃhāra krama, we must understand the primary ingredient of upāsanā, which is anugraha or grace.

> ***Ultimately, the progression of upāsanā is a non-linear process that is driven entirely by anugraha.***

There tends to be no logical reason for why we are born and raised in the particular circumstances that facilitate the meeting with the Guru and the vidyā. To even behold a Śrīcakra is an auspicious event catalyzed by anugraha. To develop a curiosity about it and to be guided to upāsanā is nothing short of *camatkāra* or a miracle.

One can be born in a family of Śrīvidyā upāsakas and not be interested in it. One can be so fascinated with rituals and techniques that they become the modes of preserving a self-image at the periphery, keeping us trapped in the very thing we seek to transcend. One can be blessed with both the opportunity to dig deeper and receive dīkṣā and guidance from the teacher and yet miss the radius. On the other hand, one can come to the Śrīcakra entirely naïve of its vidyā and find themselves squarely on the radius, blazing through the āvaraṇas as if lassoed in by Devī's noose.

This is a roundabout way of saying there is no prescriptive line of inquiry that ensures we will arrive at the Trikoṇa. At the Vasukoṇa, the Vāgdevatās open us to the ultimate question, "What am I, really?" Of course, we can ask this question any time on our journey, and anugraha will determine where we land. Prematurely asking this question has the high possibility of resulting in spiritual bypassing or creating a mental construct of what the I is, and this is even more hardy and difficult to dissolve.

Devī determines when she is ready to return to her original form in the Bindu. Perhaps she is done enjoying herself as you with the juicy drama of your many lives. Maybe she's not done yet and wants to continue to play as the unique ray of light that is you. As useful as inquiry is, surrendering to her will is more valuable. This is a misnomer, as we have just seen in the description of the perception states – Devī's will prevails... only 100 percent of the time.

The Trikoṇa

Lalitā Devī is Mahātripurasundarī – the great beauty of the three cities symbolizing the triads that make up creation and are present in every āvaraṇa of the Śrīcakra from the Bindu to the Bhūpura (see Figure 51). Pervading all the triads of every āvaraṇa is the primary triad or the Trikoṇa.

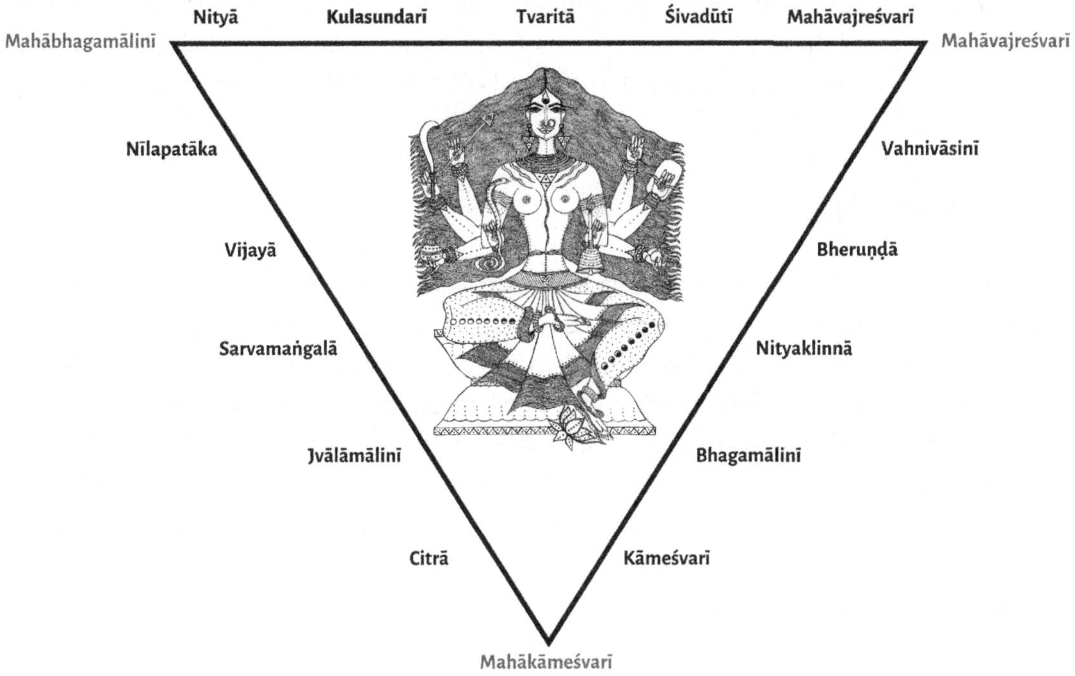

Figure 51. Trikoṇa with Atirahasya Yoginī

The Trikoṇa symbolizes the primordial triad of Śiva, Śakti and the relationship between them, which is the source of all the other triads in creation. It is presided by the three *Atirahasya* (extremely secret) Yoginīs who represent the unique aspects of each triad. The Trikoṇa is known as the Sarvasiddhipradā (sarva = all, siddhi = attainment, pradā = bestower) cakra.

In the Śrīcakra, the Trikoṇa is Śiva experiencing himself as Śakti in every āvaraṇa, yoginī, sandhi, marma, psychosomatic characteristic, and attainment. Here at the Trikoṇa, the fundamental relationship between Śiva-Śakti as the Aham-Idam is established. We have traversed the other āvaraṇas successfully, moving from the gross to the subtle, and here, we first understand and then transcend even the subtlest aspect of creation.

Atirahasya Yoginī

The majestic Atirahasya Yoginī is red-hued and six-armed (see Figure 52), bearing a range of implements befitting her sovereignty over the Śrīcakra. In her right lower hand is a snake-noose, signifying her discursive and uniting force as Prāṇakuṇḍalinī and Parākuṇḍalinī. In her left lower hand is a bell, resounding across creation as vāc.

In her middle hands are a knife that cuts through the dense veils of Māyā and a shield that casts the protective field of vidyā. She bears a bow and an arrow in her upper hands, indicating her mode of action throughout the Śrīcakra as the primordial forces of icchā, jñāna and kriyā.

Figure 52. Atirahasya Yoginī

The three Atirahasya yoginīs are situated in the anti-clockwise direction beginning at the east portal (see Figure 53) and are the personification of the countless triads of creation. The Trikoṇa is surrounded by the fifteen magnificent Nityā Devīs, whom we will meet later in this chapter. It's important to note here that each of the triads is manifested against the background of a fourth principle, which is Śiva-Śakti as the Absolute Reality (see Table 18). In other words, every triad is considered in the context of a fourth element that is the driver of that triad and is situated in the Bindu, which we will examine closely in the next chapter.

Table 18. Selected Triads Represented in the Trikoṇa

Bindu	Side 1	Side 2	Side 3	Attribute
Devī (Śiva-Śakti)	Fire	Sun	Moon	Bindus
Devī (Śiva-Śakti)	Pramāṇa	Prameya	Pramātṛ	Primordial powers
Devī (Śiva-Śakti)	Icchā	Jñāna	Kriyā	Primordial powers
Devī (Śiva-Śakti)	Mahākāmeśvarī	Mahāvajreśvarī	Mahābhagamālinī	Primordial powers
Devī (Śiva-Śakti)	Avyakta	Mahat	Ahaṅkāra	Vimarśa
Ambikā	Vāmā (sṛṣṭi/creation)	Jyeṣṭhā (stithi/ maintenance)	Raudrī (saṃhāra/ dissolution)	Creative powers
Parā	Paśyantī	Madhyamā	Vaikharī	Language
Śrīṃ	Ka E I La hrīṃ	Ha Sa Ka Ha La hrīṃ	Sa Ka La hrīṃ	Mantra
Turya/ Turyatītā	Jāgrata	Svapna	Suṣuptī	Consciousness
Oḍḍiyāṇa	Kāmarūpa	Pūrṇagiri	Jālandhara	Pilgrimage sites
Guru	Guru	Devī	Self	Guru

At the outset, we must establish that the triads don't correspond with each other. For example, the triad of the attributes of Vimarśa (*avyakta*, mahat and ahaṅkāra) don't neatly correspond with the triad of guṇas or the primordial powers. They are not intended to be examined as corresponding with each other. Instead, each triad stands on its own as the source of Self-knowledge and becomes the basis for understanding the other triads. For example, if we focused on the triad of the primordial powers of icchā, jñāna and kriyā śaktis in our sādhanā, there would be no need to delve into the triad of the pīṭhas. A deep and holistic understanding of the primordial powers of creation will eventually lead us to understand the pīṭha triad. If we take each triad as the building block of creation, the fourth element is the screen upon which the blocks arrange and rearrange themselves to become the movie of creation. The fourth subsumes and pervades the triad.[208]

208 See The Fourth and the Fifth in Chapter 17.

Mahākāmeśvarī

Mahākameśvarī (mahā = great, kāma = desire, īśvarī = sovereign) is seated at the eastern point of the Trikoṇa and symbolizes avyakta or the unmanifest. She is not to be confused with Mahātripurasundarī as Kāmeśvarī in the Bindu, or Kāmeśvarī the Nityā Devī (see below). Mahākāmeśvarī rules supreme over desire as icchā Śakti that brings creation into manifestation.

The three yoginīs at the corners of the Trikoṇa are personifications of three aspects of Vimarśa at the subtlest level. Avyakta is the yet-to-manifest potential of creation and the first spark of separation.

> ***Mahākāmeśvarī as avyakta holds creation within herself like a seed that contains the potential of a tree.***

Among the primordial powers of Śiva-Śakti, she is icchā Śakti (see previous chapter), where creation is present as only an intent, a desire or longing, with no specific direction or goal. As this potential, she bursts forth as Vāmā in the creative process and is known as Brahmā. In the Kāmakalā, she is the principle of agni or fire.[209] She is paśyantī, having

209 Note that we explored the fire principle in Kāmakalā. Think of it again as levels. Śiva and Śakti as the white and red bindus of fire and moon, and their interpenetration in the sun are more upstream (samaṣṭi rūpa) in the Bindu. Here at the Trikoṇa the same principles are slightly more differentiated (vyaṣṭi rūpa).

devolved from parāvāk as the receiving word, yet to become manifest as madhyamā.

Among the states of consciousness, she is ajaḍa jāgrata, Devī's fully awake avasthā that is devolved from turya, and yet to evolve into her dream state that will eventually become the predominant state of creation. If Oḍḍiyāṇa is the Bindu, she is Kāmarūpa, the pīṭha of intention that then devolves into Pūrṇagiri.

The three corners of the Trikoṇa represent the three kūṭas (peaks) of the Pañcadaśī mantra – Vāgbhava, Kāmarāja and Śakti.[210] If the mystical Śrīṃ is the Bindu, Mahākāmeśvarī symbolizes the Vāgbhava kūṭa.

210 See 'Devī in the Kulas', K. Chinnaiyan, *Glorious Alchemy: Living the Lalitā Sahasranāma* (New Sarum Press, 2020).

Mahāvajreśvarī

From her seat at the northwest corner of the Trikoṇa, *Mahāvajreśvarī* (mahā = great, *vajra* = diamond, īśvarī = sovereign) rules over the mahat aspect of Vimarśa. Her diamond-like resilience maintains creation between the two endpoints of birth and dissolution, endowing it with linearity and continuity.

Mahat is the first manifestation of Prakṛti prior to individualization or ahaṅkāra, where the guṇas are in perfect equilibrium. They have been emitted but have not fully differentiated, which is why she represents madhyamā vāk that will differentiate fully as vaikharī. From the perspective of the primordial powers, she is jñāna śakti that is the slight crystallization of icchā śakti, which will devolve into kriyā śakti. Creation has begun, and must now be maintained, which is why she assumes the form of Jyeṣṭhā, the one who will sustain and come to be known as Viṣṇu.

The idea of continuity is the result of the Devī's svapnā avasthā, personified by Mahāvajreśvarī that is in the jaḍājaḍa state, straddling the ajaḍa at the center and the jaḍa at the periphery and bridging the two. Continuity is an illusion – time as we ordinarily think of it is an imagined idea of carrying over of the past into the present that then becomes the future. Every event is discrete, arising and dissolving in the eternal Now.

> ***Memories and samskārās of the past as well as expectations of the future provide the framework for continuity when it doesn't exist.***

Our attachments and sentimentality become the basis for the linearity of our lives, where there is a continuous unfolding of karma. Every action leads to consequences in this scheme of continuity. When freed from the linearity of time, we are freed from karma.[211] As svapnā, Mahāvajreśvarī provides this framework that propagates creation through the impression of change and evolution.

211 See 'Kali' in K. Chinnaiyan, *Shakti Rising* (Nonduality Press, 2017).

She is the Kāmarāja kūṭa of the divine Pañcadaśī mantra. In the Kāmakalā, she is the sun and among the pīṭhas, she is Pūrṇagiri.

Mahābhagamālinī

Mahābhagamālinī (mahā = great, *bhaga* = fire, mālinī = garland) wears the garland of fire and rules over the Trikoṇa from her seat in the southwest corner. She is the great power of dissolution that brings everything in creation to its most manifest form so that it can disintegrate and begin again.

Among the creative powers, she is kriyā śakti, which fully crystallizes intention and knowledge into objects and activity that are fully manifest. For kriyā śakti to come into play, creation must become fully manifest (*vyakta*), which occurs through individualization. When examining the tattvas in Chapter 4, we saw that when Prakṛti is permeated by Puruṣa, the guṇas go out of balance and this state of imbalance explodes into the material universe. At the macrocosmic level, the functioning and structure of the cosmos is determined by the guṇas in specific proportions. All subsequent tattvas after Puruṣa and Prakṛti are nothing but the precise combination of guṇas, starting with the ahaṅkāra. When the unfolding of guṇas is set in motion at the level of mahat, every form becomes individuated, separate, and distinct from all others – a rock, a tiger, a coconut – each having its own unique signature, which is the ahaṅkāra. Because of the differentiation that occurs at this level of vaikharī, we would never mistake a rock for a tiger, or a coconut for a parrot.

> ***Diversity and demarcation of individual forms is the manifestation of kriyā śakti.***

At this stage, the differentiation is complete and to move forward in the cycle of creation, the objects of the material universe must die and recycle. We could say that the whole process of creation is moving toward its own self-destruction, joyfully and willingly dying to be reborn again and again. Take your own life as an example. When an idea you had for a project comes to fruition, it no longer remains in its original form. Instead, it evolves or develops into other ideas that materialize as other results. As soon as our children who began as our dreams or desires are born, they give rise to new dreams and desires that evolve as they grow up. In fact, the very idea of time is based in dissolution of the past that gives rise to the present, and a future that's birthed in the now. Mahābhagamālinī assumes this power of dissolution as Raudrī and comes to be known as Rudra. Among the states of consciousness, she is ajaḍa suṣuptī, Devī's deep sleep.[212]

212 See Avasthās in Chapter 6.

Suṣupti is the state of absorption, and we can see its intricate relationship with kriyā śakti in the moment-to-moment unfolding of our lives as well. Say you are in a conversation with someone. When you're listening to them, your mind begins to form a response, which arises as a vague idea that then crystallizes into what you want to say. As soon as you say it, your words and you become one – you are *absorbed* in your words and what will come of it will be your cross to bear. Even though you are not your words, in the instant they leave your mouth, they become your identity. The world sees us according to what we say and how we express our icchā and jñāna śakti – our kriyā śakti.

> ***No matter how great our intention (icchā) or knowledge (jñāna), our action (kriyā) is our legacy and our identity because of this principle of absorption or suṣuptī avasthā.***

Of the three kūṭas of the Pañcadaśī mantra, she is the Śakti kūṭa, and among the pīṭhas, the Jālandhara. In the Kāmakalā, she is the moon.

Nityā Devīs

While the three corners of the Trikoṇa symbolize the crystallization of everythingness from nothingness, the cyclical nature of time that drives creation is represented by the Nityā Devīs situated along the lines connecting the three points of the triangle. The significance, understanding, practice and ritual worship of the Nityās are at the core of Śrīvidyā sādhanā, and this vidyā must be learned directly from the Guru.

The Nityā Devīs are also known as Nitya Kalā Devīs because each represents a kalā or phase of time and space. They are 16 in number,[213] where the 16th is Mahātripurasundarī in the Bindu. The other 15 surround the Trikoṇa (see Figure 53) and are considered in the anti-clockwise direction beginning at the eastern portal, each representing a moon phase or tithi. Beginning at the new moon with Kāmeśvarī and ending with *Citrā* at the full moon is the paddhati or method of practice or worship.[214] Starting on the full moon with Citrā to end at Kāmeśvarī in the opposite or clockwise direction on the new moon is a continuation of this method of worship and contemplation. Lalitā Devī as the 16th digit is always unchanging and whole (full), directing the unfolding of time and space in each direction as the Nityās, who are her various forms.

The Nityās are seen as the combination of the three guṇas and the five mahābhūtas that give rise to 15 variations in time and space, which are most readily observed as the phases of the moon.[215] Although the moon itself never changes and is always full, we observe its changes in the night sky with the passage of time and the relationship between the sun, earth, and moon in space. The sequence of the Nityās, when observed in relation to the body, breath, and mind provides deep insights into the nature of unfolding reality as Mahākāmeśvarī, Mahāvajreśvarī and Mahābhagamālinī in both the macrocosm and microcosm.

The new moon represents the dissolution of the separation between Aham and Idam. Śakti is fully absorbed in Śiva and "nothingness" prevails. Kāmeśvarī, the first Nityā, is the first stir of icchā śakti, where Śakti begins to detach herself from Śiva with the arising of intention. Over the next five tithis, icchā condenses to become jñāna as the moon progressively "grows." It continues to swell from jñāna to kriyā over the subsequent five tithis. Citrā on the full moon signifies the completion of Devī's *unmeṣa*, where she has turned away from Śiva to become fully absorbed as the objects of the universe.

213 In some Kaula traditions, there is a 17th that transcends and subsumes the 16 Nityās.

214 It is also acceptable to go from the full moon to the new moon. This is highly sampradāya-specific and text-dependent, which is why it must be learned from your Guru.

215 See also Chapters 4 and 8.

The opposite cycle is observed where she begins to withdraw into *nimeṣa* on the full moon, turning back to Śiva and becoming progressively absorbed in his essence. On the new moon, she is so fully dissolved in him that she is totally turned away from creation. In her absorption in Śiva, it is as if her eyes are closed and she revels in him; in her absorption in the world, her eyes are open, and she celebrates her seeming separation from Śiva.[216] In this fashion, the cycle of creation continues, pulsing between absorption at both ends of the spectrum of time and space. Devī's expression as unmeṣa-nimeṣa is the grand display of the moon phases as the Nityā Devīs, which is why they are deeply revered and worshiped in Śrīvidyā. In fact, Devī is known as the one who is understood through the lunar phases that teach us everything we need to know about ourselves and the world around us, leading us to vidyā.

216 See *Lalitā Sahasranāma*, N281: unmeṣa nimiṣotpanna vipanna bhuvanāvaḷiḥ (Devī is described as the one whose blinking causes worlds to appear and disappear).

One of the most important insights of Nityā sādhanā is the understanding of the subtle variations in the totality of experience, beginning with Kāmeśvarī as the inkling of desire on new moon day. On the path of upāsanā, as the desire grows, it becomes more intense, as if on fire, symbolized by *Bhagamālinī* and turning into a delightful flow with *Nityaklinnā*. The flow of the fire of desire breaks through the armor of our inertia (at least temporarily) as *Bheruṇḍā*, fanning the flames to a frenzy as *Vahnivāsinī*. Vahnivāsinī purifies desire with her blazing force, crystallizing it through diamond-like determination as Mahāvajreśvarī. Now, jñāna is firing up the icchā that needs to be directed toward our awareness. *Śivadūtī* is the fierce goddess who directs Śiva, the embodiment of awareness towards the fructification of icchā and jñāna.

When icchā is purified by the removal of karmic traces, the results are immediate as Tvaritā Devī takes her place in the sky as the perfect half-moon. With clarity directing pure icchā and jñāna, Kuṇḍalinī is activated as the joyful *Kulasundarī*. This eternal pattern that enlivens all processes of creation is the play of Nityā Devī, who shows us that the foundational building blocks of the macrocosm are identical with those of the microcosm. With this realization, we arrive at the feet of the pristine *Nīlapatāka*, whose austere blue is reminiscent of unconditioned space. With the correct application of vidyā in kriyā, we become victorious through the grace of the next Nityā, *Vijayā*, who empowers us to conquer our inner demons.

Our inner struggle finally leads us to the propitious *Sarvamaṅgalā*. Our vṛttis come to a rest with the realization of this all-encompassing auspiciousness, leading us to the fiery *Jvālāmālinī*, who ensures that the auspiciousness is maintained through the fire of ongoing insight. As agni, she transforms ordinary experience into delight and auspiciousness, leading us to Citrā, the multi-variegated goddess who reveals the underlying rasa of bliss in the infinite variety of experience.

In the reverse sequence, there is an unravelling of experience from Citrā to Kāmeśvarī, where kriyā, jñāna and icchā are resorbed into Śiva. Even though this sequence is demonstrated here in correlation with the moon phases, it occurs in contracted or expanded forms in every aspect of creation and is applicable to every experience. We may become stuck at any given phase for days, months or years, or even lifetimes, until the next Nityā pulls us into her orbit. Given that every experience or form has its own unique lifespan, the understanding of this sequence is more important than the exact timeline.

Mahātripurasundarī is the 16th Nityā, who remains hidden in the Bindu as the sum totality of the Nityās. Like the moon that is always full but reveals only parts of itself throughout the month, she remains full (*pūrṇam*) while revealing various aspects of herself as the Nityās, representing the limitations that she imposes upon herself. Devī in the Bindu takes on these limitations at the Trikoṇa even while subsuming them.

> ***The Nityās also symbolize the vowels of the Sanskrit alphabet and the syllables of the Pañcadaśī mantra.***

Each Nityā is invoked through her own Khaḍgamālā Stotra, and mantras infused with specific sequences of bījas that must be learned from the Guru.

Cakreśvarī: Tripurāmbā

In the Trikoṇa, we have the fundamental triad of reality and the Atirahasya Yoginīs hold the ultimate secrets of creation. They bestow their grace by way of *all* attainments, which is why this āvaraṇa is known as the Sarvasiddhiprada cakra. All siddhis become ours if we arrive at the Trikoṇa, which occurs when all three malas dissolve. The kārma mala dissolves in the Bahirdaśara and the māyīya mala at the Vasukoṇa. The Trikoṇa dissolves the āṇava mala that creates both the māyīya and kārma malas, preparing us for the Bindu.

Here, we must examine the relationship between attainments or siddhis and the Trikoṇa. Our ordinary way of interacting with the world is transactional, where the Aham or "I" here is taking in the Idam or "not I" there. The I that we take to be the self is usually the citta which resides in the artha sphere that we examined in the last chapter. This becomes important in understanding siddhis or attainments.

Ordinarily, we think of attainment as an acquisition, where external powers and abilities (Idam or objects) are gathered and assimilated by me (Aham or subject) through rituals, mantras, and other processes. In this situation, however, the Aham is the ahaṅkāra that lives in the sphere of Prakṛti (see Figure 48 in Vasukoṇa, Chapter 14), and both the attainment and the one who attains it are objects of the Puruṣa.

Moreover, whether it is an attainment or a material object, we always remain at the mercy of external forces in this situation, where it's entirely possible to lose what is gained in sādhanā. Remember that the āṇava mala doesn't care how it is fulfilled. Although seemingly disparate, making millions of dollars in insider trading, harming others, or attaining siddhis is the same in the ultimate analysis. In all these examples, the sense of completion for the āṇava mala arises from the world of objects.

Even highly advanced practitioners who have made the difficult journey through the Śrīcakra can become stuck here in the quest for powers and attainments. Their sense of doership as the kārma mala and uniqueness as the māyīya mala may have dissolved, but the primordial sense of being limited as the āṇava mala is still present. The āṇava mala cannot be assuaged without seeing the fundamental difference between Aham and Idam.

It is relatively easy to see the difference between an object like a table or a pen and the self. As our practice deepens, we can see that even thoughts are objects to the self, where the self is their perceiver. Furthermore, everything we take to be the I can be seen as objects perceived by the self. We look for the self and find that it can't be found! This is because the self is not an object.

> ***Anytime we say, "I know myself," there is a split between I as the subject and myself as the object. Any "thing" we assume to be the self isn't "it" because the self is the one that knows.***

In sādhanā, we arrive at the Trikoṇa when we start progressing from transactional knowledge to Self-knowledge (see Figure 53).

Transactional knowledge begins at our ordinary level of awareness, where the I is the ahaṅkāra, interacting with the objects of the world as the other. This is at vaikharī or the gross level of interaction between Aham and Idam. Here, we are unable to distinguish between the objects of the mind such as our thoughts and feelings and our sense of self. Our sense of self is a mass of stories, emotions, and thoughts that we take to be the Aham.

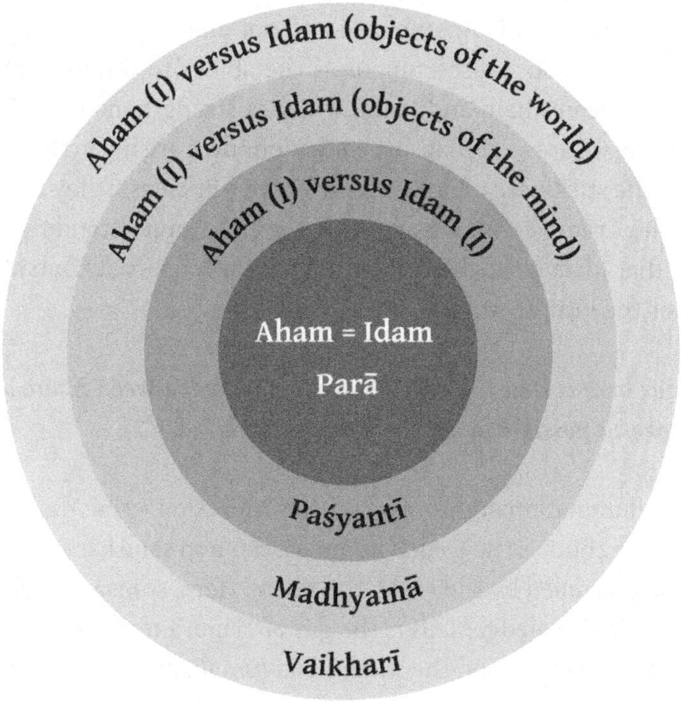

Figure 53. The Trikoṇa in Practice

As our introspection progresses, we begin to distinguish the contents of the mind from the self, understanding that thoughts and emotions are not what we are; this is at the madhyamā level. Even though we understand that we are not our thoughts and emotions, our identity is strongly associated with our stories and personal history, where we take our deep-rooted samskārās to be the Aham. We are unable to discern between Aham and our samskārās.

With ongoing cultivation of discernment and dispassion, we arrive at paśyantī, which is at the level of the Trikoṇa. Here, awareness is at the most refined level, where even the subtlest samskāra is seen to be Idam, an object apprehended by the subject or Aham. Here, the I (Self) is observing itself (self) at the subtlest level, stripped of stories, thoughts, emotions, and patterns. Objects take on an ephemeral quality, arising and subsiding in pure awareness, the I, which is Ahambhāva and not ahaṅkāra. Here, there is supreme discernment and dispassion – discernment as the ability to differentiate between the subtle boundary between Aham and Idam, which is strengthened by dispassion in the drama of Idam. Here, we are so self-absorbed that our own arising vṛttis have nowhere to adhere – without the stickiness of our interest in their juiciness, they dissolve.

It is here at the Trikoṇa that we arrive at the lived understanding of Prakāśa and Vimarśa, seeing that Idam exists because of Aham. Nothing exists outside of the Aham, which illuminates the infinite aspects of the Idam.

The paradox here is that the very ability to discern between Aham and Idam is what makes it possible to see the Idam in Aham.

Prakāśa is the illumination and Vimarśa is self-reflection – the Aham is the illuminator of Idam. What we think is the I, such as our stories and samskārās is the Idam, which is illuminated and enlivened by the real I, the Aham. Here, transactional knowledge has been replaced by Self-knowledge. This is the gift of Tripurāmbā, who is propitiated with mantra *hsraiṃ hsklrīṃ hsrsauḥ* and the mudrā bīja *hssauḥ*, corresponding with *Sarvabīja*. This supreme Cakreśvarī endows us with wholeness, where we come to see that nothing exists outside of us. Ahambhāva has replaced ahaṅkāra as the I or sense of self. This is the greatest attainment that propels us on to the next āvaraṇa, the Bindu.

Chapter 17

Bindu

निरुपाधिकसंविदेव कामेश्वरः ॥ २६ ॥
सदानन्दपूर्णः स्वात्मैव परदेवता ललिता ॥ २७ ॥

nirupādhika-saṁvideva kāmeśvaraḥ || 26 ||
Sadānandapūrṇaḥ svātmaiva paradevatā lalitā || 27 ||

"Unconditioned awareness is Kāmeśvara
The supreme, ever-blissful Lalitā Devī is one's own Self."
~ Bhāvanopaniṣad, verses 26-27

As we arrive at the threshold of the Bindu, our journey up to this point is like a distant dream. The Bhūpura, where we started, seems unreal where we were bound in our interactions by our dense samskārās. Even though we traversed the Trivṛtta that separated the gross and the subtle worlds, we gained a very different understanding of the gross and the subtle at the Trikoṇa. From the vantage point of the Trikoṇa, our understanding of the Śodaṣadalapadma with the attractions and the Aṣṭadalapadma with the agitations has shifted greatly. We now see them as different aspects of the self. Similarly, nāḍīs of the Manvaśra, the vāyus of the Bahirdaśara and the agnis of the Antardaśara are all known as aspects of Vimarśa being illumined by the Self, Prakāśa. Our understanding of the Vasukoṇa is an orgasmic one, where the elements of language pour out in ecstatic communion of śabda and artha. We are learning to internalize Devī's implements in the ongoing exploration of the relationship between Aham and Idam.

In some traditions, the real sādhanā is said to begin here, for the transition from the Trikoṇa to the Bindu can take lifetimes and there is absolutely nothing *we* can do to facilitate this. Although we have heard that every aspect of sādhanā is a gift of grace, nowhere else do we see this truth as starkly as here at this transition.

To move from the Trikoṇa to the Bindu, the triad needs to collapse. The fundamental perception that drives our existence must shift radically, and not as an intellectual exercise. With the collapse of the Trikoṇa, nothing will ever be the same again, and the cycle of saṃsāra comes to an end. To go beyond the Trikoṇa is to ascend beyond the Māyā tattva toward the five pure tattvas and traverse the pure path or the śuddhādvan.

The Conundrum of the Trikoṇa

The challenge we eventually face in sādhanā is that of the stubborn separation between subject and object, which becomes obvious in deep meditation. Say you're meditating on a mantra, which is the object. As you get deeper into the meditation, the mantra becomes more subtle, arising in progressive cycles as a fuzzy object that loses its distinct edges. The pronunciation becomes subtle until the mantra is just a vibration that is the faintest disturbance in stillness. Until this point, the meditator (you) remains separate from the object of meditation (the mantra). You are distinctly aware of yourself as the one uttering the mantra. There is nothing *you* can do to erase this separation.

At various times during meditation, however, you may inadvertently lose awareness of yourself as a meditator. This becomes evident in retrospect when you realize that for that brief moment you were "gone" and had no awareness of that time or space. During these periods, you (the meditator) had dissolved into the mantra (the object of meditation) and the triad collapsed. However, the samskārās are so powerful that the triad reappears, separating the subject and object.

During those periods when you as the meditator disappear, you are briefly in the Bindu, and the rest of the Śrīcakra that is the elaborate pattern of your existence dissolves into it (see Figure 54). The moment awareness returns, the Trikoṇa explodes into the rest of the āvaraṇas, and your sense of self and the world reappear.

Figure 54. Bindu with Mahātripurasundarī

At this point, depending on the tradition we follow, we may have two choices. In some traditions, the separation between Self (Aham) or Puruṣa and Nature (Idam) or Prakṛti is irreconcilable, and since we have seen that the world doesn't exist as we think it did, we may remain satisfied with this dichotomy and focus on becoming absorbed in Puruṣa while ignoring Prakṛti. If we subscribe to the nondual Tāntrik traditions, however, we see that there are tattvas above Puruṣa and Prakṛti, suggesting that sādhanā needs to continue into śuddhādvan. Here, the triad will collapse and continue into progressive stages of refinement of the union of Aham and Idam.

Parāpara Rahasya Yoginī

The Bindu *is* the Śrīcakra and is presided by *Parāpararahasya* (para = the highest, *apara* = without a superior, rahasya = secret) Yoginī.

The red-hued Parāpararahasya Yoginī is Lalitā Devī in her four-armed emanation, bearing her magnificent implements of flower arrows, sugarcane bow, noose, and goad (see Figure 55).[217] Her delicate arrows are the tanmātras, while the sweet sugarcane bow is her mind. Together, the bow and arrows entangle us in the world of sense objects. Her golden noose binds creation in attachment while her shimmering goad expands it in the endless sphere of time and space.

217 See Chapter 15.

From her seat in the Bindu, Parāpararahasya Yoginī reigns over the Śrīcakra. She is the supreme Brahman who is one without a second, devolving into every element of the Śrīcakra and taking on countless names and forms while simultaneously transcending them.

Figure 55. Parāpara Rahasya Yoginī

The Bindu is the ultimate secret at the Absolute and the relative levels that holds the Śrīcakra together.

If we return to the analogy of the circle, the Bindu is the center that transcribes the circumference through the radius, without which the structure wouldn't exist.

While the circumference and the radii are conditioned, the Bindu is free and infused with svātantrya śakti. Devī here is hailed as *Parā Bhaṭṭārikā* or the Supreme Empress, one without a second. In her absolute freedom, she *chooses* to create through first splitting herself into three, descending as vāc, and exploding as the universe with its infinite forms.

As we have seen throughout this book, every āvaraṇa subsumes the subsequent āvaraṇas when viewed from the sṛṣṭi krama. The Bindu subsumes every āvaraṇa, presenting as the triad in every element of the Śrīcakra. In other words, in every triangle and lotus petal, the Bindu presents as both the Aham and Idam, where the Idam is the specific attribute of the element.

Devī as Parā Bhaṭṭārikā is both the Aham and Idam, becoming Śiva as Prakāśa and Śakti as Vimarśa. She is the Aham and becomes the Idam of the Bhūpura to the Trikoṇa, witnessing herself in her myriad forms.

Even though she seemingly splits herself in three in every element of every āvaraṇa, she remains free and unconditioned as Parāpara.

The Pure Path

Below the Māyā tattva, upāsanā progresses along the impure path or aśuddhādvan, because of the superimposition of Idam on Aham. Until we understand the essential non-separation of Aham and Idam (see Trikoṇa), our sādhanā remains in aśuddhādvan. As we saw in the previous chapter, the ability to discern between pure subjectivity without attributes (Puruṣa) and the attributes that become superimposed on it (Prakṛti) is crucial in understanding the subtlest aspect of the Trikoṇa (see CittaGunas.png in Chapter 16).

Until this point, *objects* or Idam as stories, experiences and attributes are taken to be the *subject* or Aham.

At the Trikoṇa we begin to understand Māyā tattva and the kañcukas. By systematically rejecting every attribute (Idam) and not assigning it to the Aham, greater insights rush in as to its true nature. Through the continuous process of clearing our misconceptions about the nature of witnessing awareness, we arrive at the threshold of its most subtle level. This occurs through the crucial process of non-grasping, where no attribute is taken to belong to the Aham.

At a certain point and through anugraha or divine grace, we are granted the exquisite insight of the identity between Aham and Idam. Even though we may have had glimpses of this oneness at the vijñānakalā stage (see the previous chapter), here, there is a certain degree of stability in this insight. This can only happen when we have successfully navigated all the other āvaraṇas. If we were to look at this from the standpoint of Kuṇḍalinī yoga, the Brahmā and Viṣṇu granthis are completely untangled and the free-flowing energy of ascension is perfectly poised to permanently pierce through the Rudra granthi. From the standpoint of the five kośas, we are in the ānandamaya kośa, having reabsorbed the other four. Our vṛttis are stilled and the mind is quiet. Prāṇa vāyus are flowing through unobstructed nāḍīs and agni is functioning optimally. Our karmas are resolved, with only the *prārabdha* karma remaining, which will dissolve with the body.[218] No further karma is being created. All three malas have resolved. Only at this point of quiescence and illumination can we begin our journey on the pure path. At this point we enter the Bindu.

218 See 'Kamalatmika' in K. Chinnaiyan, *Shakti Rising* (Nonduality Press 2017).

With the resolution of the Trikoṇa, we arrive at the Bindu above the Māyā tattva, where Aham and Idam are seen as a continuity of each other. *Śuddha* in śuddhādvan refers to purity of perception, which is not tainted by the malas or the kañcukas. Here, progression is guided entirely by grace where insight is nonlinear and therefore indescribable.

The top five tattvas describe the phases of śuddhādvan by way of progressive awareness (see Figure 56). Recall that the three tattvas after Śiva-Śakti are icchā, jñāna and kriyā when the tattvas are examined in the sṛṣṭi krama. In the saṃhāra krama, these tattvas are known by other names – Śuddha Vidyā, Īśvara and Sadāśiva corresponding with kriyā, jñāna and icchā, respectively.

At the Śuddha Vidyā level, Aham and Idam are one, but there is a subtle dominance of

Idam over Aham. Here, kriyā śakti is dominant because of emphasis on the manifested universe (Idam), "I am THAT!" Notice here that within the subjectivity, the emphasis is on the subjectivity of the object, which is at the level of action. As upāsanā progresses upstream to the Īśvara tattva, the emphasis is on jñāna śakti, "I am That. That I am!" Here, Idam is seen to be within Aham, and the universe arises from the Self. At both Śuddha Vidyā and Īśvara levels, linearity has mostly dissolved, with creation tending toward manifestation. With progression to Sadāśiva, Aham is in Idam, "I am That!" This is at the level of icchā śakti, which is entirely nonlinear. There is no specific way for creation to be and all possibilities exist here. If we were to think of vectors and scalars, at Sadāśiva, the vector has lost direction entirely and contains only magnitude. The ultimate state of attainment is beyond Sadāśiva, and is that of Śiva-Śakti at the level of absolute freedom or svātantrya śakti, "I Am." All the śuddhādvan states are associated with a sense of wonder, amazement, and joy, known as camatkāra.

In the iconography of the Śrīcakra, Lalitā Devī resides in the Bindu as the supreme Kāmeśvarī, seated in the lap of Kāmeśvara and in eternal union with him. Here in the Bindu, Prakāśa and Vimarśa are perpetually united, inseparable, and indistinguishable.

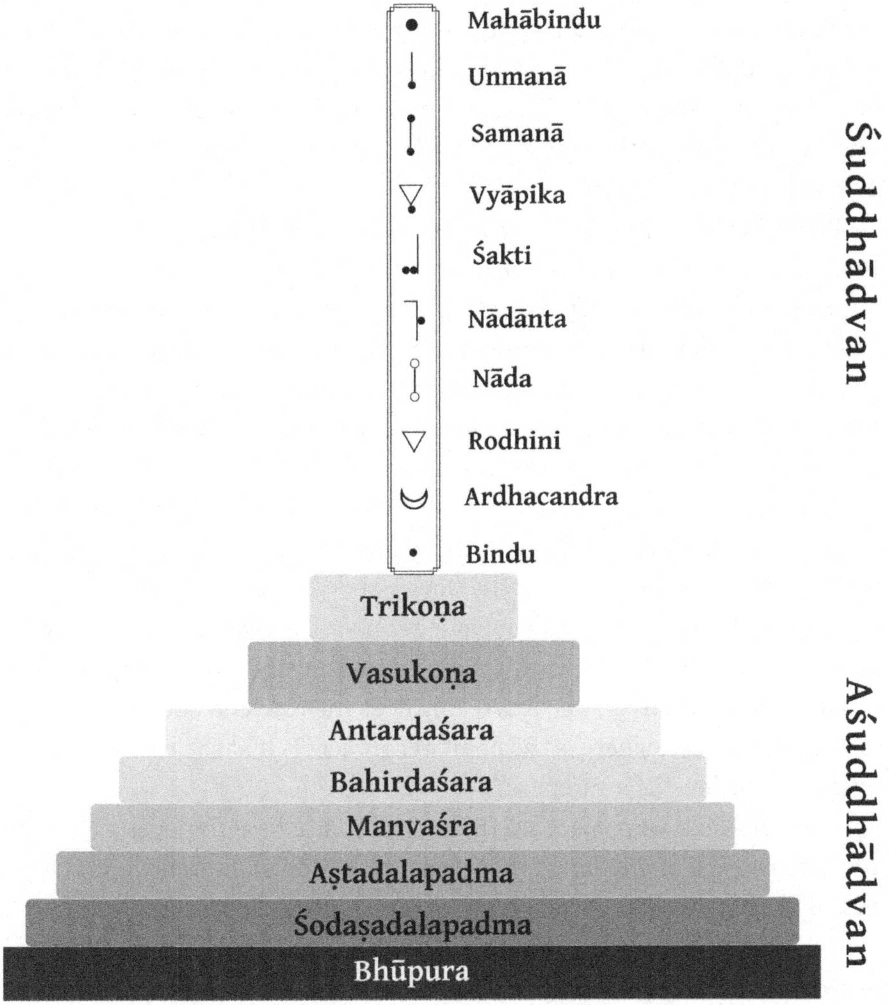

Figure 56. The Pure and Impure Paths in the Śrīcakra

The Fourth and the Fifth

As we saw in Chapter 4, the white bindu of Prakāśa pierces the red bindu of Vimarśa, resulting in the mixed bindu that tends toward creation, giving rise to Nādātmika Śakti or the primordial sound. The mixed bindu is charged with the mass of phonemes (Mātṛkā) beginning with the first, "*A*" and ending with "*Ha*" that combine to become Aham or I. The "*M*" of Aham is the contact point between the "*A*" and "*Ha*," uniting them in the orgasmic flow of creation.

While the "*A*" is the bindu or anusvāra, the "*Ha*" is the visarga. Here, the anusvāra represents the turning inward of Śakti toward Śiva or into dissolution. It's as if she closes her eyes and, in this resorption, creation ceases to exist. She becomes united with Śiva, and Prakāśa and Vimarśa collapse as one. When she opens her eyes, she turns away from Śiva in an outward movement of visarga, where he ceases to exist, and creation emits forth. Prakāśa and Vimarśa are seemingly separated, one becoming three.

This point of contact between Prakāśa and Vimarśa or Aham and Idam is one of the crucial insights that propels us into the contemplation of śuddhādvan. Say you're looking at a red rose. Here, the flower is the Idam and you, its perceiver, are the Aham. Where is the point of contact between the flower and your eyes? As you behold the shape and color of the flower, nerve cells in your retina are activated and the information is conveyed to a specific area in your brain. You register the shape and color, concluding that it is a red rose. However, *where* in seeing does the rose end and you begin? When you are looking at the rose, where is the point of contact? Is it at the rose or the eyes? Is it at the eyes or at the level of awareness?

In our bhāvanā, we come to see the point of contact is at the level of awareness, where the rose cannot exist as anything other than a reflection of awareness. This is because awareness is always perceiving itself. In other words, all sense perceptions occur at the level of awareness, where form, sound, touch, smell, and taste are being experienced by awareness *as* awareness. The lyrical way of saying this is that Śiva and Śakti are always in union, the "*A*" and "*Ha*" perpetually wedded in orgasmic union as Kāma-Kāmeśvarī, as Aham.

> ***Because of the immense importance of the syllable "m" Devī is known as Mā or mother – she is the point of contact for the universe.***

She is the sole perceiver of the universe she births.

Creation is spontaneously projected outward (sphurattā) and withdrawn into the source through the play of Vimarśa and Prakāśa. Vimarśa or self-reflection depends on Prakāśa for sphurattā and Prakāśa depends on Vimarśa to recognize itself. The Bindu is where Prakāśa and Vimarśa are pure and undifferentiated – Śiva looking at Śakti and seeing only himself – as opposed to the other āvaraṇas where he saw himself (her) as the conditioned aspects represented by their elements.

At the level of Absolute Reality is the supreme AUM, which is nonlinear and whole, with no nāda or resonance. With the separation of Śiva and Śakti within Absolute Reality, AUM tends toward linearity at Parā. Parā is still whole and nonlinear with the *propensity* for creation. Here, the nāda of AUM begins as hrīṃ. Parā tending toward creation is paśyantī, where śabda and artha *seem* to diverge, and Aham and Idam separate at the Trikoṇa.[219] Paśyantī becomes madhyamā at the Vasukoṇa, where the subtle framework of creation comes into existence as language. Vaikharī arises from madhyamā as the rest of the āvaraṇas, which become the objects of the universe. At the icchā tattva, hrīṃ is subtle, becoming progressively denser with jñāna and kriyā. At the Māyā tattva, hrīṃ is fully manifest, enveloping all of creation in this vibration, which is why it is known as the Māyā bīja.

219 See N25 śuddha vidyāṅkurākāra dvijapaṅkti dvayojjvalā - twin rows of teeth of pure knowledge, in K. Chinnaiyan, *Glorious Alchemy: Living the Lalitā Sahasranāma* (New Sarum Press, 2020).

Remember the different triads with a "fourth" overarching principle in the previous chapter? It turns out there's an even more upstream fifth principle that subsumes the fourth, Absolute Reality that subsumes all the other levels, including the fourth. In this scheme, we can think of Parā having two opposing aspects of wholeness – tending toward AUM is the nonlinear Bindu and tending toward hrīṃ is the linear visarga.

Guṇatīta transcends the three guṇas, and *lokātīta* transcends the three worlds as the fourth principle of each triad that is its ground of being. Among the avasthās, turya corresponds to parā tending toward creation while the fifth is turyatītā, corresponding to Absolute Reality or parā tending toward the nonlinear whole or AUM.

Devī in the Bindu is the fourth/fifth principle that subsumes every triad and infuses it with her essence or I-ness.

Cakreśvarī: Mahātripurasundarī

The Bindu is known as the Sarvānandamaya (sarva = all, ānanda = bliss, maya = replete) cakra, referring to the absence of the inherent strife of the objective world or the "other" that comes into play at the other āvaraṇas. Here, Devī is both the transcendent and the immanent, replete with the bliss of being whole, undivided, and saturated with the nectar of immortality. Unlike happiness derived from sense objects, ānanda is related to self-illumination.

Ānanda, the pulse of orgasmic bliss, isn't restricted to the Bindu. It pervades the Śrīcakra and is present in every aspect, tattva, and experience as the union of Śakti with Śiva as Aham. Whether it is the ahaṅkāra interacting with the objects of the Bhūpura or pure subjectivity interacting with itself at the Trikoṇa, Devī is both sides of the subject-object duality.

From our densest samskārās leading to the greatest delusion to the most elevated knowledge and wisdom, every aspect of form is Devī.

She is both the most heinous crime and the saintliest conduct, and everything in between. In every instance, she is the doer and the beholder, drenched in the bliss of the union between the two.

Mahātripurasundarī reigns over the Bindu, seated upon Kāmeśvara who takes the form of Sadāśiva as the seat of her throne that has Brahmā, Viṣṇu, Rudra and Īśāna as its four legs. She is Śiva-Śakti in union,[220] comprised of all five powers represented by the celestial throne – creation (Brahmā), sustenance (Viṣṇu), dissolution (Rudra), concealment (Īśāna), and revelation, grace or anugraha (Sadāśiva). Her face is icchā śakti, the universal will that births the cosmos. Her heart is jñāna śakti, the universal wisdom that mediates her will and action. Her glorious feet make up her kriyā śakti, the universal cascade of action that drives creation. Here in the Bindu begins the Kāmakalā, with the moon that is her mind giving rise to the idea of creation, the sun that is her power of preservation, and fire that dissolves it to continue the creative process. The universes are Devī's rays that are the powers or yoginīs of the eight āvaraṇas. From her seat in the Bindu, she emits the other eight worlds and withdraws them back into herself. She is

220 See N997 śrīmat-tripura sundarī the auspicious Tripurasundarī, N998 śrī śivā auspicious Śiva, N999 śivaśaktyaikya rūpiṇī union of Śiva-Śakti, N1000 Lalitāmbikā Mother Lalitā – Devī is the supreme beauty of the triads of creation (N997), which she pervades as the auspicious Śivā, and the auspicious union of Śiva-Śakti. As this Supreme auspiciousness, she is known as the great mother Lalitā. K. Chinnaiyan, *Glorious Alchemy: Living the Lalitā Sahasranāma* (New Sarum Press, 2020).

invoked through the Pañcadaśī mantra and the mudrā bīja *hssaiṃ* corresponding with Sarvayoni, the source of creation.

The crucial thing to remember here is that the insight one arrives at in worship or contemplative practice is that Devī isn't "out there" as a separate entity. She is our own true Self. We come to see how we create, sustain and dissolve countless universes in our moment-to-moment life with the arising of our body-mind. The body-mind with its chronic patterns of thought and chemical and electrical impulses ceases to exist in our awareness in deep sleep and arises as the maṇḍala of infinite universes as soon as we wake up. Our conflicting desires lead to the creation of parallel worlds and situations, some imagined and some tangible, which lead to more universes. Every thought has the potential to create a Śrīcakra, which rises immediately and sequentially from the Trikoṇa to the Bhūpura.

We come to see in this sādhanā that the seemingly concrete playing field of the Bhūpura is of our own making. Our current circumstances and predicaments are the result of our own choices, most of which are hidden from us. The beauty of this path is that any of the myriad worlds that we create through our own subtle processes can lead us back to the Source, the Bindu, if we follow the breadcrumb trail of the nine āvaraṇas.

> ***With quietening of discursive thought, surrendering to the force of Kuṇḍalinī as she propels us toward the Bindu, and steady application of the vidyā in day-to-day life, we arrive here at the Bindu to find that Devī is our own self.***

She had been running the show all along as Brahmā, Viṣṇu and Rudra, creating and destroying our universes. She was the delusion as Īśāna, and she is grace as Sadāśiva. We find that we hold the sugarcane bow and the flower arrows, the noose, and the goad in our multi-armed abilities. The sun, moon, and fire act through us, and most importantly – we were free all along but just didn't know it.

Worshiping the Bindu

The worship of the Śrīcakra is the worship of the Bindu. In every ācāra, paramparā and sampradāya, oblation of the Bindu is the worship of the Śrīcakra. Devī is said to be pleased with Bindu tarpaṇa,[221] which is ordinarily understood as oblations to the Bindu in ritual worship.

In moment-to-moment practice, Bindu tarpaṇa occurs through the process of favoring it in every experience. With the mantra, the sādhanā takes us to progressive levels of subtlety, subsuming experience with its vibration and frequency.[222] In contemplation or bhāvanā, Bindu tarpaṇa occurs in understanding the core of experience – the Trikoṇa – with progressive cultivation of discernment and dispassion to first know the difference between Aham and Idam and then their unity. In this tarpaṇa, the Trikoṇa collapses and the Bindu is seen in every arising experience occurring at all āvaraṇas. The shadows of the elements dissolve, revealing the Bindu at the center of every arising.

Bindu tarpaṇa takes us to the realization of Devī at the Bindu as *Mahāmahārājñī* (supreme sovereign), *Mahāmahāśakti* (supreme power), *Mahāmahāguptā* (supreme secret), *Mahāmahānanda* (supreme bliss), *Mahāmahāskandhā* (supreme support), *Mahāmahāspandā* (supreme vibration), *Mahāmahāśayā* (supreme nobility), and is hailed as the ruler of the supreme city or structure of the Śrīcakra (*Mahāmahā Śrīcakranagara Sāmrājñī*).

As the great sovereign of the Śrīcakra, Devī is now realized in its every element, delightfully playing as the self and other in the Bhūpura, as the playful attractors and agitations of the Ṣodaṣadalapadma and Aṣṭadalapadma, the highly logical and supremely intelligent design of the Manvaśra, Bahirdaśara and Antardaśara, the exquisite matrix of language in the Vasukoṇa, and the orgasmic separation and union with Śiva in the Trikoṇa and Bindu.

Bindu tarpaṇa leads us to the lived realization that Devī is all that exists as the infinite fractals of Reality.

221 See N974 bindu in tarpaṇa santuṣṭā pleased by oblations to the bindu in K. Chinnaiyan, *Glorious Alchemy: Living the Lalitā Sahasranāma* (New Sarum Press, 2020).

222 See Mantra Sādhana in Chapter 6.

Chapter 18

Fractals of Reality

On the extraordinary path of the Śrīcakra, we are bestowed with the most important insight, which is the ability to perceive the whole in its parts. The Śrīcakra is the perfect hologram, the Bindu shining in every minute aspect of its intricate structure. Accordingly, every āvaraṇa can stand alone as a complete upāsanā that takes us to the Bindu with the right stance and bhāvanā.

As our sādhanā progresses in the nivṛtti mārga, a paradoxical phenomenon occurs – the greater our dispassion for discursive movements that keep us on the surface, the more aligned we become with the lived experience that even the agitations of the surface are replete with Devī's unmistakable presence.

As we get closer to the center, the surface becomes exquisitely enjoyable because we can see the primordial pattern in its seeming diversity. The point of upāsanā in Śrīvidyā is not to shut off from the world, but to enjoy it fully and extract the rasa out of every experience. Bhukti at its highest level is the ability to fully relish the entire range of experience without the strife of owning it, dispossessing it, or creating mental and emotional modifications about it.

The gift of understanding the Śrīcakra as fractals of Reality is that no matter what field of life or study we are in, it lends itself to delight in bhukti. Being the king of cakras, the Śrīcakra contains within itself the blueprint and the path of any phenomenon, from the vast expanse of the macrocosm to the minutest subcellular processes of biological cells. The Śrīcakra's fundamental principles apply to all phenomena, beginning with the ten cosmic forces of creation known as the *Daśa Mahāvidyās.*

The Mahāvidyās

The vastness and diversity of the Śākta tradition arises from a conglomeration of pre-Vedik philosophy and tribal practices, Vedik refinement, Purāṇik accounts, Buddhist influence, the development of Tāntrik thought influenced by the scholars of Kashmir nondual Śaivism as well as Advaita Vedanta.[223]

223 See any of the books on Śākta Tantra by Arthur Avalon.

The understanding of Śiva as the ground of being and Śakti as the countless attributes of creation arises from a combination of the above traditions and in the *Mahābhāgavata Purāṇa* (8-10th century, CE), Śakti's primary creative powers were given ten main forms known as the Daśa Mahāvidyās. Over time, the Daśa Mahāvidyās were incorporated into the Śākta pantheon, each becoming a stream of philosophy, ritual, and practice. In some sampradāyas, they are worshiped as a group and in others, individually as the central deity of the tradition. The characteristic feature of this group is that they are fierce even when their iconography suggests otherwise. Being specific creative forces such as time and space, the Daśa Mahāvidyās are the primordial causes of saṃsāra. Their worship and sādhanā leads us to nirvāṇa.[224]

224 See K. Chinnaiyan, *Shakti Rising* (Nonduality Press, 2017).

Lalitā Tripurasundarī is placed in the sequence of the Daśa Mahāvidyās as the third goddess. Through a series of events in history that are beyond the scope of this book, Lalitā Devī subsequently became the central deity of Śrīvidyā and favored in the stream known as *Śrīkula* that revolves around the gentler forms of the Mahāvidyās. This is to differentiate the stream from *Kālīkula* which favors the fiercer forms of the Mahāvidyās. The critical thing to note here is that Lalitā is not different from Kālī – they are one. It's just that the approach to the one takes different forms. We find in our experience and upāsanā that Lalitā is as exceedingly fierce as Kālī, and Kālī is as exceptionally gentle as Lalitā.

Even though each of the Mahāvidyās has her own path, yantra and mantra, she is very much present in the Śrīcakra. Kālī as the force of time is the driving force of the Śrīcakra. Icchā is born in and as time, propagated to the furthest corners of the Bhūpura as the cascade of events that become karma.

From her seat in the Bindu as the timeless, nonlinear principle, Kālī weaves the web of time that becomes the Śrīcakra.

Tārā as the primordial vibration of AUM gives birth to the nāda that devolves into the structure of the Śrīcakra. Lalitā Devī as the pinnacle of śṛṅgāra and icchā drives the unfolding of creation at every step. Bhuvaneśvarī as the creative force of space provides the framework for Kālī's dance as time. *Tripura Bhairavī* is the power of agni and vāyu coming together to create the transformation of the guṇas and elements into their myriad forms as tattvas.

The magnificent *Cinnamastā* beheads herself to ensure the purpose of creation, which is for the One to become many, while the fearful *Dhūmāvatī* keeps the many anchored to the void of the One. Between them, Cinnamastā and Dhūmāvatī anchor creation in the transcendent *and* the immanent. *Baglamukhī* creates the infinite points of rest required for the unfolding of linear time and the division of past, present, and future. She presents the infinite possibilities that exist in every moment as the sandhis and marmas of the Śrīcakra. Mātaṅgī unfolds the devolution of vāc from Parā to vaikharī, infusing Tārā's pristine vibration in every element as the power of expression. *Kamalātmikā*, the tenth Mahāvidyā, infuses the Śrīcakra with harmony, bliss, and abundance; its appeal in symmetry, logic, and beauty is her joyful presence.

The upāsanā of the Śrīcakra changes our neurohormonal pathways where novel electrical and chemical pathways are forged when we overcome our habitual patterns. The Śrīcakra begins to manifest in our internal landscape as a pattern. Bit by bit, the pattern emerges during meditative practices and eventually, in daily life. The beauty of the path is that if you are a lover of Kālī and contemplate the Śrīcakra entirely from the perspective of time, the Śrīcakra will reveal her yantra to you within its pattern. The Kālī yantra has all the elements of the Śrīcakra, but they are arranged to understand Reality as the function of time. The Bindu of the Kālī yantra is the seat of Lalitā as Kālī who is recognized as the Kāmakalā who sets creation in motion. So too with the other Mahāvidyās – each is a path to the center, and to each other. In Śrīcakra upāsanā, we gain a holistic understanding of the Mahāvidyās as fractals of the whole.

Kuṇḍalinī

In many ways, it's misleading to discuss Kuṇḍalinī "in" the Śrīcakra.

By all analyses, the Śrīcakra is Kuṇḍalinī.

Even though we may think of Kuṇḍalinī as the force of transformation, when we reflect on the various aspects of the darśana such as the triads, prāṇa, agni, vāc, avasthās, sandhis and marmas, pravṛtti and nivṛtti, upasarga and apasarga, karma, and saṃsāra and nirvāṇa, we come to see that they are all aspects of Kuṇḍalinī.

Quite simplistically, the movement toward the periphery is the force of Prāṇakuṇḍalinī as Vāmā and the journey back to the center is Parākuṇḍalinī as Jyeṣṭhā. She operates at the periphery as Raudrī as the force of karma and saṃsāra. The practice of the Śrīcakra is one of deep surrender to Kuṇḍalinī, who determines the moment-to-moment flow of prāṇa toward the rim or to the center. The purpose of the sādhanā spectrum is to favor Parākuṇḍalinī so that we can stop creating the turbulence at the surface, with an evolution of vāc and avasthās through a change in the sandhis and marmas.

When we fail to surrender or when our attention is fixated on the surface with its choppiness, Kuṇḍalinī becomes a problem, causing physical, psychological, mental, and emotional conflict. The fundamental issue here tends to be a deep conflict between bhukti and mukti – we don't want liberation at *all* costs but as a cherry on top of the proverbial cake that we would like to hoard *and* eat. The clash between pravṛtti and nivṛtti and upasarga and apasarga isn't a hypothetical one. The Manvaśra and Bahirdaśara show us the exquisite logic of prāṇa and its flow.

The flow of our prāṇa is dependent on our deepest longings and not what is cool or desirable to want, which is why spiritual bypassing leads to more "Kuṇḍalinī" symptoms. It is also possible that even when we are aligned with our deepest longings, we have significant disturbances in our physiology, which brings up the topics of transition and transformation.

Transition is often violent and uncomfortable. Until we come out on the other side, we are in the marma, cooking in the heat of change that will determine the direction in which prāṇa will eventually flow. Depending on our previous situation and karma, including the formidable force of genetics (which is another manifestation of Vāmā) and conditioning, the reversal of patterns can be excruciatingly painful. However, the sandhi and marma points of transition give us the opportunity to re-evaluate our goals – would we still want liberation if it comes at the cost of this discomfort? The answer to this question determines the action of Kuṇḍalinī. If difficult transitions are used as stimuli for cultivating viveka and vairāgya and the application of the right bhāvanā, perspective and perception can transform radically, which are also the effects of Kuṇḍalinī.

> ***When Kuṇḍalinī bestows her grace, every breath becomes a mantra and a portal to the Absolute Reality.***

Prāṇa, the inward breath, brings in the world of objects from the Bhūpura through the senses, from the periphery to the center. Udāna unites the Aham and Idam at the Bindu or center. Samāna equalizes the Aham-Idam unity in all the āvaraṇas, while vyāna harmonizes and diffuses it across the sandhis and marmas. Apāna flows back to the Bhūpura, replete with śṛṅgāra rasa from the Bindu. Beauty and abundance as Śrī flow orgasmically in the upāsaka's experience devoid of the separation between me and the other.

If we were to look at the Śrīcakra as the unfolding of Kuṇḍalinī in the Kāmakalā into every one of its aspects, we would see her pulsating in her many forms in every aspect of creation, including our lives, behavior, thought and speech. Every aspect of the Śrīcakra is a fractal of Reality as this great mother, Kuṇḍalinī.

Macrocosm

The correlation of the laws of physics and quantum theories with spirituality is not new, but the subject is beyond the scope of this book. A dedicated search on the correlations of physical laws with the Śrīcakra is sure to yield something.

However, we don't need to be scientists or physicists to understand the presence of the macrocosm in the Śrīcakra. The five elements are easily available for our contemplations, each a gateway to the triad of guṇas that drive their behavior. Our moment-to-moment sense experiences provide the framework for the union of sense objects with the organs, both made of the same components and meeting because of this identity.

The cycles of day and night and seasons give us the knowledge of the invisible sandhis and marmas that drive time and space. Whether we believe in astrology or not, we can't deny that times change suddenly and mysteriously –all is going well one day, and our world falls apart the next. People change for no good reason and relationships are in constant flux, where everyone is operating under the influence of the larger forces of their life.

The play of karma as linear time becomes evident in the global effects of evolution, pollution, climate changes and natural disasters, all of which were collectively placed in motion in the near or distant past. New species are discovered while others become extinct in accordance with the triad of sṛṣṭi, stithi and saṃhāra.

> ***Icchā-jñāna-kriyā flows as prāṇa in the nāḍīs of the macrocosm, shifting and changing objects through interaction and decay, birthing newer objects, and moving creation along the linear time-space continuum in the Bhūpura.***

Death and destruction give way to new life, thought and innovation, all of creation subjugating to Devī as Vāmā. Even as new stars are born, others self-destruct and disappear into black holes, obeying her command as Jyeṣṭhā, while those created go on to generate infinite loops and variations of being, driven by her frenzy as Raudrī. The universe is expanding at a fast pace while simultaneously collapsing upon itself against the backdrop of the auspicious orgasmic union of Śiva-Śakti as Ambikā.

When we contemplate Nature as the sādhanā of the Śrīcakra, a walk in the park is enough to lead us to great insights about the play of the guṇas, mahābhūtas, icchā-jñāna-kriyā, avasthās, sandhis and marmas. The sight of a fallen leaf on a windy fall day becomes a fractal of Reality, leading us to the Bindu pulsating in it, the ground, the air, and the cosmos.

Microcosm

As we have seen in the saṃhāra krama, every aspect of the microcosm – the deha (body) and the antaḥkaraṇa or citta (internal landscape) is accounted for in the Śrīcakra. Both the body and mind are made up of the five elements infused with the three guṇas that constantly show up in their gross and subtle functions. The biological functions of cell division and death, the release of appropriate chemicals and hormones through microscopic channels, and the firing of electrical pathways are synchronized with the day and night cycles. The anabolic and catabolic functions of the body are separated by different neurohormonal pathways that respond to the cycles of the moon, sun, and fire in the Kāmakalā.

From the release of acid in the stomach to the triggering of a pain receptor, every pathway without exception is driven by the triad of icchā-jñāna-kriyā. This primordial triad keeps us alive, even when we are depressed or unmotivated. The call to open our eyes in the morning, evacuate our bowels and bladder, and the involuntary functions of the heart beating and the lungs breathing go on in the incessant cycles of sṛṣṭi-stithi-saṃhāra, arising and dissolving in the vastness of eternal space and time. The food we eat and obsess over goes through the joyful process of digestion without our consent or approval, driven by the triads of creation. The breath we take for granted patiently goes through the cycle of sṛṣṭi-stithi-saṃhāra, expanding to the far corners of the Bhūpura and dissolving back into the Bindu 21,600 times a day in its silent, incessant japa from birth to death.

Our idiosyncrasies, attractions and aversions, our constant grasping and posturing are the manifestations of the deep and often underappreciated eṣaṇas. The flow of prāṇa in our nāḍīs that keeps us on the surface is a function of its flow in the sandhis and marmas as Kuṇḍalinī in the direction of upasarga or apasarga. She is both the power of concealment and of revelation appearing as the Guru that shows us how to traverse the path of the Śrīcakra.

Each element of our body-mind can become a portal for anugraha, including pain, disease, and discomfort if we give it a chance.

Even if all we did was to reflect deeply on the various aspects of body-mind that are constantly available to us, we would come to appreciate them as fractals of Reality.

Upāsanā

The various aspects of upāsanā begin to make sense as we traverse the Śrīcakra and gain its holistic knowledge. The numerous facets of each upāya fall into place as a non-sequential, non-linear process. While we began our upāsanā with a particular upāya, traversing the āvaraṇas opens us to see the beauty and depth of the advanced teachings in the basic practices.

Outwardly, the discipline of diet and lifestyle, rituals, and mantra sādhanā may look the same. However, the internal stance of practice has changed. In pūjā or ritual, we previously invoked and worshiped Devī as an external entity. Now, every act of offering is directed toward the Self. Meditation and mantra are fully internalized with no expected outcome or objective. Āṇavopāya and śāktopāya practices are suffused with the sattarka and subtlety of śāmbhavopāya, where the worshiper and worshiped are one.

So too with ācāra. While we previously adhered to a prescribed ācāra, Śrīcakra upāsanā has taken us beyond social, moral, and cultural norms. We continue to honor the rules of society and play our roles but internally, we are free. We use language, make plans, get groceries, and work and play in the Bhūpura infused with the fragrance of the Bindu. The clarity and quiescent citta is impervious to attachments and contractions. Instead, each facet of life and upāsanā becomes a fractal of Reality.

Vāc

The exposition of vāc in the sādhanā of the Śrīcakra can be life-transforming if we can meditate deeply on it in the context of the macrocosm and microcosm. If we embody the knowledge that creation is expression as language, the entire structure of the Śrīcakra and its darśana including prāṇa, karma, transmigration, evolution, and dissolution becomes clear as frequencies and wavelengths.

Each of the Daśa Mahāvidyās is a unique stream of vāc. In fact, we can think of the ten creative powers as aspects of vāc, each in its most rarefied form as Parā in the Bindu, the subtlest differentiation in the Trikoṇa, the beginning of manifestation as its matrix in the Vasukoṇa, and in its progressively denser forms as vaikharī from the Antardaśara to the Bhūpura. We meet the Mahāvidyās not only in our moment-to-moment experience as our own expression in behavior, thought and speech but also in the external world.

Kuṇḍalinī is vāc, unfolding from her supreme position of Parā in the Bindu as Śaktikuṇḍalinī and becoming Prāṇakuṇḍalinī with the rise of nāda and the Śakti praṇava, hrīṃ.

As this primordial principle, she pervades the universe with her potency, devolving to paśyantī at the Trikoṇa, madhyamā at the Vasukoṇa, and vaikharī in the rest of the āvaraṇas. The coffee cup in your hand, these words you're reading, the thoughts running in your mind, the sound of children outside, and the explosion of stars in the distant galaxy are manifestations of the Supreme Kuṇḍalinī. She is the breath of the breath, the vāc of the vāc, and the prāṇa of prāṇa, pervading and enlivening the Śrīcakra from the Bindu to the Bhūpura.

Vāc in all her forms dictates the macrocosm and the microcosm, from the creation of new galaxies to the expression of dormant traits in your genes. As the *potential* for stars or your blue eyes, she is Parā. With the rise of icchā-jñāna-kriyā, she begins to charge the potential with force and direction as paśyantī. When your eye color began to develop, she became the pattern of blue as madhyamā, and is vaikharī as the eyes you see in the mirror. Whatever you can think of in your life – your joy, sorrow, challenge, or triumph – was once in its potential form, as Parā. Through your choices and life circumstances, they were given direction and energy to become the facets that make you unique.

There is nothing in creation that escapes the scheme of vāc in the Śrīcakra. If we never performed a Śrīcakra pūjā, got dīkṣā into the mantra or studied its original texts but reflected deeply on vāc as it arises in our moment-to-moment experience, we would embody its teaching. Every expression, no matter how elevated or depraved, is thus a fractal of Reality.

If we can learn to perceive everything in existence as a fractal of Reality, Devī begins to manifest in our experience as the lived yantra that is enlivened by the mantra of the breath and prāṇa. With the meeting of yantra and mantra, we come to experience what is known as Tantra.

RESOURCES

Śrīvidyā (by no means a complete or exhaustive list):

- Avalon, Arthur. *Kāmakalā Vilāsa by Puṇyānanda Nātha with the commentary of Naṭanā*nanda *Nātha*. Madras: Ganesh and Co (Pvt) Ltd, 1961. A comprehensive examination of Kāmakalā in English.
- Avalon, Arthur, Shastri, Lakshmana. *Tantraraja Tantra*. Delhi: Motilal Banarsidass, 2000. Although the text is in Sanskrit, this version has an excellent introduction by Arthur Avalon.
- Avalon, Arthur. *Tantra of the Great Liberation: Mahanirvana Tantra*. Rockville, MD: Wildside Press, 2009. The most accessible English translation of an essential Tāntrik text.
- Bhāskararāya, Sastri, Subrahmanya, S. *Varivasyā-Rahasya and its commentary*. Chennai: Adyar Library and Research Centre, 2000. This is the most accessible English version of Bhāskararāya's Varivasyā Rahasya, which explains the manifold meanings of the Pañcadaśī mantra.
- Bowden, Michael M. *The Goddess and The Guru*. 45th Parallel Press, 2017. This book details the remarkable journey of Śrī Amritananda Natha Saraswati from his education and work as an eminent scientist to a Śrīvidyā adept and founder of the temple at Devipuram.
- Bowden, Michael M, ed. *Gifts from the Goddess: Selected Works of Śrī Amritananda Natha Saraswati*. 45th Parallel Press, 2019. This book is a much-anticipated resource of Śrīvidyā traditions and procedures as expounded by Śrī Amritananda Natha Saraswati.
- Brooks, Douglas R. *Auspicious Wisdom: The Texts and Traditions of Śrīvidyā Śākta Tantrism in South India*. Albany, NY: SUNY Press, 1992. This is an academic exploration of the tradition of Śrīvidyā and a good resource for upāsakas interested in learning more

about the context and history of the path.

- Caitanyānandā. *Śrī Vidyā Śrī Cakra Pūjā Vidhiḥ*. Rush NY: Śrī Vidyā Temple Society, 2013. This is the most comprehensive handbook on the Śrīcakra pūjā and is highly recommended for upāsakas interested in performing the pūjā as part of their sādhanā.
- Chinnaiyan, Kavitha. *Glorious Alchemy: Living the Lalitā Sahasranāma, A Practical Manual of* Śrīvidyā. New Sarum Press, 2020. A practical exploration of the Lalitā Sahasranāma in the context of the darśana of Śrīvidyā.
- Chinnaiyan, Kavitha M. *Shakti Rising: Embracing Shadow and Light on the Goddess Path to Wholeness*. Oakland, CA: New Harbinger Publications, 2017. A comprehensive exploration of the Daśa Mahāvidyās with extensive practice prompts for sādhanā.
- Dwivedi, Ramayana Prasad. *Kāmakalāvilāsa of Śrīmanmāheśvara Puṇyānanda Nātha along with 'Cidvallī' Sanskrit Commentary of Śrī Naṭanānanda Nātha and English Translation*. Chaukhamba Sanskrit Pratishthan, 2004. There are very few English commentaries on the Kāmakalā Vilāsa, and this is a very good one.
- Finn, Louise M. *The Kulacūḍāmaṇi Tantra and the Vāmakeśvara Tantra with the Jayaratha Commentary*. Otio Harrassowitz Wiesbaden, 1986. A scholarly exploration of two important Tāntrik texts of the Kaula tradition.
- Kaviraj, Gopinath M. M. *Selected Writings*. Varanasi: Indica Books, 2006. A very handy resource for understanding key concepts of Tantra.
- Kinsley, D. R. *Tantric Visions of the Divine Feminine: The Ten Mahavidyas*. Berkeley: University of California Press, 1997. Scholarly and thorough, this book describes the Mahāvidyās in detail.
- Lakshmanjoo, Swami. *Shiva Sutras, The Supreme Awakening*. Culver City, CA: Universal Shaiva Fellowship, 2007. A superb commentary on the Śiva Sūtras by one of the last lineage holders of Non-dual Śaiva Tantra.
- Mishra, G.R. *Śrī Mātṛkācakra Vivekaḥ*. Chaukhamba Surbharati Prakashan, 2016. There are no easily available English commentaries other than this one on this beautiful text that examines the relationship between vāc and avasthās in the Śrīcakra.
- Padoux, André (Translated by Jacques Gontier). *Vāc: The Concept of the Word in Selected Hindu Tantras*. Delhi: Sri Satguru Publications, 1992. Thorough and superb work on Vāc (or Vāk) in Tantra; an essential read.
- Padoux, André, Jeanty, Roger-Orphé. *The Heart of the Yogini: The Yoginihrdaya, A Sanskrit*

Tantric Treatise. Oxford, UK: Oxford University Press, 2013. The most accessible English translation of an essential Śrīvidyā text.

- *Paraśurāmakalpasūtra.* A reliable and easy-to-understand English translation is difficult to find in book form. Here is an excellent online resource to learn about this essential Śrīvidyā text: http://amritananda-natha-saraswati.blogspot.com/p/parashurama-kalpa-sutra.html (last accessed on August 19, 2019).
- Pandit, M.P. *Bases of Tantra Sādhanā*. Pondicherry: Dipti Publications, 1972. An English commentary on the *Paraśurāmakalpasūtra.*
- Pratyagatmananda Saraswati, Swami. *Sādhanā for Self-Realization*. Ganesh Publishers, 1963. A short but nice exposition on the Śrīcakra using the Gāyatrī Mantra as its sonic equivalent.
- Rao, Ramachandra S.K. *Śrīvidyā Kośa*. Delhi: Sri Satguru Publications, 2005. An exploration of Śrīvidyā and its many contexts, this is a wonderful resource for practitioners.
- Rao, Ramachandra S.K. *The Tantra of Sri-Chakra (Bhavanopanishat)*. Delhi: Sri Satguru Publications, 2008. Based on the Bhāvanā Upaniṣad, this book examines the Śrīcakra for practice.
- Sastry, Ananthakrishna R. *Lalitā Sahasranāma with Bhāskararāyas Commentary Translated Into English*. Madras: Adyar Library and Research Centre (first edition 1899, last edition 2010). This is the most accessible English translation of Bhāskararāya's commentary on the Lalitā Sahasranāma.
- Shankaranarayanan, S. *Sri Chakra*. Chennai: Samata Books, 2013. This is a short and concise explanation of the Śrīcakra.
- Shankaranarayanan, S. *The Ten Great Cosmic Powers*. Chennai, Tamil Nadu, India: Samata Books, 2013. A concise and yet superb exploration of the Daśa Mahāvidyās.
- Silburn, Lilian. *Kuṇḍalinī: Energy of the Depths*. Albany, NY: SUNY Press 1988. An excellent work on the concept of Kuṇḍalinī in Tāntrik traditions.
- Singh, Jaideva (Edited by Bettina Bäumer). *Parā-triśikā-Vivaraṇa. The Secret of Tantric Mysticism*. Delhi: Motilal Banarsidass, 8th Reprint 2017. An accessible English translation and commentary on a very dense and essential Tāntrik text.
- Tapasyananda, Swami. *Saundarya Lahari of Sri Śaṅkarācārya*. Ramakrishna Math, 1987. An excellent commentary on an essential Śrīvidyā text.
- Tapasyananda, Swami. *Śrī Lalitā Sahasranāma: The Text, Transliteration and English*

Translation. Mylapore, Chennai: Śrī Ramakrishna Math Printing Press, 2006. This is a text of the Lalitā Sahasranāma with a concise introduction.

- Wallis, Christopher D. *The Recognition Sutras: Illuminating a 1,000-Year-Old Spiritual Masterpiece*. Mattamayura Press, 2017. A modern commentary on the Pratyabhijñā Hṛdayam, useful for practitioners of Śrīvidyā and Non-dual Śaiva Tantra.

Other Relevant Books

- Amazzone, Laura. *Goddess Durga and Sacred Female Power.* Hamilton Books, 2010.
- Dyczkowski, Mark S. G. *The Doctrine of Vibration. An Analysis of the Doctrines and Practices of Kashmir Shaivism.* Albany, NY: SUNY Press, 1987. Excellent academic exploration of the principle of spanda in Non-dual Śaiva Tantra.
- Johari, H. *Tools for Tantra.* Rochester, VT: Destiny Books, 1988. This is a practical handbook for those interested in traditional practices of Tantra, including sacred sound and geometry.
- Kali, Devadatta. *In Praise of the Goddess: The Devīmahātmaya and Its Meaning.* Berwick, ME: Nicolas-Hays, 2003. This is an excellent commentary and analysis of the Devī Mahātmyam, particularly useful for sādhanā.
- Kempton, S. *Awakening Shakti: The Transformative Power of the Goddesses of Yoga.* Boulder, CO: Sounds True, 2013. This book contains comprehensive descriptions of Shakti in her different forms, including practices to realize them.
- Kempton, Sally. *Doorways to the Infinite: The Art and Practice of Tantric Meditation.* Boulder, CO: Sounds True, 2014. A modern and accessible exploration of the Vijñāna Bhairava Tantra, an essential text of Non-dual Śākta-Śaiva Tantra
- Lakshmanjoo, Swami. *Vijnana Bhairava: The Manual for Self- Realization.* New Delhi: Munshiram Manoharlal Publishers Pvt. Ltd., 2011. Well-organized commentary on an essential text of Non-dual Śaiva Tantra.
- Lakshmanjoo, Swami. *Kashmir Shaivism: The Secret Supreme.* Universal Shaiva Fellowship, 2007. An overview of the darśana of Kashmir Shaivism, which overlaps with Śrīvidyā.
- Muller-Ortega, Paul Eduardo. *The Triadic Heart of Śiva. Kaula Tantricism of Abhinavagupta*

in the Non-dual Shaivisim of Kashmir. Albany, NY: SUNY Press, 1989. Comprehensive work on Abhinavagupta's teachings on Non-dual Śaiva Tantra.

- Odier, D. *Tantric Kali: Secret Practices and Rituals.* New York, NY: Inner Traditions, 2016. An exploration of the left-handed path of goddess worship.
- Rai, Ramkumar. *Mantra Mahodadhih, 2 volumes.* Benaras: Prachya Prakashan, 1992. The most accessible English translation of one of the authoritative texts on mantra sādhanā.
- Svoboda, Robert. *Aghora Trilogy.* Rupa, 1998. A compilation of the teachings of Aghori Vimalananda, spanning the breadth of Tantra. A fascinating and inspiring read, and a must for all aspiring upāsakas.
- Swami, Om. *The Ancient Science of Mantras: Wisdom of the Sages.* Black Lotus, 2017. An excellent resource for understanding the science and practice of mantras.
- Wallis, Christopher D. *Tantra Illuminated: The Philosophy, History, and Practice of a Timeless Tradition.* Mattamayura Press, 2013. A comprehensive examination of Tantra and its myriad nuances, and much-needed resource for those interested in learning about classical Tantra.

Websites (last accessed on July 2021)

- http://amritananda-natha-saraswati.blogspot.com/. A comprehensive blog with articles by Śrī Amritananda Natha Saraswati, my Parama Guru and founder of the temple at Devipuram in India.
- https://www.devipuram.com/. The official website of the Devipuram temple in India.
- https://grdiyers.weebly.com/. An excellent resource for learning chants, pujas and other nuances of Santana Dharma.
- https://hareesh.org. This site contains excellent articles and blog posts by Hareesh (Christopher) Wallis on Non-dual Śaiva Tantra.
- https://www.kamakotimandali.com/. A superb resource for Śrīvidyā and related texts, practices and articles.
- https://manblunder.com. An informative website for Śrīvidyā-related articles and practices.
- http://omswami.com/. An excellent resource for living spirituality, with posts

written by Om Swami. Swamiji is a dynamic example of the fruit of Śrīvidyā sādhanā.

- https://sabda.institute. This is the website where I post frequently about Śrīvidyā, Non-dual Śaiva Tantra and non-duality.
- http://www.shivashakti.com/. An excellent resource for Śrīvidyā-related texts, practices and articles.
- https://sreenivasaraos.com. An informative website for Śrīvidyā-related articles and practices.
- https://srividyasadhana.com. An informative website for Śrīvidyā-related articles and practices, dīkṣa information and events.
- https://srividya.org. The official website of the Rājarājeśvarī Pīṭham in Rush, NY.

GLOSSARY

ācāra: conduct to be followed in accordance with prescribed rules; precept
ādhāra: base, foundation, support
adharma: not living according to one's individual guṇa, aptitude and stage of life; disharmony
agni: God of fire; principle of transformation; fire of transformation. The energy of transformation/consciousness
aham: I; Self-consciousness
ahambhāva: Recognition or apprehension of Self as a distinct existence
ahaṅkāra: I-maker; ego; (Aham - I; kārā - maker)
āhuti: Offering, oblation
aiśvarya: prosperity, wealth, riches
ajaḍa: wise; not inanimate; not torpid; not dense
ajapa: japa occurring without the conscious effort of *japa* (*Japa* is the process of working with a mantra)
ājñā: third eye; command; summoning
ākarṣaṇa: attraction; the power to attract others
ākāśa: ether
amṛta: nectar
anāhatā: heart chakra; unstruck (sound)
ānanda: bliss
anaṅga: incorporeal; limbless
āṇava: minute; relating to aṇu (atom)
aṅkuśa: goad
annamaya: physical body made up of cells, organs, and organ systems; referring to the body sustained by food (anna)
antaḥkaraṇa: seat of thought and feeling; the mind, the heart, the conscience, the spirit, or soul; inner landscape

anugraha: grace
anusvāra: an after-sound; the nasal sound which is marked by a dot above the line and which always belongs to a preceding vowel
apaḥ: water
apasarga: the process by which the surface tendency is traced back to its root and is destroyed in the process. (apa = destruction, sarga = tendency)
artha: money; wealth
āsana: practices to enable stability and resilience of the body
aṣṭa: eight
ātma: Self, imperishable Soul, the experiencer of the world through the body
āvaraṇa: coverings, the nine layers around the bindu in the Śrīcakra; layers or coverings in a yantra
avasthā: stage, condition
avidyā: ignorance; ignorance of our own true Divine Self; entrapment in the saṃsāra
avyakta: unmanifest; formless; beyond sriśṭi, stithi and saṃhāra
āyudhas: weapons; implements
bāṇa: arrow
baudha: intellectual understanding of knowledge/wisdom without practical application or experiential knowledge
bhāvanā: right contemplation
bhojana: food, meal
bhū: earth
bhukti: enjoyment
bībhatsa: the "odious" sentiment (rasa)
bīja: (seed); single syllable (the bīja of the Deity is the Deity)
bindu: the point in center of a yantra; the crown of the deity; the union of Śiva-Śakti
Brahmā: principal deity of creation
Brahman: highest Universal Principle; the Supreme Being; Unmanifest, formless Supreme Being
brahmāṇḍa: macrocosm
buddhi: the discerning faculty, the one that chooses, decides between this and that, and reasons

cakra: wheel; focal point/nerve center within the subtle body; focal centers of energy stored in the body where there is dynamicity and movement within its construction and structure
camatkāra: wonder, an astonishing event
cāpa: bow (weapon)
cara: movable
cit: Consciousness, Bliss
citta: the tool/awareness through which the external world is perceived; the field of thinking and feeling that gives rise to the me-story
dakṣiṇa: south; right; right-handed path, a path that conforms to moral and social norms
darśana: the view of the path, that has a particular roadmap. The road map lays out the view, the way to practice and the goals of the path.
deha: living body
devatās: deities
Devī: Goddess; The Supreme Goddess
dhaneṣaṇā: longing for resources and wealth
dharma: the order that makes life and universe possible; Cosmic law, the rules that created the universe and maintain its harmony; to be in alignment with rightful purpose
dhyāna: meditation
dīkṣā: initiation by the Guru - the process by which the śiṣya becomes initiated into the practice, the philosophy, and the lineage
divya: divine, refers to the bhāva of exquisite viveka (discernment) and vairāgya (non-attachment)
doṣa: principle humors that drive the body and all of nature; literal meaning is fault, distortion
duḥkha: suffering
eṣaṇā: fundamental human longing; universal desire
ghee: clarified butter
granthi: knots of saṃskāras that keep us bound in ignorance or avidyā. They are the mass of nādis that are so obstructed that there is no free flow of prāṇa
gūḍārtha: secret meaning transmitted orally from the Guru to the student

guṇa: the three universal qualities of creation: tamas, rajas, sattva; three modes of existence - sattva: pure essence, intelligence; rajas: movement, dynamism; tamas: structure, static

guru: the one who sheds the light of Self-knowledge that dispels the darkness of ignorance (*gu*, means darkness, and *ru*, means confining or obstructing darkness)

homa: a ritual where in offerings are made into consecrated fire

hṛdaya: heart

icchā: power of will or desire; Śakti's creative energy in the form of intention; the desire to create

jaḍa: inert

jāgrata: waking state of consciousness

japa: systematic repetition of a mantra

jīva: the vital principle

jīvanmukta: liberation while embodied

jñāna: wisdom

jñānendriyā: sense organ

kalā: digit; limited action as a kañcuka

kāla: time

Kāma: God of desire

kañcuka: five factors of limitation that occur during the process of creation

kanda: bulb; the origin of nāḍis in some texts

kāraṇa: causal

karma: action; seeds of impressions or actions that fuel the cycle of saṃsāra

karmendriya: organ of action

khaḍga: sword

koṇa: corner created by the meeting of two lines, an angle

kośa: sheath; layer

krama: sequence

kriyā: action

kula: group; family

Kuṇḍalinī: the potential to turn inward to discover the true nature that lies dormant in favor of outward turned prāṇa

kuṅkuma: red turmeric powder used ceremonially in sacred rituals and cosmetically for making distinctive mark on the forehead
kūṭa: peak
Lalitā: Great Goddess and central deity of the Śrīvidyā tradition
lokeṣaṇā: longing for validation and to be seen and recognized
madhyamā: middle; speech at the level of thought
mahat: great; large, intellect at the macrocosmic level
Mahātripurasundarī: Supreme form of the Goddess Tripura-sundarī; the Absolute Reality
maithuna: sexual practice
mala: impurity
mālā: prayer beads/rosary
māṃsa: meat
manas: mind
maṇḍala: aggregation of individual elements; field or domain delineated in space
mantra: sacred sound that results in the expansion of the mind
marma: point where three lines meet; vital point
mātṛ: personified energies of the principal deities reckoned variously as seven, eight, nine or sixteen in numbers; mother
mātrā: measure of time
mātsarya: envy
meru: three-dimensional form of Śrīcakra (or any yantra)
mokṣa: liberation
mṛtyu: death
mudrā: hand gesture; symbol/gesture of the hand used in particular ways in sādhanā
mukti: salvation
mūrti: idol
nāda: primordial vibration/force of creation; resonance
nādānta: end of nāda or sound
nāḍī: channel
nāmarūpa: name and form
navarātra: Hindu festival of nine nights in honor of the Goddess

nidrā: sleep
nimeṣa: small unit of time measured by the wink of an eye
nirvāṇa: freedom from saṃsāra
Nityās: Goddesses representing phases of the moon cycle
nivṛtti: path of dissolution or cessation of vṛttis
niyati: space
nyāsa: to place; procedure of inviting the deity into various body parts through ritual touch
ojas: vigor; strength; essence of longevity and immunity
padārtha: category
paddhati: method, system, custom
pañcadaśi: The central mantra of Śrīvidyā; a mantra of 15 syllables
paralokeṣaṇā: The longing to transcend all the desires; the desire for a favorable future outcome of the actions we engage in today
paramparā: tradition, lineage
pāśa: noose
paśu: animal; one who follows the herd
piṇḍāṇḍa: microcosm
piṅgala: energetic nerve channel on the right side of the body, the Sun or hot channel, also known as sūrya nāḍi
pīṭha: sacred seat/place where a Goddess or Yoginī resides
Prakāśa: illuminating principle; Śiva; subjective awareness
Prakṛti: materiality that makes up everything witnessed by the Puruṣa (subject); manifestation
pralaya: Process of dissolution when all of creation is reabsorbed into the seed form and becomes unmanifest; deluge
pramāṇa: means of knowledge
pramatṛ: subject of knowledge
prameya: object of knowledge
prāṇa: life force
praṇava: primordial
prāṇeṣaṇā: inherent desire for survival, longevity, and health

prārabdha: results of previous actions which have already begun to bear fruit in one's lifetime
prasāda: Divine grace; consecrated offering
pravṛtti: path of action that is externally turned where *vṛttis* are produced in an explosive and exponential pattern, each layer of creation giving rise to infinite other layers
pṛthvī: earth
pūjā: ritualistic worship of a Deity
pūrṇadīkṣa: final level of initiation
pūrṇam: fullness
Puruṣa: pure consciousness; witnessing awareness; knowing subject, the one that witnesses the body, mind and the world that make up Prakṛti
puryaṣṭaka: grouping of eight
rajas: movement and dynamism, which drives the expansion of the universe
rāga: passionate desire; attachment
rakṣa: guard, protector
rasa: taste; juice of an experience
ṛṣi: sage
ṛtam: mechanism of natural order that regulates satyam or truth/being; order of the Universe in which the truth is expressed
rūpa: form
śabda: sound; source of all names and forms; expressive power of the Supreme
sādhaka: spiritual practitioner
sādhanā: spiritual practice
sahasranāma: hymn of a thousand names of a deity
Śaiva: devotee/follower of Lord Śiva
Śākta: devotee/Follower of Śakti or Goddess
Śakti: primordial creative power
samādhi: absorption in the object of meditation
sāmānyārghya: offering used for the invocation of various śaktis, deities and kalās (digits of the fire, sun, and moon into them through mantras and nyāsas; reverential offering used to oblate the Śrīcakra
samaṣṭi: aggregate; all-pervading

saṃhāra: dissolution
sampradāya: lineage; tradition; line of succession of spiritual masters
saṃsāra: cycles of joy and suffering; cycles of death and rebirth to which life in the material world is bound
samskāra: subtle impressions accumulated over time through our actions and experiences that determine our choices and the course of present and future action; remnants of all prior choices and actions
sandhi: the point where two lines intersect; union of the perceiver and the perceived
saṅgha: community
sankṣobhaṇa: agitation
sarga: nature; tendency
śarīra: body
ṣaṭcakra: the six energy centers (cakras) that reside in the subtle body
sattarka: sound reasoning
sattva: pure essence; inherent intelligence of the cosmos; essence of clarity that is inbuilt in the design of creation
satyam: truth; fundamental self-evidence of consciousness
saubhāgya: good fortune
sevā: selfless service
siddhi: perfection; attainment
śiṣya: student
Śiva: ground of being; principal deity who maintains equilibrium in creation through destruction
spanda: primordial throb; movement between bindu and visarga
sparśa: touch
sphurattā: joyful bursting forth of luminosity
śraddhā: faith
Śrī: auspiciousness
Śrīcakra: geometric form of Lalitā Devī
Śrīvidyā: path of philosophy and practice centered on the goddess Lalitā Mahātripurasundarī

Śrīyantra: another name for the Śrīcakra as a device or contraption that is fueled by the Śrīvidyā mantra
śṛṅgāra: essence/nectar/juice of the beauty of a life experience; erotic creative power of Śiva- Śakti in union
sṛṣṭi: creation
sthūla: the gross; most differentiated
stithi: sustenance
stotra: ode; hymn of praise to a deity
śuddhādvan: pure path; I (subject) and That (object) are one
sukha: happiness
sūkṣma: subtle
śūnya: void; nothingness; emptiness
suṣupti: deep sleep
sūtra: aphorism
svadharma: one's unique prescribed duty or purpose
svapna: dream state
svarūpa: essential nature
svātantrya: freedom; independence
tamas: inertia; structure of matter; heaviness
tanmātra: sense perception associated with the sensory organ (sound, touch, form, taste and smell)
tantra: instrument for expansion. on the nature of Reality through the particulars of philosophy, code of conduct, and the use of ritual, mantra, and yantra (tan -to expand; tra -instrument)
tapas: penance; perseverance; heat of sustained effort; intense practice
tarpaṇa: offering
tattva: 'that-ness' or 'such-ness; a principle of Reality
tejas: radiant energy
tirodhāna: state of concealment, disappearance
tithi: digit; days of the Vedic calendar measured according to the phases of the moon
Trika: school of non-dual Śaiva-Śākta Tantra
trikoṇa: triangle

turya: witnessing awareness; the one in which all other three states (waking, dream, and deep sleep) occur
unmeṣa: opening
upadeśa: instruction, precept
upāsakā: practitioner who is continuously in the presence of the object of worship
upāsanā: devoted spiritual practice
upasarga: process where tendencies beget tendencies
upāya: means
vāc: speech; language (vāk: singular, vāc: plural)
vairāgya: non-attachment, disinterest; dispassion
varga: division
varṇa: color; attribute; class
vasu: eight
Vāyu: God of wind; air
vid: all-encompassing knowledge
vidhi: law; manner; method; system
vidyā: knowledge
vikalpa: mental construct
Vimarśa: Self-reflection; Śakti
vīra: valorous, (vīrā: feminine)
visarga: sending forth; emission
viśeṣārghya: special offering used to oblate the Śrīcakra
Viṣṇu: principal deity of mainenance
viveka: discernment
vṛtti: mental modification
vyakta: manifest
vyaṣṭi: derivative; individuality
yantra: device; contraption
yoga: union (with the Divine); practices that facilitate the state of union
yoginī: deities of the Śrīcakra; female practitioner who is in the state of yoga; supernatural forces that facilitate the attainment of knowledge
yoni: womb; place of origin; source

APPENDIX I

MEDITATION

This meditation utilizes the the bīja mantra of auspiciousness – Śrīṃ. Here, we will explore a meditation on the central channel (suṣumnā nāḍī) with this mantra, which facilitates a gentle and yet powerful opening of the nāḍīs while simultaneously instilling sweetness and wholeness in them.

श्री Sit comfortably, ensuring that the spine is erect. If sitting on a chair, have your feet on the floor. If sitting on the floor, place a small cushion if needed under your buttocks to help support the spine.

श्री Close your eyes and take a few deep breaths, relaxing your face, shoulders and the rest of your body.

श्री Visualize three spheres of light – at the perineum (between the anus and genital organs), heart (center of the chest), and between the eyebrows (see Figure 57).

श्री Place your attention at the spine, imagining a vertical thread of light connecting the three spheres.

श्री Bring your attention to the sphere at the perineum. Silently chant Śrīṃ once, prolonging the sounds Ś---ṛ---ī---ṃ. Trace the thread upward to the heart with the ṃṃṃ of the Ś---ṛ---ī---ṃ (See Figure 28).

श्री Silently chant Śrīṃ once at the heart, prolonging the sounds Ś---ṛ---ī---ṃ. Trace the thread upward to the eyebrow center with the ṃṃṃ of the Ś---ṛ---ī---ṃ.

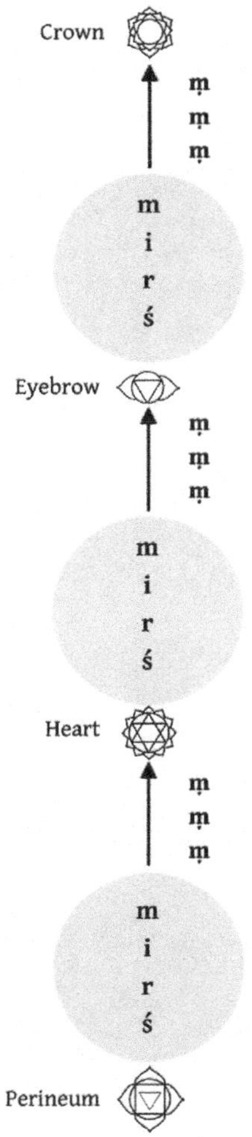

श्रीं Silently chant Śrīṃ once at the eyebrow center, prolonging the sounds Ś---ṛ---ī---ṃ. Trace the thread upward to the crown with the ṃṃṃ of the Ś---ṛ---ī---ṃ.
श्रीं Bring your attention back to the perineum.
श्रीं Repeat this cycle for 10-15 minutes.
श्रीं End the practice by lying down on the floor and resting for a few minutes.

APPENDIX II

KHAḌGAMĀLĀ STOTRA

asya śrī śakti-sambuddhyanta-mālā-mantrasya |
upasthendriyādhiṣṭhāyī varuṇāditya ṛṣiḥ |
gāyatrī chandaḥ |
sāttvika kakārabhaṭṭāraka-pīṭhasthita
śiva kāmeśvarāṅka-nilayā śrī lalitā mahātripurasundarī devatā |
aiṃ bījaṃ | klīṃ śaktiḥ | sauḥ kīlakaṃ | khaḍgasiddhau viniyogaḥ |

"The Khaḍgamālā Stotra begins with the declaration of the intention, invoking its seer or ṛṣi, the meter (Gāyatrī), the deity (Lalitā Devī), the seed mantra (aiṃ), the power mantra (klīṃ), the key mantra (sauḥ) and the siddhi, which is the garland of swords."

ṛṣyādinyāsaḥ
upasthendriyādhiṣṭhāyī varuṇāditya ṛṣaye namaḥ śirasi | (*top of the head*)
gāyatrī chandase namaḥ mukhe | (*mouth*)
sāttvika kakarābhaṭṭāraka-pīṭhasthita śiva kāmeśvarāṅka-nilayāyai
śrī lalitā mahātripurasundarī devatāyai namaḥ hṛdaye | (*heart*)
aiṃ bījāya namaḥ guhyam | (*genitals*)
klīṃ śaktaye namaḥ nābhim | (*navel*)
sauḥ kīlakāya namaḥ pādau | (*feet*)
khaḍgasiddhau viniyogāya namaḥ | (*hands together*)

(Nyāsa: the procedure must be learned from the Guru. The above nyāsa involves touching the parts of the body noted in the parentheses while chanting the associated mantras.)

aṅganyāsaḥ
hrāṃ - aṅguṣṭhābhyām namaḥ (*thumbs*)
hrīṃ - tarjanībhyām namaḥ (*index fingers*)
hrūṃ - madhyamābhyām namaḥ (*middle fingers*)
hraiṃ - anāmikābhyām namaḥ (*ring fingers*)
hrauṃ - kaniṣṭhikābhyām namaḥ (*little fingers*)
hraḥ - karatalakarapṛṣṭhābhyām namaḥ (*palms*)
hrāṃ - hṛdayāya namaḥ (*heart*)
hrīṃ - śirase svāhā (*top of the head*)
hrūṃ - śikhāyai vaṣaṭ (*crown of the head*)
hraiṃ - kavacāya huṃ (*hands across chest*)
hrauṃ - netratrayāya vauṣaṭ (*eyes and third eye*)
hraḥ - astrāya phaṭ *(strike left palm with right fingers)*
bhūrbhuvassuvarom *(circle around the head in the clockwise direction and snap fingers)*
iti digbandaḥ *(cross index fingers)*

(Nyāsa: the procedure must be learned from the Guru. The above nyāsa involves touching the parts of the body noted in the parentheses while chanting the associated mantras.)

dhyānam
tadṛśa khaḍgam āpnoti yena hastasthitena vai |
aṣṭādaśa mahādvīpa sāmrājya bhoktā bhaviṣyati ||

(Meaning: The one whose hand is graced by the sword (of Devī, bestowed by this stotra) becomes the ruler and enjoyer of the island (the universe) in all eight directions Meditate on Devī with closed eyes.)

mānasa pūjā
laṃ - pṛthviyātmane gandhaṃ kalpayāmi (*little fingers - earth - sandalwood paste*)
haṃ - ākāśātmane puṣpam kalpayāmi (*thumbs - space - flowers*)
yaṃ - vāyavyātmane dhūpaṃ kalpayāmi (*index fingers - air - incense*)
raṃ - agniyātmane dīpaṃ kalpayāmi (*middle fingers - fire - camphor*)
vaṃ - amṛtātmane amṛtaṃ kalpayāmi (*ring fingers - water - food*)
saṃ - sarvātmane samastopacārān samarpayāmi (*joined palms - all elements - all offerings, including self*)

(Internal worship with offering of the five great elements to Devī. Visualize offering each element while chanting the associated mantra and touching the parts of the hands as noted above.)

śrī devī sambodhanaṃ
oṃ aiṃ hrīṃ śrīṃ aiṃ klīṃ sauḥ oṃ namas-tripurasundari |

(Offer a pinch of kuṅkuma to the Bindu)

nyāsāṅgadevatāḥ
hṛdayadevi, śirodevi, śikhādevi, kavacadevi, netradevi, astradevi |

(Offer a pinch of kuṅkuma to the Bindu)

tithinityādevatāḥ
kāmeśvari, bhagamālini, nityaklinne, bheruṇḍe, vahnivāsini, mahāvajreśvari, śivadūti, tvarite, kulasundari, nitye, nīlapatāke, vijaye, sarvamaṅgale, jvālāmālini, citre, mahānitye |

(Offer a pinch of kuṅkuma to the each of the Nityā Devīs around the Trikoṇa)

divyaughaguravaḥ
parameśvara-parameśvari, mitreśamayi, ṣaṣṭhīśamayi, uḍḍīśamayi, caryānāthamayi, lopāmudramayi, agastyamayi

(Offer a pinch of kuṅkuma to the Guru Maṇḍala above the horizontal line of the Trikoṇa)

siddhaughaguravaḥ
kālatāpa-śamayi, dharmācārya-mayi, muktakeśīśvara-mayi, dīpakalānātha-mayi

(Offer a pinch of kuṅkuma to the Guru Maṇḍala above the horizontal line of the Trikoṇa)

manavaughaguravaḥ
viṣṇudeva-mayi, prabhākaradeva-mayi, tejodeva-mayi, manojadeva-mayi, kalyāṇadeva-mayi, vāsudeva-mayi, ratnadeva-mayi, śrīrāmānanda-mayi |

(Offer a pinch of kuṅkuma to the Guru Maṇḍala above the horizontal line of the Trikoṇa)

śrīcakra prathamāvaraṇadevatāḥ
aṇimāsiddhe, laghimāsiddhe, garimāsiddhe[225], mahimāsiddhe, īśitvasiddhe, vaśitvasiddhe, prākāmyasiddhe, bhuktisiddhe, icchāsiddhe, prāptisiddhe, sarvakāmasiddhe |
brāhmi, māheśvari, kaumāri, vaiṣṇavi, vārāhi, māhendri, cāmuṇḍe, mahālakṣmi |

225 Some versions of the Khaḍgamālā Stotra don't include Garimā Siddhi here. In some traditions, she is assigned to the Trivṛtta.

sarvasaṅkṣobhiṇi, sarvavidrāviṇi, sarvākarṣiṇi, sarvavaśaṅkari, sarvonmādini, sarvamahāṅkuśe, sarvakhecari, sarvabīje, sarvayone, sarvatrikhaṇḍe |
trailokyamohana cakra-svāmini prakaṭa-yogini |

(Offer a pinch of kuṅkuma to each of the Prakaṭa yoginīs)

śrīcakra dvitīyāvaraṇadevatāḥ
kāmākarṣiṇi, buddhyākarṣiṇi, ahaṅkārākarṣiṇi, śabdākarṣiṇi, sparśākarṣiṇi, rūpākarṣiṇi, rasākarṣiṇi, gandhākarṣiṇi, cittākarṣiṇi, dhairyākarṣiṇi, smṛtyākarṣiṇi, nāmākarṣiṇi, bījākarṣiṇi, ātmākarṣiṇi, amṛtākarṣiṇi, śarīrākarṣiṇi |
sarvāśāparipūraka cakra-svāmini gupta-yogini |

(Offer a pinch of kuṅkuma to each of the Gupta yoginīs)

śrīcakra tṛtīyāvaraṇadevatāḥ
anaṅgakusume, anaṅgamekhale, anaṅgamadane, anaṅgamadanāture, anaṅgarekhe, anaṅgavegini, anaṅgāṅkuśe, anaṅgamālini |
sarvasaṅkṣobhaṇa cakra-svāmini guptatara-yogini

(Offer a pinch of kuṅkuma to each of the Guptatara yoginīs)

śrīcakra caturthāvaraṇadevatāḥ
sarvasaṅkṣobhiṇi, sarvavidrāviṇi, sarvākarṣiṇi, sarvahlādini, sarvasammohini, sarvastambhini, sarvajṛmbhini, sarvavaśaṅkari, sarvarañjani, sarvonmādini, sarvārthasādhini, sarvasampattipūraṇi, sarvamantramayi, sarvadvandvakṣayaṅkari |
sarvasaubhāgyadāyaka cakra-svāmini sampradāya-yogini

(Offer a pinch of kuṅkuma to each of the Sampradāya yoginīs)

śrīcakra pañcamāvaraṇadevatāḥ
sarvasiddhiprade, sarvasampatprade, sarvapriyaṅkari, sarvamaṅgalakāriṇi, sarvakāmaprade, sarvaduḥkhavimocani, sarvamṛtyupraśamani, sarvavighnanivāriṇi,

sarvāṅgasundari, sarvasaubhāgyadāyini |
sarvārtha-sādhaka cakra-svāmini kulottīrṇa-yogini |

(Offer a pinch of kuṅkuma to each of the Kulottīrṇa yoginīs)

śrīcakra ṣaṣṭāvaraṇadevatāḥ
sarvajñe, sarvaśakte, sarvaiśvaryaprade, sarvajñānamayi, sarvavyādhivināśini, sarvādhārasvarūpe, sarvapāpahare, sarvānandamayi, sarvarakṣāsvarūpiṇi, sarvepsita-phalaprade |
sarvarakṣākara cakra-svāmini nigarbha-yogini |

(Offer a pinch of kuṅkuma to each of the Nigarbha yoginīs)

śrīcakra saptamāvaraṇadevatāḥ
vaśini, kāmeśvari, modini, vimale, aruṇe, jayani, sarveśvari, kauḻini |
sarvarogahara cakra-svāmini rahasya-yogini |

(Offer a pinch of kuṅkuma to each of the Rahasya yoginīs)

śrīcakra aṣṭamāvaraṇadevatāḥ
bāṇini, cāpini, pāśini, aṅkuśini, mahākāmeśvari, mahāvajreśvari, mahābhagamālini |
sarvasiddhiprada cakra-svāmini atirahasya-yogini |

(Offer a pinch of kuṅkuma to each of the Atirahasya yoginīs)

śrīcakra navamāvaraṇadevatāḥ
śrī śrī mahābhaṭṭārike |
sarvānandamaya cakra-svāmini parāpararahasya-yogini |

(Offer a pinch of kuṅkuma to Devī at the Bindu as the Parāpara Rahasya yoginī)

tripure, tripureśi, tripurasundari, tripuravāsini, tripurāśrīḥ, tripuramālini, tripurāsiddhe, tripurāmbā, mahātripurasundari |

(Offer a pinch of kuṅkuma to the Bindu for each of the Cakreśvarīs)

śrīdevī viśeṣaṇāni namaskāranavākṣarīca
mahāmāheśvari, mahāmahārājñe, mahāmahāśakte, mahāmahāgupte, mahāmahājñapte, mahāmahānande, mahāmahāskandhe, mahāmahāspande, mahāmahāśaye, mahāmahā śrīcakranagarasāmrājñi
namaste namaste namaste svāhā |

(Offer a pinch of kuṅkuma to the Bindu for Devī's powers)

phalaśrutī
guhyāti guhya goptri tvaṃ gṛhaṇāsmat-kṛtaṃ japam |
siddhirbhavati me devi tvat prasādān maheśvari ||

(O Maheśvarī, the most closely held secret guardian, please accept my japa and grant me your grace that bestows perfection)

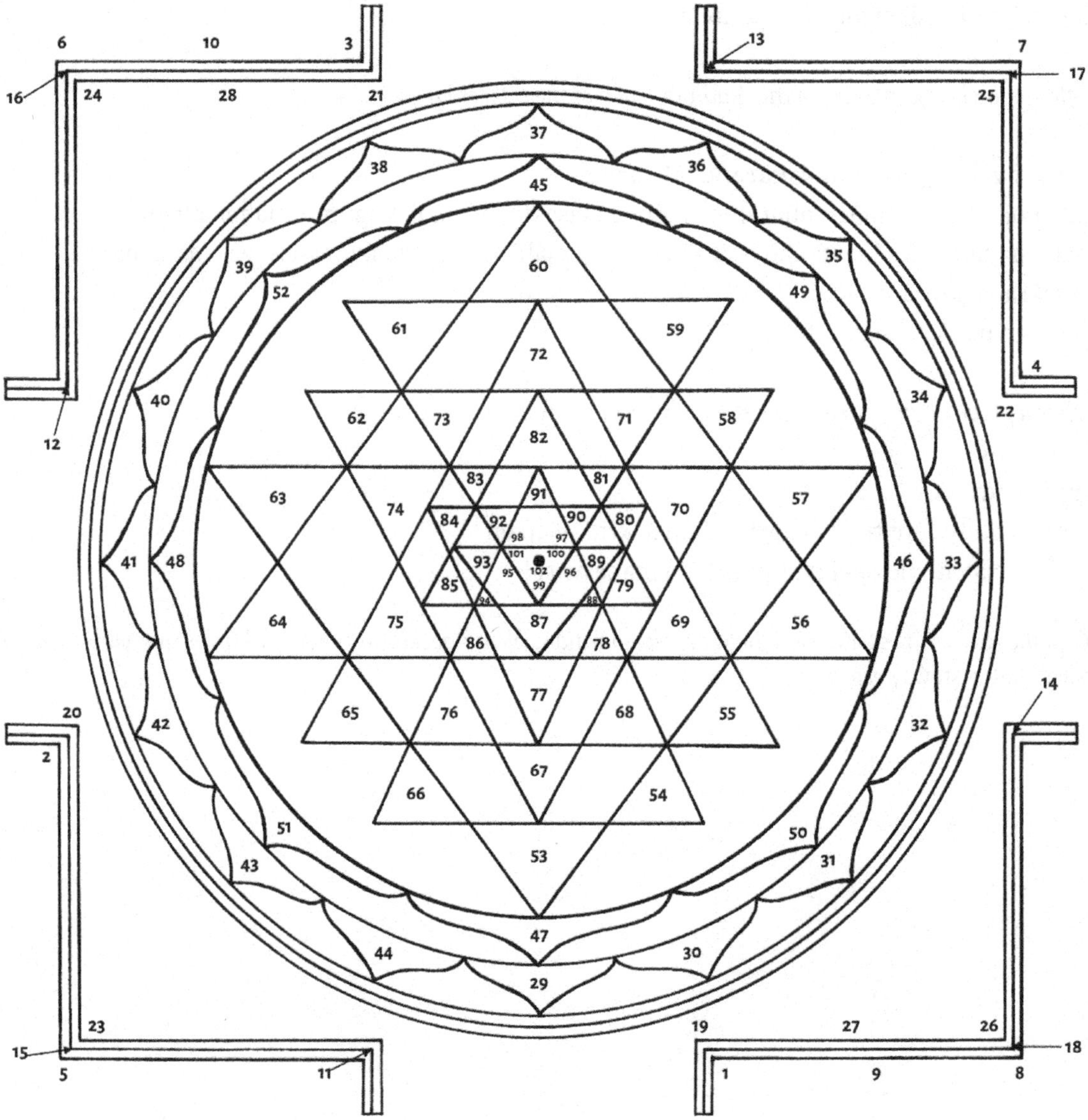

Figure 57. The Yoginīs in the Śrīcakra According to the Khaḍgamālā Stotram

1. aṇimāsiddhe
2. laghimāsiddhe
3. mahimāsiddhe
4. īśitvasiddhe
5. vaśitvasiddhe
6. prākāmyasiddhe
7. bhuktisiddhe
8. icchāsiddhe
9. prāptisiddhe
10. sarvakāmasiddhe
11. brāhmi
12. māheśvari
13. kaumāri
14. vaiṣṇavi
15. vārāhi
16. māhendri
17. cāmuṇḍe
18. mahālakṣmi
19. sarvasaṅkṣobhiṇi
20. sarvavidrāviṇi
21. sarvākarṣiṇi
22. sarvavaśaṅkari
23. sarvonmādini
24. sarvamahāṅkuśe
25. sarvakhecari
26. sarvabīje
27. sarvayone
28. sarvatrikhaṇḍe

*trailokyamohana cakra-svāmini prakaṭa-yogini

29. kāmākarṣiṇi
30. buddhyākarṣiṇi
31. ahaṅkārākarṣiṇi
32. śabdākarṣiṇi
33. sparśākarṣiṇi
34. rūpākarṣiṇi
35. rasākarṣiṇi
36. gandhākarṣiṇi
37. cittākarṣiṇi
38. dhairyākarṣiṇi
39. smṛtyākarṣiṇi
40. nāmākarṣiṇi
41. bījākarṣiṇi
42. ātmākarṣiṇi
43. amṛtākarṣiṇi
44. śarīrākarṣiṇi

*sarvāśāparipūraka cakra-svāmini gupta-yogini

45. anaṅgakusume
46. anaṅgamekhale
47. anaṅgamadane
48. anaṅgamadanāture
49. anaṅgarekhe
50. anaṅgavegini
51. anaṅgāṅkuśe
52. anaṅgamālini

*sarvasaṅkṣobhaṇa cakra-svāmini guptatara-yogini

53. sarvasaṅkṣobhiṇi
54. sarvavidrāvini
55. sarvākarṣiṇi
56. sarvahlādini
57. sarvasammohini
58. sarvasthambhini
59. sarvajṛmbhini
60. sarvavaśaṅkari
61. sarvarañjani
62. sarvonmādini
63. sarvārthasādhini
64. sarvasampattipūraṇi
65. sarvamantramayi
66. sarvadvandvakṣayaṅkari

*sarvasaubhāg-yadāyaka cakra-svāmini sampradāya-yogini

67. sarvasiddhiprade
68. sarvasampatprade
69. sarvapriyaṅkari
70. sarvamaṅgalakāriṇi
71. sarvakāmaprade
72. sarvaduḥkhavimocani
73. sarvamṛtyupraśamani
74. sarvavighnanivāriṇi
75. sarvāṅgasundari
76. sarvasaubhāgyadāyini

*sarvārtha-sādhaka cakra-svāmini kulottīrṇa-yogini

77. sarvajñe
78. sarvaśakte
79. sarvaiśvaryaprade
80. sarvajñānamayi
81. sarvavyādhivināśini
82. sarvādhārasvarūpe
83. sarvapāpahare
84. sarvānandamayi
85. sarvarakṣāsvarūpiṇi

86. sarvepsitaphalaprade
*sarvarakṣākara cakra-
svāmini nigarbha-yogini
87. vaśini
88. kāmeśvari
89. modini
90. vimale
91. aruṇe
92. jayani
93. sarveśvari
94. kau‌ḻini
*sarvarogahara cakra-
svāmini rahasya-yogini
95. bāṇini
96. cāpini
97. pāśini
98. aṅkuśini
99. mahākāmeśvari
100. mahāvajreśvari
101. mahābhagamālini
*sarvasiddhiprada cakra-
svāmini atirahasya-yogini
102. śrī śrī mahābhaṭṭārike
sarvānandamaya cakra-svāmini
parāparārahasya-yogini
*tripure
*tripureśi
*tripurasundari
*tripuravāsini
*tripurāśrīḥ
*tripuramālini
*tripurasiddhe
*tripurāmbā
*mahātripurasundari
*mahāmaheśvari
*mahāmahārājñe
*mahāmahāśakte
*mahāmahāgupte
*mahāmahājñapte
*mahāmahānande
*mahāmahāskandhe
*mahāmahāspande
*mahāmahāśaye
*mahāmahā śrīcakranaga-
rasāmrājñi namaste
namaste namaste svāhā

Dedication

Etat pūjā phalam sarvam
Śrī Rājarājeśvarī devatārpanaṃastu
Śrī Parameśvaramārpaṇamastu
Śrī Guru devatārpanaṃastu
Svātmārpaṇamastu ||

"I offer the fruits of my pūjā (worship) to Devī (Rājarājeśvarī), to the Supreme Reality, to my Guru, and to my highest Self."

Index

*Note: *n* indicates marginal notes; **Bold** indicates tables; *italics* indicates figures

Dakṣiṇāmūrti, 59
Darśana, 77, 190
as nonlinear, 76
Daśa Mahāvidyās, 393, 394, 401
Devī, 44, 54, 127, 142, 313, 364
descent into creation, 199
Icchā, 200
Devi-Guru-Self triad, 101
Devī's āyudhas, 351–358, 353, 359
as vāc, 137–138
Dhairyākarṣiṇī, 215–216
Dhaneṣaṇa, 116
Dharma, 51, 94, 95, 314
as a function of harmony, 195–196
Dhūmāvatī, 395
Dhyāna, 71
Dīkṣā, 48, 53–54, 142
Discernment, loss of, 181
Discipline, as remedy for lust, 177
Divine, 37–38
Divine Śiva-Śakti, 76
Divine Will, 62, 355
Divya, 50–51
Divyaugha Guru, 101
Dvāpara, 76n
Dynamism, 339

E
Envy, 182–183
Eros, 227
Eṣaṇas, 116–117, 220

F
Fearlessness, development of, 302
Fractals of reality, 393–402

G
Gaṇapati, 48
Gandha, 214
Gandhākarṣiṇī, 214
Gandharva Tantra, 67
Garimā Siddhi, 158n
Ghee, 315, 316
Granthia, 252, 253–255
Grasping, 223–224
Gūḍārtha, 33
Gunas, 341
correlations of the Rahasya Yoginīs with, 331
of Prakṛti, 341, 342
Guṇatīta, 389
Guptatara Yoginī, 229–230, 231, 297
Aṣṭadalapadma with, 228
grace of, 242
Gupta Yoginī, 205, **206**
Śodaṣadalapadma with, 204
Gupta Yoginīs, 297, 351
Guru, 46–48
as example of maṇḍalas, 64
guidance of, 52, 108
importance of, 54
Supreme, 54
Guru Maṇḍala, 54–55, 55, 71, 101
Guru paramparās, 331
Guru-śiṣya relationship, 46–48, 49, 101

H
Happiness, as goal, 28
Hārdakalā, 82
Harmony, dharma as function of, 195–196
Hastijihvā, 263
Hastijihvā nāḍīs, 262
Havyavāhinī, 316
Heat, 336
Hlādhana, 262
Homa, 299, 317, 318
Human condition, uniqueness of, 30
Humiliation versus humility, 159, 160
Humility
as antidote to Buddhyākarṣiṇī's Māyā, 209
humiliation versus, 159, 160
importance of, on the spiritual journey, 159
Hunger, 261

avasthās and, 128–129
avasthās as sandhis and marmas, 136, 137
avasthās in saṃhāra kramas, 132–135, 135
avasthās in sṛṣṭi krama and, 130–131, 132
avasthās in the Śrīcakra, 129–130
defined, 127
devolution of Devi's avasthās as, 137–138
levels of, 127–128
mantra in aśuddhādvan and śuddhādvan, 145–147
Mantra sādhanā, 141–143, 142
path of Bhukti and Mukti, 143–145
in practice, 346–349
in sādhanā, 147
in the Śrīcakra, 138–140, 139
in the trivṛtta, 197, 197–198
Vāgbhava, 85
Vāgbhava kuta, 370
Vāgdevatās, 323, 331, 349, 352, 364
Vāgdevatā Kāmeśvarī, 335
Vāgdevatās, 346
Vahnivāsinī, 373, 374
Vaikharī, 128, 250
Vairāgya, 124, 125, 318, 342
Vaiṣṇavācāra, 51
Vaiṣṇavī, 181
Vāk, 328–329
Vāmā, 127, 141, 142, 143, 146, 196, 212, 369, 398
Vāmācāra, 52
Vāmakeśvara Tantra, 42, 67
Vārāhī, 48, 181–182
Vaśaṅkara, 264
Vaśinī, 332–333
Bhāvanā on, 334
Vaśitva Siddhi, 164–165
Vasukoṇa, 71, 92, 100–101, 105, 126, 139, 142, 143, 319, 320, 321–350, 324, 325, 352, 360, 364, 375, 379
Artha and, 326–327, 327
Aruṇā and, 339–340
Bhāvanā on Vaśinī, 334
correlation of the phoneme groups with the Tattvas, 327, 328
explosion at creation, 302
inquiry in, 322–323
Jayanī and, 341–343, 342
Kāmeśvarī and, 335–336
Kaulinī and, 345–346
Modinī and, 336–337
Rahasya Yoginī and, 319, 320, 321, 324
Śabda and, 326–327, 327
Sarveśvarī and, 343–345
Vāc and, 346–349
Vaśinī, and, 332–333
Vimalā and, 338–339
Yoginīs of the, 332
Vasukoṇa, 325, 325
Vāyu, 102
Vedācāra, 51
Vedānta, 21, 245
Vedas, 41, 44
Veda Vyāsa, 41n
Vedic philosophy, 19
Vidhi, 23n
Vidrāvaṇa, 262
Vidyā, 41, 134, 200, 201, 306, 363
transmission of, 47
Vidyārṇava Tantra, 67
Vijñānakalā, 362
Vijñānamaya kośa, 245
Vikalpa, 233
Vimalā, 338–339
Vimarśa, 77–78, 79, 81, 131
attributes of, 369
Viparya, 225–226
Vīrā, 51, 62, 163–164
Virtue, 184, 185, 314
Vīrya, 164
Visarga, 127, 131, 140
resonance of, 82
Viśeṣārghya, 49
Viṣṇu, 97, 253
Viṣṇu granthi, 254
Visphuliṅginī, 312

Made in the USA
Monee, IL
14 July 2024

61778146R00247